Charles V and the Castilian
Assembly of the Clergy

Studies in the History of Christian Traditions

VOLUME 141

Charles V and the Castilian Assembly of the Clergy

Negotiations for the Ecclesiastical Subsidy

By

Sean T. Perrone

BRILL

LEIDEN • BOSTON
2008

Cover illustration: The procession of Pope Clement VII, and the Emperor Charles V, after the coronation at Bologna on the 24th February MD.XXX, call number *58C-93 PF, by permission of the Houghton Library, Harvard University.

The copyright of the cover image belongs to the Houghton Library, Harvard University, and no reproduction may be made without written permission.

This book is printed on acid-free paper.

Library of Congress Cataloging-in-Publication Data

Perrone, Sean T.
   Charles V and the Castilian Assembly of the Clergy : negotiations for the ecclesiastical subsidy / by Sean T. Perrone.
       p. cm. — (Studies in the history of Christian traditions ; 141)
   Includes bibliographical references and index.
   ISBN 978-90-04-17116-9 (hardback : alk. paper) 1. Church and state—Spain—History—16th century. 2. Spain—Church history—16th century. 3. Charles V, Holy Roman Emperor, 1500–1558. I. Title.

   BX1584.P47 2008
   322'.1094609031—dc22

                                                                2008029084

ISSN 1573–5664
ISBN 978 90 04 17116 9

To my parents,

Vito and Carmel Perrone

CONTENTS

LIST OF TABLES AND MAPS

Tables

Maps

ACKNOWLEDGMENTS

I am indebted to many people in both the United States and Spain for the completion of this book. It is impossible to express my gratitude to everyone who has helped me along the way, but I would like to mention a few.

At the University of Wisconsin-Madison, I am grateful to Professor Stanley G. Payne who took me on as a graduate student and has continued to support me in my academic endeavors. I would also like to thank Professors Robert M. Kingdon, Domenico Sella, Johann P. Sommerville, Suzanne M. Desan and Raymond Harris for their feedback and suggestions on the earliest version of this book (that is, my dissertation).

I am also indebted to several Hispanists, colleagues, and friends who expressed interest in my research and provided useful suggestions over the years. In particular, I would like to thank Adonica Y. Lui, Brian Bunk, Laura Canabal Rodríguez, Dan Crews, Teófanes Egido, Pablo Fernández Albaladejo, Ward Holder, Alistair Malcolm, Constance J. Mathers, J.B. Owens, Phil Pajakowski, Silvia Shannon, and Bartolomé Yun Casalilla. C. Scott Walker, Digital Cartography Specialist at the Harvard Map Collection, Harvard University, kindly helped me to prepare the three maps, and Benjamin Waterhouse helped me to put the final draft in order.

Thanks to generous grants from the Fulbright Commission, the Program for Cultural Cooperations between Spain's Ministry of Culture and United States' Universities, and the Tinker Foundation, I was able to do my archival research in Spain. The cathedral archivists in Burgos, Granada, Seville, and Toledo kindly opened their collections to me and facilitated my research. I especially want to thank the staff at the Archivo General de Simancas, particularly Isabel Aguirre, who kindly helped a young researcher during his first visit to the archives. I am also grateful to Saint Anselm College for a summer research grant and semester sabbatical that made it possible for me to write this book.

Over the years, I have presented several conference papers and published articles based on aspects of this work or related themes. I am grateful to the fellow panelists, audience members, and reviewers for their feedback. I am also thankful to Ashgate Publishing for permission to republish in part or wholly material in chapters 1 and 5 that first appeared as articles: "The Castilian Assembly of the Clergy in the Sixteenth Century," *Parliaments, Estates and Representation* 18 (1998): 53–70 and "The Road to the *Veros Valores*: Verification and Redistribution of the Ecclesiastical Subsidy in Castile, 1540–1542," *Mediterranean Studies* 7 (1998): 143–165.

ABBREVIATIONS

Data for this study have been gathered from the following collections and archives:

ACB *Archivo Catedralicio de Burgos*
      R—Registro

ACG *Archivo Catedralicio de Granada*
      AC—Actas Capitulares

ACS *Archivo Catedralicio de Sevilla*
      Sec.—Seccion

ACT *Archivo Catedralicio de Toledo*
      AC—Actas Capitulares
      O.F.—Obras y Fabrica

AGS *Archivo General de Simancas*
      CC—Comisario de Cruzada
      CJH—Consejos y Juntas de Hacienda
      E—Estado
      PR—Patronato Real

AHN *Archivo Historico Nacional*
      Clero

BN   *Biblioteca Nacional* (Madrid)

leg. legajo (bundle)
lib. libro (book)

INTRODUCTION

During the Middle Ages, a complex financial relationship developed in the Iberian Peninsula between the church and the state. To help finance the wars against the Muslims, the church readily provided monetary aid to the crown in one form or another over the centuries. Without those financial contributions, the monarchy would have had insufficient fiscal resources to fund the *Reconquista* and the Granada War. Even after the fall of Granada in 1492, the crown continued to receive ecclesiastical contributions to help underwrite its campaigns against the Turks. By the early sixteenth century, the popes usually granted the Spanish crown an ecclesiastical contribution of a *décima* (a tenth of a year's rents), a *quarta* (a quarter of a year's rents), *dos quartas* (a quarter of two years' rents), or *medios frutos* (half of a year's rents). Charles V received ecclesiastical contributions totaling 3,666,000 ducados between 1519 and 1555.[1] These contributions were crucial for Charles to carry out his ambitious foreign policy in the Mediterranean and northern Europe.

Such ecclesiastical contributions were not limited to the Iberian Peninsula. By the fifteenth century, princely authorities throughout Europe had acquired the right to large portions of ecclesiastical rents. The Reformation accelerated this process in both Catholic and Protestant countries. Princes, however, did not simply impose a levy on the church; they often had to negotiate with the clergy for the contribution.[2] These

---

[1] He received papal concessions in 1519, 1523, 1529, 1532, 1536, 1539, 1543, 1546, 1551, and 1555. These contributions constituted roughly 7.3 percent of the crown's Castilian revenues in 1540. They do not include the sale of indulgences (*cruzada*), the sale of ecclesiastical lands, or the confiscation of silver and gold plate from the church. I used Tarsício de Azcona's figures to calculate the total contribution made during Charles V's reign and James Tracy's figures to determine what percentage of the crown's Castilian income the ecclesiastical contribution was in 1540. See Tarsício de Azcona "Estado e Iglesia en España a la luz de las asambleas del clero en el siglo XVI," *Actas del congreso internacional Teresiano*, coordinated by Teófanes Egido Martínez (Salamanca: Ediciones Universidad de Salamanca, 1983), pp. 314–315; James D. Tracy, *Emperor Charles V, Impresario of War: Campaign Strategy, International Finance, and Domestic Politics* (Cambridge: Cambridge University Press, 2002), p. 102.

[2] Many Protestant clergy continued to convene Assemblies to vote ecclesiastical contributions. The English Convocation, for example, continued to grant ecclesiastical subsidies until 1664. For more on the English Convocation, see William Gibson, *The Church of England, 1688–1832: Unity and Accord* (New York: Routledge, 2001), chapter 3.

negotiations for ecclesiastical contributions and the conditions under which money was transferred to princes have received little scholarly attention to date.[3] My in-depth investigation of the negotiations between Charles V (1516–1556) and the Castilian Assembly of the Clergy sheds new light on political practice, royal finance, and church-state relations in sixteenth-century Castile. The Castilian Assembly of the Clergy was an important political and religious institution, and to accord it a central place in the historiography of the modern state, parliamentary institutions, and taxation is long overdue.[4]

The Assembly of the Clergy also deserves a central place in the historiography of the Castilian church. Scholars have studied different aspects of the institutional church and its influence on all aspects of Spanish life: religion, politics, ideology, economy, and culture.[5] Yet the Assembly has received scant attention from church historians, even though it often spoke loudest and most stridently in defense of ecclesi-

---

[3] While the historiography on the Castilian Assembly of the Clergy has grown in recent years, it is still mainly limited to references in larger works on cathedral chapters, church-state relations, or royal finances. The most important works are by Tarsício de Azcona, "Las Asambleas del clero de Castilla en el otoño de la Edad Media," *Miscelánea José Zunzunegui (1911–1974)* I (Estudios Historicos, I)Vitoria, Editorial ESET, 1975, pp. 203–245 and "Estado"; Lucía Carpintero Aguado "La congregación del clero de Castilla en el siglo XVII" (Ph.D. diss., Universidad Autónoma de Madrid, 1993); Elena Catalán Martínez, "El fin de un privilegio: La contribución eclesiástica a la hacienda real (1519–1794)," *Studia Historica. Historia Moderna* 16 (1997), pp. 177–200 and "La participación de la Iglesia en el pago de las deudas de la Corona, 1543–1746," in *Iglesia, sociedad, y estado en España, Francia e Italia (ss.XVIII al XX)* ed. Emilio La Parra López and Jesús Pradells Nadal (Alicante: Diputación Provincial de Alicante, 1991), pp. 41–57; and Ángel Iturrioz Magaña, *Estudio del Subsidio y Excusado (1561–1808). Contribuciones económicas de la Diócesis de Calahorra y La Calzada a la Real Hacienda.* (Logroño: Instituto de Estudios Riojanos, 1987). There are also important references to the Assembly and the negotiations for subsidies in works by Ramón Carande, *Carlos V y sus banqueros: La Hacienda Real de Castilla,* (Madrid: Sociedad de Estudios y Publicaciones, 1949); Modesto Ulloa, *La hacienda real de Castilla en el reinado de Felipe II.* 3rd. ed. rev. (Madrid: Fundación Universitaria Española Seminario "Cisneros", 1986); Rafael Marín López, *El cabildo de la catedral de Granada en el siglo XVI* (Granada: Universidad de Granada, 1998); and Bartolomé Yun Casalilla, *Marte contra Minerva: El pricio del imperio española, c. 1450–1600* (Barcelona: Crítica, 2004). Other relevant works can be found in the bibliography.

[4] For the most current discussion of the historiographical trends in late fifteenth- and early sixteenth-century Castile, see David Alonso García, "Poder y Finanzas en Castilla en el tránsito a la modernidad (Un apunte historiográfico)," *Hispania* 66 (2006), pp. 157–197.

[5] For a review of the historiography see Carmen Soriano Triguero, "Iglesia, poder y sociedad: Notas historiográficas sobre el clero española en la edad moderna," in *Poder y mentalidad en España e Iberoamérica* coord. Enrique Martínez Ruiz (Madrid: Ediciones Puertollano, 2000), pp. 359–370.

astical liberties and economic rights.[6] The Assembly has probably been overlooked in the historiography because much of the documentation that relates to it is found in cathedral archives, and research on cathedral chapters has been negligible until recently. The failure to examine the Assembly has distorted our view of the Castilian church and the power relations within it. An institution that coordinated the transfer of 3,666,000 ducados from the church to the crown between 1519 and 1555 and countless millions more in the centuries that followed surely had influence with other clergy—the way the Assembly apportioned those monies affected the livelihoods of many people and defined relationships within the ecclesiastical estate. Without understanding the Assembly and its mechanisms for transferring money to the crown, we really cannot understand two of the Tres Gracias (Cruzada, Subsidio, and Excusado) and therefore much of the fiscal interaction within the church and between the church and the crown.[7] Moreover, the Assembly addressed issues besides finance. In 1586, for instance, the Assembly sought a papal dispensation so that the clergy could consume eggs and milk during Lent,[8] while in 1602 it presented Philip III (1598–1621) with a strongly worded memorial against the city of Soria's request to

---

[6] See J.A. Álvarez Vázquez, "El memorial del estamento eclesiástico en 1691 sobre la baja de la tasa de interes en fueros y censos," *Hispania* 38 (1978), pp. 405–435; and Theodoro Martín Martín, "La resistencia fiscal del clero en el antiguo regimen: Análisis de un manifesto-protesta," *Hispania* 48 (1988), pp. 1075–1084.

[7] The *cruzada* refers to the sale of indulgences within Spain to finance the crusade against the Muslims. The Assembly negotiated the payment of the *subsidio* and *excusado*. The *subsidio* was a monetary contribution from the ecclesiastical estate to the crown. Prior to 1562, the pope granted a monetary contribution ranging from a tenth to half of the ecclesiastical rents for a year; the Assembly then negotiated a payment less than the percentage that the pope had conceded. After 1562, the popes conceded a fixed monetary sum of 420,000 ducados annually to the crown, in what is known as the *subsidio de las galeras* or the subsidy of galleys. In the seventeenth and eighteenth centuries, the popes occasionally conceded *subsidios extraordinarios*, either a tenth or a fixed rate of ecclesiastical rents, in addition to the *subsidio de las galeras*. The *excusado* refers to a concession made originally in 1567 to transfer to the crown the rents from the third richest benefice of each diocese for the war in Flanders. In 1571, the *excusado* was revised to transfer to the crown the rents from the richest benefice of each diocese for the war effort against the Turks, and later against Flanders. See Manuel Teruel Gregorio de Tejada, *Vocabulario Básico de la historia de la Iglesia* (Barcelona: Crítica, 1993), pp. 115–117, 152, and 415–418.

[8] Biblioteca Nacional-Madrid, 3/18355, "Congregación de las yglesias metropolitanas y catedrales de los reynos de Castilla, y León, que se celebro en la villa de Madrid el ano de mil y quinientos y ochenta y seys, con occasion del quatro quinquenio de Excusado," ff. 50–51.

be made into a bishopric or vicariate general.[9] The Assembly also challenged the Hieronymites privilege to print reformed texts at both the
royal and papal courts for decades.[10] The importance of the Assembly,
then, requires that we incorporate it into the narrative of the Castilian
church to better understand internal developments within the church,
differentiate the shifting interests and goals of divergent ecclesiastical
actors, and emphasize the crucial role cathedral chapters played in
ecclesiastical and secular politics in early modern Castile.

The origins of the Assembly go back to the Great Schism (1378–1415)
when Henry II (1369–1379) convened the clergy in Toledo to legitimize
his political decision to break with the Roman pope and to recognize the
Avignon pope. Again in 1380 and 1399, the Castilian kings convened
the clergy to sanction their political decisions in relation to the Schism.
These early Assemblies apparently did not provide an ecclesiastical
contribution to the crown. During the fifteenth century, however, the
Assembly addressed both fiscal and political interests. The first-known
Castilian Assembly of the Clergy to grant an ecclesiastical contribution was convened in 1462.[11] Sixteen years later, in 1478, Ferdinand
and Isabel (1574–1504) convened the Assembly to secure ecclesiastical
support for Isabel's succession to the Castilian throne, to begin ecclesiastical reforms, and to extract financial concessions from the clergy.
In addition to these new functions, the Assembly also experienced a
major change in its composition. Until 1505, both prelates and representatives of the chapters attended the Assemblies. After 1505, only
the chapters sent representatives.[12] These changes left ample room for
disputes over the organization and structure of the Assembly and its
functions. For example, the absence of episcopal representations after

---

[9] Juan Loperraez Corvalan, *Colección diplomática citada de la descripción histórica del
obispado de Osma* (Madrid: Imprenta Real, 1788), vol. 3, pp. 395–401.
[10] Timothy J. Schmitz, "The Spanish Hieronymites and the Reformed Texts of the
Council of Trent," *Sixteenth Century Journal* 37 (2006), pp. 375–399; Fermín de los Reyes
Gómez, "Los libros de nuevo rezado y la imprenta española en el siglo XVIII," *Revista
General de Información y Documentación* 9 (1999), pp. 117–158.
[11] The contribution of 1462, however, was not the first ecclesiastical contribution.
The church had provided the crown with numerous contributions throughout the
Middle Ages. Such contributions should not be confused with loans, which technically
the crown had to pay back.
[12] José Manuel Nieto Soria, *Iglesia y génesis del estado moderno en Castilla (1369–1480)*
(Madrid: Editorial Complutense, 1993), pp. 407–408; Carpintero, "La congregación,"
pp. 6–7, 21–30; Azcona, "Las Asambleas," pp. 203–245.

1505 may explain the Assembly's equivocal position on church reform in the sixteenth and seventeenth centuries.[13]

The Assembly's main functions, however, were never in doubt: to defend the privileges of the church and to negotiate the fiscal obligations of the church with the crown.[14] It convened at least 43 times in the sixteenth and seventeenth centuries.[15] The present study examines several assemblies during Charles V's reign in detail, because only in this way can we glimpse the complex relationships between the church and crown and, to a lesser extent, within the ecclesiastical estate itself. In turn, this study will allow us to better understand the extent to which the clergy were incorporated into the royal government and the extent to which the clergy maintained autonomy of action. José Manuel Nieto Soria, for instance, suggests that the crown used the Assembly to integrate the clergy into the governmental structure of the monarchy. For him, the fifteenth-century Assembly was a way for the crown to reform the clergy and gain greater control over the clergy's rents.[16] To a certain extent, Nieto Soria's assessment is correct: the Assembly was integrated into the governmental structure, providing an institutional means to collect the subsidy. Some level of integration, however, does not equal royal control. The present study argues that the Assembly defended ecclesiastical liberties and hampered royal attempts to extract more money from the church.[17] More importantly, the study reveals the institutional mechanism through which a privileged group within the church sustained itself and its privileges for nearly four centuries through collaboration and negotiation with the crown.

---

[13] The French Assembly, which retained episcopal representation, played an active, though not always a successful, role in church reform and in arresting the spread of Protestantism in France. See M. Péronnet, "Les assemblées du Clergé de France et la révocation des édits de religion (1560–1685)," *Bulletin de la Société de l'Histoire du Portestantisme Français* 131 (1985), pp. 453–479; Cyril B. O'Keefe, "The French Assembly of the Clergy and the Provincial Councils, 1750–1788: A Frustrated Proposal for Ecclesiastical Reform in the Ancient Regime," *Proceedings of the Annual Meeting of the Western Society for French History* 6 (1978), pp. 144–152.

[14] Carpintero "La congregación," p. 1. In the early sixteenth century, however, the Castilian Assembly of the Clergy normally represented only thirty dioceses.

[15] See Azcona, "Estado," pp. 303–313 and Carpintero, "La congregación," pp. 76–114, 208–248.

[16] Nieto Soria, *Iglesia y génesis*, pp. 406–412.

[17] In a larger discussion of the fiscal burden throughout Europe, Juan Gelabert briefly noted that the Spanish clergy strongly opposed the subsidy in the first half of the sixteenth century. The present study confirms his observation. See Juan Gelabert, "The Fiscal Burden," in *Economic Systems and State Finance* ed. Richard Bonney (Oxford: Clarendon Press, 1995), p. 555.

Rethinking Politics and Church-State Relations

At its heart, this book is about political practice in the sixteenth century. How did the king interact and negotiate with his subjects? How did the king react to the actions of others? In the process of answering these interrelated questions through the prism of the Assembly and the cathedral chapters, I found that the master narratives of absolutism and state-building failed to describe adequately early sixteenth-century political practice.[18] Historians and social scientists have long associated the foundation of the modern state with the rise of the 'new monarchies' in the late fifteenth- and early sixteenth-century Europe. They have seen the configuration of bureaucratization, monopolization of force, creation of legitimacy, strengthened confessional unity, and homogenization of the subject population as the keys to state building. These levers supposedly allowed the 'new monarchies' to centralize authority and break down the feudal order. A shift in the locus of political power from feudal to centralized authority, then, is the hallmark of the modern state. Even though this paradigm has been a useful tool to understand historical developments in western Europe between the late fifteenth and eighteenth centuries, it can lead to the use of concepts that obscure important aspects of political life and over-generalizations that do not stand up under closer scrutiny. This book examines issues such as fiscal policy, coercion, and bureaucratization in the exercise of royal authority in Castile and concludes that the state-building paradigm is inappropriate for understanding political developments there.

Instead, it posits a paradigm that emphasizes pluralism in the political sphere.[19] That is, the kingdom consisted of multiple autonomous political organizations, such as the Assembly, and the keystone of the Habsburg monarchy's policies was to seek consensus with these political organizations for the common good.[20] This approach differs slightly

---

[18] For a discussion on the usefulness of a revised concept of absolutism, see Wolfgang Schmale, "The Future of 'Absolutism' in Historiography: Recent Tendencies," *Journal of Early Modern History* 2 (1998), pp. 192–202.

[19] For a succinct discussion of the pluralistic nature of power in early modern Europe see John Rogister, "Some New Directions in the Historiography of State Assemblies and Parliaments in Early Modern and Late Modern Europe," *Parliaments, Estate and Representation* 16 (1996), pp. 1–16.

[20] José Manuel de Bernardo Ares, "Parliament or City Councils: The representation of the kingdom in the Crown of Castile (1665–1700)," *Parliaments, Estates and Representation* 25 (2005), pp. 34, 36.

from that of an earlier generation of scholars who also confronted the inability of state-building to explain the documentation. These historians concluded that the monarch was not strong enough to impose his will and therefore ruled through and with autonomous, intermediate bodies.[21] Their argument indirectly suggests that a stronger monarch would have imposed his will and thus leaves in place the centralization versus decentralization framework. Moreover, it implies that the monarch's failure to impose his will *ipso facto* led to the supremacy of the municipality, parliament, or aristocracy. A pluralistic interpretation of the political sphere, however, suggests that the monarchs not only lacked the means to centralize their power, but also had no intention of imposing their will as state-building theorists argue. Rather, monarchs and the elites sought to work out through consultation and consensus "the compromises necessary to maintain their privileged positions within the commonwealth."[22]

Despite this difference in approach, the present study relies heavily on earlier scholarship on intermediate bodies that has focused on the city councils and the Cortes (parliament).[23] Historians such as Charles Hendricks, I.A.A. Thompson, Pablo Fernández Albaladejo, and José Ignacio Fortea Pérez, among others, have transformed our understanding of government and finance in sixteenth- and seventeenth-century Castile, restoring the Cortes to center stage in national affairs and demonstrating that local government continued to control taxation.[24] The Cortes, however, was not the only representative body that contributed to the royal coffers.[25] The Assembly also provided substantial

---

[21] Jaime Vicens Vives, "The Administrative Structure of the State in the Sixteenth and Seventeenth Centuries," in *Government in Reformation Europe, 1520–1560* ed. Henry J. Cohn (London: MacMillan Press, 1971), pp. 63, 69.

[22] J.B. Owens, *"By My Absolute Royal Authority": Justice and the Castilian Commonwealth at the Beginning of the First Global Age* (Rochester, NY: University of Rochester Press, 2005), p. 6.

[23] See Constance Jones Mathers, "Relations between the City of Burgos and the Crown, 1506–1556" (Ph.D. diss., Columbia University, 1973).

[24] Charles David Hendricks, "Charles V and the Cortes of Castile: Politics in Renaissance Spain," (Ph.D. diss., Cornell University, 1976); I.A.A. Thompson, *Crown and Cortes: government, institutions, and representation in early modern Castile* (Brookfield, Vermont: Variorum, 1993); Pablo Fernández Albaladejo, *Fragmentos de Monarquía* (Madrid: Alianza Universidad, 1992); José Ignacio Fortea Pérez, *Monarquía y Cortes en la Corona de Castilla: Las ciudades ante la política fiscal de Felipe II* (Salamanca: Cortes de Castilla y León, 1990).

[25] The Cortes and the Assembly both met thirteen times during Charles's reign. The crown consequently had to deal with one or the other institution on almost a yearly basis. The Cortes met in 1518, 1523, 1525, 1528, 1532, 1534, 1537, 1539, 1542, 1544,

aid to the crown, and through the Castilian Assembly of the Clergy, the cathedral chapters maintained effective local control over ecclesiastical rents.[26] Even as its influence ebbed in the early eighteenth century, the Assembly still administered the collection of the ecclesiastical contribution. The crown consequently could not disregard this institution and, more importantly, never managed to usurp control over the collection process.

By providing an important addition to the literature on Castilian governance and finance that has focused almost exclusively on secular parliamentary systems and city councils, my research also offers a sounder foundation to compare royal efforts to secure financial support from the cities and the church. Such comparisons are necessary to understand fully political practice and royal finance in Castile.[27] They also will help us to understand better how politics proceeded without formal meetings of representative institutions and therefore resolve historiographical debates over 're-feudalization' in Castile in the second half of the seventeenth century.[28]

This book also addresses church-state relations and the internal dynamics of the church in early modern Castile. Research on the Assembly suggests that royal appointments of prelates and attempts to reform the clergy did not give the crown greater control over the church. The cathedral chapters remained autonomous and staunchly defended their jurisdictions from the intervention of prelates. Moreover, the Castilian church itself was not a centralized, monolithic, or unified

---

1548, 1552, and 1555. The Assembly of the Clergy met in 1517, 1519, 1520, 1523, 1530, 1533, 1536, 1540, 1541, 1543, 1546, 1551, and 1555.

[26] In the mid-sixteenth century, the royal income from unfixed rents, which had to be negotiated with the estates or individuals, was: servicio—177,000,000 maravedís; cruzada and subsidy—207,000,000 maravedís; and the Indies—367,000,000 maravedís. Income from church sources, i.e., the cruzada and subsidy, exceeded the servicio at this time. See P. Fernández, *Fragmentos*, p. 161.

[27] For an initial effort at such a comparison see Aurelio Espinosa, "The Spanish Reformation: Institutional Reform, Taxation, and the Secularization of Ecclesiastical Properties under Charles V," *Sixteenth Century Journal* 37 (2006), pp. 3–24.

[28] For discussions on representation outside the Cortes and Assembly, see Bernardo Ares, "Parliament or City Councils," José I. Fortea Pérez, "Las ciudades, las Cortes y el problema de la representación política en la Castilla moderna," in *Imágenes de la diversidad: el mundo urbano en la Corona de Castilla (s.XVI–XVII)*, ed. José I. Fortea Pérez (Santander: Universidad de Cantabria, 1997), pp. 421–445, Xavier Gil, "Parliamentary Life in the Crown of Aragon: Cortes, Juntas de Brazos, and other Corporate Bodies," *Journal of Early Modern History* 6 (2002), pp. 379, 391–393, and Sean T. Perrone, "The Procurator General of the Castilian Assembly of the Clergy, 1592–1741," *Catholic Historical Review* 91 (2005), pp. 26–59.

institution. Persistent conflicts within the church over local interests and jurisdictions significantly influenced the pace and course of the negotiations for subsidies and the eventual agreements with the crown. Internal division and lack of centralization within the church undermined the crown's attempts to extract swift compliance from the Castilian clergy. The crown had to negotiate and work with the Assembly, and accommodate the local interests represented by the chapters. The current state-building literature has overlooked the complex internal dynamics of the church as a critical factor that impinged church-state relations. Furthermore, the overlap of interests and functions between royal and ecclesiastical officials also defies a clear and simplistic demarcation of church and state because, in many cases, the clergy were the principal agents on both sides of the negotiations. The Castilian Assembly of the Clergy provides an ideal focal point to reexamine church-state relations and rethink the issue of royal control over the church.

In an attempt to illustrate both sides of the negotiations between the crown and the Assembly, I have conducted research in both royal and ecclesiastical archives. For royal documentation, this book draws principally on the Archivo General de Simancas, which contains the bulk of royal documentation from the sixteenth century. Documentation from the Assembly of the Clergy proved harder to find, because it is scattered and often incomplete for the first half of the sixteenth century. Through investigations in the cathedral archives of Burgos, Granada, Seville, and Toledo, however, I gathered sufficient documentation to explain how the Assembly worked.

The Assembly was not recognized in canon law and should not be confused with a synod or council, or with the ecclesiastical estate's representation in the Cortes. The term Assembly might sound anachronistic, but Tarsício de Azcona finds the sixteenth-century term, *congregación* or congregation, used in the documents to be equivocal because it can refer to civil meetings, inquisitorial meetings, or other high level gatherings. Furthermore, similar meetings of the clergy in France and elsewhere were called Assemblies of the Clergy. Azcona consequently feels that the term Assembly is more intelligible.[29] Following his example, I use the term Assembly of the Clergy instead of congregation throughout this book to refer to the national body of clergy that voted funds to the king.

The monetary system in Castile was rather complex, as it included both money of account (or imaginary money) and money of payment

---

[29] Tarsício de Azcona, "Estado," pp. 298–299 and "Las Asambleas" p. 205.

(or real money). The negotiations for subsidies discussed here were primarily conducted in money of accounts (florin and ducado) and then converted into money of payment (maravedí). The conversion rates are 1 florin = 265 maravedís; 1 ducado = 375 maravedís. The maravedí could then be broken down into smaller units, such as the blanca (1/2 maravedí). Money of payments could make the burden of the subsidy lighter or heavier for the clergy and determine how much real money the king obtained from these concessions. At a much later date, for example, the clergy reached agreements to pay more of the contribution in copper *vellón* than in gold and silver coins and thus lightened their burden even though the money of account was the same or greater than before.

Chapter Summaries

Chapter one provides an overview of the participants in the negotiations, the structure of the Assembly (how it was convened and functioned), and the collection process. This information should provide the reader with the necessary background for the subsequent case studies.

Chapter two examines the negotiation between the crown and the Assembly in 1530. The principal issues in the negotiations between the crown and the Assembly were the size of the subsidy and the length of the payment period. The crown, naturally, wanted the largest subsidy possible in the shortest payment period, while the Assembly wanted the smallest subsidy possible in the longest period. The give and take during these negotiations suggests the importance of consensus in the political process. If the two sides did not reach an agreement, the peaceful collection of the subsidy was unlikely.

Chapter three examines the ecclesiastical estate's response to coercion in 1533. Far from being docile when the crown abrogated its privileges, the ecclesiastical estate defended itself by a *cesación a divinis*, that is, a suspension of Holy Offices. The simple threat of a suspension created much agitation within the regency government of Isabel of Portugal throughout the spring of 1533. The regency government initially hesitated to use force, which in this case would have entailed sequestering and embargoing ecclesiastical rents, for fear of a *cesación*. When the crown finally resorted to coercion, the ecclesiastical estate responded by suspending Holy Offices. This chapter provides a description of the *cesación a divinis* as well as an analysis of how the ecclesiastical estate pressured the crown.

Chapter four describes the arduous negotiations for the subsidy from October 1533 to March 1534. In the aftermath of the *cesación a divinis*, the differences between the Assembly and the crown were so great that nearly five months passed before the two sides reached an agreement. The main challenge in the negotiations was the king's demand that the clergy declare the size of the subsidy without conditions and the Assembly's refusal to declare the size of the subsidy until the king responded to its conditions. When the Assembly finally did declare the size of the subsidy first, it still demanded that the king accept certain conditions. In the end, the parties reached a compromise, but only after many threats by both sides. Further complicating matters was the royal ministers constant need to consult the king, who was in Aragon, and the Assembly's accusations that the ministers were purposefully delaying the negotiations.

Chapter five addresses the verification of the diocesan rents to ensure an equitable apportionment of the subsidy among the dioceses. The chapter centers on divisiveness within the Assembly over how to verify the values of the diocesan rents and thus calculate a fair apportionment of the subsidy. An examination of the Assembly of 1541 reveals the rancor between representatives on the best method to verify the values—a process which could impinge on various diocesan rights. This analysis suggests that local interests hindered the ecclesiastical estate's ability to address larger concerns. Moreover, royal attempts to pressure the clergy to verify the values completely failed.

Chapter six examines the negotiations between the crown and the clergy in 1546, providing details of events before, during, and after the Assembly. It discusses the crown's reluctance to convene an Assembly as well as the clergy's desire to do so. Further, the chapter analyzes the actual negotiations through which the representatives sought redress of grievances before supply, which royal ministers firmly opposed, and briefly addresses the acceptance of the agreement in each diocese.

Chapter seven looks at the breakdown of negotiations in 1555. The Assembly hesitated to negotiate a subsidy after learning that a rule of the papal chancery revoked Pope Julius III's concession on his death, although royal officials claimed that the bull was still valid. Eventually, the Assembly dissolved without an agreement, and royal officials sequestered ecclesiastical rents several months later only to be stymied by ecclesiastical resistance (via a *cesación a divinis*) and papal intervention. As a result, the crown finally had to return the monies it had collected.

Chapter eight expands the investigation from Castile to Rome. Since the concessions required papal approval, Spanish ambassadors and representatives of the Assembly constantly bombarded the popes with requests either to grant or revoke a concession. As the previous case studies indicated, a pope's attitude toward the concession could greatly affect negotiations in Castile. This chapter also indicates that other princes sought papal concession for ecclesiastical contributions. Through an examination of Spanish diplomacy and the church subsidy, the chapter connects a particular Spanish institution to the wider European context. Contrary to John A.F. Thomson's arguments about the growth of princely control over ecclesiastical rents in the fifteenth century, the cases discussed in this chapter suggest that the movement toward princely control still had not taken full form in the first half of the sixteenth century.[30] For many principalities that remained Roman Catholic, negotiations with the papacy were essential to obtain access to ecclesiastical rents. The papacy continued to hinder princes' ability to gain control over the national church's financial resources.

Chapter nine concludes the book. Through a detailed analysis of the negotiations for ecclesiastical subsidies during the reign of Charles V, my work provides a further contribution to our limited understanding of the Castilian Assembly of the Clergy. I argue that, in the first half of the sixteenth century, the crown attempted to build consensus with the Assembly and reach an accord that was acceptable to both sides. In many ways, the situation described here corresponds to what Gerhard Oestreich calls the 'finance state'—a partnership between the ruler and the estates.[31] State-building theories and concepts of absolutism do not effectively capture this partnership between the ruled and the ruler

---

[30] John A.F. Thomson argues that in the fifteenth century, the Renaissance papacy made concessions to secular rulers to buttress papal authority against conciliarism. Moreover, the popes had to cooperate with princes to ensure the flow of ecclesiastical rents to Rome. Such cooperation normally entailed conceding subsidies to the princes or letting the princes collect annates. Financial concessions, then, served as a bargaining chip. Thomson suggests that, in time, these practices led to a situation where, in regard to clerical taxation, "the limitations on lay action were slight." If a prince decided to tax the clergy, a pope could do little to stop him; the princes desired papal concessions only to bring "additional pressure to bear on reluctant clerical taxpayers." See his *Popes and Princes, 1417–1517: Politics and Polity in the Late Medieval Church* (London: George Allen & Unwin, 1980), Chapter 8 and p. 180.

[31] Gerhard Oestreich *Neostoicism and the early modern state*. eds. Brigitta Oestreich and H.G. Koenigsberger. trans. David McLintock. (Cambridge: Cambridge University Press, 1982), p. 194.

and consequently push aside important institutions, like the Assembly, that do not neatly fit the interpretative model. A pluralistic view of the political sphere, however, provides an interpretive framework centered on consensus between the crown and autonomous, intermediate corporate bodies, and thus provides a truer understanding of political practice and life in the sixteenth century.

CHAPTER ONE

STRUCTURE OF THE ASSEMBLY

This chapter examines the institutional structure and function of the Castilian Assembly of the Clergy in the early modern period. First, I will introduce the major agents in the negotiations. Second, the chapter discusses the convocation of the Assembly from the notification of the papal bull to the election of representatives. Third, I explore the Assembly's functions, costs, and purpose. Fourth, the chapter addresses the process for the actual collection of the subsidy, including discounts, lawsuits, and other obstacles to collection. By examining the participants and the stages of the Assembly from its convocation to the payment of the contribution by individual dioceses, this background material provides a foundation for comprehending the Assembly and makes the detailed case studies of the negotiations between the Assembly and the crown easier to understand.

Major Agents

Representatives of the cathedral chapters constituted the Castilian Assembly of the Clergy.[1] Since the biographical databases necessary for a proper prosopographical study of the representatives do not exist for early modern Spain, a brief discussion of what a cathedral chapter was, what it did, and who constituted it should provide a general idea of the type of men who attended the Assembly.

A *cabildo eclesiástico* was a corporation of beneficiaries attached to a particular church to celebrate Holy Offices in the choir and to administer the *mesa capitular* (rents of the chapter). There were two types of *cabildos eclesiásticos*—cathedral chapters and collegiate chapters. The cathedral chapter is the focus here. In the early church, priests serving in the cathedral church lived a common life with the bishop. In time, the cathedral clergy or canons independently administered the chapters'

---

[1] During Charles V's reign, thirty-three cathedral chapters sent representatives to Assemblies, and a representative of the abbey of Agredo attended the Assembly of 1546. See Table I.

properties and no longer lived the common life, but instead owned personal property and had separate homes and prebends. The cathedral canons became known as 'secular canons.' The number of canons and dignitaries (dean, *chantre*, *maestrescuela*, archdeacons, etc.) varied from cathedral to cathedral, often determined by the rents. Other clergy also served the cathedral and received their salaries from the *mesa capitular*, but they did not have a vote in the cathedral chapter. At the beginning of the sixteenth century, for example, the cathedral of Seville had nine dignitaries, 40 canons, 20 *racioneros* (prebendaries), and 20 *medios racioneros* (half-prebendaries), plus a large number of chaplains. Together, the archbishop and the chapter consumed nearly half the ecclesiastical rents received by the secular clergy in Seville. Most chapters, however, were not as large as Seville. Santo Domingo de la Calzada, for instance, only had three dignitaries, ten canons, and six *medios racioneros*. Regardless of their numbers, canons had three obligations: to maintain residency, to attend Holy Offices, and to attend chapter meetings. In addition to their religious and administrative obligations in the cathedral, canons helped the prelate carry out his pastoral duties and acted as his senate. Moreover, in times of *sede vacante* (vacancy of the episcopal see), the chapter administered the diocese until a new prelate was named. Some chapters also had seigniorial rights, possessing villages, forts, vassals, and the right to administer civil law in their *señorios*.[2]

During the Middle Ages, chapters were autonomous bodies, exempt from the bishops' jurisdiction, and constituted a near parallel power to the bishops in the dioceses. In fact, the Fourth Lateran Council (1215) officially recognized the chapters' right to elect bishops. In the fifteenth century, the popes began to deny chapters the right to nominate bishops, and Hadrian VI (1522–1523) finally conceded this right to Charles V (1516–1556) in the Spanish kingdoms. The Council of Trent

---

[2] For more details see Manuel Teruel Gregorio de Tejada, *Vocabulario Básico de la historia de la Iglesia*, (Barcelona: Crítica, 1993), pp. 31–56; J. Gilchrist, "Cathedral Chapter," *New Catholic Encyclopedia* (New York: McGraw-Hill Book Company, 1967), vol. 3, pp. 249–250; M.A. Ladero Quesada, *El siglo XV en Castilla: Fuentes de renta y política fiscal* (Barcelona: Editorial Ariel, 1982), pp. 202–203; Maximiliano Barrio Gozalo, "La iglesia peninsular de los Reyes Católicos a Carlos V (1490–1530)," in *De la union de coronas al Imperio de Carlos V*, coor. by Ernest Belengeur Cebriá (Madrid: Sociedad Estatal para la Conmemoración de los Centenarios de Felipe II y Carlos V, 2001), vol. 1, pp. 229–231; Rafael Marín López, *El cabildo de la catedral de Granada en el siglo XVI* (Granada: Universidad de Granada, 1998), p. 15; Ignasi Fernández Terricabras, *Felipe II y el clero secular: La aplicación del concilio de Trento* (Madrid: Sociedad Estatal para la Conmemoración de los Centenarios de Felipe II y Carlos V, 2000), p. 294.

(1545–1563) further challenged the cathedral chapters' independence by passing several decrees that increased episcopal authority over them. In response, the Castilian cathedral chapters convened an Assembly of the chapters in 1553 to defend their privileges. The bishops, in turn, assembled in 1554 to discuss how to enact the Tridentine decrees in their dioceses. In the end, the chapters persuaded the popes not to enforce certain Tridentine decrees and maintained a fair amount of independence vis-à-vis their prelates, especially in regard to negotiations for ecclesiastical contributions. For the rest of the century, the chapters continued to aspire to power equivalent to the bishop's on the diocesan level and were often able to exercise significant authority during *sedes vacante*, which lasted on average just over nine months during the reign of Philip II (1556–1598).[3] The prelates, however, were not without influence over their chapters. The chapters of both Seville and Granada periodically consulted their archbishops concerning the subsidy, and the archbishop of Seville and the bishop of Jaén persuaded their respective chapters to accept the terms of payment for the subsidy in the summer of 1540 (see chapter five). In this particular case, however, the chapters probably consented to the prelates' requests out of self-interest.[4] Nonetheless, scholars' assumptions of episcopal centralization in the early modern period obscure the continued importance and autonomy of cathedral chapters, even after Trent, especially in the negotiations discussed here. The negotiations for subsidies, in turn, may have helped the chapters to maintain their position.

Tensions existed not only between prelates and chapters but also between the chapters and the other clergy (secular and regular) and the military orders, especially over the apportionment of the subsidy. In fact, in 1592, the military orders initiated a lawsuit to be admitted to the Assembly for the general apportionment of the subsidy.[5] Nevertheless, the chapters and other clergy did maintain a fair amount of cooperation and coordination on certain occasions, such as the *cesación a divinis* in 1533 (see chapter three). Scholars have paid even less attention to these interactions between the chapters and the other clergy than they

---

[3] See J. Gil Sanjuán, "Lucha de los cabildos castellanos por su autonomía y libertad (1553–1555)," *Espacio, Tiempo y Forma, Serie IV, Historia Moderna* 7 (1994), pp. 275–295; Fernández Terricabras, *Felipe II y el clero secular*, p. 291.

[4] See Lucía Carpintero Aguado, "La congregación del clero de Castilla en el siglo XVII" (Ph.D. diss., Universidad Autónoma de Madrid, 1993), p. 16; AGS, E 49, f. 135; ACG, AC lib.3 ff. 13v, 201, 245v; and ACS, Sec.I, lib.13, f. 203v.

[5] ACT, OF lib. 1350, f. 110v.

have to those between prelates and chapters. Such interactions, though, further demonstrate the fractious nature of the ecclesiastical estate. Thus, when the chapters represented the church in the Assembly of the Clergy, they represented men and women with different interests than the cathedral canons. Nonetheless, the other clergy grudgingly recognized the Assembly's authority to make binding decisions for the entire ecclesiastical estate and occasionally asked the Assembly to petition the king or the pope on their behalf.[6]

To better understand the internal dynamics of individual chapters, it is useful to explore the canons' social background, how they obtained their offices, and what percentage of canons came to office due to the patronage of popes, kings, or bishops. Drawing a composite picture of the cathedral canons is difficult, however, because there was no typical chapter or canon. Still, a few general comments may be helpful.

Popes, prelates, kings, and chapters could all fill vacant offices under certain conditions; the king himself could never name a sufficient number of canons to control a cathedral. Even in Granada, where the king had the right to name all the canons, he did not always do it: often leaving the selection to the archbishop. In general, though, few canonries fell vacant, because it was possible to pass the office from person to person by resignation. Such a tactic, however, could be expensive: in the mid-sixteenth century, a papal bull of resignation for a canonry in Burgos cost 250 *ducados*. Furthermore, the system of resignation often meant that the canonry passed to relatives or descendents of previous officeholders, many of whom were mediocre men without university degrees. Only the *magistral* (theology), *doctoral* (canon law), *lectoral* (lecturer on moral themes), and *penitenciaria* (confessor) canonries were filled by open competition, and these posts usually served as steppingstones to higher office. Most canons were members of the urban commercial and political elites, and they remained in their hometowns and were not destined for great things. They often served in the cathedral chapters with relatives and gained their position through the system of resignations, especially in smaller, poorer chapters.

The situation was somewhat different in wealthier chapters. The kings often used those vacant canonries to reward loyal servants. For example,

---

[6] The collegiate chapter of Valladolid, for example, asked the Assembly to seek the revocation of the exemption of certain monasteries and hospitals from paying tithes. See ACS, Sec. VII, lib. 85 "Congregación de las Santas Iglesias...1555," Session 37, August 19, 1555.

Diego de Saavedra Fajardo, the diplomat and author, was named canon of Santiago in 1617. Many nobles also tried to obtain canonries for their offspring and, like the urban elites, often used the system of resignations to keep the post in the family. No matter how they obtained their office, canons were overwhelmingly from the superior classes. Data from the cathedral of Barcelona in the seventeenth century reveal the elite character of a cathedral chapter: 62 percent of the canons were nobles or urban gentry, 11 percent were urban professionals, and the rest were descendents of laborers and artisans. These figures indicate that cathedrals did offer some social mobility. The composition of the diocesan clergy of Barcelona, however, was the exact inverse.[7]

Canons' social background could vary, but all had to meet certain educational requirements. In Granada, for instance, the cathedral's constitution established that candidates for the office of dean had to have either a master's degree or else be a licenciado in theology, or be a doctor or a licenciado in canon law. Other dignitaries had slightly lower educational requirements, such as a minimum of a bachelor's degree in theology or canon law. A canon needed to have at least two years in theology or canon law at the university. In Granada, the canons were roughly divided between theologians and lawyers. In Burgos, the educational requirements were less stringent: canons were supposed to be literate in Castilian and Latin.[8] Despite differences in education levels within a cathedral and educational requirements between cathedrals, the cathedral canons were nonetheless among the most educated people in society.

On the whole, most representatives to the Assembly of the Clergy came from the elite and highly educated. The personal data on just a few of the representatives confirms this assessment. Diego López de Ayala, one of Toledo's representatives in 1533, was the son of the count of Fuensalida and translated the works of Boccaccio and other Italian writers into Spanish, while García Manrique de Lara, one of

---

[7] See María Isabel Nicolas Crispin et al. *La organización del cabildo catedralicio Leones a comienzos del s.XV (1419–1426)* (León: Universidad de León, 1990), pp. 53–61; Antonio Domínguez Ortiz, *Las clases privilegiadas en el Antiguo Régimen* (Madrid, 1985 edn), pp. 239–46; Constance Jones Mathers, "The Life of Canons in Sixteenth-Century Castile," in *Renaissance Society and Culture: Essays in Honor of Eugene F. Rice, Jr.*, eds. John Monfasani and Ronald G. Musto (New York: Italica Press 1991), pp. 161–176; Barrio, "La iglesia," p. 232; Marín López, *El cabildo*, pp. 77, 151–155; Fernández Terricabras, *Felipe II y el clero secular*, pp. 294, 297–298.

[8] Marín López, *El cabildo*, pp. 17–18, 59; Mathers, "Life," p. 174.

Toledo's representatives in 1541, was the son of the count of Belarcázar and the marquise of Ayamonte.[9] Several representatives from Burgos came from prominent urban families. Don Agustín de Torquemada, who attended the Assembly of 1533, and Andrés Ortega de Cerezo, who attended the Assembly of 1541, were both related to Pedro de Melgosa, a *regidor* (municipal councilor) in Burgos from 1523 until 1558. Diego Díez de Arceo Miranda, who attended the Assemblies of 1551 and 1555, was a descendent of a prominent fifteenth-century Burgos family. Palencia's representative in 1533, Francisco Ruiz de la Mota, had ties to both the ecclesiastical elite and the urban elite; his uncle was Bishop Pedro Ruiz de la Mota, who had been Charles V's favorite, and his brother and other relatives were members of the city council in Burgos.[10] Some canons also served as royal officials or at court. For example, Cristóbal Hernández de Baltodano, one of Badajoz's representatives in 1555, was on the Council of the Inquisition, and Alvaro de Caravajal, Plasencia's representative in 1592, was chaplain mayor to Princess Juana.[11] Other representatives were intellectuals and scholars, such as Dr. Pedro de Lerma, one of Burgos's representatives in 1533, who defended Erasmus at the conference of Valladolid in 1527. These representatives' status gave them contacts throughout the highest political and intellectual circles in Castilian society.[12]

Greater knowledge of the representatives will also explain more fully networks within the ecclesiastical estate and the mobility of canons. José Sánchez Herrero suggests, for example, that Dr. Juan Egido, one of Seville's representatives in 1555, might have had the secret intention of meeting with members of the Protestant cell in Valladolid.[13] Generally,

---

[9] Ángel Fernández Collado, *La catedral de Toledo en el siglo XVI: Vida, arte y personas* (Toledo: Diputación Provincial de Toledo, 1999), pp. 80–83.

[10] I am grateful to Constance Jones Mathers for providing me with the biographical information on the canons from Burgos who attended the Assembly (September 1997).

[11] ACS, Sec. VII, lib. 85 "Congregación de las Santas Iglesias...1555," Session 1, June 25, 1555; ACT, OF lib. 1350, f. 12v.

[12] For more on the linkage between the chapters and the local oligarchies, see Fernández Terricabras, *Felipe II y el clero secular*, p. 298.

[13] In 1549, Charles V planned to nominate Dr. Egido to be bishop of Tortosa. The nomination was withdrawn within two months, because Dr. Egido was accused of preaching errors. The Inquisition did not convict him at this time. In 1559, four years after his death, however, he was burnt in effigy. See José Sánchez Herrero, "Sevilla del Renacimiento," in *Historia de la Iglesia de Sevilla*, ed. Carlos Ros (Sevilla: Editorial Castillejo, 1992), pp. 372–373; Robert C. Spach, "Juan Gil and Sixteenth-Century Spanish Protestantism," *Sixteenth Century Journal* 26 (1995), pp. 857–879.

however, representatives' goals were less surreptitious: for example, they received the Assembly's permission to compete for open canonries at nearby cathedrals. In 1628, the representative from Córdoba competed for the canonry *magistral* in Toledo, and in 1638 the representative from Orense competed for the canonry *penitenciaria* in Ávila.[14] By attending the Assembly, canons also had the opportunity to meet with the king and royal ministers, which may have increased their chances of promotion. The representative of Burgos in 1530, for example, was tapped by the Council of the Indies for a bishopric in the New World, while another canon was named bishop of Lugo during the Assembly of 1560.[15] A century later, two representatives were elevated to bishoprics during the Assembly of 1664.[16]

Interaction at the Assemblies also allowed representatives to make contacts with fellow canons from distant chapters. Some of these contacts may have developed into friendships, because many representatives attended multiple Assemblies. Francisco Vélez, for example, represented Granada at the Assemblies of 1530, 1533, 1536, 1540, 1541, and 1543, while Dr. Bartolomé de la Plaza represented the chapter at the Assemblies of 1575, 1582, and 1587.[17] Frequent attendance also guaranteed that a handful of representatives at any given Assembly would have had previous experience with the Assembly's business and procedures. Personal contacts and the creation of social networks probably helped the chapters to organize resistance to the subsidy, but it may also have created new rivalries between chapters. Further research on the representatives will provide a better understanding of the negotiations between the Assembly and the crown, internal disputes between canons, and mobility and advancement of the clergy.

Such research is necessary because, as Neithard Bulst has pointed out, the negotiations of representative institutions often had as much to do with the individuals involved in the negotiations as with the institutional framework in which the negotiations took place. For example, Alonso de Mendoza, a strident opponent of Philip II, was the president of the

---

[14] BN 3/14341, *Assientos de la congregación que celebraron las santas iglesias de la corona de Castilla y León...de 1637*, f. 67v.

[15] Dr. Juan de Aceves apparently did not go to America, but he eventually obtained the bishop's mitre of Ciudad Rodrigo (1546–1549), Mathers, September 1997.

[16] BN, VE 24–1, ff. 1v–2.

[17] Marín López, *El cabildo*, pp. 160–162, 444–445; ACG, AC lib. 2, f. 323; For a short note from the archbishop of Granada recommending Vélez to the king see AGS, E leg. 45, f. 195.

Assembly of 1586 and doubtless made trying negotiations even more difficult by refusing to hand over certain papers to royal officials and circulating documents that attacked Philip's fiscal policy. Yet, in light of the sparse personal data for most representatives, the present study examines these negotiations from an institutional perspective. This undoubtedly will make the Assembly appear more monolithic than it actually was, but the perennial conflict between the Assembly and the crown over nearly three centuries indicates that the structure and politics of the negotiations for subsidies explain much of the conflict; the individual representatives and their personal animosities toward the crown only exacerbated underlying tensions.[18]

The principal agent for the crown in these negotiations was the Comisario General de la Cruzada, who was also the ecclesiastical official in charge of the Council of the Cruzada. The office of Comisario General had existed since at least 1482. Prior to 1529, the king nominated individuals to the office, but the pope had the final say on appointments. The commission of the Comisario General was originally valid only during the sale of indulgences for a crusade (*cruzada*) or the negotiations for and collection of a specific subsidy.[19] After 1529, the title became permanent; it was independent of the crusade or the subsidy.[20] Furthermore, the king now appointed each Comisario General, but a new Comisario General still needed papal confirmation within six months of appointment to exercise the office.[21] The popes did not always scrutinize the royal candidate. In 1546, for example, Pope Paul III (1534–1549) authorized Giovanni Poggio, the nuncio, to confer the office on whomever the king named.[22] During Charles V's reign, there were three principal Comisarios General: Francisco de

---

[18] See Neithard Bulst, "Rulers, Representative Institutions and their Members as Power Elites: Rivals or Partners?" in *Power Elites and State Building*, ed. Wolfgang Reinhard (Oxford: Clarendon Press, 1996) pp. 41–58; Richard L. Kagan, *Lucrecia's Dreams: Politics and Prophecy in Sixteenth-Century Spain* (Berkeley: University of California Press, 1990), p. 106.

[19] In the case of a subsidy, the commission could last two to three years, because the Comisario General held office until all the money was collected.

[20] Yet, the Assembly contested the permanency of the office at least once. See ACS, Sec. VII, lib. 85, "Congregación del clero...1555," Session 22, July 23, 1555.

[21] José Martínez Millán and C. Javier de Carlos Morales, "Los orígenes del consejo de Cruzada (siglo XVI)," *Hispania* LI/3, no. 179 (1991), p. 912; Juan Miguel de los Ríos, *Historia de las Tres Gracias pontificias de Crusada, Subsidio y Excusado* (Madrid, 1849), vol. 1, f. 25.

[22] AGS, E leg. 873, ff. 47–48, 52.

Mendoza (Bishop of Oviedo, Zamora, and Palencia), 1525–March 29, 1536; García de Loaysa (Bishop of Sigüenza and Archbishop of Seville), May 20, 1536–April 22, 1546;[23] and Juan Suárez de Carvajal (Bishop of Lugo), April 22, 1546–1562. Between 1525 and 1608, there were twelve Comisarios General, and on average they each held office for eight years.[24]

Prior to 1525, two to four prelates periodically occupied the office of Comisario General jointly when it existed. Thereafter, the trend was for one cleric, typically a prelate, to occupy the office. Nevertheless, on several occasions, an additional prelate, most often the papal nuncio, shared authority with the Comisario General for certain matters. This arrangement may have resulted from papal efforts to maintain some control over the contribution or from royal efforts to better administer its collection. In 1532, for instance, treasury officials recommended that more than one Comisario General would be necessary for the good dispatch of the *cruzada* and the *quarta* (quarter of the year's rents).[25]

The Comisario General had both spiritual and temporal prerogatives. He could deprive clergy of their benefices for failing to pray the canonical hours properly. He could confiscate money gained through usury or price gouging and use it for the war against the infidels. He had jurisdiction over cases of homicide, simony, apostasy, and other ecclesiastical crimes. He had the right to halve the pecuniary fines imposed

---

[23] For a biography of Loaysa, see Kristen Kuebler, "Cardinal García de Loaisa y Mendoza: Servant of Church and Emperor" (Ph.D. diss., Oxford University, 1997), especially chapter 5 where she discusses his role as Comisario General.

[24] Francisco de Mendoza (Bishop of Oviedo, Zamora, and Palencia) 1525–March 29, 1536; Cardinal García de Loaysa (Bishop of Sigüenza, Archbishop of Seville, and President of the Council of the Indies) May 20, 1536–April 22, 1546; Juan Suárez de Carvajal (Bishop of Lugo and President of Hacienda) April 22, 1546–1562; Bernardo de Fresneda (Bishop of Cuenca, Council of State, and Confessor of King) July 1, 1562–1571 or Pedro Deza y Guzmán, 1563–1572; Francisco de Soto Salazar (Bishop of Segorbe y Albarracin) December 1, 1572–1576; Pedro Velarde (Council of the Inquisition) August 1576–July 14, 1582; Tomás de Salazar (Canon of Seville and Council of the Inquisition) July 26, 1582–June 26, 1585; Pedro Puertocarrero (Royal Council, Inquisitor General, Bishop of Calahorra, and Bishop of Cuenca) June 27, 1585–July 6, 1589; Cardinal Francisco de Ávila (Canon of Toledo and Council of the Inquisition) 1589–July 31, 1596; Juan de Zuñiga (Canon of Toledo, Bishop of Cartagena, and Inquisitor General) August 1, 1596–August 31, 1600; Felipe de Tarfis (Council of the Inquisition and Bishop of Palencia) September 1, 1600–May 27, 1608. See Alonso Pérez de Lara, *Compendio de las Tres Gracias de la Santa Cruzada, Subsidio y Excusado* (Madrid, 1610), Book 1, pp. 18–19; Martínez Millán and Carlos Morales, "Los origenes," pp. 931–932.

[25] AGS, E leg. 25, f. 174.

by ecclesiastical courts. The Comisario General could allow priests to celebrate Mass at non-canonical hours in oratories and authorize private Masses in oratories during an interdict. He also had authority to grant dispensations for marriages within four grades of consanguinity.

The Comisario General's most important prerogatives, however, related to the administration of the papal concessions known collectively as the Tres Gracias: Cruzada, Subsidio, and Excusado. For example, he could suspend interdicts to allow for the promulgation of the *cruzada*. During the preaching of the *cruzada*, he could suspend and later revalidate the indulgences granted by specific churches, monasteries, confraternities, or other ecclesiastical institutions. He had the right to translate the bulls of the *cruzada* to each kingdom's vernacular, as well as to interpret them. He was responsible for the bulls' publication at the Prado monastery in Valladolid and the monastery of San Pedro Mártir in Toledo, and their distribution through Spain. He had the right to appoint administrators of the *cruzada* and had jurisdiction over all crimes or abuses committed by members of the Council of the Cruzada or its agents. The Comisario General also had jurisdiction over all lawsuits related to the Tres Gracias. He could promulgate ecclesiastical censures against the clergy and others for not complying with his orders. Finally, he oversaw the outfitting of the galleys maintained by ecclesiastical contributions and presided over the Council of the Cruzada.[26]

In the negotiations between the crown and the Assembly for ecclesiastical contributions, the Comisario General played a central role. He often headed the royal delegation that conferred with the Assembly on the terms of payment. He could also bypass the Assembly and negotiate for contributions directly with the chapters. Once the parties reached an agreement, the Comisario General worked directly with the chapters for the collection and payment of their share. Such work was not always easy. The Comisario General and the chapters often sparred over the appointment of commissioners and other officials responsible for collecting the subsidy and *excusado* in each diocese. The Comisario General technically had the right to name his own commissioners, judges, and other officials, but in practice the chapters made selections from among the canons and the Comisario General simply confirmed the appointments. The result was a constant struggle between

---

[26] Pérez de Lara, *Compendio de las Tres Gracias*, Book 1, pp. 52–63 and Book 2, pp. 94–95; Ríos *Historia de las Tres Gracias*, vol 1, ff. 27–32.

the Comisario General, who tried to exert greater influence over the collection of ecclesiastical contributions at the diocesan level, and the chapters, who defended their right to administer the collection.[27]

The Comisario General de la Cruzada presided over the Council of the Cruzada, which was formed sometime between 1509 and 1534 but went without Ordinances until 1544. The council's central administration consisted of roughly 20 people, both lay and clerical. Under normal circumstances, the council met three times a week—for two hours on Tuesday, Thursday, and Saturday afternoons—in the Comisario General's residence. The revised Ordinances of 1554 circumscribed the Comisario General's authority, however. Clause 3, for example, stated that the Comisario General could not dispatch any decree, provision, or sentence without consulting his council's assessor. That clause meant that the Comisario General could no longer function without his council.

On the local level, the number of people involved with the Tres Gracias was far greater. By the end of the sixteenth century, approximately 8,795 people in Castile alone worked for the Council of the Cruzada. Royal officials occasionally augmented these numbers. To prevent delays in collecting the Tres Gracias, for example, the crown ordered secular magistrates to assist in collecting from recalcitrant clergy or laymen who possessed ecclesiastical rents. Several royal decrees from Philip II, however, suggest that the local magistrates did not always comply. Peru and New Spain each had a Comisario General *subdelegado* with their own bureaucracies to administer the Tres Gracias in the American colonies, with any appeals sent to the Comisario General de la Cruzada.[28] Although the following case studies will not address the council directly, it played a major support role to the Comisario General and had an important place within the nascent Castilian administration, as one of three councils that held both spiritual and temporal jurisdiction.[29]

---

[27] For more details on the conflicts over appointments and the number of officials, see Carpintero, "La congregación," pp. 153–159.

[28] See Dolores Cruz Arroyo, "El Consejo de la Cruzada: Siglos XVI–XVII" (Tesina, Universidad Autónoma de Madrid, 1988); Pérez de Lara, *Compendio de las Tres Gracias*; Ríos *Historia de las Tres*; Martínez Millán and Carlos Morales, "Los origenes," pp. 901–932; Carpintero, "La congregación," pp. 149–172; ACG, leg. 458, pieza 7, "A las justicias del arcobispo de granada que executen los mandamientos que los juezos subdelegados del comisario general…"; and Teruel, *Vocabulario*, p. 116.

[29] Pablo Fernández Albaladejo notes that Spain and Portugal were the only kingdoms where state councils—Inquisition, Cruzada, and Orders—had both spiritual and temporal jurisdiction. See "Iglesia y configuración del poder en la monarquía católica

Interestingly, when Fray Antonio de Sotomayor was Inquisitor General (1632–1643), someone suggested merging the councils of the Cruzada and of the Inquisition, primarily to cut costs for the government, but also as a way to extend the reach of the Inquisition.[30]

Throughout the formation of the office of Comisario General and the Council of the Cruzada in the early sixteenth century, the crown continually intervened to exert greater influence over them. In 1509, for example, the Comisario General's accountants were placed under royal jurisdiction to help coordinate the financing of the military campaign against Oran. This move allowed the crown to count revenues from ecclesiastical contributions together with its other extraordinary income. Ultimately, the crown hoped to eliminate all restrictions on the use of ecclesiastical contributions. Through the treasury ordinances of 1523, 1524, and 1525, Charles V placed the disbursement of ecclesiastical contributions almost completely under the jurisdiction of the royal treasury. These changes allowed the monarch to transfer more easily money raised through ecclesiastical contributions to causes that were distinct from the original papal concession, but also led to jurisdictional conflicts between the Comisario General and the Treasury. These clashes were temporarily mitigated when the same person was both Comisario General and president of the Treasury, as was the case with Francisco de Mendoza and Juan Suárez de Carvajal. Suárez, however, had difficulty reconciling the two positions and jealousy guarded his office as Comisario General, resisting the transfer of revenues from the *cruzada* and subsidy to the royal coffers, as the rest of the Council of the Treasury desired. Conflicts between the Comisario General and the Treasury were perennial, and the kings occasionally supported the Council of the Cruzada against the Treasury. In 1609, for instance, Philip III (1598–1621) issued a decree to keep receipts from the Tres Gracias separate from those of the Treasury. Nonetheless, the Treasury continued to infringe on the Comisario General's jurisdiction and, in time, even the Assembly complained, declaring that the Comisario

---

(siglos XV–XVII)" in *Etat et Eglise dans la Genese de L'Etat Moderne* (Madrid: Bibliotheque de la Casa de Velazquez, 1986), pp. 209–216.

[30] Memorial Library, Special Collections, University of Wisconsin-Madison, Porter Collection of Spanish Literature, Item 736, ff. 215–219. Treasury officials were already complaining about the high administrative costs of the Council of the Cruzada in the 1540s, see *Corpus documental de Carlos V*, ed. Manuel Fernández Álvarez (Salamanca: Universidad, 1975) II, pp. 263–264.

General should administer the Tres Gracias and royal officials should only assist him in forcing recalcitrant contributors to pay.[31]

The office of Comisario General not only had to withstand royal intervention, but it also became intertwined with factional politics at court. In 1538, for example Comisario General Loaysa sought to strengthen his position against the presidents of the Councils of Castile and of the Treasury by making Suárez, his nephew-in-law, an assessor in the Council of the Cruzada. José Martínez Millán and C. Javier de Carlos Morales have suggested that in 1563, while Bernardo de Fresneda was still Comisario General, Pedro Deza's appointment to the same office may have resulted from the emerging predominance of the Ebolista faction at court. Factional politics clearly swayed the appointment process, and as the office of Comisario General evolved, it "inevitably influenced the relations of power maintained between the patrons of the court—their fight to control political and administrative influence in the kingdom."[32]

Convocation of the Assembly

It was the chapters that convened an Assembly, but first the crown needed to obtain the requisite papal bull for the concession of an ecclesiastical contribution. Once the bull arrived at court, the Comisario General notified all the chapters throughout Spain via the *corregidor* (chief royal magistrate in the cities) or another royal official on the local level. The notification followed a prearranged format. In each case, the chapter met in the chapter house and four canons received the royal official in the foyer. The royal official disarmed before entering the chapter house and, upon entering, sat next to the dean or highest dignitary. Once the royal decree was read, a scribe entered and the rest of the documents were read. Three copies of the Comisario General's notification were delivered. One was nailed to the cathedral door to

---

[31] Martínez Millán and Carlos Morales, "Los orígenes," pp. 907–912, 919; BN, V.E. 186-7, ff. 7–9.

[32] Martínez Millán and Carlos Morales, "Los orígenes," pp. 914 (quote), 916–917, 929. For more on court factions and the council of the Cruzada, including a clarification on the Fresneda—Deza situation in the 1560s, see Henar Pizarro Llorente, "Facciones cortesanas en el Consejo de Cruzada durante el reinado de Felipe II (1562–1585)," *Miscelánea Comillas* 56 (1998), pp. 159–177.

notify individuals who possessed ecclesiastical rents of the contribution, another was deposited in the cathedral archive, and a third,
which acknowledged notification of the concession, was returned to
the Council of the Cruzada.[33] The various chapters, however, did not
always receive notification at the same time. In 1555, for instance, the
chapter of Toledo was notified on February 18, while the chapter of
Seville did not receive official notification until May 2.[34]

   After the notification, the cathedral chapters consulted with each
other to gauge the other chapters' positions and to coordinate a unified
stance.[35] The correspondence could be heavy; in May 1536, for example,
the chapter of Toledo appointed six canons to read and respond to
letters from the other chapters.[36] Such exchanges occurred with every
notification, as the large bundle of correspondence in the Cathedral
Archive of Granada attests.[37] The exchanges generally addressed the
nature of the concession, the ecclesiastical estate's response, preparations to appeal the bull, and whether or not to convene an Assembly
of the Clergy.

   An appeal to either the Comisario General or the pope was usually
the first action the chapters took. In their appeals, the chapters generally
argued that the church was exempt from taxation in accordance with
the Bible, teachings of church fathers, decrees of Councils, and papal
encyclicals. Further, they argued that the church was to aid princes in
their wars through prayers; that paying the contribution would severely
hinder the church's ability to carry out its religious and charitable duties;
and that the church already provided the crown with excessive economic aid.[38] The chapters also charged that the crown inappropriately
used the contributions; for example, instead of equipping galleys in the
Mediterranean, the crown used the contributions to guarantee loans in
northern Europe.[39] Such arguments, however, rarely convinced either
the king or the pope that the concessions were illegitimate or needed
to be completely revised. Still, the appeals demonstrate the ecclesiasti-

---

[33] Carpintero, "La congregación," pp. 32–33.
[34] ACT, AC lib. 9, f. 239v; ACS, Sec. I, lib. 23 ff. 38rv and 39v.
[35] ACT, AC lib. 9, f. 242; ACS, Sec. I, lib. 23 f. 25v.
[36] ACT, AC lib. 5, f. 226v.
[37] ACG, leg. 69, pieza 1.
[38] ACS, Sec. IX, leg. 107, no. 12.
[39] Ángel Iturrioz Magaña, *Estudio del subsidio y excusado (1561–1808): Contribuciones
económicas de la Diócesis de Calahorra y La Calzada a la Real Hacienda* (Logroño: Instituto
de estudios riojanos, 1987), pp. 16–22.

cal estate's determination to defend its liberties and prerogatives from royal infringement.

The chapter of Toledo had the primatial right to convene an Assembly, but traditionally only with the consent of all or a majority of the chapters.[40] In 1532, for example, Segovia prepared a list of questions for Toledo on the courses of action to pursue in the absence of an Assembly.[41] Even when a particular chapter insisted on calling an Assembly, it often encountered resistance. In May 1536, Seville pressed for an Assembly, even sending representatives to Toledo, only to discover that the other chapters were not ready to assemble. It took the chapters three months to agree finally to an Assembly in August 1536.[42]

Despite the royal convocation of several Assemblies in the fourteenth and fifteenth centuries, the role of royal permission in convoking an Assembly is unclear. As noted above, the initiative to convene an Assembly came from the chapters themselves. Nevertheless, a canon in Toledo vigorously argued against convening an Assembly in 1523 because neither the pope nor the king had ordered it. Even if the pope approved an Assembly, he maintained, the chapter still needed to consult the king, and without his permission it should not proceed. Moreover, the canon did not think there was just cause to convene an Assembly, and his argument convinced some other canons, who promptly changed their position.[43] The Assembly eventually did meet from July 17 to August 27, but whether the crown consented to the Assembly of 1523 is unknown. In 1545, Toledo's attempt to convene an Assembly to address the upcoming Council of Trent faltered in part perhaps because the chapter had not asked for royal permission. In fact, Prince Philip, regent of Spain in Charles V's absence, had written to all the chapters, urging them not to attend. A further obstacle in 1545 was that the Council of Trent potentially lay outside the Assembly's parameters. According to the chapter of Granada, the Assembly only had authority on issues related to the ecclesiastical contribution and not on doctrinal issues.[44]

---

[40] In 1575, however, the chapter of Toledo convened an Assembly without the approval of the majority of the chapters. In response, the Assembly of 1575 decreed that in the future Toledo could not do so without the consent of a majority of the chapters. See Carpintero, "La congregación," p. 34.

[41] ACS, Sec. I, lib. 13, f. 216v.

[42] ACS, Sec. I, lib. 15, f. 32rv. ACT, AC lib. 5, f. 231v. ACB, R lib. 45, f. 13rv.

[43] AGS, E leg. 11, f. 181.

[44] ACG, leg. 69, pieza 2. See also AGS, E legs. 70–72. Yet, 25 years earlier, Granada had sent a representative to an Assembly convened to address a brief allowing secular

Nevertheless, the documents confirm that in general the chapters did convene Assemblies without royal permission. In an attempt to divide the chapters in 1555, for example, the Comisario General pointed out that the chapter of Toledo had convened the Assembly without royal permission.[45] Apparently, despite many ambiguities, lack of royal permission was not an obstacle if the chapters were determined to meet. Once they reached an agreement, the chapter of Toledo notified the other chapters of the Assembly's date and location.

Even if royal permission had been required to convene an Assembly, the chapters' ability to circumvent it indicates the Castilian Assembly of the Clergy's initiative. The Assembly did not meet only at the whim of the king; instead, its mandate usually came from below, from the chapters themselves.[46] In fact, at the Assembly of 1533, a representative from Toledo proposed that the Assembly meet every three years to address the ecclesiastical estate's grievances.[47] While nothing came of his proposal, similar proposals emerged periodically and at no point did any representative bring up the need for royal permission.[48]

With the convocation of an Assembly, the chapters elected their representatives, assigned them a salary, and drew up their powers and instructions. The election process varied from chapter to chapter. The canons could choose their representative(s) by consensus on the most qualified candidate(s) or by a vote of acclamation, but normally they used secret ballots. Those elected did not always accept the office enthusiastically, and many managed to avoid the post by citing other obligations or health. Throughout most of the sixteenth century, the chapters could elect dignitaries, canons, or prebendaries as their representatives to the Assembly. In 1596, Pope Clement VIII (1592–1605) ordered

---

judges to try and punish clergy who had committed crimes. The chapter of Granada must therefore have recognized that the Assembly's jurisdiction was not limited to only ecclesiastical contributions. See ACG, AC lib. 2, ff. 20v–21.

[45] ACT, Documentos Secretaria Cabildo, Caja 1, "Al dean y cabildo de Toledo de capellan mayor de Toledo y Francisco de Silva. Valladolid 30 junio 1555."

[46] The French king recognized the French Assembly of the Clergy's right to convene on its own accord in 1579; in 1595, the Assembly initiated regular meetings at five year intervals. See R. Doucet, *Les institutions de la France au XVIᵉ siécle* (Paris: Editions A. Et J. Picard, 1948), p. 850.

[47] ACS, Sec. VII, lib. 85, "Congregación del clero…1533," November 24, 1533.

[48] Corporate bodies in the crown of Aragon also met on their own initiative in the early seventeenth century. See Xavier Gil, "Parliamentary Life in the Crown of Aragon: Cortes, Juntas de Brazos, and other Corporate Bodies," *Journal of Early Modern History* 6 (2002), pp. 383–384.

that only canons and dignitaries could represent the chapters at the Assembly. Later, in 1622, Pope Gregory XV (1621–1623) ordered that representatives must be ordained *in sacris*. Except for bishops *in partibus infidelium*, who had the title of bishop but no actual diocese, bishops could not attend the Assembly after 1505. In 1560, for example, the Assembly discharged a representative from Toledo of his duty when he was named bishop of Lugo; it was considered inappropriate for a prelate to attend the Assembly.[49]

For each Assembly, the number of chapters in attendance and the number of representatives sent by chapters varied. Hence, the total number of representatives present changed from Assembly to Assembly (see Table I). Failure to attend an Assembly, however, did not always mean that a chapter lacked representation. Some absent chapters delegated their authority to another chapter in attendance, even though this practice was frowned upon. The Assembly of 1530, for example, ruled that, in the future, representatives could not represent chapters other than their own.[50] Despite the Assembly's decision, chapters continued to delegate their authority to other chapters. In 1533, the chapter of Toledo had power of attorney for Cartegena. That Assembly subsequently renewed its predecessor's decision and ordered that future letters of convocations state clearly that those who granted power of attorney and those who accepted it would be fined. Furthermore, that Assembly instituted fines on absent chapters.[51] Absenteeism, however, was a perennial problem. The Assembly of 1586 drew up regulations to fine chapters for each day their representatives were absent and applied the money raised from those fines to the common costs of the Assembly. Notwithstanding fines and other reprimands, some chapters still absented themselves from the Assembly entirely or they only attended the negotiations for either the subsidy or the *excusado*.[52]

Most chapters who attended the Assembly sent one or two representatives. Toledo, for example always sent two representatives, while Segovia sent two representatives in 1530, 1533, 1541, and 1555 and only one representative in 1546 and 1592 (Table I). The chapters

---

[49] Carpintero, "La congregación," pp. 37–38; Iturrioz, *Estudio del subsidio*, pp. 138–139. For examples of canons declining the position, see ACT, AC lib. 4, f. 286v and AC lib. 9, ff. 259–260, 261v–262v.

[50] ACS, Sec. II, lib. 1577 (77), Session 9.

[51] ACS, Sec. VII, lib. 85, "Congregación del clero...1533," November 22, 1533.

[52] Carpintero, "La congregación," pp. 45–49.

Table I. Representatives at Assemblies.

Dioceses	1530*	1533	1541	1546	1555	1592†
Toledo	2	2	2	2	2	2
Seville	2	2	2	2	2	1
Santiago	2	2	2	1	1	1
Burgos	2	1	2	1	1	
León	1	1	2	1	1	1
Córdoba	1	1	1	2	2	1
Salamanca	2	2	Attended	2	2	1
Zamora	1	1	1	1	2	1
Segovia	2	2	2	1	2	1
Ávila	2	2	2	1	2	1
Cuenca	2	1	1	1	2	1
Palencia	2	1	1	1	2	S (1)
Sigüenza	2	1	1	1	1	S (1)
Plasencia	2	1	1	1	2	1
Calahorra	1	1	1	1	2	1
La Calzada	1	1	1	1	1	
Jaén	1	1	Attended	1	1	1
Astorga	1	1	2		1	1
Cartegena	1	p. Toledo	1		2	S (1)
Ciudad Rodrigo	1		1	1	1	1
Coria	1	1	1	1	1	S (1)
Oviedo	p. Toledo‡	2	1	1	2	1
Badajoz	p. Plazencia	1	Attended	1	2	
Tuy	1	1	1	1	1	S (1)
Lugo	1	1	1	1	1	S (1)
Osma	1	1	1	1	1	S (1)
Orense	1	1	1	1	1	S (1)
Cádiz		1	p. Toledo	1	1	1
Mondoñedo		1	1	1	1	S (1)
Granada	2	1	1			S (1)
Málaga		1				
Pamplona	3					E
Guadix		1				S (1)
Agredo				1		
Total	40	37	34	32	43	32

Sources: ACS, Sec. II, lib. 1157(77); Sec. VII, lib. 85, 86 and 87; Lucía Carpintero Aguado "La congregación del clero de Castilla en el siglo XVII" (Ph.D. diss., Universidad Autónoma de Madrid, 1993), pp. 45–46.

* A blank space indicates that there is no evidence of a chapter attending the Assembly.

† Two Assemblies were held in 1592—one for the subsidy and one for the excusado. Those chapters whose representatives only attended the Assembly for the subsidy are indicated by S, while those whose representatives only attended the Assembly for the excusado are indicated by E.

‡ Indicates that a chapter granted power of attorney to another chapter to represent it at the Assembly.

were free to decide on the number of representatives. In 1536, for example, the chapter of Burgos discussed sending two representatives but finally voted to send only one; a few years later, in 1541, it sent two.[53] Representatives from the Kingdom of Navarre, the Kingdom of Granada, and the Canaries occasionally augmented the number of representatives at the Castilian Assembly of the Clergy in the first half of the sixteenth century. For most of the sixteenth century, the total number of representatives attending any given Assembly was between 32 and 43, and the Assembly's expenses increased with each additional representative (see below). In order to control the spiraling costs, the crown tried on several occasions to limit each chapter to sending one representative.[54]

There was no uniform remuneration for representatives. Each chapter individually compensated its own representative(s), and salaries within a chapter could change from year to year, as representatives of different ranks received different salaries. In 1523, the chapter of Toledo paid its representatives three ducados a day. In 1530, the chapter of Seville paid the *chantre* (choir master) four ducados a day and a canon two ducados a day, while in 1533 it paid both representatives only two ducados daily. Representatives' salaries occasionally led to conflicts between the chapters and the rest of the diocesan clergy, who had to pay a portion of the salary. In Calahorra, for example, the chapter paid its representatives four ducados a day in 1562. This led to a lawsuit before the Comisario General between the chapter and the rest of the clergy, including the bishop. Finally, in 1584, the parties reached a resolution to reduce the salary to three ducados a day. Regardless of the amount assigned, the salary did not always cover the costs of attending the meeting. In 1546, for example, the representative of Burgos lost his mule en route to the meeting and requested further compensation from the chapter for his mule. The chapter willingly agreed to pay him but only after the apportionment of the subsidy and its costs. Some chapters, like Granada, occasionally provided a gratuity to representatives who successfully carried out their charge.[55]

With the representatives elected and their salaries determined, the chapters drew up powers and instructions for them. The specific powers

---

[53] ACB, R lib. 45, f. 13v and R lib. 46, f. 208v.

[54] See Carpintero, "La congregación," pp. 43–44 and Tabla I, pp. 45–46. The Comisario General also tried to limit each chapter, except Toledo, to one representative in the 1570s. See ACS, Sec. IX, leg. 111, ff. 6–12.

[55] ACT, AC lib. 4, f. 286v; ACS, Sec. I, lib. 12, f. 116v and lib. 13, f. 265; Iturrioz, *Estudio del subsidio*, pp. 139–140; ACB, R lib. 48, f. 318rv; Marín López, *El cabildo*, p. 161.

granted are not exactly clear from the documents, except that each representative needed to possess certain powers to participate in the Assembly. In 1530, for example, the representatives from Pamplona were only allowed to participate conditionally in the Assembly until they received the proper powers from their chapter.[56] To avoid the continual problem of representatives arriving with incomplete or insufficient powers, the Assembly of 1582 ordered the chapter of Toledo to send a prototype of the powers each representative should have with future letters of convocation. Either Toledo failed to comply with the order or chapters continued to send representatives with incomplete powers, because the Assembly of 1592 again charged Toledo with this task.[57]

Each chapter gave its representatives specific instructions. The details differed from diocese to diocese, but there were many shared concerns. The chapter of Granada's instructions for its representatives provide insight into the types of issues chapters wanted their representatives to address. First, the Granadan representatives were instructed to strive for the smallest subsidy payable over the longest period and to make sure the Kingdom of Granada paid no more than 8,000 ducados. Second, the representatives were asked to secure a discount of 1,000 ducados from Granada's share of the subsidy. To achieve this objective, they brought copies of previous royal decrees that stipulated the discount. Third, the Granadan representatives were to seek specific ordinances to facilitate the collection and apportionment of the subsidy on the diocesan level. The chapter, for example, wanted all local judges of the Council of the Cruzada to be cathedral canons. It further demanded the right to censure people who did not pay their portion of the subsidy, the right to summon royal officials against lay people who possessed ecclesiastical rents and refused to pay their portion of the subsidy, and royal decrees to prohibit the *Chancillería* of Granada (high court) from meddling in business relating to the subsidy. They also wanted the subsidy and its cost to be collected simultaneously. Fourth, the representatives were instructed to include in the apportionment those orders or individuals who were normally exempt from paying the subsidy. If this failed, they were to seek a further discount for the exempt orders or individuals from the amount allotted to the Kingdom of Granada. At times, the chapter of Granada ordered its representatives not to enter the Assembly, believing

---

[56] ACS, Sec. II, lib. 1157 (77), Session 10.
[57] Carpintero, "La congregación," pp. 40–41; ACT, OF lib. 1350, f. 134.

that the chapter could negotiate betters terms with the crown directly or to protest perceived or real harms done to it by other chapters in the Assembly. At other times, the chapter instructed its representatives to enter the Assembly specifically to defend it from injury.[58] Although the instructions may have differed from diocese to diocese, all chapters basically pursued the same goals in the negotiations—smallest payment over the longest period, discounts, rules for collection, exemptions, and protecting the chapter's local interests in the Assembly.

Assembly

The Castilian Assembly met at least 33 times during the sixteenth century, and the location of the Assembly normally corresponded to that of the court.[59] During Charles V's reign (1516–1556), five Assemblies convened in Madrid, three in Valladolid, one in Aranda de Duero, one in Alcalá de Henares (later transferred to Illescas and then Toledo), and one in Barcelona. After 1563, the Assembly convened in Madrid, except for the Assembly of 1602, which met in Valladolid. The representatives generally met in either the chapter house of a monastery, such as the Prado monastery in Valladolid (1523), or the chapel of a church, such as the parish of San Martín in Madrid (1530).

Each Assembly began with certain formalities. The representatives made an oath not to reveal the sessions' proceedings and to defend the church's liberties and immunity. They presented to the entire Assembly the powers granted by their chapters to make an agreement.[60] The representatives appointed a secretary or secretaries. The secretary was

---

[58] ACG, leg. 29, pieza 4. "Lo que el senor Doctor don Pedro de Vibero…" and "Ynstrucion para el senor licenciado Pero Lopez de Caravajal…"; Marín López, *El cabildo*, pp. 163–164 and 169–191.

[59] The chapters convened Assemblies in the following years: 1502 or 1503, 1506, 1508, 1510, 1512, 1517, 1519, 1520, 1523, 1530, 1533, 1536, 1540, 1541, 1543, 1546, 1551, 1555, 1560, 1563, 1565, 1572, 1575, 1577, 1582, 1586, 1587, 1591, 1592, 1596, and 1597. There were two Assemblies in 1565, 1582, and 1592 because the Assemblies for the subsidy and the *excusado* overlapped and took place in the same year. For a short description of each Assembly, see Tarsício de Azcona "Estado e Iglesia en España a la luz de las asambleas del clero en el siglo XVI," *Actas del congreso internacional Teresiano*, coordinated by Teófanes Egido Martínez (Salamanca: Ediciones Universidad de Salamanca, 1983), pp. 303–313 and Carpintero, "La congregación," pp. 76–114.

[60] In the sixteenth century, the representatives only presented their powers to the Comisario General after an agreement was reached. In 1634, however, the king finally forced the representatives to present their powers at the beginning of the Assembly.

usually another representative, but at times other prebendaries who were not representatives received the position. The representatives also appointed chaplains and doorkeepers. They established voting procedures and a seating hierarchy for the Assembly. The hierarchical order was used to place the chapters' names in the minutes and agreements, and to determine the processional order to kiss the royal hands. The seating arrangement often created conflicts within the Assembly. Starting as early as 1519, Seville and Santiago argued over whose representatives would sit at Toledo's right hand. Although the Assembly decided in 1551 and 1555 that the two churches would alternate the seat next to Toledo daily, the conflict continued to cause problems into the seventeenth century.[61] In another example of tension, Palencia and Oviedo disputed the seat after Burgos.[62]

Once the opening formalities were settled, the Assembly began to negotiate with the crown on the size of the subsidy and the terms of payment. The Assembly also made the general apportionment of the subsidy among the dioceses, abbeys, and military orders. The representatives formed committees to prepare appeals and petitions, draw up agreements, communicate with the chapters, negotiate with royal ministers, and attend to other business.[63]

The Assembly reached all major decisions by votes, and a majority was usually sufficient.[64] Since each representative had a vote, the extra representative sent by the wealthier chapters may have given them a greater voice in the Assembly. In an attempt to address this problem, a statute of the Assembly of 1572 determined that the presence of more than one representative did not entitle a chapter to more than one vote. Toledo immediately challenged this decision and sued to retain its two votes; the lawsuit or an appeal was still pending nearly 70 years later in 1639. Possibly in an effort to placate Toledo, the Assembly in that year agreed to let Toledo have two votes, one for each representative,

---

[61] For more on the conflict between Santiago and Seville, see ACS, Sec. II, lib. 1157 (77), Session 20 ff.; Sec. VII, lib. 85, "Congregación del clero...1533," October 10, 1533; and Sec. VII, lib. 85, "Congregación del clero...1555," Session 12, July 9, 1555.

[62] For more on the conflict between Palencia and Oviedo, see ACS, Sec. VII, lib. 85, "Congregación del clero...1533," October 10–November 13, 1533.

[63] Carpintero, "La congregación," pp. 40–41.

[64] In the case of the Assembly of 1541, it will be possible to address the voting patterns within the Assembly and analyze its implications. In general, we should keep in mind that the individual chapters often had divergent views on how to proceed in the negotiations and even representatives from the same chapter did not always agree. These differences, however, possibly created space for compromise in the negotiations.

without prejudice to its pending lawsuit. Although the outcome of this case is unknown, its very existence indicates the importance of an extra vote in the Assembly. Since the Assembly did not admit votes *in absencia*, a chapter that sent two representatives increased the likelihood that at least one of its representatives was present at every session.[65]

At times, the chapters were even able to influence the Assembly's proceedings. For example, in the midst of tense negotiations in 1530, the representatives addressed the problem of bishops appointing mendicant friars to carry out the visitations of the churches.[66] The chapter of Toledo admonished the Assembly to focus on reaching a settlement for the *quarta* and not to address other issues.[67] It was trying to keep the deliberations on track, fearing that other issues might distract the Assembly from the principal negotiations. The chapter apparently prevailed, since no further references to the friars or other unrelated issues appeared in the Assembly's minutes.

Other chapters also influenced the negotiations. The Assembly directly sought the chapters' feedback on its initiatives, and individual representatives were in constant contact with their chapters. Sometimes, the chapters even sent new powers or instructions to their representatives in light of developments, as Seville did in September 1533. Moreover, representatives often had to consult with their chapters before accepting an agreement. Thus, although the Assembly was the focal point of the negotiations, the negotiations were not limited to the Assembly and the proceedings could be influenced from outside. Royal officials realized this as well, and on at least three occasions in 1533 the archbishop of Toledo wrote his chapter regarding the state of the negotiations in Alcalá de Henares.[68] The constant communications and at times micromanagement of the representatives by their chapters could delay the negotiations, which is why the king asked that the representatives come with full powers to negotiate. For their part, the chapters likely limited their representatives' authority in order to maintain some control over the negotiations.

---

[65] Carpintero, "La congregación," pp. 43–44; ACS, Sec. IX, leg. 111, n. 1, ff. 6–7; BN 3/14341 "Assientos de la congregación que celebraron las santas iglesias...desde 19 noviembre de 1637 hasta 28 de junio de 1639," f. 18.

[66] ACS, Sec. II, lib. 1157 (77), Session, February 25, 1530. The secular clergy apparently felt that it was inappropriate for regular clergy to evaluate their churches.

[67] ACT, AC lib. 5 f. 35v (of small book).

[68] ACS, Sec. I, lib. 13, ff. 270, 279, 282, and 288; ACG, leg. 10, pieza 1 "Minuta de la carta del cabildo a la congregación"; AHN Clero, leg. 7216, n°2, Cardinal of Toledo to chapter of Toledo, September 6 and 12, and December 4, 1533.

The Assembly's main objective was to negotiate the size of the subsidy and the period of payments with the crown. In the early sixteenth century, the popes normally conceded to the crown a proportion of the Spanish ecclesiastical rents, ranging from a tenth to a half. During Charles V's reign, the most common concessions were the *quarta* and *dos quartas*. The *quarta* was a quarter of the ecclesiastical rents for one year, and the *dos quartas* was a quarter of the ecclesiastical rents for two years. The *dos quartas* should not be confused with the *medios frutos*, half the ecclesiastical rents for one year. The Assembly of the Clergy and the crown then reached an agreement on a monetary sum less than the papal concession. By a previous agreement with the Catholic Kings, the Assembly had converted a *décima* (a tenth) into a 'subsidy' of 100,000 florins. When contributions of a *quarta, dos quartas,* or *medios frutos* were introduced after 1519, the Assembly reduced these concessions to multiples of a *décima* and then converted them into 'subsidies.' Thus, in 1523, when the Assembly agreed to pay 210,000 florins, the amount was calculated as two subsidies, and in 1533, according to Granada's representative, the Assembly's initial offer of 400,000 florins was equivalent to four subsidies.[69] In spite of these variations, I will hereafter use the term 'subsidy' to refer to the total amount agreed upon between the Assembly and the crown.

After 1562, the popes conceded a fixed monetary sum of 420,000 ducados annually to the crown for five years (*quinquenio*). This amount was known as the *subsidio de las galeras*, or the subsidy of the galleys, because it was for the maintenance of 60 galleys in the Mediterranean.[70] Once the amount of the subsidy was fixed, the negotiations often centered on discounts, the period of payments, and the type of money (gold, silver, *vellón*) used to make payments. Through these negotiations, the Assembly was often able to lower the amount paid in real terms. In 1567, the pope conceded a new imposition, the *excusado* (a tax on the richest benefice of each diocese), which, once again, the Assembly was responsible for collecting and apportioning; the Assembly also negotiated the new tax down to 250,000 ducados annually. During the seventeenth

---

[69] ACG, leg. 22, pieza 5, "de dos del presente rescebi la letra de v.m. y en lo que me enbian a mandar que les avise...." For more on the terminology, see Ramón Carande *Carlos V y sus banqueros: La Hacienda Real de Castilla* (Madrid: Sociedad de Estudios y Publicaciones, 1949), pp. 466–467.

[70] Ivan Cloulas has skillfully examined the negotiations for the first subsidy of galleys. See "Le 'subsidio de las galeras,' contribution du clergé espagnol a la guerre navale contre les infidèles de 1563 à 1574," *Melanges de la Casa de Velazquez* 3 (1967), pp. 289–326.

century, the *décima* (tenth) was added, and the Assembly negotiated and administered its payment.[71] The Assembly continued to represent the ecclesiastical estate in negotiations involving papal concessions into the eighteenth century. Although the negotiating strategies changed with the latter concessions, the basic framework for negotiations was established during the reign of Charles V.

Once the subsidy was agreed upon, the Assembly apportioned the money among the dioceses, abbeys, and military orders (see Table II).[72] The general apportionment of the contributions was supposed to be proportional to the wealth of individual dioceses. Even as the size of the subsidy increased, the Assembly successfully kept the apportionment proportional overall. Toledo, the richest diocese, paid 11.85 percent of the total subsidy in 1457, approximately 12 percent in 1530, 14 percent in 1546, 15 percent in 1551, and 15.6 percent of the combined total of the subsidy and *excusado* in 1630. Tuy, a poorer diocese, on the other hand, paid only 0.61 percent of the total subsidy in 1457, 0.65 percent in 1530, 0.63 percent in 1546, 0.56 percent in 1551, and 0.48 percent of the combined total of the subsidy and *excusado* in 1630.

An equitable apportionment among the dioceses, however, did not necessarily guarantee relief from the fiscal burden. While Palencia's share of the general apportionment decreased from 1530 to 1551, the amount that the diocese had to pay increased by over 1,866 ducados. There were also some anomalies. Santiago, for example, managed to have its share of the subsidy in the general apportionments reduced from 8.9 percent in 1457 to 2.69 percent in 1551. It still only paid 3 percent of the combined total of the subsidy and *excusado* in 1630 even though it was the third richest diocese in the kingdom of Castile. Orense, on the other hand, was allotted more than double what nearby dioceses with similar rents paid, and it was one of the most burdened dioceses in 1630. Thus, despite efforts to apportion the subsidy equitably and to modify the apportionment over time (Table III), the apportionment was never truly equitable, although the overall fiscal burden slowly shifted from Galicia and Old Castile to the richer dioceses in New Castile and Andalucia (Map 1).[73]

---

[71] See Carpintero, "La congregación," pp. 359–385; Elena Catalán Martínez, "El fin de un privilegio: La contribución eclesiástica a la hacienda real (1519–1794)," *Studia Historica. Historia Moderna* 16 (1997), p. 195.

[72] Between 1502 and 1597, the Spanish Assemblies apportioned 27,540,000 ducados in subsidies and *excusados*. Azcona, "Estado," p. 315.

[73] Catalán Martínez, "El fin de un privilegio," pp. 192–193.

Table II. Division of the Subsidy in 1530, 1533, 1546, and 1551.

Diocese	1530‡	1533	1546†	1551
Toledo	14,572,800□	14,572,800	21,801,340	23,807,590
Seville	10,351,423	10,351,423	15,299,924	16,061,174
Burgos	10,413,398	10,413,398	11,727,756	10,977,753
Palencia	7,797,618	7,697,618	8,964,293	8,514,293
Cuenca	3,823,441	3,873,441	6,279,530	6,598,280
Calahorra	5,783,067	5,683,067	6,037,129	5,268,379
León	5,470,245	5,480,245	5,852,412	5,083,662
Ávila	4,060,326	4,509,326	5,663,077	5,513,077
Córdoba	3,275,642	3,275,642	5,408,487	5,719,737
Segovia	4,041,471	4,041,471	5,150,000	4,962,000
Salamanca	3,519,551	3,509,151	4,907,500	5,076,250
Osma	3,602,843	3,602,843	4,812,500	4,812,500
Sigüenza	3,283,650	3,283,650	4,687,500	4,848,750
Santiago	8,308,000	8,208,000	4,216,087	4,216,087
Zamora	2,777,017	2,758,017	3,863,680	4,062,430
Plasencia	1,845,671	1,845,571	3,450,000	3,825,000
Jaén	1,887,398	1,887,398	3,013,500	3,063,500
Badajoz	1,982,905	1,984,900	2,812,500	2,842,500
Oviedo	2,874,519	2,874,519	2,774,990	2,212,420
Cartagena	1,487,417	1,487,415	2,677,983	3,087,982
Coria	1,548,726	1,548,726	2,662,500	2,850,000
Astorga	2,558,460	2,558,360	2,592,938	2,366,838
Orense	2,558,160	2,558,160	2,503,937	2,138,837
Ciudad Rodrigo	933,493	933,493	1,237,500	1,312,500
Lugo	1,094,420	1,094,420	1,070,437	676,688
Cádiz	705,888	705,888	1,050,000	1,136,250
Mondoñedo	2,270,880	2,270,880	1,030,000	667,250
Tuy	819,856	809,856	1,000,000	887,500
Abbey of Agreda	266,759	266,759	375,000	262,500
Abbey of Alfaro	119,016	119,016	150,000	150,000
Order of Calatrava	5,875,746	5,875,747	7,312,500	7,312,500
Order of Alcántara	4,733,800	4,733,801	6,375,000	6,375,000
Total	124,815,007°	124,815,001	156,760,000	156,750,000

Sources: ACS, Sec. II lib.1157(77) and Sec. VII libs. 85, 86, and 87.

‡ Although not included in the above calcuations, the division of 1530 included 41 tarines and the division of 1533 included 43 tarines.

□ All figures are in maravedís (1 ducado = 375 maravedís).

° The total for 1530 is from the document. My calculations give a total of 124,815,606.

† Except for Palencia receiving 10,000 mrs. less and Cartagena 10,000 mrs. more, the 1546 division corresponds to the 1541 division.

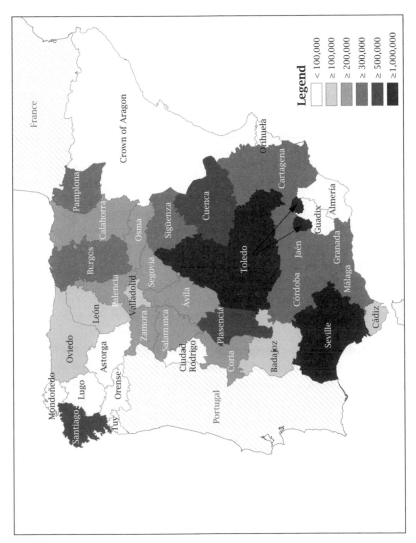

Map 1. Value of Rents in Ducados, 1630.

Table III. Proportional Apportionment of Subsidy and *Excusado*.

Dioceses	1457	1530	1546	1551	1630
Toledo	11.85%	12%	14%	15%	15.6%
Seville	10.03%	8.29%	9.79%	10.24%	10.26%
Santiago	8.90%	6.65%	2.69%	2.69%	3%
Cuenca	4.21%	3.06%	4.0%	4.2%	4.39%
Plasencia	2.18%	1.47%	2.2%	2.44%	2.44%
Burgos	6.09%	8.34%	7.48%	7.0%	5.5%
Cartagena	2.13%	1.19%	1.7%	1.96%	1.628%
Palencia	5.7%	6.25%	5.7%	5.44%	3.7%
Tuy	0.61%	0.65%	0.63%	0.56%	0.48%
Orense	3.09%	2%	1.59%	1.36%	1.3%
Mondoñedo	1.79%	1.8%	0.657%	0.425%	0.325%

Source: José Manuel Nieto Soria, *Iglesia y génesis del estado moderno en Castilla (1369–1480)* (Madrid: Editorial Complutense, 1993), pp. 331–332; Sean Perrone *Charles V and the Castilian Assembly of the Clergy*, pp. 40 and 43 Tables II and IV.

Due to imprecise data and constantly changing economic conditions, the actual burden of the subsidy and *excusado* on individual dioceses is harder to calculate, especially in the sixteenth century. A petition of the Assembly to the pope in 1630 indicates the value of the Castilian rents and the burden of the subsidy and *excusado* on the dioceses. Overall, the subsidy and *excusado* consumed only 5.6 percent of the ecclesiastical revenues. The burden, however, could vary between dioceses: León, for example, contributed approximately 13.3 percent of its total revenues of 120,000 ducados to the subsidy and *excusado*, while the Canaries contributed only 2 percent of its total revenues of 200,000 ducados. Even though Toledo was apportioned the largest share of the subsidy and *excusado* in 1630, it did not shoulder the heaviest burden (at 6.4 percent). The most burdened dioceses were still in northern Castile in 1630 despite the redistribution of the subsidy from the north to the south, and many poorer dioceses contributed a larger percentage of their income than wealthier dioceses (Table IV and Map 2). The burden of the subsidy many have been roughly the same throughout the early modern period. José Antonio Vázquez, for example, finds that between 1500 and 1800, the subsidy and *excusado* never exceeded 7 percent of the chapter's revenues in Zamora.[74] Thus, the total burden

---

[74] See "La contribución de subsidio y *excusado* en Zamora, 1500–1800," *Haciendas forales y hacienda real: Homenaje a D. Miguel Artola y D. Felipe Ruiz Martín*, ed. E Fernández de Pinedo (Bilbao: Servicio Editorial Universidad del Pais Vasco, 1990), p. 135.

Table IV. Rents of Churches of Castile and Léon, 1630 (in ducados).

Dioceses	Rents of Diocese in 1630	Share of subsidy and *excusado* in 1630	Burden of subsidy and *excusado* to rent in 1630
Toledo	1,500,000	96,000	6.4%
Seville	1,000,000	63,000	6.3%
Santiago	600,000	18,000	3.0%
Cuenca	550,000	27,000	4.9%
Plasencia	500,000	15,000	3.0%
Burgos	450,000	34,000	7.5%
Córdoba	450,000	23,000	5.1%
Sigüenza	400,000	17,000	4.3%
Jaén	350,000	15,000	4.3%
Granada	350,000	10,000	2.9%
Cartagena	300,000	10,000	3.3%
Pamplona	300,000	10,000	3.3%
Málaga	300,000	9,000	3.0%
Segovia	250,000	18,000	7.2%
Osma	250,000	15,000	6.0%
Coria	250,000	11,000	4.4%
Palencia	220,000	23,000	10.5%
Ávila	200,000	20,000	10.0%
Calahorra	200,000	18,000	9.0%
Salamanca	200,000	15,000	7.5%
Zamora	200,000	14,000	7.0%
Canaries	200,000	4,000	2.0%
Badajoz	180,000	11,000	6.1%
Valladolid	150,000	11,000	7.3%
León	120,000	16,000	13.3%
Oviedo	120,000	7,000	5.8%
Cádiz	120,000	4,000	3.3%
Astorga	100,000	8,000	8.0%
Tuy	100,000	3,000	3.0%
Orihuela	100,000	3,000	3.0%
Ciudad Rodrigo	90,000	4,000	4.4%
Orense	80,000	8,000	10.0%
Lugo	80,000	3,000	3.8%
Guadix	70,000	2,000	2.9%
Almería	40,000	2,000	5.0%
Mondoñedo	40,000	2,000	5.0%
Order of Santiago	306,000	19,000	6.2%
Order of Calatrava	127,000	14,000	11.0%
Order of Alcántara	109,000	12,000	11.0%
Total	10,952,000	614,000	5.6%

Source: Quintín Aldea, "Patrimonio Eclesiastico", eds Quintín Aldea Vaquero, Tómas Marín Martínez, José Vives Gatell, *Diccionario de Historia Eclesiástica de España* (Madrid, 1972), v. 3, p. 1897.

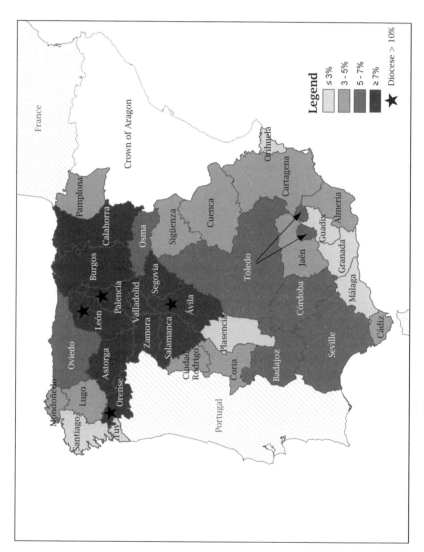

Map 2. Burden of the Subsidy and *Excusado*, 1630.

of 5.6 percent derived from the petition of 1630 probably provides a reasonable indication of the overall burden for the subsidy and *excusado* in the early modern period.

Why then did the clergy constantly complain that the contributions were a huge onus? Was it simply empty rhetoric or was there any truth to their grievances? The available data suggest that the contribution to the crown did not constitute a particularly heavy burden on the Castilian ecclesiastical estate as a whole.[75] The number and the stridency of complaints on both the diocesan and national levels in the early sixteenth century, however, belie the view that the grievances were groundless.[76] Many of these complaints might have resulted from a reduction in the percentage of the diocesan rents to a fixed sum. At the Assembly of 1533, for example, many representatives claimed that, given the current agricultural sterility, their dioceses would contribute less if they paid the full *medios frutos* than the fixed sum apportioned them by the Assembly. In fact, the chapter of Badajoz planned to pay the *medios frutos* and not participate in the subsidy agreement that year.[77] The challenge in negotiating the reduction of the papal concession to a fixed sum was to ensure that the fixed sum was not a burden and was significantly less than paying the *quarta, dos quartas,* or *medios frutos* under normal economic conditions.[78] Despite the Assembly's best efforts, this was almost impossible given the fluctuations in the agrarian economy, which accounted for 90 percent of ecclesiastical rents.[79] The evidence thus suggests that the onus on individual chapters and dioceses could be significant and that the complaints were not mere hyperbole. Much of the debate concerned issues of equity between the chapters on the national level and between individual chapters and their diocesan clergy on the local level. To understand the rhetoric, the issue of equity

---

[75] In fact, the burden may have actually decreased slightly in real terms for most dioceses between the late sixteenth and early eighteenth centuries. See Catalán Martínez, "El fin de un privilegio," p. 196.

[76] The volumes of appeals in the Archivo Catedralicio de Burgos attest to the many diocesan clergy who felt unduly burdened with every new ecclesiastical contribution. See ACB, *Repartimiento de subsidio y concesión... de subsidio.*

[77] ACS, Sec. VII, lib. 85, "Congregación del clero... 1533," December 13, 1533.

[78] Issues such as these were not limited to the clergy; many city councils did not like the *encabezameinto* because if the sum was set too high or there was an economic crisis, the city would not be able to pay without hardship. See Constance Jones Mathers, "Relations between the City of Burgos and the Crown, 1506–1556" (Ph.D. diss., Columbia University, 1973), p. 209.

[79] See Carpintero, "La congregación," pp. 115–118.

on both the national and the local levels must be examined. A closer
examination of the issues may help explain the chapters' positions on
the size of the subsidy and its apportionment.[80]

In addition to apportioning the subsidy, the Assembly also divided
among the chapters the common costs of the meeting and of sending representatives to Rome to petition the pope. The common costs
included the salaries of the doorman, secretaries, and chaplains; the
costs of liturgical acts and of supplies, such as paper and ink, and mail;
and any usage fees to the monastery or parish where the Assembly
convened. The length of an Assembly was a major factor in these
costs; during Charles V's reign, most Assemblies appear to have lasted
between two and three months. Compared with the size of the subsidy
granted, the common costs of the Assembly were small (see Table V).
The chapter of Toledo paid the entire common costs up front, and the
other chapters were obligated to pay their share later. Although most
chapters repaid punctually, some did not. In such cases, Toledo would
send letters reminding delinquent chapters of their obligations. On
February 3, 1531, after receiving one such letter, the chapter of Seville
promptly decided to pay Toledo to avoid being the only delinquent.[81]
Delinquency was not the only problem. At the Assembly of 1555,
Cartagena's representative inquired how the commons costs would be
collected in the absence of a subsidy, since the common costs were normally added to the subsidy payment and then apportioned among the
diocesan clergy. This problem was resolved when the chapters received
a papal brief in late 1555 that allowed them to collect the common
costs from two cathedral benefices that year.[82] Appeals to Rome, then,

---

[80] To understand the clergy's complaints, we also need to look more closely at the
mechanisms of collection on the local level and its apportionment, the unequal distribution of rents within the dioceses, and the additional taxes the clergy had to pay on
top of the subsidy (for example, *sisas* and *tercias*). Similar points are discussed regarding
the *alcabala* and *encabezameinto* in Ubaldo Gómez Álvarez, *Revisión histórica de la presión
fiscal castellana (siglos XVI–XVIII)* Tomo I: Análisis tributario del caso de la provincia de
León, sus partidos y concejos en el s. XVII. (Oviedo: Universidad de Oviedo, 1996),
pp. 17–18, 20, 27, 209, 215. For a discussion of the unequal distribution of ecclesiastical rents in the eighteenth century, see Antonio Domínguez Ortiz, "Un alegato de los
párrocos de la dioceses toledana contra el desigual reparto de los diezmos," *Hispania
Sacra* 33 (1981), pp. 533–539.
[81] ACS, Sec. I, lib.13, f. 10v. Seville was tardy in its payments on other occasions as
well. See ACS, Sec. I, lib. 11, ff. 56, 57v; lib. 14, f. 21v; and lib. 21, f. 48v. For a more
detailed description of the common costs, see Carpintero, "La congregación," pp. 59–74.
[82] ACS, Sec. VII, lib. 85, "Congregación del clero…1555," Session 80, October
16, 1555; BN, Ms. 9937, f. 163v.

not only addressed the negotiations for subsidies but also the Assembly's internal organizational issues, and the costs of sending representatives to Rome were significant. In 1546, for example, the Assembly allocated 3,344 ducados to pay the salaries and expenses of its representatives to Rome, and a century later, in 1648, it spent 7,779 ducados.[83] The representatives were primarily sent to Rome to petition the pope for a repeal of the concession or at least a favorable revision of the terms of the subsidy. Based on the amount of money invested and the frequency with which they sent representatives to Rome, the clergy apparently thought that this was a worthwhile endeavor.

Not only did the individual chapters and dioceses have to contribute their portion of the subsidy and share in the common costs of the Assembly, but, as noted earlier, they also had to pay their representatives' salaries to attend the meeting. The salaries constituted the bulk of the expenses for each chapter. An estimate of the expenses for representatives' salaries and the share of the common costs provides a general idea of the fiscal burden for individual chapters to attend the Assembly.

For Seville, the common costs for the entire Assembly of 1533, which lasted roughly five months, came to approximately 77 ducados (1 ducado = 375 maravedís). Seville's representatives each received two ducados a day, or 600 ducados for five months, for both. Between the common costs and the salaries of two representatives at court for five months, Seville's expenses for attending the Assembly of 1533 would be approximately 2.4 percent of its share of that year's subsidy, which would be collected with the subsidy from all the clergy of the diocese. In 1546, the common costs accrued by Toledo were 29 ducados, and that chapter's representatives each garnered roughly 90 ducados from the month-long Assembly.[84] Toledo's expenses, then, would be approximately 0.36 percent of its share of the subsidy in 1546. Since the exact number of days for which the representatives received salaries is unknown, given that they received a salary during their journey to and from the Assembly, the above calculations seek only to illustrate

---

[83] ACS, Sec. VII, lib. 86, "Congregación del clero...1546," Session 34. See also Carpintero, "La congregación," pp. 69–70.

[84] The chapter of Toledo also offered each representative a further 50 ducados on their return because of the extraordinary costs of living in Madrid, due to dearth. This figure, however, has not been added into the above calculation. See ACT, AC lib. 7, f. 183.

Table V. Division of the Assembly's Costs in 1533 and 1546.

Diocese	1533	Diocese	1546
Toledo	37,709	Toledo	10,900
Seville	28,692	Seville	7,650
Burgos	28,762	Burgos	5,864
Palencia	21,262	Palencia	4,482
Cuenca	10,692	Cuenca	3,140
Calahorra	15,884	Calahorra	3,018
León	15,181	León	2,926
Ávila	12,455	Ávila	2,831
Córdoba	9,048	Córdoba	2,704
Segovia	11,162	Segovia	2,575
Salamanca	9,684	Salamanca	2,453
Osma	9,971	Osma	2,406
Sigüenza	9,072	Sigüenza	2,344
Santiago	22,900	Santiago	2,108
Zamora	7,655	Zamora	1,932
Plasencia	5,093	Plasencia	1,725
Jaén	5,738	Jaén	1,507
Badajoz	5,478	Badajoz	1,406
Oviedo	7,967	Oviedo	1,387
Cartagena	4,409	Cartagena	1,334
Coria	4,241	Coria	1,331
Astorga	7,117	Astorga	1,296
Orense	6,426	Orense	1,252
Ciudad Rodrigo	2,580	Ciudad Rodrigo	618
Lugo	3,036	Lugo	535
Cádiz	2,027	Cádiz	525
Mondoñedo	6,011	Mondoñedo	515
Tuy	2,235	Tuy	500
Abbey of Agreda	739	Abbey of Agreda	187
Abbey of Alfaro	326	Abbey of Alfaro	75
Pamplona	5,000	Order of Calatrava	3,656
Kingdom of Granada	13,220	Order of Alcántara	3,187
Total	331,772	Total	78,369

Source: ACS, Sec. VII, libs. 85 and 86.
† All figures are in maravedís (1 florin = 265 maravedís, 1 ducado = 375 maravedís).
  80 tarines were also divided among the dioceses in 1533, while 55 tarines were
  divided among the dioceses in 1546.

the large size of the representatives' salaries compared to the common costs, and the small cost for the wealthier chapters compared to their share of the subsidy.

For a poor chapter, such as Lugo, the expenses for attending the Assembly would not be so small compared to its share of the subsidy. Lugo's share of the common costs was 8 ducados in 1533 and 1 and a half ducado in 1546. Assuming that the representative from Lugo received at least a ducado daily, Lugo would have paid its representative 150 ducados in 1533 and 30 ducados in 1546. Lugo's expenses compared to its share of the subsidy were thus approximately 5.4 percent for the five-month long Assembly in 1533 and 1.1 percent for the month-long Assembly in 1546. Paying a further 1 to 5 percent for the costs of the Assembly beyond a diocese's share of the subsidy itself might have been significant for the poorer dioceses and explain why some did not send any representatives. Even though the overall costs of the Assembly were not extravagant, the crown's interest in limiting each chapter to one representative and curtailing the negotiations are understandable.[85]

The Assembly generally dissolved once it reached an agreement with the crown for the payment and collection of a subsidy, though in 1530 the Assembly was on the verge of dissolving without an agreement. If it had dissolved without an agreement, the crown could still have collected the papal concession in accordance with the papal bull. A royal collection of the subsidy, however, was often plagued with difficulties, as in the summer of 1540 (see chapter five). So it was generally in the best interests of the crown and the Assembly to reach an agreement before the Assembly dissolved itself.

The individual chapters then ratified the national agreement and prepared their own separate obligations with the crown for payment. The various obligations contained the conditions under which the subsidy would be collected within the diocese, which generally corresponded to the conditions in the agreement reached between the Assembly and the crown.[86]

---

[85] N.B. The Assembly of 1533 appears to be the longest of Charles V's reign, while the Assembly of 1546 appears to be the shortest. Unlike the Cortes, there is no indication that the crown bribed representatives or provided them with gifts. Thus, it would seem that the crown was truly concerned that the Assembly's costs might burden the poor clergy as a memorandum from 1555 indicates. See AGS, PR, leg. 20, f. 34 (I).

[86] For examples of the obligations from various years during the reign of Charles V, see AGS, CC legs. 1–4.

Collection Process

Since the crown made discounts to dioceses, orders, hospitals, and individuals, the ecclesiastical estate never completely paid the agreed upon amount. The crown, however, did not always enthusiastically make these discounts. On July 8, 1530, for example, Charles V wrote Isabel of Portugal, his wife and the acting regent, that his present needs prevented him from offering the customary charity and graces. Instead, he would deduct 16,000 ducados from what all the religious orders, hospitals, and churches had to pay, taking special care for the observant Franciscan monasteries, the poor monasteries of reformed nuns, and the poor churches and monasteries of the kingdom of Granada.[87] This discount, 4.8 percent of the subsidy, paled compared to the royal auditor Juan de Vozmediano's suggested 45,333 ducados discount to monasteries and hospitals, roughly 13.6 percent of the total subsidy in 1530.[88] Vozmediano apparently wanted to keep the discount of 1530 uniform with the discount of 1523, roughly 13.9 percent of the total subsidy.

On August 16, 1530, Isabel reproved Charles for only offering a discount of 16,000 ducados in a time of dearth and dire poverty in the hospitals, monasteries, and colleges. She stressed that the parsimonious discount would create an uproar and advised him to increase it.[89] On November 22, despite his financial needs, Charles increased the discount from 16,000 ducados to 20,000 ducados.[90] The extra 4,000 ducados certainly lightened the load for some needy clergy, but it did not prevent others from feeling deep stress. Unfortunately, the king's demand for a subsidy coincided with poor harvests in Castile, and the monasteries and hospitals were consequently in greater need of a discount than ever. Although the discounts were often essential for the monasteries and hospitals to retain enough funds to carry out their duties, as the General of the Hieronymites argued to Charles's adviser Francisco de

---

[87] AGS, E leg. 21, f. 339. The discount for individual monasteries and hospitals could be significant. Between 1554 and 1556, monks in the crown of Castile were apportioned 18,168 ducados and had 12,925 ducados discounted or 71 percent, see Azcona, "Estado," p. 328.

[88] AGS, E leg. 20, f. 113.

[89] María del Carmen Mazarío Coleto, *Isabel de Portugal: Emperatriz y Reina de España* (Madrid: Consejo Superior de Investigaciones Científicas, 1951), p. 289. For a similar opinion expressed by Tavera and Mendoza, see AGS, E leg. 20, f. 143.

[90] AGS, E leg. 21, f. 296.

los Cobos in 1530, the king continued to limit the size of the discount so that the subsidy would not be reduced even further.[91] Nonetheless, economic realities forced him to continue making discounts, and by the 1550s, royal officials basically anticipated a 12 percent discount (that is, 60,000 ducados out of 500,000 offered by the clergy in the Crowns of Castile and Aragon).[92] From subsidy to subsidy, the size of discounts and who received them were continually addressed, and the size of the discounts could be large. Discounts, however, were generally negotiated directly with dioceses, orders, hospitals, and individuals, outside the Assembly of the Clergy. Moreover, they could also be retroactive.[93] Discounts, then, were a further avenue through which the ecclesiastical estate might limit the fiscal demands placed on it by the crown.[94]

Moreover, sometimes the clergy simply did not pay what was apportioned them. In 1530, the churches of Santiago and Mondoñedo and the military orders of Alcántara and Calatrava had been apportioned 79,569 florins, but only paid 25,388. As a result, the crown lost 54,181 florins out of the 471,000 florins (11.5 percent) granted in the subsidy of 1530. Cardinal Tavera, president of the royal council, advised the king in 1533 that between discounts and the inability of the dioceses to pay, the crown could anticipate at least 100,000 florins less than what the Assembly offered. It was imperative for the royal treasury that the apportionment be based on economic realities. Otherwise, the king would again lose a similar amount of money, because over-assessed dioceses would once more be unable to pay.[95]

It is not farfetched to assume that the representatives understood this and consequently refused to reapportion the subsidy, even though it would have helped burdened clergy in Santiago and Mondoñedo (because an equitable reapportionment would have allowed the crown to extract more money from the clergy in other dioceses). Agreements between the Assembly and the crown, then, did not necessarily mean

---

[91] AGS, E leg. 20, f. 60.

[92] AGS, E leg. 103, f. 56.

[93] For more on discounts, see Carpintero, "La congregación," pp. 144–149.

[94] Discounts, rebates, and 'graces' were a normal part of subsidy negotiations with both secular and ecclesiastical bodies. Other bodies appeared to have been more successful at this than the Castilian clergy. In the Netherlands, graces ate away a large portion of the ordinary subsidy granted in 1531. In Flanders, for instance, the nominal value of the subsidy was reduced by 34.82 percent. See James D. Tracy, *Emperor Charles V, Impresario of War: Campaign Strategy, International Finance, and Domestic Politics* (Cambridge: Cambridge University Press, 2002), p. 72.

[95] AGS, E leg. 27, f. 121.

that all that money was collected, and it is possible that many of the aggrieved churches never paid their full share of the subsidy. More detailed work on the collection process in the individual dioceses is necessary, however, before any definitive conclusions can be reached.

The cathedral chapters were responsible for collecting the subsidy. A memorandum of 1520 from the chapter of Jaén to the chapter of Granada illustrates the general procedures for collection. That memorandum explained how the subsidy should be apportioned and collected on the diocesan level. First, who was to pay and from what revenues? The bishop paid the subsidy on all his rents, whether from tithes, possessions, dependencies, parishes, and rights of court. The chapter paid the subsidy on its tithes, possessions, Masses and anniversaries celebrated in the cathedral, the value of the food distributed among the chapter, and the fees received for all services during the year. All the collegiate churches and parishes paid the subsidy in a similar manner, as well as for first fruits and the rents accrued by benefices. Even priests without benefices, chaplaincies, or earnings from Masses had to pay the subsidy on their income. Except for the observant Franciscans and Clares, all monasteries regardless of Order paid the subsidy on all their rents and possessions, Masses, and the value of the food distributed among the monks or nuns, and offerings. The confraternities, hospitals, and pious places also paid the subsidy on all their rents, possessions, and charity that they had received. Chaplains and priests, as well as laymen in possession of royal *tercias* (a share of the tithe), paid the subsidy. Hermitages and houses of devotion would also pay on income they received from charity. Clergy also paid the subsidy from the tithes and other rents pertaining to the maintenance of the cathedral, collegiate churches, and parishes.[96] In sum, they had to pay on practically every source of income.

Second, the memorandum explained how the subsidy was apportioned within the diocese of Jaén. The judges of the subsidy were to direct the clergy and laymen either to make an oath attesting to the true values of their rents to the last blanca (i.e., a very small monetary unit) before them or to send an affidavit attesting to the values. The judges would then apportion the subsidy, common costs of the Assembly, and the representative's salary among the clergy and laymen according to their income.[97]

---

[96] ACG, AC, lib. 2, f. 16rv.
[97] Ibid.

Third, the memorandum addressed the chapter of Jaén's sole responsibility to collect the subsidy. The chapter named the collectors and scribes of the subsidy. The judges of the subsidy were to inform the clergy and laymen who were in possession of ecclesiastical rents to pay the persons named by the chapter. The *repartidores* (distributors) helped the judges to make the local apportionment. Secretaries and notaries were also employed to collect the subsidy. The chapter paid the officials as well: judges received a salary of 10 and a half ducados, scribes received 16 ducados, distributors received 8 ducados, and the notary received 4 ducados, for a total of 38 and a half ducados.[98] The collection procedures and remunerations certainly varied from diocese to diocese and from subsidy to subsidy. Granada itself modified its procedures in 1533, but the procedures outlined here give an approximate sense of a process that took place across Castile.[99]

Although the collection process sounds simple enough, it was often rife with controversy and conflict. Take, for example, the chapters apportioning the subsidy among all the diocesan clergy, the regular clergy, and others who held ecclesiastical rents in the dioceses. Like the general apportionment of the subsidy on the national level, the diocesan apportionment was supposed to be equitable, each person or institution paying in proportion to income.[100] The chapters, however, did not always apportion the subsidy equitably. In 1530, for instance, the Hieronymite Order petitioned the Assembly for permission to name two representatives in each diocese as observers when the chapters made the local apportionment of the subsidy. Through their representatives at the chapters, the Hieronymites clearly hoped to prevent their Order from being unfairly burdened. The Assembly replied that such a decision was outside its jurisdiction and that the Order would need to talk with the individual chapters.[101] Isabel of Portugal's royal decree of March 13, 1531, ordered the chapter of Seville to provide her with details of the diocesan apportionment and how it was calculated. The crown's interest in the diocesan apportionment suggests that some complaints about the division of the subsidy reached it.[102]

---

[98] Ibid.

[99] Marín López, *El cabildo*, pp. 392–393.

[100] For an overview of the local apportionment in seventeenth-century Seville, see José Julián Hernández Borreguero, "Impuestos sobre la renta de los eclesiásticos: El subsidio y excusado (Diócesis de Sevilla, mediados del siglo XVII)," *De Computis: Revista Española de Historia de la Contabilidad* 7 (December 2007), pp. 87–99.

[101] ACS, Sec. II, lib. 1157 (77), Session, March 15, 1530.

[102] ACS, Sec. I, lib.13, f. 25.

Complaints against the local apportionment even made it to Rome.
Kenneth Setton noted that:

> On 6 July 1536 the pope was obliged to restrain the excessive enthusiasm
> of the chapters from apportioning an undue share of the burden of the
> subsidies and tithes upon the incomes of 'persons and places regular,'
> obviously sparing their own resources in the process.[103]

Individual chapters, then, were often unscrupulous in apportioning
the subsidy within their dioceses. The orders, the crown, and even the
pope had to be vigilant to assure an equitable apportionment of the
subsidy on the diocesan level.

Even if the chapters honestly apportioned the subsidy, the cathedral
canons, some of the richest clergy in the diocese, were rarely burdened
by the contribution, because the subsidy agreements often gave chapters
the privilege to sell their grain free of taxation. In many cases, this privilege generated more money for the chapters than they contributed to
the crown. Such privileges were limited to the chapters, creating further
tension with the other clergy and reinforcing the unequal distribution
of ecclesiastical wealth between the higher and lower clergy.[104]

Exemptions were a further hindrance to a controversy-free collection. Some clergy and ecclesiastical institutions were exempt from
paying the subsidy or, in the case of the military orders, had different
arrangements for paying the crown. In other cases, the popes exempted
certain clergy for a single contribution. In the *medios frutos* of 1532, for
instance, Clement VII (1523–1534) exempted all benefices worth less
than 12 ducados per year and ordered that benefices worth less than
24 ducados only be obliged to pay a *décima* (tenth) and not the *medios
frutos* (half).[105]

The actual number of exemptions is hard to calculate, because they
varied over time and from diocese to diocese. For example, the churches
in the kingdom of Granada were briefly exempted after the Morisco
uprising (1568–1570). Much later, the Archpresbytery of Fuenterrabía
in the diocese of Calahorra y La Calzada was exempted from paying
the *subsidio* and *excusado* from roughly 1648 to 1668 due to the ravages
of war.[106] Such changes likely created a fair amount of confusion over

---

[103] Kenneth M. Setton, *The Papacy and the Levant (1204–1571)*, vol. III (Philadelphia:
American Philosophical Society, 1984), p. 414.

[104] See Álvarez Vázquez, "La contribución," p. 135.

[105] AGS, E leg. 27, f. 354 and CJH leg. 11, f. 210.

[106] Marín López, *El cabildo*, p. 390; Iturrioz, *Estudio del subsdio*, pp. 106–107.

who was exempt from subsidy to subsidy. Possibly to avoid such confusion in the diocesan apportionment, a Benedictine monk presented the Assembly with a papal brief in 1533, stating that the Order of Saint Benedict was exempt from the subsidy and threatening to excommunicate those who apportioned or collected subsidies from the Order. The Assembly dismissed the monk, saying he needed to present his brief to the individual chapters.[107]

To make matters worse, the crown periodically exempted clergy after the collection had already begun. In 1552, the Comisario General ordered the chapter of Toledo to cease collecting the subsidy from the archbishop of Toledo and to return anything already collected to him, because in exchange for being exempted from the subsidy until 1554, the archbishop had agreed to pay 40,000 ducados annually to the crown. The chapter apparently did not comply, and a further order was issued in 1554.[108] In that same year, Prince Philip informed the chapter of Granada that the chaplains, their servants, and other officials of the Royal Chapel in Granada were exempt from paying the subsidy; any money already collected was to be returned and their portion of the subsidy reapportioned among the other diocesan clergy.[109] These exemptions narrowed the base on which the chapters could apportion the subsidy, placing further fiscal pressure on the rest of the clergy.

Exemptions may also have led to fraud in the subsidy's collection. The Comisario General warned in November 1533 that the papal order that exempted all benefices worth less than 12 ducados and allowed benefices worth less than 24 ducados to pay a *décima* (tenth) instead of the *medios frutos* (half) would lead to fraud and lawsuits; he feared that everyone would claim that their benefices were worth less than 12 or 24 ducados, even if they were worth 100 ducados.[110] The extent of fraud is unknown, but the Comisario General's warning must be taken seriously, because fiscal fraud was endemic in Castile even among the clergy.[111]

---

[107] ACS, Sec. VII, lib. 85, "Congregación del clero…1533," October 15 and 16, 1533.

[108] AGS, CC, leg. 1, "la dicha Toledo, traslado de la carta que se dio para que no se pide subsidio al arcobispo de Toledo de lo que le cabia en los anos de 1552–1554 quanto el principe nro senor ha mando no se cobre del."

[109] ACG, leg. 458, pieza 5, "Al cabildo de Granada que no repartan ni cobren subsidio de los capellanes y servidores de la capilla real…".

[110] AGS, E leg. 27, f. 122.

[111] For clerical opposition to and evasion of the *millones* and other public taxes, see David Alonso García, "¿Pagar o no pagar? En torno al fraude fiscal eclesiástico en el Madrid del antiguo régimen," *Cuadernos de Historia de España* 77 (2001–2002),

When the chapters did apportion shares of the subsidy to those truly exempt from payment on the diocesan level, complaints and lawsuits followed. In June 1531, the friars of San Pablo in the archdiocese of Seville complained that their assessment went against custom and should be canceled. Later in August, a judge for the Council of the Cruzada ordered the chapter of Seville not to allocate any part of the subsidy to the friars. If the chapter had already collected anything from them, it should return those sums. Instead of complying with the judge's order, the chapter of Seville appears to have initiated a lawsuit in the royal *Chancillería* of Granada.[112] Although some chapters apparently initiated lawsuits, others petitioned for royal decrees prohibiting secular judges from hearing cases relating to the subsidy.[113] The crown complied and continued to issue such decrees.[114] Lawsuits clearly exacerbated the collection and increased costs. Moreover, they gave royal officials more input into a collection process, which the chapters wanted to keep under their control. Lawsuits and appeals were supposed to be limited to the chapters on the local level and to the Comisario General on the national level. Still, as the case of San Pablo indicates, the ecclesiastical estate was often incapable of abiding by its own judges' resolutions, opening the door to protracted lawsuits and appeals.

Further complicating the subsidy's apportionment on the diocesan level was that rents sometimes belonged to a church in another diocese. The chapel of La Concepción de Nuestra Señora in the church of San Andrés in Jaén, for instance, held rents within the archdiocese of Seville. In August 1531, a judge for the Council of the Cruzada decreed the chapel's rents in Seville exempt from the subsidy. The chapter of Seville appealed the order and was prepared to go to Rome if neces-

---

pp. 187–206; Antonio Irigoyen López, "El clero murciano frente a la presión fiscal. Un documento de 1668," *Contrastes: Revista de Historia* 11 (1998–2000), pp. 183–208; Francisco Marcos Burgos Esteban, "El poder de la fe y la autoridad de la palabra. Iglesia y fiscalidad en la época del conde duque de Olivares," in *Iglesia y Sociedad en el Antiguo Régimen*, eds., Enrique Martínez Ruiz and Vicente Suárez Grimón (Las Palmas: Universidad de las Palmas de Gran Canaria, 1994), pp. 429–438; and Beatriz Cárceles de Gea, "La contribución eclesiástica en el servicio de millones (1621–1700)" in Idem, pp. 439–449.

[112] ACS, Sec. I, lib. 13, ff. 48v, 67, and 102v.

[113] ACG, leg. 29, pieza 4. "Lo que el senor Doctor don Pedro de Vibero…" and "Ynstrucion para el senor licenciado Pero Lopez de Caravajal…"

[114] For an example of the 1536 decree see ACG, leg. 1, pieza 30, "Real Cedula ordenando que el presidente y oidores no se mezclan en los asuntos regentes al subsidio." For an example of the 1543 decree, see ACG, leg. 458, pieza 17, "Presidente e oydores de la audiencias y chancilleria que reside en la cibdad de granada…".

sary. Until January 12, 1532, the chapter defied the judicial order not to collect the subsidy on the chapel's rents in Seville. The canons then backed down and ordered that the money already collected from the chapel's rents be returned and that no further payments be collected from its rents in Seville.[115] The chapel's exemption from paying the subsidy, however, continued to be a sore point, and the Assembly of 1533 unsuccessfully asked the Comisario General to include the chapel's rents in the subsidy.[116] In another example in 1555, Santiago's representative to the Assembly complained that its suffragan churches and Salamanca had included the *votos de Santiago* in their diocesan apportionment of the subsidy. The representative explained that this was unfair, because the Assembly had included the *votos* in Santiago's rents for the general apportionment of the subsidy, so now these rents were taxed twice, once in Santiago and once in their place of origin. He asked the Assembly to correct the matter before other chapters assessed the *votos* in their dioceses.[117]

In addition to lawsuits and complaints, clerical reluctance to pay also held up the collection process. On November 13, 1534, for example, Diego Hernández de Sevilla, canon and collector of the subsidy in Seville, brought grievances before the chapter concerning its steward. Hernández had asked the steward to pay him the 2,376 ducados that fell to the *mesa capitular* (rents of the chapter), but with the second payment due in two days, he still had not received anything. He asked the chapter to order its steward to pay immediately, adding that if the payment was not made, he would not be responsible because he had already made a sufficient effort to collect.[118] On another occasion, it was the archbishop's steward who proved reluctant. On October 9, 1545, the *maestrescuela* asked the archbishop of Seville to direct his steward to pay the portion of the subsidy corresponding to the *mesa episcopal*. Collecting the archbishop's portion of the subsidy may not have had a happy ending, because on November 4 the chapter informed the archbishop of what had occurred in the recent collection.[119] The chapter

---

[115] ACS, Sec. I, lib. 13, ff. 63v and 119v.

[116] AGS, E leg. 27, ff. 332–333.

[117] ACS, Sec. VII, lib. 85 "Congregación de las Santas Iglesias…1555," Session 16, July 15, 1555. The *voto de Santiago* was an ecclesiastical tax that the Castilian and Galician farmers paid to the archbishopric of Santiago and its benefices. For more details see, Teruel, *Vocabulario básico*, pp. 456–458.

[118] ACS, Sec. I, lib. 14, f. 18rv.

[119] Ibid., lib. 19, f. 253v and 257. The chapter of Toledo had similar problems, see ACT, AC lib. 7, ff. 138v, 144.

of Granada also fell behind in its payments. In 1556, the Comisario General threatened to auction the chapter's goods if it did not pay 21 ducados and 125 maravedís still outstanding from the subsidy payment in 1547.[120]

The final step was to pay the king or his collectors, although the crown regularly sent commercial bills of exchange to the chapters directing them to pay a third party or whomever the third party named. In July 1541, the Comisario General told the chapter of Seville to pay a portion of the upcoming subsidy to Rodrigo de Dueñas, a merchant from Medina del Campo, and to an Italian merchant. The chapter directed a canon to comply with the order.[121] In December 1541, the bishop of Lugo wrote to the chapter of Seville, explaining that, for the defense of the cities and the outposts in Africa, the king had borrowed 100,000 ducados from an individual, who asked that the repayment be made to a third party, and the chapter of Seville was then ordered to pay 346 and a half ducados from the next payment of the subsidy due in June 1542 to the third party. The chapter was also to ensure that the person was paid in full and did not lack a maravedí because of discounts. If the chapter did not comply, the judges of the Cruzada would proceed against it with ecclesiastical censure; if the chapter still did not comply, the judges would possibly invoke the secular arm.[122] The bishop's firmness on full payment, as well as his threat, indicates that chapters did not always comply with alacrity. Such foot dragging might have been easier when the payment went to a merchant or banker and not a royal official, as indeed much of the subsidy did go directly to repay royal loans to merchants or bankers without even passing through the royal coffers. The policy, however, was probably wise, even with ecclesiastical foot dragging, because sending the money to court would have involved further expenses that most likely would have been paid from the king's pocket.

On the other hand, the payment of the subsidy directly by the chapters to bankers, especially foreign bankers, may have increased the ecclesiastical estate's concern that the money was being used for purposes

---

[120] Marín López, *El cabildo*, p. 393.

[121] ACS, Sec. I, lib. 17, f. 94v. Kristen Kuebler provided me with this citation.

[122] ACS, Sex. IX, leg. 195, no. 2, "para que el dean y cabildo de la santa iglesia de sevilla en lo que an de pagar en la quarta paga de fin de junio de dxlii..." The section of Comisario de Cruzada in the Archivo General de Simancas contains many examples of royal orders for the chapters to pay merchants or bankers from the payment of the subsidy; legajos 1–6 correspond to Charles V's reign.

beyond those for which it was granted. The clergy had a valid reason to be concerned, because even before agreements were reached for paying subsidies, the crown took loans using the subsidy to guarantee repayment, almost as though it was regular income. However, the crown had little choice but to do so, because the subsidy along with the *cruzada* and income from American treasure fleets were its only sources of unmortgaged income on which bankers wanted their loans assigned.[123] The crown's international financial dealings then could negatively affect its domestic politics in Castile, creating further opposition among the clergy to the misappropriation of the subsidies and other ecclesiastical contributions.

Through this overview, a few observations can be made about royal finances and tensions within the church and between the church and state. First, the crown relied on intermediary agencies, such as the Assembly, for the collection of subsidies. The crown failed to collect its own rents because it lacked the administrative apparatus and apparently never intended to form a group of permanent functionaries paid by the royal treasury. This observation is directly at odds with master narratives of royal centralization in the early modern period.[124] The clergy benefited from this situation, because the crown needed to reach an agreement with the Assembly of the Clergy for payment of the subsidy, and, through agreements and obligations, the clergy nominally excluded the crown from participating in the collection process. Ecclesiastical control over the collection limited the amount of money that the state could exact from the church. In the mid-eighteenth century, for example, royal officials briefly collected the *excusado* and took in almost eight million reales more than the clergy would have collected according to the agreement with the Assembly.[125] The Assembly clearly was able to limit royal fiscal demands, and this favored all the clergy, not just the cathedral chapters.

Second, the subsidy was a focal point for conflicts within the church, and these conflicts provide further evidence that the Castilian church

---

[123] See Carande, *Carlos V y sus banqueros*, p. 476; Tracy, *Emperor Charles V*, pp. 95 and 104; Elena Catalán Martínez, "La participación de la Iglesia en el pago de las deudas de la Corona, 1543–1746," in *Iglesia, sociedad, y estado en España, Francia e Italia (ss. XVIII al XX)* ed. Emilio La Parra López and Jesús Pradells Nadal (Alicante: Diputación Provincial de Alicante, 1991), pp. 41–57.

[124] Gómez Álvarez, *Revisión histórica*, p. 58.

[125] The actual amount collected was 7,777,625 reales and 11 maravedís. See Iturrioz, *Estudio del subsidio*, pp. 186–189.

was not a monolithic institution. A number of these conflicts have been discussed, particularly those relating to apportionment and exemptions. These conflicts were rarely resolved on the local level and often led to the intervention of the crown or the papacy. The collection process also exposed the chapters' inability to coerce even their own canons at times to perform their duties. Otherwise, Diego Hernández de Sevilla would not have had to lodge a grievance against the chapter of Seville's own steward for his failure to pay the subsidy promptly. Thus, the subsidy provides a window for the further study of the internal dynamics of the church, and royal relations with ecclesiastical institutions. More important, the continual independence of the cathedral chapters to negotiate and collect the subsidy indicates that prelates did not gain complete control over their diocesan clergy after the Council of Trent. Consequently, royal appointments of prelates did not lead to greater royal control over the ecclesiastical estate or the easier transfer of funds from the church to the crown.

This chapter has only addressed the Castilian Assembly of the Clergy and is based primarily on data collected from four cathedral archives: Burgos, Granada, Seville, and Toledo. It cannot consequently claim to be a comprehensive study of how Assemblies of the Clergy functioned elsewhere in the Spanish monarchy or how the subsidy was divided and collected in all dioceses. Nonetheless, it should provide a solid foundation to understand the negotiations for ecclesiastical contributions and the process by which the subsidy was apportioned and collected on the diocesan level. This will enhance understanding of the case studies in the subsequent chapters.

CHAPTER TWO

NEGOTIATIONS FOR THE SUBSIDY OF 1530

In 1529, Charles V made separate treaties with the king of France and the pope, bringing the Italian wars to an end. Peace with the pope paved the way for papal concessions of both a *cruzada* and a *dos quartas* in the Spanish kingdoms. The immediate result of the papal concessions was to embroil Isabel's regency government in acrimonious negotiations with the Assembly of the Clergy for the *dos quartas*. The negotiations between the Assembly and the crown illustrate royal reluctance to use coercion to obtain payment as well as ecclesiastical ability to limit royal fiscal demands and keep control of taxation in the hands of local entities. This chapter suggests that, as with its negotiations with the Cortes and cities, the crown's ability to access ecclesiastical rents relied on consultation with and the consensus of the Assembly of the Clergy.[1]

The Notification of the Contribution

In December 1529, corregidores throughout Spain notified the chapters of the *dos quartas* Pope Clement VII had recently conceded to Charles V, delivering a royal letter and instructions from Francisco de Mendoza, Comisario General de la Cruzada and the bishop of Zamora, for collecting the *dos quartas* from the ecclesiastical rents of 1529 and 1530. The corregidores also nailed a copy of the bull to the cathedral door, which notified both the diocesan clergy and the lay people who held church benefices of the papal concession. Some corregidores even had public notaries testify that they had followed orders, presumably to verify to the crown that royal instructions had been carried out.[2]

After receiving notification of the *dos quartas*, the chapter of Toledo

---

[1] For a general overview of the Cortes and the development of the state, see Pablo Fernández Albaladejo, *Fragmentos de Monarquía* (Madrid: Alianza Universidad, 1992), part II.

[2] AGS, E leg. 19, ff. 128, 269. N.B.: f. 269 is dated December 30, 1530. I assume, however, that this conforms to the custom of dating the last days in December as the next year.

wrote to the Castilian chapters to convene an Assembly in Madrid at the end of January. Receiving Toledo's letter on January 4, 1530, the chapter of Seville immediately elected its representatives and sent its reply. In their instructions, Seville's representatives were authorized to convert the *dos quartas* into a subsidy.[3] Around the same time, the other chapters elected representatives to attend the Assembly in Madrid as well.[4] The chapters do not appear to have consulted each other about the appropriateness of convening the Assembly in this year, and the speed with which the Castilian chapters sent representatives to Madrid surprised even the empress.[5]

In the other Spanish kingdoms, the chapters also received notification of the new contribution. The chapter of Granada, for example, received notification on December 31, 1529, and immediately decided to send representatives to meet with Isabel. On January 3, 1530, the archbishop of Granada and the chapter authorized the chapter's representatives to reach an agreement for payment and promised to abide by it.[6] Although the representatives from Granada eventually joined the Castilian Assembly of the Clergy, in early January the chapter apparently planned to negotiate separately. The ecclesiastical estates in Navarre and the Crown of Aragon presumably made preparations to send deputies to meet with either the empress or the Viceroy of Aragon.[7]

Between the notification and the Assembly of the Clergy, the chapters also appealed the bull to the crown. The chapters of Toledo, Salamanca, Palencia, Segovia, Ávila, Sigüenza, Osma, Córdoba, and Granada formally appealed both the bull and the bishop's instruction before the

---

[3] ACS, Sec. I, lib. 12, ff. 115 and 118.

[4] For examples from Burgos, Toledo, and Córdoba, see ACB, R lib. 43 f. 259; ACT, AC lib. 5 f. 31 (of small bound in AC lib. 5); Juan Gómez Bravo, *Catalogo de los obispos de Córdoba, y breve noticia historica de su Iglesia Catedral, y obispado* (Córdoba: Juan Rodríguez, 1778) vol. I, p. 431.

[5] See María del Carmen Mazarío Coleto, *Isabel de Portugal: Emperatriz y Reina de España* (Madrid: Consejo Superior de Investigaciones Científicas, 1951), p. 269.

[6] ACG, AC lib. 2, ff. 197v–198. The archbishop of Granada's involvement in granting powers to the representatives may well have been an anomaly. Prelates clearly were consulted but did not usually play such a prominent role.

[7] Although the papal concession was for the Spanish Monarchy, negotiations took place between the crown and the ecclesiastical estates in each of the various kingdoms. In the Crown of Aragon, for instance, there were separate Aragonese, Catalan, and Valencian Assemblies of the Clergy, while in the Crown of Castile, there were separate Castilian, Granadan, and Navarrese Assemblies. Representatives from the kingdoms of Granada and Navarre occasionally joined the Castilian Assembly to negotiate with the crown. Prior to the creation of the diocese of Vitoria in 1862, parishes in the Basque Provinces belonged to the dioceses of Pamplona (96 parishes) and Calahorra.

bishop of Zamora, while other chapters lodged appeals before judges of the Cruzada. Some judges immediately denied the chapters' request; others consulted the bishop of Zamora before responding. The bishop himself did not respond at all. The bishop of Ciudad Rodrigo, on the other hand, advised the king to respond positively to the appeals, because the chapters were ready to grant a subsidy if he did so. Even though a positive response would have slightly reduced the size of the subsidy, the bishop said, the cost was worth paying to avoid the inevitable delays and expenses that would result from consulting the king who was outside of Spain. In the end, however, the crown rejected the chapters' appeals.[8]

Had the crown responded positively to their appeals, a quick resolution was not guaranteed, because the chapters did not agree on the size of the subsidy to offer. Some thought it would be enough to pay the *décima*, while others proposed paying 210,000 florins, since the present bull supposedly conformed to the *quarta* Pope Hadrian VI (1522–1523) had conceded in 1523. Still others believed the reference to Hadrian's bull in the announcement sent to the chapters was deceptive, because the florins would be converted into ducados, which would end up being slightly more each year. The chapters then began negotiating with the crown without a clear agreement among themselves on a suitable offer.[9]

Disagreement also emerged between the king and his ministers on how to proceed in the negotiations. The king wanted to reach an agreement quickly for the most money in the shortest period of payments,[10] but the bishop of Ciudad Rodrigo reported that, due to dearth, the period of payments would have to be longer than in the previous subsidy.[11] The bishop also warned Charles that if he provided discounts to individuals and monasteries, the king should take care not to err with the discounts based on what the Treasury said had been done in 1523. Whether the bishop feared the Treasury would suggest too large or

---

[8] AGS, E leg. 20, f. 37.

[9] Ibid.

[10] AGS, E leg. 21 f. 233. Charles V to the Archbishop of Santiago, January 21, 1530.

[11] The bishop's comments on the payments make clear the connection between the current economic situation of the churches and their position in the negotiations. Since agricultural output was down, the clergy would be unable to pay quickly. Even if they had a bumper crop, the clergy preferred longer periods of payment to lessen the burden. Economic hardships were not limited to Castile. On June 6, 1530, Tavera advised Charles V to make the best resolution possible with the Assemblies of Aragon, Catalonia, and Valencia in view of widespread pestilence and hunger (see AGS, E leg. 20, f. 15).

too small a discount is unclear, but in the end, the Treasury suggested a discount much larger than what Charles finally made.[12] The bishop also proposed obtaining a brief from the pope to make an agreement with the Assembly to reduce the *dos quartas* to a subsidy and another brief authorizing ecclesiastical censures to force payment.[13] Much of his advice guided royal policy once the negotiations began in earnest.

The Council of the Orders, on the other hand, tried to protect the interests of the military orders. It advised Charles that the Order of Santiago traditionally did not pay the *quarta* or indeed any subsidy; the councilors recommended other ways for the Order to help defend Christendom, especially Spain, than by contributing to the subsidy. These councilors also warned Charles that even though the current bull's inclusion of the Order in the *quarta* was in the king's interest, the pope might require the Order to contribute another *quarta* in the future for ends contrary to the king's.[14] The councilors' logic suggests that the king's drive to acquire ecclesiastical rents might allow the pope to access previously inaccessible rents. By temporarily alienating a portion of the military orders' rents to the crown, the popes might actually open new sources of revenue for themselves to exploit at a later date. Royal policy was not equivalent to the demands of the king; the various ministers and councils, who often had contradictory objectives, often sparred over the best policy and obstructed policies that were detrimental to their council's prerogatives.[15]

Differences between the royal ministers over policy and its implementation even led to personal attacks. In mid-March, for example, tempers flared over a new bull that authorized prelates to help determine the size of the ecclesiastical contribution. In a letter of March 12, 1530, Alonso de Fonseca, the archbishop of Toledo, advised the king to shelf the bull because prelates had not actively participated in

---

[12] See chapter 1, pp. 50–51.

[13] AGS, E leg. 20 f. 37.

[14] Ibid., f. 29.

[15] I.A.A. Thompson has suggested that, by protecting their own judicial rights and prerogatives, the royal councils in Castile, not representative institutions, were the true guarantors of societal liberty. The Council of the Order's case that the Order of Santiago should not pay clearly bolsters Thompson's argument. Nevertheless, the majority of the evidence uncovered for the Assembly of the Clergy indicates that representative institutions did guarantee corporate liberty in Castile. See I.A.A. Thompson, "Castile: Absolutism, Constitutionalism, and Liberty" in *Fiscal Crises, Liberty, and Representative Government, 1450–1789,* ed. Philip T. Hoffman and Kathryn Norberg (Stanford: Stanford University Press, 1994), p. 217.

the Assembly since 1505. To announce a bull that gave them a greater role in determining the size of the ecclesiastical contribution, he feared, would only irritate the Assembly, making the negotiations for the *dos quartas* more difficult. He then blasted an unnamed minister, presumably either Tavera or Mendoza, saying that this was neither the first nor last problem that minister had caused in the subsidy negotiations and in other affairs entrusted to him. He reviled that minister's conduct as unworthy of a minister of princes, who should act with prudence and authority.[16] The archbishop of Toledo's personal attack on a colleague suggests a deeper animosity than differences over the current negotiations. Royal ministers continually struggled over the best policy; these disagreements often spilled over into conflicts of personality between the people involved.[17]

Changing royal demands affected policy, as well, for Charles was not inhibited in pressing the clergy for further aid. On April 4, he told Tavera that he would be pleased if the pope ordered the prelates, the ecclesiastical estate, the monasteries of Castile and Aragon, and the military orders of Santiago, Calatrava, Alcántara, and San Juan to contribute a moderate number of galleys for a year without prejudicing the *quarta*.[18] Charles's suggestion demonstrates his desire to acquire as much money as possible from the clergy without jeopardizing the *quarta*.[19] He quickly determined, however, that this initiative was

---

[16] B.N., Ms.1778, f. 60v. Tensions between the archbishop and other members of the council of state date to at least the fall of 1529, when the archbishop had been sidelined and denied access to the cipher system used in correspondence with the king. See Peter Marzahl, "Communication and Control in the Political System of Emperor Charles V. The First Regency of Empress Isabella," in *The World of Emperor Charles V*, edited by Wim Blockmans and Nicolette Mout (Amsterdam: Koninklijke Nederlandse Akademie van Wetenschappen Verhandelingen, Afd. Letterkunde, Nieuwe Reeks, deel 188, 2004), pp. 87–88.

[17] In a possible attempt to defend his role in the negotiations, Tavera related to Cobos on June 14 the Licenciado Alarcón's exchange with the canons of the chapter of Toledo. Even though the empress, their archbishop, the bishops of Zamora and Ciudad Rodrigo, and other royal ministers were involved in the negotiations, the canons blamed Tavera alone for forcing them to offer more than 200,000 ducados. Furthermore, they said that no one demonstrated more diligence to benefit the royal treasury than Tavera. B.N., Ms. 1778, ff. 206rv. In 1533, the archbishop of Toledo hesitated to become involved with the negotiation for the *medios frutos* because he was blamed for the errors in the negotiations for the subsidy of 1530. See AGS, E leg. 27, f. 178.

[18] AGS, E leg. 21, ff. 267–270.

[19] The next reference to asking the ecclesiastical estate to finance galleys appears in a letter of June 14 from Tavera to Cobos. Tavera had not yet broached the issue with other prelates at court, because the last time he discussed it their response had been unenthusiastic. He recommended that the king himself order the ecclesiastical estates in

detrimental and thus abandoned it. Political expediency partially determined royal policy; whatever was reasonably within its grasp, the crown did not hesitate to obtain.

A final factor preventing the formulation of a coherent royal policy was that Charles's imperial worldview often clashed with his ministers' peninsular perspective. Despite the frequent exchanges between Charles and his regency governments, the regency governments often lacked adequate information on the king's wishes, which delayed important decisions. The regents thus frequently had to decide for themselves the correct course of action, and, in these cases, they often followed the governing precept shared by both courts: maintain domestic tranquility.[20]

It is hard to draw an accurate picture of royal and ecclesiastical policy going into the negotiations in 1530 from a few scattered documents. Nevertheless, it is safe to say that the crown did not have a coherent policy, except for the standard objective of gaining the largest amount of money in the shortest period of payments, which many ministers thought was not a viable option, given the current economic hardships. Despite unanimous opposition to the contribution, however, the chapters could not agree on the size of a counter-offer. Although the focus here is on the negotiations between the crown and the Assembly, the divergent voices within both camps on what policies to pursue are important to note. The presence of such divergent views did not necessarily hinder successful negotiations. On the contrary, they may have allowed the Assembly and the crown to bridge certain impasses with an adroit shuffling of negotiators.

The Assembly of the Clergy

On February 2, 1530, the Assembly convened in Madrid, though representatives from only 14 chapters attended the initial session.[21] In

---

the Crowns of Castile and Aragon as well as the military orders to finance some galleys for a year. He also recommended obtaining a papal concession and did not believe this request would be an obstacle to collecting the subsidy (B.N. ms. 1778, ff. 204v–205). On July 8, however, Charles told Tavera that in the present circumstances, he declined to ask the ecclesiastical estate to provide galleys (AGS, E leg. 21, ff. 342–344). Tavera concurred with him on July 31, saying that it was best not to ask the church to supply galleys until the subsidy was completely paid (AGS, E leg. 20, ff. 176–177).

[20] Marzahl, "Communication and Control," pp. 88, 92, and 96.

[21] The chapters were: Toledo, Seville, Burgos, León, Córdoba, Salamanca, Zamora, Segovia, Ávila, Cuenca, Plasencia, Calahorra y La Calzada, Sigüenza, Jaén, and Astorga. See ACS, Sec. II., lib. 1157 (77), Session 1.

time, all 28 Castilian chapters sent representatives, as did Granada, Navarre, and the orders of the Kingdom of Valencia.

On February 3, the representatives met with Isabel of Portugal, the empress and regent of Spain in Charles's absence, to inform her that paying the *dos quartas* would severely hamper their ability to perform their religious duties. They argued that, as mediators between God and men, the clergy's duties were to pray and make continual sacrifices for all Christians—especially for the king. Moreover, in a time of dearth, the collection of the *dos quartas* would strain the clergy's ability to maintain themselves and their churches, hinder their ability to perform their duties, and reduce the amount of money available for charity. The clergy begged the king to forsake the contribution. Isabel responded that the king's great need afflicted everyone, not just the ecclesiastical estate. She would do whatever she could to help the ecclesiastical estate, however, and promised to name ministers to negotiate with the Assembly.[22]

The representatives also presented a further petition to the bishop of Zamora on February 4. To the representatives' consternation, the bishop immediately rejected it. The bishop's hard-nosed attitude made many representatives fearful that he might bypass the negotiations altogether and execute the collection without an agreement. On February 5, the Assembly consulted its lawyers concerning the appropriate response to take should the bishop collect the *dos quartas* without its consent. The lawyers advised them to suspend Holy Offices, but the Assembly apparently thought this was too bold a step; on February 7, it formed a committee to discuss further the proper response to a forcible collection.[23] Such an action would be a serious challenge to the authority of the Assembly and to ecclesiastical liberty. The lawyers clearly thought that a forced execution would breach ecclesiastical law (or the Comisario General's powers) and warrant the suspension of Holy Offices.[24] The Assembly's discussion on how to resist a forcible collection indicates that the ecclesiastical estate would not permit the crown to appropriate its rents 'illegally' without a fight, but it also shows the representative's reluctance to suspend Holy Offices. The decision to suspend Holy Offices, then, was not taken lightly by the clergy.

---

[22] Ibid., Session 4.

[23] Ibid., Sessions 6, 8, and 9.

[24] In April, a papal brief arrived granting the Comisario General power to execute the *quarta*. This brief significantly undercut the legal argument for a suspension of Holy Offices. See ACS, Sec. II, lib. 1157 (77), Session April 2, 1530.

Because its appeal to the bishop of Zamora produced no results, the Assembly prepared an appeal to Rome. It reasoned that, although the pope had granted the ecclesiastical contribution to the crown, he could also place restrictions on the crown's ability to collect it. The Assembly also elected two representatives who were knowledgeable of the clergy's liberties and their religious duties to delivery the appeal personally in Rome.[25] In the fourteenth and fifteenth centuries, as Nieto Soria points out, the Castilian church had turned to the crown to resist the centralization of papal power. At that time, the Castilian church had protested more loudly about fiscal demands from outside the kingdom than from within. Although the Castilian church gained greater independence from Rome, it also became more tightly tied to the internal politics of Castile and open to royal intervention.[26] The tables had been turned by the 1530s, with the Castilian church seeking papal protection from ceaseless royal demands.

The crown also wanted the pope to amend the original concession. Some military orders, for example, had not been included in the bull, and a papal brief was necessary to remedy that situation. The crown also solicited and received briefs to reduce the *dos quartas* to a subsidy and collect it by force if necessary.[27] These briefs were necessary because, although the crown had gained considerable control over ecclesiastical rents from popes in the previous century, it still depended on papal authorization to carry out the collection.[28] The pope, then, could never be completely marginalized in the negotiations for ecclesiastical contributions. Even after the original papal bull was granted, Rome continued to play a crucial role: both the crown and the Assembly looked to the pope either to expand or to limit the contribution.

While the Assembly discussed methods of resistance and prepared appeals to Rome, a messenger notified it on February 7 that the empress had named the archbishop of Santiago, the bishop of Zamora, and

---

[25] Ibid., Session 12. One representative elected, Dr. Juan de Aceves, so impressed members of the Council of the Indies that they thought he had the right qualities to be a prelate and suggested a bishopric in America for him (AGS, E leg. 19, f. 16). The Assembly of the Clergy thus provided individual canons an opportunity to gain royal recognition and maybe even promotion.

[26] José Manuel Nieto Soria, *Iglesia y génesis del estado moderno en Castilla (1369–1480)* (Madrid: Editorial Complutense, 1993), pp. 22, 34, 251, 342.

[27] For more details on these briefs, see AGS, E leg. 21 ff. 59, 256, and 270.

[28] John A.F. Thomson, *Popes and Princes, 1417–1517. Politics and Policy in the Late Medieval Church* (London: George Allen & Unwin, 1980), chapter 8.

the bishop of Ciudad Rodrigo to negotiate on behalf of the crown. The Assembly then named four deputies to negotiate with the royal ministers.[29]

On February 10, the Assembly offered to provide Charles with a voluntary contribution if the king promised neither to request nor to accept another ecclesiastical contribution from the pope in the future.[30] This proposition did not entice the crown, for although she wished the ecclesiastical estate well, the empress lacked the authority to accept the offer. She then admonished the Assembly not to advance new terms for an agreement, saying that the Assembly would be better served negotiating within the framework of the present concession. In response, the Assembly presented the royal negotiators with decrees from Toro, Barcelona (1519), and Valladolid (1523) in which both King Ferdinand and Charles V promised not to ask for further contributions and to convert any future papal concessions into subsidies of 100,000 florins.[31] The Assembly apparently felt the earlier decrees set a precedent for its offer, so its proposition was not an innovation.

The past royal decrees had little effect on the royal negotiators. After a protracted discussion on February 14, they told the Assembly that they were not judges, but the Assembly did not accept their response.[32] The next day, the Assembly's deputies informed the archbishop of Santiago, bishop of Zamora, and bishop of Ciudad Rodrigo that it intended to comply with the earlier decrees and offer the crown 100,000 florins.[33] The bishops of Zamora and Ciudad Rodrigo asserted that the amount was minuscule, especially since the Moors had just attacked Cartagena and were raiding the countryside around Cádiz. Nevertheless, they communicated the offer to the empress.[34]

Isabel denounced the offer of 100,000 florins for failing to meet royal needs, declaring that she would hear no more about this sum.

---

[29] ACS, Sec. II, lib. 1157 (77), Session 10.

[30] Ibid., Session 13. The Assembly made a similar offer in 1533. Although the Assembly's rationale for offering a voluntary contribution is not clear from the documents, it may well have seen turning the contribution into a voluntary grant as the best way to limit royal demands. By the 1540s, though, the Assembly's position had changed, and it rejected the king's proposal that the clergy make a voluntary grant.

[31] Ibid., Session 16, February 14, 1530. For a copy of the decrees see Ibid., "Capitulacion de ciertas cedulas que las iglesias tienen cerca de las quartas."

[32] Ibid., Session 17.

[33] Ibid., Session 18.

[34] Ibid., Session 19. The Archbishop of Santiago was not present at the meeting.

The Assembly subsequently withdrew from the negotiations.[35] Its initial strategy to rely on past royal decrees to limit royal demands had failed. The crown clearly was not prepared to recognize the validity of the decrees or to accept such a small sum. Although it wanted to reach an agreement by consensus, the crown would not allow earlier decrees to curtail the contribution's size. Prior to the Assembly of 1523, the chapters had also discussed using past decrees to limit royal demands.[36] In 1530, the Assembly used the same strategy with apparently the same result. Clearly, the crown did not feel bound by previous decrees, but such arbitrary action posed serious challenges for the crown because it could weaken royal authority in the long run, reducing the support for the crown on which royal government was build.[37] In this case, the crown apparently rejected the previous decrees in an effort to pressure the Assembly to increase its offer. The arbitrary use of absolute royal authority thus might in fact have been a stratagem to reach a consensus. In turn, by breaking off the negotiations, the Assembly probably hoped to pressure the crown to accept its offer.

The Assembly's boycott of the negotiations, however, did not last long, for on February 22, the representatives discussed renewing them. The next day, a representative from Toledo declared that the boycott was counterproductive and urged the Assembly to return to the negotiating table. Hoping to allay fears that the deputies might make an agreement with the crown behind the Assembly's back, he proposed requiring the deputies to consult the Assembly before reaching an agreement with the crown. He also recommended charging them with obtaining the inclusion of the military orders, cardinals, vacant sees, dioceses in the kingdoms of Navarre and Granada, and the nuns of Santa Clara in the agreement. A majority of the representatives favored this proposal. They also discussed sending deputies to meet the archbishop of Toledo, who was sympathetic to the Assembly, and to seek his aid to bring moderation to the negotiations.[38] The representatives again

---

[35] Ibid., Session 22. February 19, 1530.

[36] AGS, E leg. 11, f. 182. Whether the chapters actually presented Charles V with the royal decrees in 1523 is unknown. In making an agreement with the crown, however, the Assembly did manage to get Charles V to sign a decree limiting his right to future contributions.

[37] J.B. Owens, *"By My Absolute Royal Authority": Justice and the Castilian Commonwealth at the Beginning of the First Global Age* (Rochester, NY: University of Rochester Press, 2005), p. 242.

[38] The bishop of Ciudad Rodrigo commented that upon learning about the new contribution, the archbishop was upset. See AGS, E leg. 20, f. 37.

presented the bishop of Zamora with their appeals and copies of past royal decrees.[39] This combination of boycott and further appeals may in fact have produced results—the royal ministers did not deny the Assembly's appeal outright.[40]

The Assembly's insistence that the royal decrees be honored and its reluctance to make a larger offer, however, frustrated the ministers. In a letter of February 25, Tavera complained to Charles that the Assembly constantly presented the royal decrees issued in Barcelona (1519) and in Valladolid (1523). He also informed Charles that he had rejected the Assembly's offer of 100,000 florins, asking the representatives instead to provide the *quarta* or an honest subsidy. According to Tavera, the representatives did not mince words in their response, so he harshly reprimanded them. His rebuke apparently chastened the representatives; after his outburst, Tavera reported that the Assembly was more benign and ready to negotiate. Still, he was uncertain how this would end. To expedite negotiations, Tavera asked Charles to tell the royal negotiators what he would consider an acceptable offer.[41] Tavera's remarks indicate that the Assembly did not freely relinquish ecclesiastical wealth to the crown. This evidence belies the notion that negotiations with corporate bodies were simple formalities. Moreover, without clear orders, the royal ministers did not necessarily know how to proceed. This, of course, was a problem that faced administrators in all of Charles's realms. Making timely decisions and carrying them out with authority sometimes required the king's presence.[42]

At the end of February, the Assembly learned that the court would leave for Segovia within ten days, and it consequently felt pressured to reach an agreement, for moving the Assembly to Segovia would be toilsome and expensive. So it asked the archbishop of Toledo to intervene with the royal negotiators, apparently in the belief that the archbishop would be able to convince the regency government to accept its offer. How the archbishop replied, however, is unclear.[43]

Given the empress's impending departure, the Assembly offered a larger amount on March 2, expecting the crown to reduce its demand.

---

[39] ACS, Sec. II, lib. 1157 (77), Sessions 24 and 25.

[40] AGS, E leg. 20, f. 36. Bishop of Ciudad Rodrigo to King, February 26, 1530.

[41] Ibid., ff. 94–95.

[42] Communications were a serious problem for the regency government, especially considering Charles's desire to have the final say on most major decisions. See Marzahl, "Communication and Control," p. 83.

[43] ACS, Sec. II, lib. 1157 (77), Session, February 28, 1530.

When the crown did not budge, the representatives decided to authorize their deputies to offer up to 300,000 florins in the longest possible period of payment. In addition to the dioceses of Castile, the apportionment of the 300,000 florins would include the military orders, the cardinals, vacant sees, dioceses in the kingdoms of Navarre and Granada, and the Order of Santa Clara. If this proposal was rejected, the Assembly ordered, the deputies were to speak no further with the royal negotiators. The meeting with the royal negotiators on March 3 was unproductive; the only noteworthy development was Tavera's announcement that he would ask the empress to replace him, because he had many other things to do.[44]

Negotiations were no more fruitful the next day. The deputies met with the bishops of Zamora and Ciudad Rodrigo and with licenciado Polanco, who had replaced the archbishop of Santiago, and slowly raised their offer to 250,000 florins, but the royal negotiators curtly told them that anything less than 600,000 florins was unacceptable. The Assembly thought that the crown's demand was exorbitant, and the representatives proposed sending a dispatch to Rome and obtaining license from the empress to leave.[45] On March 5, the Assembly voted to end the negotiations. The representatives knew that their offers were insufficient for the royal negotiators, who would not honor Ferdinand or Charles V's decrees. Moreover, by ending the negotiations, the representatives would avoid further costs from futile talks. They consequently sent a deputy to obtain license from the empress to depart and named other deputies to remain at court, as well as someone to handle the dispatch to Rome. The representatives also wrote to the archbishop of Toledo. To protect the churches from royal coercion, a representative proposed that if one diocese suspended Holy Offices, all the other dioceses should do likewise even if the crown had not yet proceeded against them.[46] Since there was no clear obligation to seek license from the empress to leave, the Assembly may have used the notification of its imminent departure to pressure the crown to accept a smaller subsidy. Departing without an agreement, however, was dangerous, because the crown might forcibly collect the contributions. The representatives clearly were

---

[44] Ibid., Sessions, March 2–3, 1530.
[45] Ibid., Session, March 4, 1530.
[46] Ibid., Session, March 5, 1530. Isabel's letter of October 13, 1532, indicates that some chapters had started to suspend Holy Offices in 1530 and that discussions to suspend Holy Offices were sincere. See Mazarío, *Isabel*, p. 363.

aware of this danger but apparently believed that leaving was the best way to proceed under the circumstances.

Both the empress and archbishop of Toledo responded negatively to the Assembly's request. The empress told the Assembly that leaving without an agreement would be counterproductive and asked the representatives to wait while she summoned the archbishop of Toledo to bring the negotiatations to a suitable conclusion.[47] The archbishop of Toledo, for his part, urged the representatives to reach some resolution before departing, saying that, with a resolution, they would leave happier and the ecclesiastical estate would have greater tranquility. To expedite a resolution, he offered to aid the Assembly, which declined his offer, determined, as it was to leave and end the negotiations. Despite the empress's and archbishop's comments, the Assembly again asked the empress for license to leave. At the same time, it prepared instructions and an appeal for its deputies to Rome.[48] At this point, the Assembly clearly thought that negotiations with the crown had reached a dead end, so it turned to the pope for aid.

Unaware of the representatives' preparations to depart, Charles informed Isabel on March 8 that the pope had sent one brief to authorize the bishop of Zamora to carry out an execution and another to permit the crown to reduce the *dos quartas* into a subsidy. These briefs gave Isabel an opportunity to reach an accord with the Assembly. Charles clearly told Isabel that the paramount concerns for the agreement were his current needs and the amount necessary to meet them. To reach a successful outcome, Charles advised keeping the second brief secret until using it became necessary.[49] These new briefs made it unlikely that the pope would favor the clergy's appeal. More importantly, the first brief allowed the crown to collect the *dos quartas* lawfully without an agreement with the Assembly.

As the representatives prepared to depart, the Assembly re-swore the oath it had made on February 28 that individual dioceses were not to make separate agreements with the crown to pay the *dos quartas*.[50] To hold royal encroachment at bay, all the chapters had to stay together.

The empress still tried to engage the representatives in serious negotiations, asking them on March 10 to wait until the archbishop of

---

[47] ACS, Sec. II, lib. 1157 (77), Session, March 6, 1530.
[48] Ibid., Session, March 7, 1530.
[49] AGS, E leg. 20, f. 278.
[50] ACS, Sec.II, lib. 1157 (77), Session, March 10, 1530.

Toledo arrived.[51] The archbishop apparently arrived that day or the next, because on March 11 he asked the Assembly to send its deputies to meet with him, the licenciado Polanco, and the Provincial of the Dominicans. These eleventh hour negotiations, however, saw no concessions from either side. The clergy would only offer 300,000 florins, while the archbishop asked them to pay 700,000 florins. Despite the impasse, the deputies agreed to further negotiations mediated by the archbishops of Toledo and Santiago and the Provincial of the Dominicans.[52] Interestingly, the Assembly did not want the Comisario General involved in the negotiations.

Although the Assembly remained in session, its position had not changed. On March 12, a representative of Seville announced that the empress had left in the morning, leaving the archbishop of Toledo, the archbishop of Santiago, and the Provincial of the Dominicans in charge of negotiating an agreement. By appointing these three, the empress demonstrated her willingness to keep communications open, but, having resigned from the negotiations just nine days earlier, Tavera, the archbishop of Santiago, was probably not enthusiastic about his reappointment. Since the royal negotiators were in Alcovendas, the Assembly sent its deputies there. The deputies, however, were not permitted to offer more than 300,000 florins even though the royal minister had already rejected that sum. If the sum was not accepted, the Assembly planned to ask the empress again for license to dissolve itself.[53]

In February, the Assembly had unsuccessfully tried to limit royal demands by using previous royal decrees. In mid-March, the Assembly used a new strategy, threatening to leave if the crown did not accept its offer. The Assembly's effectiveness in early March, however, is hard to gauge, because the regency government was attempting to keep the Assembly in Madrid until news arrived from the king.

A major breakthrough finally occurred in mid-March. At Alcovendas, the deputies once again offered the crown 300,000 florins, but the royal negotiators turned the tables on the Assembly, saying that if it did not offer a larger amount, the representatives could return to their dioceses. At the same time, as an incentive for the Assembly to increase its offer, they indicated that the crown planned to reduce its demand. Each side

---

[51] Ibid.

[52] Ibid., Session, March 11, 1530.

[53] Ibid., Session, March 12, 1530. The empress apparently left to make arrangements for the exchange of the French princes at the border. See Mazarío, *Isabel*, p. 269.

strategically threatened to dissolve or dismiss the Assembly to pressure the other either to raise or lower its proposal for the subsidy. In view of the crown's position, the Assembly decided on March 15 to offer up to 420,000 florins. It preferred a payment period of six years, but would settle for four. Moreover, it reiterated its request that the military orders, cardinals, vacant sees, the Order of Santa Clara, and the kingdoms of Navarre and Granada be included in the sum.[54]

On March 27, the deputies reported on their meeting in Alcalá de Henares with the archbishops of Toledo and Santiago and other royal negotiators. On behalf of the Assembly, they had offered to pay the crown 400,000 florins over ten years. The offer did not include the military orders, cardinals, vacant sees, and the Order of Santa Clara, but it did include the dioceses in the kingdoms of Navarre and Granada in the division with those of Castile. The royal ministers, however, backed away from this offer, explaining that they lacked the authority to make an agreement and were waiting for further instructions from Charles V. After so many days, they hoped the representatives would wait a little longer. The Assembly was perturbed that the royal negotiators had duped it into raising its offer when they did not have authorization to make an agreement. The representatives were also angry about the amount of money they had spent on the negotiations and decided that 400,000 florins was their final offer.[55]

The empress's report to Charles at the end of March differed from the Assembly's minutes. She related that the parties agreed on 420,000 florins for both *quartas*, or 210,000 florins for each, as in the last contribution. The representatives argued that they had made a larger contribution than they intended to and determined to leave before they were pressured to give more money. The empress, on the other hand, wanted to detain the representatives until a messenger arrived with the king's orders, which fortunately arrived two days later. She also advised Charles that all the councilors, both secular and ecclesiastical, thought it would be difficult to break the Assembly's resolve and that it would be wiser for him to accept the Assembly's offer rather than endure the inconveniences of a forcible collection.[56] Slow communications clearly complicated the negotiation process, especially when the regency

[54] ACS, Sec. II, lib. 1157 (77), Session, March 15, 1530.
[55] Ibid., Session, March 27, 1530.
[56] Mazarío, *Isabel*, p. 269.

government did not have firm orders from the king and limited freedom
to act without his approval.

In the meantime, the Assembly agreed to send agents to Rome
within thirty days with or without an agreement and to create a fund
to pay them. It granted complete powers to the dean of Plasencia
and a canon of Burgos to bring to Rome the general appeal and the
responses of the bishop of Zamora and his subordinate judges. If
an agreement was reached, the agents would receive new orders. By
sending agents to Rome, the Assembly sought to preserve the liberty
of all the Spanish clergy. On March 31, the Assembly learned that the
king's messenger had finally arrived, and it immediately sent deputies
to learn the mail's contents.[57]

The messenger brought both orders from Charles and the papal
briefs (discussed above). The royal orders did not satisfy Isabel, because
Charles failed to state the exact amount of money he needed. Nevertheless, she believed that the brief for execution would probably
prompt the Assembly to offer more. Royal plans to keep the contents
of the second brief secret, however, were foiled. According to Isabel,
the Assembly knew of both briefs even before the messenger arrived.[58]
As a result, the briefs' arrival did not bolster the regency government's
negotiating position. Though the briefs, especially the one to collect
the *dos quartas*, clearly armed the state, Charles's failure to specify a
monetary amount left the regency government in the same quandary.
Isabel nonetheless did an about face with the arrival of the briefs.
Although she already knew their contents from an earlier letter, she
believed she could coax a larger offer from the Assembly now that she
had the briefs in hand, whereas two days earlier she had been ready
to accept 420,000 florins.

On April 2, the Assembly officially learned the contents of the recent
mail from Charles V. The papal brief to make an agreement was not as
favorable as the Assembly had hoped, but it sufficed. The papal brief
for the bishop of Zamora to execute the *dos quartas*, however, was unacceptable. The Assembly's deputies indignantly told the royal negotiators
that there was no need for a forcible collection, stressing that the lack
of an agreement after almost seventy days of negotiations was not the
Assembly's fault and the ecclesiastical estate's goodwill was well known.

---

[57] ACS, Sec. II, lib. 1157 (77), Sessions, March 30 and 31, 1530.
[58] Mazarío, *Isabel*, p. 271. April 1, 1530. For more on briefs, see AGS E leg. 20, f. 278.

The royal negotiators replied that they desired neither to use that brief nor to frighten the Assembly, but that the brief rendered the Assembly's appeals redundant. From the royal and papal viewpoints, there were no valid arguments against paying the *dos quartas*. Since the Assembly was determined not to spend more time or money in these negotiations and would not offer a larger amount, its deputies implored the royal negotiators to accept its offer. The royal negotiators contended that the empress had already mercifully reduced the crown's original demand to 600,000 florins. The deputies retorted that, in Alcovendas, they had offered 300,000 florins, while the negotiators demanded 500,000 florins. After that exchange, the deputies stated, the royal negotiators had promised to ask for less if the Assembly offered more than 300,000 florins. Consequently, the Assembly was persuaded to increase its offer to 400,000 florins. The empress, it argued, offended the Assembly by requesting 600,000 florins without even responding to its previous offer of 400,000 florins. The representatives stuck to their offer and decided to depart that afternoon.[59]

The Assembly's decision to dissolve itself infuriated the empress.[60] She told the Assembly that its request was a further example of its insolence and that she had ordered the bishops of Zamora and Ciudad Rodrigo to make preparations for the execution of the bull. She was displeased, she wrote to Charles, that these negotiations had gotten so out of hand. If the Assembly had been reasonable and reached an agreement, she would have offered it largesse, and the clergy would have avoided the difficulties and expenses associated with a forcible collection. Despite her angry outburst, the empress still thought that even if the contribution did not exceed 500,000 florins, it would be better for the chapters themselves to collect the money.[61] The Assembly's reluctance to offer more than 400,000 florins left her government little option but to prepare for the execution, yet the empress was ready to forgo the execution if the chapters began the collection on their own—even if this meant a smaller subsidy.

---

[59] ACS, Sec. II, lib.1157 (77), Session, April 2, 1530.
[60] The norms for convening and dissolving an Assembly were vague at this time. Generally, the Assembly would request license from the crown to convene and dissolve. Yet there are many cases, such as this one, where the Assembly did as it pleased without royal license. See chapter 1, pp. 29–30.
[61] Mazarío, *Isabel*, p. 272.

Although his response to the letter arrived after the parties had already reached an agreement, Charles was also reluctant to use coercion. Like Isabel, he was displeased that the Assembly would not offer more. Still, he preferred an agreement, because even though he would collect less, an agreement would allow him to make discounts and avoid lawsuits and other complications. If there were no agreement, however, Charles ordered the collection of the *dos quartas* by the most suitable method.[62] Although the crown had papal authority to use force, the king and the regency government showed a clear preference to avoid confrontation.

As the Assembly's representatives prepared to leave, the archbishop of Toledo pleaded with them to stay longer and to reach an agreement favorable to God and king. Knowing his goodwill toward them, those representatives still present reconvened.[63] In appreciation of the renewal of the negotiations, the empress reduced her offer of 600,000 florins by 50,000 and apparently joined the military orders of Santiago and San Juan with the Assembly for purposes of the apportionment. On April 4, however, the deputies told the archbishop that they still would not offer more than 400,000 florins, adding that this amount should include all the military orders, the Order of Santa Clara, cardinals, vacant sees, and the dioceses in the Kingdoms of Navarre and Granada. The archbishop asked them to consult the entire Assembly. Later, the majority in the Assembly voted that if all the military orders, the Order of Santa Clara, cardinals, vacant sees, and the dioceses in Kingdoms of Navarre and Granada were included with them, they would offer up to 500,000 florins. If the military orders were removed, they would only offer up to 420,000 florins. If the dioceses in the kingdoms of Navarre and Granada and the Order of Santa Clara were included, they would offer 430,000 florins.[64]

At this point, the size of the subsidy was contingent on the number of ecclesiastical bodies that would be included with the Castilian dioceses for payment. On April 5, the deputies reported that they had offered 480,000 florins if all the military orders, the Order of Santa Clara, cardinals, vacant sees, and the dioceses in the Kingdoms of Navarre and Granada were included. Without the military orders of Santiago

---

[62] AGS, E leg. 21, f. 316.
[63] ACS, Sec. II, lib. 1157 (77), Session, April 3, 1530. The representatives from Santiago and Astorga had left already.
[64] Ibid., Session, April 4, 1530.

and San Juan, they offered 450,000 florins. Without any military orders, they offered 420,000 florins. For the Kingdoms of Granada and Navarre and the Order of Santa Clara, they added 10,000 florins more.[65] The crown proposed that the Assembly give 500,000 florins without the military orders of Santiago and San Juan, the dioceses in the Kingdoms of Navarre and Granada, and the Order of Santa Clara. The deputies replied that neither the dioceses in the kingdoms of Navarre and Granada nor the Order of Santa Clara should be separated from the Assembly. Including these and the military orders of Calatrava and Alcántara, they offered 480,000 florins on behalf of the Assembly. The deputies originally proposed a six-year payment period, which they then lowered to four years. The crown, however, insisted on two. In the end, they compromised on three years and scheduled the last payment for June 24, 1532. A majority of the representatives voted for this agreement, but several representatives voted against it. The representative of Coria, for example, noted that the earlier offer of 300,000 florins had included all the military orders, the Order of Santa Clara, and the dioceses in the kingdoms of Navarre and Granada. The Assembly's offer then had increased substantially while the number of contributors had remained the same. Indeed, the final agreement did not include all the military orders.[66]

On April 7, the crown and the Assembly prepared to draw up the agreement.[67] On April 8, the royal negotiators and the Assembly signed a nine-point understanding that stipulated the following.

1. The Assembly agreed to reduce the *dos quartas* to two subsidies of 100,000 florins each (1 florin = 265 maravedís in 1530). Due to the king's great need, the Assembly offered a further 280,000 florins, for a total contribution of 480,000 florins. The Assembly's agreement included the dioceses of Castile, Navarre, and Granada, and the military orders of Calatrava and Alcántara. The contribution did not include the dioceses of the Canaries and Indies and the military orders of Santiago and San Juan.
2. The payments were to be made as follows: 66,666 florins and 2 tarines would be paid on July 8, 1530, another 66,666 florins and 2 tarines

---

[65] Ibid., Session, April 5, 1530.
[66] Ibid., Session, April 6, 1530.
[67] Ibid., Session, April 7, 1530.

on September 8, 1530, and a further 66,666 florins and 2 tarines at the end of December 1530; three payments of 66,666 florins and 2 tarines would likewise be paid in 1531; and in 1532, there would be two payments of 40,000 florins, one at the end of April and the other at the end of August. Each diocese was responsible for collecting the subsidy at its own expense. There were to be no general discounts, only specific arrangements for individual churches, benefices, and pensions of cardinals, vacant sees, and whatever discounts the king should make in the future.

3. The king had the option to make separate agreements with the dioceses in the kingdoms of Navarre and Granada. If he did so, the amount that corresponded to those dioceses would be deducted from the 480,000 florins.

4. Since Santiago and Mondoñedo complained of injuries from past apportionment of the subsidy, the Assembly agreed to reassess their shares of the present subsidy. Since the first payment was soon due, those dioceses would be apportioned their share based on the assessment used in the previous subsidy, but the second payment would be adjusted more equitably. If the dioceses paid more than they should have in the first payment, the difference would be deducted from the second payment.

5. The chapters were to ensure that parishes, benefices, and poor clergy were not overburdened in the local apportionment.

6. Two months were given for the chapters and the king to be notified of and accept the agreement. If the king did not accept it, he was to notify the chapter of Toledo; if the chapters did not accept, they were to notify the Comisario General. If chapters did not reply, it was assumed that they accepted the agreement and were obligated to obey its terms.

7. The king would confirm the previous decrees of Barcelona and Valladolid, limiting his right to ask the pope for ecclesiastical contributions and automatically converting any future concession into a subsidy of 100,000 florins.

8. At the time of or before the first payment, the Assembly requested that a further papal brief to reduce the *dos quartas* to a subsidy be sent to the chapter of Toledo. The papal brief would be necessary in order for the clergy to avoid incurring ecclesiastical censures.

9. Even though they had not paid the last subsidy, the monasteries of the Order of Santa Clara would add a further 1,000 florins to the contribution.

The actual agreement differed on some points from what the Assembly had discussed on April 7 and on the morning of April 8. For instance, the representatives agreed to remedy the complaints of Santiago, Mondoñedo, and other churches before the collection began and only to offer 600 florins more to include the monasteries of the Order of Santa Clara. Even with the final agreement, then, the Assembly accepted compromises that probably did not satisfy all representatives. The agreement, however, was not the last word. Just as the cities retained final say in the Cortes, the individual chapters had final say on the agreement for the subsidy.[68] The documents do not make clear, however, what the consequences would have been had either the crown or chapters rejected the agreement.[69]

Isabel wrote to Charles on April 14 to inform him of the agreement, explaining that the threats of execution had compelled the clergy to return to the negotiating table. The agreement guaranteed payment without any of the inconveniences of a forcible collection. Isabel also sent Charles the new agreement along with that of 1523 to show him the similarities, as well as past royal decrees as examples of what he would prepare for the current subsidy. She asked the king to approve the agreement immediately and sign the orders. Nothing would be gained from delays or further negotiations, she stated, because the Assembly had granted more than previously and was determined not to offer more, and due to dearth there was no more to be extracted. The ministers therefore thought the agreement suitable and better than a forcible collection.[70]

For its part, the Assembly clearly feared that an execution would be far worse than negotiating a settlement. There are two possible reasons: first, the crown would collect the highest amount possible, and second, laymen in the royal service would carry out the collection. On the other hand, a forcible execution did not necessarily favor the crown, either. In her letters to Charles, Isabel stressed the many problems with a forceful collection and advocated accepting the accord. An agreement, then, served both the crown and the clergy's interests.

---

[68] In fact, Fernández Albaladejo suggests that any attempt of the Cortes to move beyond specific urban concerns was not permitted by the cities. *Fragmentos*, p. 165.

[69] ACS, Sec. II, lib. 1157 (77), April 8, 1530. For the division of 471,000 florins (124,815,007 mrs.) among the dioceses of Castile see Table II.

[70] Mazarío, *Isabel*, pp. 273–274.

Charles sent his approval on April 26. He ordered Isabel to complete everything promised by the crown within the timeframe and
expected that the chapters would do the same. If, at the end of two
months, they did not abide by the agreement and remained obstinate,
he thought that it would be very harmful. Further, he did not address
point three of the agreement—whether the dioceses in Navarre and
Granada should be entered into the agreement or remain outside of it
for collection purposes; rather, he allowed the regency government to
decide the course that would be most advantageous to the crown. He
also confirmed the decrees as stipulated in point seven. Even though the
regency government already had the brief to reduce the *dos quartas* to a
subsidy and another brief was probably superfluous, he would ask the
pope to send one more in response to point eight. If the new brief did
not arrive before the first payment, he stated, there was still no excuse
not to pay. According to Charles, the original brief that reduced the *dos
quartas* to a subsidy was sufficient. With regard to the discounts made to
monasteries and individuals, he wanted a report within two months on
what was customarily done, what had been done in the last subsidy, and
what ought to be done in the current one.[71] Although the negotiations
were intense, a consensus finally emerged and the parties agreed on
the most convenient way to proceed. The king's response also suggests
a willingness to work within the framework of the agreement.

Post-Assembly

Even though the Assembly and the crown had reached an agreement in
April, loose ends still remained into the summer. Isabel wrote to Charles
on June 7 to express her gratitude that the agreement satisfied him.
The chapters, she added, had also approved it. They still demanded
the brief to reduce the *dos quartas* to a subsidy in compliance with the
agreement, and Isabel therefore asked Charles to send it.[72] On July 8,
the date that the first payment was due, Charles wrote Isabel that Micer
Mai, the ambassador in Rome, had finally obtained and sent the papal

---

[71] AGS, E leg. 21, ff. 229–230. For the king's letter to the chapters, see ACS, Sec.II,
lib. 1157 (77), "Capitulación de ciertas cedulas que las iglesias tienen cerca de las
quartas."
[72] Mazarío, *Isabel*, p. 277.

brief. Charles ordered her to do whatever was necessary so that the chapters would consent to the payment without this brief.[73]

The regency government decided to make a separate agreement with the Kingdom of Granada. In July, the chapter of Granada elected a canon to negotiate with the crown for the payment of the subsidy and to provide for its equitable apportionment.[74] On August 2, the canon agreed to pay 2,625,000 maravedís, or roughly 9,905 florins, over two years. On some points, the agreement differed greatly from that reached between the crown and the Castilian Assembly. First, if a chapter failed to pay the entire amount on time, it would be obligated to pay the entire *quarta* conforming to the papal bull. The Comisario General's sub-delegated judges would have authority to carry out an execution. Second, there were to be no discounts unless the king made them to a specific church, hospital, monastery, or individual. Third, for the conscience of the clergy, each canon would receive an authentic copy of the papal brief that reduced the *dos quartas* to a subsidy. Fourth, nothing was to be assessed to the military orders of Santiago, Calatrava, or Alcántara or to any monastery of the Order of Santa Clara. Fifth, the corregidores were authorized to collect any portion of the subsidy assessed to seigniorial lands.[75] The crown's right to carry out the collection gave it greater leverage against the dioceses in the Kingdom of Granada to force them to complete the payment. The agreement in the Kingdom of Granada indicates that the various ecclesiastical bodies that negotiated with the crown often obtained different terms and conditions. Such differences might indicate the relative negotiating strength of various bodies vis-à-vis the crown.

Conclusion

The negotiations for the *dos quartas* in 1530 demonstrate the importance of consensus in the governing process in sixteenth-century Castile. The crown needed to negotiate with the Assembly of the Clergy and could not simply impose its will on the ecclesiastical estate. Even when the crown had the right to use force, it was reluctant to do so because

---

[73] AGS, E leg. 21, f. 339.
[74] ACG, AC lib. 2, f. 198v.
[75] ACG, leg. 11, pieza 7.

of potential resistance. If we understand the absolutist state to mean that the crown was above the law, these negotiations suggest that this definition is not entirely accurate. Although the regency government did not have any qualms about overlooking the royal decrees of Toro, Barcelona, and Valladolid, the crown was confined by canon law as it waited for the papal brief that allowed it to reduce the *dos quartas* to a subsidy. The negotiations for the subsidy certainly continued without that brief, but the Assembly clearly wanted authorization from the pope, and the documents suggest its reluctance to pay if the brief did not arrive. Royal authority was limited and could be impeded at many points by legal technicalities and a determined opponent.

The Assembly of the Clergy clearly was such a determined opponent. From the outset of the negotiations, it tried various strategies to limit royal demands. Although no one strategy completely succeeded, together the strategies did pressure the crown and create tense negotiations. The crown finally accepted 480,000 florins, a sum significantly lower than the 700,000 florins that it had requested in mid-March. Moreover, the regency government continually stated its desire to reach an agreement rather than forcibly collect the money, which would have entailed numerous difficulties. The Assembly also offered the clergy a united front to resist royal demands. The oath not to make individual agreements with the crown suggests that the Assembly's negotiating position was only strong if all the chapters stuck together. The Castilian clergy's determination first not to pay and then to pay as little as possible highlights two important facts: regalism had not yet triumphed in Spain, and the Castilian clergy did not necessarily support the king's wars, especially when they had to pay the bills.

CHAPTER THREE

CLERICAL RESISTANCE AND THE
SUSPENSION OF HOLY OFFICES

According to long-held convention, the state gained a 'monopoly on force' in the early modern period through the creation of standing armies. Many historians and social scientists have seen this development as the central pillar of the state-building process, because it allowed the state to forcibly extract revenue from its subjects. The crown's ability to force individuals to pay, however, was often circumscribed; royal authority was not always strong enough to force any unified group to provide the monetary resources necessary to meet the state's expenses. A more appropriate paradigm to understand the state's ability to finance itself is not coercion but rather consensus between the state and corporate bodies. An examination of negotiations in Castile for the ecclesiastical contribution between the fall of 1532 and the fall of 1533 clearly indicates the Castilian crown's failure to force a resisting corporate body to contribute.[1] Moreover, the church's use of a *cesación a divinis* (suspension of Holy Offices) demonstrates that corporate bodies were not without recourse when they faced royal coercion. Only when the state relaxed coercion, in fact, did the church reach an agreement with the crown for paying the contribution. This chapter provides further evidence that the financial pillar of the state rested on consensus, not coercion, between the crown and, in this case, the church.

The Clergy's Reaction to the Papal Bull of 1532

In the fall of 1532, Pope Clement VII (1523–1534) conceded a further ecclesiastical contribution to the crown: the *medios frutos* of the current year's rents in two payments, half in three months and the rest at the end of six months. When the clergy learned of the new papal concession,

---

[1] Juan Gelabert incorrectly refers to a "strike against the tax" in 1532. The suspension actually occurred in the summer of 1533. See Juan Gelabert, "The Fiscal Burden," in *Economic Systems and State Finance*, ed. Richard Bonney (Oxford: Clarendon Press, 1995), p. 555.

they immediately appealed the bull, believing that it was excessive and a violation of their exemption from taxation. Indeed, they threatened to suspend Holy Offices if the crown tried to enforce the concession. Isabel, the empress and regent of Spain in Charles's absence, took the clergy's threat seriously.[2] Writing to Charles on October 13, she said: "It is certain that the clergy and prelates will take very harshly this *medios frutos*. There is now talk that they will suspend Holy Offices, as... was done in some parts of Italy, and as some chapters of [Castile] had begun to do when the past *quarta* was granted." She advised Charles that "the *medios frutos* should be changed to a *dos quartas* in two years; concurrently, the amount paid should be increased from last time. This change would satisfy the subjects."[3] Instead of demanding that the clergy pay in six months, Isabel suggested extending the period of payments over two years to ease the burden. In turn, she claimed that the crown would be compensated by a larger subsidy from the churches.

Even if the crown had succeeded in changing the terms of payment from the *medios frutos* to a *dos quartas*, such action might not have appeased the clergy, for the real issue was royal infringement on clerical rights. A letter from the chapter of Burgos to the archpresbyterate of Melgar y Campo on December 18, 1532, clearly expressed the clergy's sentiments. It charged, on behalf of several Castilian chapters, that Clement VII's order for the Spanish dioceses to pay half their rents within six months was an intolerable imposition. Further, the letter claimed that the pope did not have the right to turn the church into a tributary estate, essentially arguing that the contribution was becoming a regular tax. If the Comisario General censured the clergy for appealing the bull and not paying promptly, the letter stated, the chapters would abstain from Holy Offices. The chapter of Burgos acknowledged that such a decision would weigh heavily on the consciences of those who daily celebrated the offices but urged them to act in unity with the cathedral. The letter closed: "Upon hearing that this church abstains, all other churches of the bishopric should do likewise; censure of one

---

[2] Catholic clergy in Italy had suspended Holy Offices in 1530 to protest a contribution, and the Castilian Assembly had discussed suspending Holy Offices in protest to the contribution of 1530. Some chapters may even have begun to do so. (See chapter 2, p. 67.) Isabel did not mention the clerical strike of 1519, but surely the king still recalled those events.

[3] María del Carmen Mazarío Coleto, *Isabel de Portugal: Emperatriz y Reina de España* (Madrid: Consejo Superior de Investigaciones Científicas, 1951), p. 363.

is censure of all.... We have just cause to ask of you the abstention; we are so sworn to defend our ecclesiastical liberty."[4]

Without doubt, the clergy saw the ecclesiastical contribution as an affront to their liberties; the pope had permitted the church to be turned into a taxable estate. To defend their freedoms, the clergy had one recourse—refusing to say Mass. The chapter of Burgos, however, advocated abstaining from Holy Offices instead of a cessation, apparently because an abstention would not plague the clergy's conscience as much.[5] Burgos also tried to convince the archpresbyterate to suspend services if the situation warranted doing so, arguing that any infringement on ecclesiastical liberties concerned all the churches and clergy. The chapter of Burgos (and other chapters) sent out similar letters to other ecclesiastical bodies within their dioceses to organize support. In fact, the chapter of Burgos found help in its letter writing campaign from the city's association of parish priests.[6]

In their appeals to the crown and the pontiff, the chapters used a wide variety of arguments. The appeal to the crown in 1532, for example, contained thirty-two clauses. Most of these clauses fell within four categories:

---

[4] AGS, E leg. 24, f. 364. This and another letter to the archpresbyterate ended up in royal hands. As we will see, the corregidor of Toledo also intercepted correspondence between the chapters. The crown, then, was aware of some developments taking place among the chapters.

[5] The clergy and the crown used different terminology to describe the suspension. The clergy used *abstenerse*, that is, to abstain from, while the crown used *cesar*, that is, to cease or to suspend. Each word gave a slightly different nuance to the situation. The clergy used the term abstain from offices because the failure to carry out religious duties tormented the conscience of those who said Mass. Moreover, the pope had explicitly prohibited a *cesación a divinis* and threatened to use ecclesiastical censure against the clergy. He said nothing, however, about abstaining from Holy Offices. The clergy, then, found a linguistic loophole. Furthermore, an abstention still allowed for the celebration of some Sacraments. The crown, of course, used the term 'cease' to place the suspension in a negative light and to justify censuring the clergy. This distinction of terms, however, was not complete, for at times the clergy also used 'cease.' Still, the clergy's use of 'abstain' is important, as the *maestrescuela* of Toledo's speech before the king in 1519 attests. For more details, see Prudencio de Sandoval, *Historia de la vida y hechos del Emperador Carlos V*, ed. Carlos Seco Serrano (Madrid: Biblioteca de Autores Españoles, 1955) vol. I, p. 155.

[6] Heliodoro García briefly describes the participation of the Universidad de Curas y Beneficiados of the city of Burgos in the preparations for the suspension and the suspension itself. See Heliodoro García, "El reformismo del 'Pastor Bonus' de Juan Maldonado," *Hispania Sacra* 35 (1983) p. 194, footnote 3. I am grateful to J.B. Owens for directing me to this work.

1. That the church was exempt from taxation in accordance with the
   Bible, teachings of Church Fathers, decrees of Councils, and papal
   encyclicals;
2. That the church was to aid princes in their wars through prayers;
3. That paying the contribution would severely hinder the church's
   ability to carry out its religious and charitable duties; and
4. That the church already provided the crown with excessive economic aid.

The chapters also argued that the bull was void because it had not
been made public.[7] They possibly hoped to delay the bull's administration through their appeals, and in this particular case such delays
might have nullified the concession, because the present bull was for
defense against the advance of the Turks. Turkish naval forces, however, had withdrawn by the time it was issued, and any further delays
likely would have made it even more difficult for the crown to justify
the contribution.[8]

The Crown's Response—Spring 1533

The royal council feared that all or most of the chapters of the kingdom
would, like Burgos, cease Holy Offices and resist the contribution.[9] With
the first payment a month away in March, the situation was clearly
serious, and the regency government spent February and March weigh-
ing its options. Cardinal Tavera, archbishop of Santiago and president
of the royal council, wrote Charles that, in the king's absence, many
royal officials feared acting against the clergy because, they believed, the
ecclesiastical estate's reaction—an actual strike or refusal to pay—would
undermine royal authority. He advised the king to order the bishop of
Zamora to execute the bull and censure the clergy for its resistance. A
forceful execution, or sequestration of ecclesiastical rents, he believed,
would signal the crown's resolve to the ecclesiastical estate and compel
them to compromise.[10] Tavera thought that the clergy would buckle
under pressure and come to an agreement. Francisco de Mendoza, the

---

[7] ACS, Sec. IX, leg. 107, no. 12; B.N. Ms. 1293, f. 45.
[8] Mazarío, *Isabel*, p. 365; November 19, 1532.
[9] Ibid., p. 375; February 4, 1533.
[10] AGS, E leg. 26, f. 17; Tavera to Charles, March 21, 1533.

bishop of Zamora and Comisario General de la Cruzada, disagreed, believing that enforcing the bull against the will of the ecclesiastical estate would lead to a suspension of Holy Offices.[11] The damage a suspension would cause, Mendoza noted, far outweighed any advantage a sequestration could bring. He believed instead that the crown should further justify its demands to the chapters and allow them an opportunity to negotiate in good faith. Specifically, he argued, the chapters should be given twenty days either to start payment or, at least, to appoint their own collectors. The bishop also proposed that, since Charles was expected to return to Spain shortly, the matter should wait until he arrived.[12] In short, the royal administration was divided on whether to use force against the clergy or to negotiate. The king's absence also influenced their decision; lingering memories of the Comunero revolt possibly made the empress and some advisors reluctant to undertake any policy that might result in an open challenge to royal authority.[13] From the regency government's perspective, then, royal authority was not unquestionable.

The advocates of further negotiations prevailed. On May 7, Charles sent letters from Barcelona to the archbishops of Granada and Toledo, and presumably to other prelates as well, in the hope that a personal appeal by the bishops would win the chapters over. The archbishop of Granada succeeded in doing so, and his chapter agreed to cooperate with the crown.[14] The archbishop of Toledo, however, failed. His chapter replied that although it had some influence with the other churches with regard to the right to convene the Assembly of the Clergy, it did not dare make a decision of this nature without first consulting with the other chapters. To the ire of the bishop of Zamora, the archbishop did not pursue the case any further. The bishop wanted the chapter of Toledo to convene the Assembly, because he thought it would be

---

[11] These views were not isolated. On May 29, 1533, *mariscal* Pedro de Navarra, corregidor of Toledo, expressed concern to the bishop of Zamora that in response to the sequestration, the clergy would suspend Holy Offices. If they did so, he would carry out the bishop's commands. He felt that any force used after they began to suspend would be just because their action would be disrespectful of royal authority; AGS, E leg. 26, f. 286.

[12] Mazarío, *Isabel*, p. 382; March 22, 1533.

[13] Fear of another revolt like that of the Comuneros was a constant concern throughout Charles's reign. Philip II, for example, referred to it in his letter of March 25, 1545 to the king. See *Corpus documental de Carlos V*, ed. Manuel Fernández Álvarez (Salamanca: Universidad, 1975), vol. II, p. 359.

[14] AGS, E leg. 27, f. 208.

easier to negotiate with the chapters as a group than separately. The archbishop, on the other hand, felt that he lacked the proper commission to pursue these negotiations. Furthermore, as he saw it, even though some chapters might come to an agreement with the crown, some would always continue to resist.[15] In view of the failure of the negotiations with the individual chapters, the bishop of Zamora began to embrace the idea of an Assembly. Believing that the crown did not have a legitimate right to a contribution, however, the chapters refused to convene one.

At the end of May, the crown offered the chapters nine days to negotiate a settlement or face a sequestration of their rents. The corregidores of Segovia and Toledo brought the king's offer to their respective chapters. The chapter of Segovia, however, would not reply until it heard from the other chapters, particularly from Toledo.[16] Segovia's response was nearly identical to the response that Toledo had given its archbishop earlier in the month. The chapters may have used the need to consult with the others as a ploy to delay responding to the crown. In Toledo, the chapter apologized profusely to the corregidor for its apparent disservice to the king and wrote to Charles to explain the legitimate reasons for its actions.[17] Half way through the grace period, neither the chapter of Segovia nor that of Toledo would openly come to terms. In the end, the chapters refused to negotiate any payment, thus facing a sequestration of their rents.

The Royal Sequestration

The crown frequently sequestered various rents and monies from its subjects. At times, it simply seized all the bullion that arrived from America to meet its financial obligations.[18] Of course, it was simpler to seize bullion from a ship than to sequester ecclesiastical rents, and the royal officials responsible for carrying out the sequestration in the

---

[15] Ibid., f. 176. The archbishop was reluctant to proceed because the errors in negotiating for the contribution of 1530 had been attributed to him. See also AGS, E leg. 27, f. 178, Archbishop of Toledo to King.

[16] AGS, E leg. 26, f. 285; May 27, 1533.

[17] AGS, E leg. 27, ff. 172–173; May 28 and 29, 1533.

[18] Manuel Fernández Álvarez, *Poder y sociedad en la España del Quinientos* (Madrid: Alianza Universidad, 1995), p. 207; Constance Jones Mathers, "Relations between the City of Burgos and the Crown, 1506–1556" (Ph.D. diss., Columbia University, 1973), pp. 315, 318, 321, and 324.

dioceses had many concerns.[19] What could they sequester? Which years' rents should they sequester? Should they treat the clergy as laymen? How should they carry out and pay for the sequestration?

To make matters worse, the clergy apparently began to hide their account books during the nine-day grace period. The corregidor of Segovia, for example, believed that some clergy were even collecting and spending the year's rents and that they would not declare under oath where they had concealed money and goods. If the clergy did not cooperate, the corregidor would not be able to continue his investigations. Given this situation, he wanted to know if he should proceed against them as if they were laymen; as a civil official, the corregidor had jurisdiction over secular, not ecclesiastical, affairs. He could not technically proceed against clerics because they had their own courts and judges, and he was wary of overstepping his jurisdictional bounds.[20] Furthermore, he worried that the sequestration would be expensive and require many agents to carry out; without access to the clergy's account books or to the money and goods they had hidden, royal officials would have to survey the ecclesiastical holdings of the entire bishopric to determine their worth and scour the countryside for caches. The corregidor believed that the threat of censure and excommunication from the bishop of Zamora might prompt the clergy to cooperate and sought instruction from the bishop on how to proceed.[21]

At the same time, *mariscal* (marshal) Pedro de Navarra, the corregidor of Toledo, wanted the bishop to clarify how he should carry out the sequestration. He asked if he should sequester moveable goods and how to pay the bailiffs and scribes who went outside the city.[22] He also wanted the bishop to specify which year's rents he should seize. Because the papal bull conceded the *medios frutos* for the rents of 1532,

---

[19] I.A.A. Thompson finds that even in the seventeenth century some corregidores "seem to have felt a certain unease at the way they were expected to conduct the exaction of forced loans." See his "Castile: Absolutism, Constitutionalism, and Liberty," in *Fiscal Crises, Liberty, and Representative Government, 1450–1789*, ed. Philip T. Hoffman and Kathryn Norberg (Stanford: Stanford University Press, 1994), p. 215.

[20] The crown was aware of this problem. In 1531, for example, to keep the clergy in line, Tavera recommended obtaining a papal brief for royal agents to arrest them. See B.N., ms. 1778, ff. 88–89.

[21] AGS, E leg. 26, f. 285.

[22] In later years, the sequestration was paid for from the subsidy. It consequently diminished royal revenues from the subsidy, because if the chapters collected it, they paid the collection costs. In 1544, for instance, a sequestration that had lasted 73 days in Jaén cost 26,375 maravedís. See AGS, CC leg. 2.

Navarra wondered what to collect in June when the previous year's rents had basically been paid and the current year's rents were not due until August.[23] Moreover, like the corregidor of Segovia, he realized that income already collected would be much harder to sequester than outstanding rents. The corregidores of Segovia and Toledo were not alone in writing for more information; on June 8, the bishop of Zamora informed Francisco de los Cobos that he and an assistant had worked continually for five or six days responding to the corregidores.[24]

In response to the corregidores' inquiries, the crown drew up a memorandum that outlined procedures to follow in the sequestration of the *medios frutos*. This document instructed the corregidores to:

1. Obtain the account books of past subsidies to calculate the rents and investigate their worth.
2. Procure other rent books for the past and the present year, as well as any books the tenants possessed. The tenants were then to declare under oath any information that pertained to these negotiations.
3. Announce publicly that all lessees of ecclesiastical rents of the past year must declare what the rents were, from whom they rented, at what price, and for how long.
4. Name two collectors to receive the ecclesiastical rents until the quantity specified in the bull of the *medios frutos* had been paid.
5. Announce that all rents be brought only to the two collectors and only when both were present.
6. Tell tenants and others who might possess ecclesiastical rents to conform to the papal bull until the *medios frutos* were paid.
7. Pay for the sequestration from the rents of the chapter of the city and of the other churches.
8. Sequester only the present rents of 1533 and not moveable goods. The rationale was that these rents could not be paid until August.

Finally, the memorandum recommended that the bishop of Zamora send bailiffs from court to aid the corregidores, especially in Toledo and Salamanca where the crown believed the chapters were more resistant.[25]

---

[23] AGS, E leg. 26, f. 286.
[24] AGS, E leg. 27, f. 184.
[25] AGS, E leg. 26, f. 284.

The chapters meanwhile continued to discuss among themselves the proper response. Navarra noted that "the chapter of Toledo had sent mail to all the other chapters," but he did not know its contents. He did manage, however, to intercept the chapter of Cuenca's response to Toledo and send a copy of it to the king. The corregidor also believed that he might be able to intercept communications from the other chapters, though we cannot ascertain fully whether it was common for corregidores to intercept letters.[26]

In the meantime, Navarra prepared to enforce the sequestration, beginning the execution on the final day of the Easter season, in conformity with the bishop's instructions. The canons had until now only responded with evasive words, and the six months the papal bull stipulated for paying the *medios frutos* had elapsed by June.[27] Through their tactics, however, the clergy had successfully delayed payment to the crown, which thus felt forced to proceed against them.

The corregidor of Toledo began the sequestration on June 3, ordering the cathedral steward to turn over the account books. The steward, however, had placed the books for 1532 and 1533 in the cathedral tabernacle and hid the key to his office. For these actions, the corregidor jailed the steward until he turned over the missing books. When Navarra's agents broke down the door to the steward's office and seized the remaining account books, they found books for 1530 and 1531, as well as others. Without all the books, however, it was impossible to investigate the rents thoroughly. There were also certain documents on rents in the cathedral archives, and the corregidor consequently wanted the bishop's approval to seize these items. He also asked the bishop to grant him special permission to arrest clergymen without giving cause, believing that the threat of punishment would deter further resistance. He ordered that all ecclesiastical rents be embargoed until the clergy paid the *medios frutos* and announced to the various lessees, tenants, and others involved not to pay their rents to the clergy. Lacking complete information on the ecclesiastical rents, however, Navarra feared that the embargo would not be properly executed.[28]

---

[26] AGS, E leg. 27, f. 181 June 1, 1533; for Cuenca's letter see AGS, E leg. 26, f. 287. The letter that Navarra intercepted from Cuenca was its response to a letter that Toledo sent after meeting with the archbishop on May 14. AGS, E leg. 27, f. 176.

[27] AGS, E leg. 27, f. 181.

[28] AGS, E leg. 26, f. 288. Navarra also arrested several other canons and clergy involved in the administration of ecclesiastical rents. See ACT, AC lib. 5, f. 121.

The cesación a divinis

The corregidor's actions outraged the chapter of Toledo, which on June 4 decided to suspend Holy Offices immediately. The canons declared that they were suspending Holy Offices because the corregidor and his assistants' actions were prejudicial to ecclesiastical liberty and the legal exemption that the clergy enjoyed. According to both divine and natural law, they argued, secular magistrates could neither sequester ecclesiastical rents nor do anything that prejudiced the ecclesiastical estate; arresting members of the clergy violated its liberty. The canons decided that there were just reasons to suspend Holy Offices, especially because they had only decided to abstain from Holy Offices and not completely cease their performance. Moreover, those individuals who wanted to celebrate Holy Offices could still do so secretly. The clergy would continue to celebrate Mass conforming to the calendar in the chapel of Santiago, and they would administer the Sacraments to those who wished to receive them. The administration of Sacraments, however, would be done without public display. The dead would be buried without pomp and marriages would be conducted secretly. The clergy would also preach sermons, and the canons would cease neither the ordinary nor the other chapter meetings. The canons, however, had to attend without their habits. After much deliberation, the chapter reached this decision, stipulating that the *cesación a divinis* was done to serve God, the pope, and the emperor. The abstention began on the morning of June 4, 1533.[29]

Although it was not a complete suspension of Holy Offices, the restricted administration of the Sacraments could place the souls of the king's subjects and family in danger. The lack of public religious services might be trying for both laypeople and the clergy, and in Toledo the Corpus Christi procession posed a difficult problem. On June 6, the corregidor reported that the city council feared that the lack of a procession would lead to pestilence and thus had asked the chapter to conduct the procession as usual, but the chapter refused. The city council then asked four unspecified religious orders to lead the procession, but the orders hesitated; parading in the street without a clear order from the archbishop or royal council would be prejudicial to the primacy of

---

[29] ACT, AC lib. 5, f. 121, June 4, 1533.

the cathedral. Navarra urged the bishop of Zamora to provide such a decree, especially after the orders had requested it.[30]

Corpus Christi was one of the most important religious festivals of the year, and the procession had both religious and political significance. The religious implications related to the body of Christ and to the superstition that failure to conduct the procession would result in pestilence. Politically, the marching order reinforced the communal hierarchy and not holding the procession could weaken the body politic.[31] The Corpus Christi incident in Toledo also indicates that the religious orders' resolve to participate in the suspension was weak; with an order from the bishop, they would say Holy Offices once again.

The most trying moment for the ecclesiastical estate's corporate conscience probably came at the end of June when the empress suddenly lay near death. The crown continually ordered the ecclesiastical estate to say prayers and lead processions for her health, and the chapters found themselves in a quandary. The chapter of Toledo, for example, decided to lead a solemn procession to the Monastery of Nuestra Señora de la Merced. On June 29, the canons made it absolutely clear that this procession did not compromise their appeals or the suspension of Holy Offices. Other chapters apparently did the same.[32]

Navarra's report to the king describing the suspension in Toledo and what he thought should be done further indicates the difficulties involved. According to Navarra, the chapter of Toledo had ordered an end to the celebration of Holy Offices in the city and the entire archdiocese, and the canons had persuaded the other cathedral chapters to do likewise. Navarra thought that the chapter's action was disrespectful of the pope, who had specifically ordered the chapters not to place an interdict or cease Holy Offices. He added that the suspension was also a disservice to the king; lack of Holy Offices created disturbances throughout the kingdom and led many people to commit crimes punishable by the death penalty. Navarra appealed to the chapter not to suspend Holy Offices and also warned it to expect appropriate punishments for its

---

[30] AGS, E leg. 26, f. 288.
[31] See Miri Rubin, *Corpus Christi: The Eucharist in Late Medieval Culture* (Cambridge: Cambridge University Press, 1991).
[32] ACT, AC lib. 5, f. 124. Alonso Fernández de Madrid, *Silva Palentina*, ed. Jesús San Martín Payo (Palencia, Ediciones de la Excma. Diputación Provincial, 1976) p. 457. I am grateful to Teófanes Egido for directing me to this work.

disobedience.[33] The ecclesiastical estate was a central pillar to royal authority and legitimacy; an open division between the crown and church might undermine that authority, as some ministers feared, and create a breakdown of law and order.[34]

The chapters had been discussing the potential for a suspension among themselves and with other clergy in their dioceses since December 1532, and had decided to act together if the liberties of any church were infringed. Within a week or two of Toledo's suspension on June 4, 1533, most other churches had joined in. The minutes of the chapter of Burgos of Tuesday, June 10, illustrate how the suspension was organized on the diocesan level. First, the canons discussed whether they should suspend Holy Offices and unanimously decided to do so the next day before vespers. Second, they sent canons to speak with the friars and nuns in the monasteries, the parish priests, and other clergy in the city of Burgos, asking them also to suspend Holy Offices. The canons also sent letters to all the churches in the diocese.[35] In the letter to the archpresbyterate of Melgar y Campo, for example, the chapter of Burgos described the situation in Toledo and insisted that since the cause was common to all, the ecclesiastical estate needed to stand together against such challenges to its rights. In this case, solidarity meant suspending Holy Offices.[36] While there was consensus among the chapters, each diocesan chapter still had a final say on whether or not to participate. Once the cathedral chapter had decided on the suspension, the canons had to ask all the other religious groups, such as parish priests, friars, and monks in the dioceses, to participate as well.

Some of the clergy turned to the chapter for guidance and leadership, and on June 10, a canon in Toledo responded to queries of local priests about how to conduct themselves during the suspension.[37] At the same time, other clergy rebuffed the chapter's request; the Franciscans and Dominicans continued to celebrate Holy Offices.[38] This relationship

---

[33] AGS, E leg. 26, f. 288.

[34] Joseph Pérez has suggested a connection between the anti-Habsburg sermons of 1518–1519 and the Comunero revolt of 1520–1521. See "Moines frondeurs et sermons subversifs en Castille pendant le premier séjour de Charle-Quint en Espagne," *Bulletin Hispanique* 67 (1965), pp. 5–24.

[35] ACB, R lib. 43, f. 566. The association of parish priests met shortly thereafter on June 13 and agreed to suspend Holy Offices. They, however, resumed services on July 2. See García, "El reformismo," p. 194, footnote 3.

[36] AGS, E leg. 27, f. 222.

[37] ACT, AC lib. 5, f. 122.

[38] AGS, E leg. 26, f. 288. A possible explanation for why the Dominicans and Franciscans did not participate is that they were not diocesan clergy and consequently not

between the chapters and the diocesan clergy, on the one hand, and the chapters and the religious orders, on the other hand, influenced the suspension's effectiveness and duration.

Navarra's letters from early June to the bishop of Zamora shed further light on how the chapters negotiated with the diocesan clergy. The chapter of Toledo asked the priors and guardians of the religious orders to join it in abstaining from Holy Offices, while Navarra tried to persuade them not to participate. He warned that should they suspend Holy Offices, the bishop would punish them, as was his right. His pleading and threatening, however, did not dissuade them, and the guardian of San Juan de los Reyes told him that they would begin the suspension that same evening, June 4. Unless the bishop countermanded the chapter's order, the guardian stated, they must conform to the cathedral's demand. Navarra consequently asked the bishop to send an order to that effect, hoping that divisions within the ecclesiastical estate could provide an opportunity for the crown to pressure or persuade certain clergy within the diocese to perform Holy Offices again.[39]

Differences of opinion also existed within and among chapters. Some canons, for instance, received their offices from the crown. In Toledo, these royally appointed canons told Navarra that they would not suspend services.[40] Navarra also informed the king on June 6 that certain canons would readily serve him and work to reach an agreement for a contribution similar to that of 1530 if they were rewarded.[41] A bribe or favor by the crown to individual clergy then could undermine the chapter's unity and bring the suspension to an end. Royal attempts to manipulate factions or individual canons within a chapter were not new. In 1523, for example, the corregidor of Toledo, Martín de Córdoba, had asked the king to write to two canons who had voted against convoking an Assembly; they did so because neither the pope nor king had ordered it.[42] Although some rewards might have come

---

subordinate to the chapter. Although diocesan clergy might have felt obliged to follow the chapter's lead, they did not always do so. On June 26, 1533, Navarra reported to the bishop of Zamora that the priest and clergy of the rural districts continued to celebrate the Holy Offices and had made no changes in them. See AGS, E leg. 27, f. 212.

[39] AGS, E leg. 26, f. 288.

[40] Ibid., Navarra to Bishop of Zamora, June 4, 1533. To ensure this, Navarra asked that orders be sent.

[41] AGS, E leg. 27, f. 182.

[42] AGS, E leg. 11, f. 181. Although the corregidor only suggested a letter acknowledging their service, it is plausible that the king would also have enclosed a token of his appreciation.

their way, those canons who supported the crown in 1523 likely did so out of conviction and not for personal gain.

Even without royal meddling, divisions within chapters could quickly undo the suspension. In Seville, for example, a minority of the canons opposed the suspension, speaking passionately against it and defiantly celebrating Holy Offices. Within a week, the chapter of Seville lifted the suspension. Supporting the crown, however, was not without risks. The chapter sought to remove those canons who opposed the suspension of Holy Offices from their offices and punish them in other ways. In response to their plight, Tavera asked Charles to order the chapter not to mistreat those canons or remove them from their offices. Finally, he suggested that the archbishop of Seville convey to his chapter how the king expected loyal canons to be treated. If the majority of the canons would not comply, Tavera said, the archbishop should punish them.[43]

In Granada, the crown successfully intervened in the internal politics of the chapter and prevented a suspension. The archbishop of Granada had convinced the chapter in mid-May to pay the *medios frutos*, as the king had ordered, and the canons agreed to the royal demands prior to the ultimatum at the end of May. Nevertheless, the crown still embargoed ecclesiastical rents in Granada. The canons were infuriated and complained that the archbishop had tricked them. Due to their poverty and their continued celebration of Holy Offices, they had believed that the king would make a separate agreement with them.[44]

Even after the crown apparently broke its word by embargoing the ecclesiastical rents, however, the canons still did not suspend Holy Offices. Why? The corregidor in Granada provided a plausible explanation. With the tombs of the Catholic Kings, the president and judges of the *Chancillería* (high court), and the Captain General of the Kingdom all located in the city, many viewed the archbishop and chapter as direct servants of the king as well as obedient sons of the pope.[45] The direct royal presence in Granada may have been stronger than in any other cathedral city. Regardless of the mid-May agreement between the crown and chapter, once the sequestration was underway, the strong royal presence possibly prevented the clergy from suspending services in June. Moreover, since most canons in Granada received

---

[43] ACS, Sec. I, lib. 13, ff. 252v–254v, 272v. AGS, E leg. 27, f. 136; Tavera to Charles August 1, 1533.

[44] AGS, E leg. 27, f. 208.

[45] Ibid., f. 209.

their benefices directly from the crown, they might succumb more easily to royal pressure. The archbishop had played a pivotal role in convincing the chapter to cooperate with the crown in May, and the canons possibly thought that the archbishop could sway the crown to honor the earlier agreement. The archbishop and the corregidor both urged the crown to change its policy towards the clergy in Granada, who had been very obedient and helpful with the collection, and to make an agreement with them for a peaceful payment. Nevertheless, the corregidor declared that he would carry out the sequester until he received a new order. As this experience makes clear, at least one chapter did not follow Toledo's lead.

The pope and the local bishops also played an influential role. The clergy had sent representatives to Rome as early as March 28, 1533, to appeal the contribution.[46] Although they probably realized that, as an ally of the crown, Clement VII would not easily support their resistance, the clergy clearly did not think winning papal support was completely impossible.[47] In fact, the pope partially responded to their complaints by asking the crown to reduce the contribution. The crown in turn knew that it could not rely completely on Clement VII and closely watched the developments in Rome. Its ambassador actively worked to prevent the pope from dispatching any brief against the *medios frutos* or the sequestration.[48] The crown was concerned that the clergy could win over certain circles in Rome, if not completely, at least enough to complicate royal negotiations for the *medios frutos*.

In this case, Charles had little to fear. In a brief of July 2, Clement VII expressed his displeasure and exhorted "the cathedral of Toledo and the clergy of Spain to come to a concordance with his majesty about the *medios frutos*."[49] The same brief also stated the papal position on the suspension of Holy Offices:

---

[46] ACT, AC lib. 5, ff. 110v and 111v.

[47] When he granted the contribution in the fall of 1532, the pope stipulated that Giovanni Poggio, his nuncio in Spain, was to serve as judge and collector with the bishop of Zamora. Tavera suggested that the pope wanted to play an active role in the process. AGS, E leg. 24, f. 224. Clement, then, may have been allied with the king but he was not under the king's thumb.

[48] AGS, E leg. 27, ff. 29 and 184; E leg. 860, ff. 3, 6, 7, 49, 51, 55, 56, and 61.

[49] ACT, AC lib. 5, f. 129. By the time the papal brief arrived on August 7, the suspension had ended. Papal opposition thus did not play a significant role in the final outcome.

> Even though we want to satisfy your desire and petition...there is nothing more foreign to our office and yours than to plead with his majesty and by occasion of this dispute to introduce a *cesación a divinis* which brings serious scandal to [Castile]....It is better for you...to reach some agreement with his majesty and to end this fight....If we have postponed the reason of your appeal by the said respects...we will seek to lighten the amount of the imposition.[50]

The pope opposed the *cesación a divinis* as a proper means to negotiate with the crown. At the request of the chapters' representatives, however, he wrote to the king, presumably exhorting him to reach an agreement with the ecclesiastical estate by reducing the payment, just as he urged the clergy to come to an agreement with the crown. In his brief, the pope acknowledged the Castilian clergy's difficulties with this contribution, but he insisted that it was necessary for the defense of Christendom. Moreover, the Italian clergy, including those from the Papal States, also contributed in this time of great need.

Within Castile, the attitudes of individual prelates were mixed. As mentioned above, the archbishop of Granada persuaded his chapter to cooperate. The cardinal of Burgos did not consent to suspending Holy Offices in his diocese, but the documents do not indicate whether he took further action against the clergy.[51] The archbishop of Toledo, on the other hand, was ambivalent. In his letter of June 6 to the bishop of Zamora, he expressed concern that the corregidor was still holding the steward prisoner, even after he had surrendered the books. While the archbishop believed the corregidor's action was unlawful, the bishop of Zamora contradicted him. Since the king had given the chapters many months to comply with his order, their disobedience left royal officials no other choice but to respond with force. Furthermore, due to the suspension, the religious orders would have to celebrate the festival of Corpus Christi in place of the chapter. This, the bishop argued in his letter of June 7 to the archbishop, would lead to even greater scandal. Moreover, the chapter's actions were a clear affront to the archbishop's authority. By suggesting that the chapter had overstepped its bounds, was the bishop trying to cajole the archbishop to take a tougher stance against the clergy? If so, he failed. In his response, the archbishop insisted that Navarra's execution was unjust. By ordering the tenants not to pay their rents and holding clergy prisoners at their expense even

---

[50] B.N. Ms. 1293, ff. 44v–45.
[51] AGS, E leg. 27, f. 184.

after they had surrendered their books, the corregidor had insulted the clergy. Given these and other atrocities, the archbishop thought that the clergy had a valid reason to suspend Holy Offices.[52]

A rift had developed between the archbishop of Toledo and the bishop of Zamora. The bishop focused on the great damage caused by the suspension to the ecclesiastical jurisdiction of the archbishop and the harm done to the people, while the archbishop felt the corregidor's action was a clear violation of ecclesiastical liberties. The reaction of individual prelates could thus vary. The local bishop could help or hinder the royal officials in carrying out the sequestration and embargo of ecclesiastical rents, just as he could encourage or undermine the clergy's resistance to the crown.

Ending the cesación a divinis

Due to internal divisions within the chapters, the bishop of Zamora used a carrot and stick approach to undermine the suspension. To weaken the canons' resolve, the bishop asked Francisco de los Cobos to send him enough letters in blank to address to all canons.[53] Based on Navarra's reports on the situation in Toledo, he thought that such letters would be useful.[54] With the letters on hand, the bishop could quickly punish and reward particular canons, allowing the crown to manipulate the internal divisions of the chapters. Writing to the king on June 12 from Madrid, Tavera repeated the bishop of Zamora's request for letters.[55] Although the suspension was still limited in scope, all the chapters of Castile, except Granada, had agreed to it in principle; it was only a matter of time before more churches took action. Either the letters did not materialize or they arrived too late to halt the suspension, and the crown's first effort at breaking the strike failed.

Navarra's letter of June 26 to the bishop of Zamora indicates that the crown had offered the chapters another opportunity to negotiate, while preparations were underway to break the suspension. In Toledo, the corregidor had received orders to bring in members of the religious orders to celebrate Mass in the parishes and to pay their salaries from

---

[52] AGS, E leg. 26, f. 288.
[53] A letter in blank refers to a royal decree complete in all aspects except for the name of the person it is directed toward and date.
[54] AGS, E leg. 27, f. 184; Bishop of Zamora to Cobos, June 8, 1533.
[55] Ibid., f. 132.

the benefices of the suspending priests.[56] The evidence, however, does not indicate whether the replacements ever took part.

The corregidor in Córdoba dealt with the orders from the royal council and the bishop somewhat differently than did his counterpart in Toledo. He notified the chapter of the crown's intent on June 26, ordering the clergy to attend to their ecclesiastical duties immediately or face serious sanctions and even excommunication. The clergy then appealed to the pope, and the corregidor realized that despite the royal orders, the canons still would not renew Holy Offices. He warned the canons that, in order to force them to celebrate Mass again, the people might take the matter upon themselves and resort to violence. Apparently the canons complied and resumed services on June 27.[57] The suspension had stirred up resentment and hostility in secular society, and the corregidor of Córdoba shrewdly manipulated this hostility to the crown's favor. In the face of potential violence, the clergy of Córdoba buckled, but the threats of punishment from the crown did not seem to have an immediate impact.

In Toledo, threat of censure could not bring the clergy to resume Holy Offices. After many days of discussion, the chapter finally agreed to send two canons to meet the king or, if that was not possible, Cardinal Tavera and Bishop Mendoza. The deputies were also commissioned to speak with the archbishop of Toledo. High-level negotiations were apparently once again opened between the chapters and the crown. The corregidor of Toledo anticipated a ripple effect throughout Castile. If the chapter of Toledo came to the negotiating table, others would soon follow. At the same time, he warned of punitive measures if the chapters failed to renew negotiations within the grace period.[58] These various threats were sufficient to pressure the chapters back into negotiations but not to renew Holy Offices.

Throughout the spring, the royal council had discussed the possibility of summoning an Assembly. Only on June 7, however, did the archbishop of Toledo outline for the king the different options for doing so; thereafter momentum slowly built toward convening an Assembly.[59]

---

[56] Ibid., f. 212.

[57] Juan Gómez Bravo, *Catalogo de los obispos de Córdoba, y breve noticia historica de su Iglesia Catedral, y obispado* (Córdoba: Juan Rodríguez, 1778) vol. I, pp. 433–434. The canons reported the threat of violence to the pope. The pope later wrote to the king that this was unacceptable, and Charles V yielded and tried to calm the situation in Córdoba.

[58] AGS, E leg. 27, f. 212; Mariscal de Navarra to bishop of Zamora, June 26, 1533.

[59] AGS, E leg. 27, f. 174. See also AGS E leg. 27, f. 184. The king apparently wrote

At the end of June or in early July, the king responded that, although the dioceses continued to defy his authority with the suspension and so gave him just cause not to negotiate, he desired that the subsidy be granted by their own volition. To avoid the harms and vexations that the sequestration inflicted on the ecclesiastical estate, and following the archbishop's suggestions, Charles V asked the chapters to convene an Assembly. When representatives of the chapters arrived, he gave the archbishop of Toledo complete authority to negotiate with them.[60] Charles, then, was aware of the harm the sequestration had caused. Even though he was reluctant to talk to the clergy, he realized that such a conversation was unavoidable if he wished to obtain a voluntary concession.

The negotiations with the chapters got underway after July 22, 1533. Although he had not kept completely abreast of the developments since early June, the archbishop of Toledo was eager to serve the king and, by this point, was certain that an Assembly would facilitate negotiations. In his letter of June 7, the archbishop's principal concern was how to convoke the clergy without undermining royal authority if they refused to assemble. By mid-July, this was no longer a concern, for several chapters had come together on their own without royal prompting. Discussions were already underway among the chapters to convene an Assembly.[61] Since the impetus already existed, the crown only needed to push it along. An Assembly would make it much easier for the crown and the clergy to hammer out an agreement despite their differences.

The chapters may have had no other option but to plan for an Assembly by late July, because between the punitive threats, the renewed attempts at negotiation between the crown and the chapters, and the empress's illness, the glue holding the suspension together began to weaken. Some cathedral chapters voted on whether to continue the suspension. On July 26, 1533, for instance, the chapter of Burgos voted

---

to the archbishop earlier about assembling the chapters. The archbishop's position had changed from May, when he did not think that an Assembly would alter the stances of the chapters; by early June, he was devising methods to assemble the clergy.

[60] AGS, E leg. 27, f. 29; This draft is probably the letter of July 9 referred to by the archbishop of Toledo in AGS, E leg. 27, f. 220. For a similar letter to Tavera, see AGS, E leg. 27, f. 14.

[61] Ibid., f. 220; Archbishop of Toledo to King, July 22, 1533. For a copy of Fonseca's letter of July 30 urging his chapter to convene an Assembly, see ACG, leg. 69, pieza 1, "Toledo de la carta que el senor obpo de Toledo embia a su iglesia sobre la congregación/ copia de la carta del senor arcobispo de Toledo para su yglesia."

24 to 9 not to lift the abstention, with two canons choosing not to vote. The chapter also wrote to the nearby chapters of Palencia and Santo Domingo to gauge their resolve.[62]

On August 4, the chapter of Burgos again discussed the suspension, but by this date the suspension was unraveling. Canons were sent out to confirm whether certain monasteries had lifted it. Not only were local parishes and religious organizations within the diocese celebrating Holy Offices, but even some of the cathedral chapters such as the 'bad churches' of Salamanca, Palencia, and Santo Domingo had resumed services. Given this situation, the chapter of Burgos decided to resume Holy Offices.[63] Most dioceses would not stick it out alone once the others decided to lift the suspension. Broad coordination and unity were necessary to maintain local churches' resolve. Most of the clergy nonetheless had held ranks for roughly two months in 1533, long enough to pressure the crown to agree to lift the sequestration and reopen negotiations.

Alonso Fernández de Madrid, a contemporary historian, described the situation at the end of July as follows:

> Finally, after so many fears of censures and loss of goods, and the corruption of the kingdom...the chapters not being able to suffer more, lifted the suspension and interdict, opened the churches, and returned to celebrate Mass, some sooner and some later. In Palencia, the suspension lasted 50 days, from June 19 to July 31.[64]

Many churches were simply worn out and could not resist any longer. Economic losses had mounted and would increase even more with the fall harvest. Moreover, many clerics had very small rents and lived on minuscule salaries. They probably had little money left. Although they evidently did not fear censure enough to lift the suspension promptly, the threat probably created a fair amount of anxiety. Moreover, the clergy may have feared that they had contributed to the corruption of the kingdom. Navarra was quick to attribute a breakdown in law and order to the suspension.

On August 5, the chapter of Toledo decided to convene an Assembly at the end of September. Although progress was being made, the corregidor of Toledo would continue the sequestration until the king

---

[62] ACB, R lib. 43, f. 589.
[63] Ibid., f. 598v.
[64] Fernández de Madrid, *Silva*, pp. 457–458.

ordered otherwise.[65] The convening of an Assembly, of course, was what the bishop of Zamora had advocated since the spring, but some royal officials thought that the ecclesiastical estate would only negotiate after force had been used against them. The chapters, on the other hand, might have believed that only after the crown saw their resolve would it come around to their position. In any case, by August, the parties had returned to the negotiating table.

Although the chapters ended the suspension believing that the sequestration would then be lifted, the crown did not do so immediately. On August 19, the canons of Toledo sent a messenger to the archbishop of Toledo, and letters to Tavera and the bishop of Zamora, inquiring when the sequestration would be lifted. When, on September 10, the crown still had not raised the sequestration, the chapter of Toledo sent a further messenger to Madrid demanding action.[66] The end of the suspension and the lifting of the sequestration obviously did not go hand in hand; the chapter of Seville, for instance, did not receive notification that the sequestration was lifted until October 20.[67]

Conclusion

Although the clerical suspension was over by early August, the acrimonious negotiations for the ecclesiastical contribution continued into the next year. Dealing with the Assembly of the Clergy did not bring as quick a resolution as the royal administrators had anticipated. Eventually, in March 1534, the chapters agreed to pay 471,000 florins between 1533 and 1536. These negotiations are examined in the next chapter.

The clergy organized to suspend Holy Offices in the fall of 1532 because they saw continual royal efforts to obtain ecclesiastical contributions as a threat to ecclesiastical liberties and an attempt to turn the church into a tributary estate. Ecclesiastical exemption from taxation was at stake. In 1533, amid an already inflamed situation between the crown and clergy, the sequestration became the catalyst for the suspension. As Alonso Fernández de Madrid described the situation:

---

[65] AGS, E leg. 27, ff. 218–219.
[66] ACT, AC lib. 5, ff. 130 and 132.
[67] ACS Sec. I, lib. 13, f. 279v.

In Palencia as in the other diocese, the corregidor ordered that the people
not come with tithes to the beneficiary and placed embargoes on debts
etc. In the end, there were so many vexations that the chapters of all of
Spain almost at the same time agreed to suspend Holy Offices...and so
they abstained as they did before in 1519, even though then there was
not extortion from the secular arm.[68]

In 1519, secular authorities had not applied force, meaning that the
sequestration was not the only possible cause for a suspension. Nevertheless, it was an immediate trigger in 1533. The underlying cause for
the conflict—whether in 1519, 1533, or 1556—was royal encroachment
on ecclesiastical liberties.

For the suspension to be effective, the dioceses needed to remain
united, and such unity may have stiffened many clergy's resolve. The
chapter of Burgos had suggested in December 1532 that the ecclesiastical conscience would be safe if they all acted together. Although the
participants could never be certain that all the chapters or diocesan
clergy would go along, the suspension's momentum had a ripple effect
throughout the kingdom. Once one chapter began to suspend, the
others followed suit according to earlier agreements. The end of the
suspension followed a similar pattern.

The complex relationship between the clergy on the diocesan level
made them susceptible to royal pressure, and internal divisions undermined the suspension. On the diocesan level, the crown tried to end
the suspension through threats and bribes. Moreover, the clergy's
resolve did not always last. The chapter of Burgos, for example, voted
unanimously to suspend Holy Offices on June 10; later, on July 26,
24 canons voted to continue the suspension, 9 voted to resume Holy
Offices, and 2 abstained. Certain canons had either grown tired of the
suspension or thought that it had served its purpose. Similar changes
in voting patterns probably took place in all the chapters of Castile.
In chapters with loyal minorities, it was probably easier to garner the
necessary votes to end the suspension. The crown wanted to break the
suspension at the diocesan level, expecting that once one diocese lifted
the suspension, the others would soon follow.[69] When the chapter of
Burgos learned that the nearby chapters had lifted the suspension, it

---

    [68] Fernández de Madrid, *Silva*, p. 457.
    [69] José Ignacio Fortea Pérez describes a similar process among the cities in the Cortes.
See *Monarquía y Cortes en la Corona de Castilla: Las ciudades ante la política fiscal de Felipe II*
(Salamanca: Cortes de Castilla y León, 1990).

did likewise. The chapters' failure to suspend Holy Offices when the crown sequestered rents in other years, such as 1539–1540 and 1544, may also have been due to a lack of coordination among chapters. If many chapters decided not to suspend Holy Offices, the suspension would have been difficult to execute and thus ineffective.

For the *cesación a divinis* to be an effective means of resistance, it had to create enough disturbances to put pressure on the crown. In his letter of June 12 to the king, Tavera reported, "[the kingdom] is all well thanks to God. There only is this disgrace of the suspension of Holy Offices that those of the chapters have made."[70] At this early stage, he clearly did not believe that the suspension was causing great havoc. Tavera, of course, had advocated using force against the ecclesiastical estate in the spring, and his nonchalant attitude toward the suspension differed from other royal officials. The simple threat of a *cesación a divinis*, for instance, made the empress advocate amending the bull, while the corregidor of Toledo reported that the suspension brought a breakdown in social order and consequently had to be brought to a prompt end. Moreover, Charles continually asked the clergy to celebrate Mass and preach in support of his endeavors; the failure of these public displays of faith in the crown would be a blow to royal authority.[71] If the church was a central pillar upon which the monarchy based its right to rule, an open and public dispute of this nature threatened to undermine the crown.[72]

The suspension's effects were not limited to the crown. Although clergy still conducted services in private or without pomp, the suspension clearly harmed the religious and public life of cities, towns, and villages. The Corpus Christi procession, for example, was an important service to the citizens of Toledo, who believed that without

---

[70] AGS, E leg. 27, f. 132.

[71] For example, on August 16, 1535, the city council of Burgos asked the chapter to ring the bells and give thanks for the king's success at La Goleta and Tunis. ACB, R lib. 44, f. 236rv.

[72] José Manuel Nieto Soria addressed the important role played by the clergy and religion in strengthening the Castilian monarch in the late medieval period, and he notes that religious propaganda firmly identified the Hispanic monarchy as a *respublica christiana* by the sixteenth century. Serious conflicts between the church and the state, such as the use of the *cesación a divinis*, undoubtedly threatened to undermine the political ideology of the state and a source of the state's legitimacy. See José Manuel Nieto Soria, "Propaganda and Legitimation in Castile: Religion and Church 1250–1500," in *Iconography, Propaganda, and Legitimation*, ed. Allan Ellenius (Oxford: Clarendon Press, 1998), pp. 105–119.

a celebration, pestilence would follow that year. Furthermore, funeral processions and the dispensing of alms played an important role in the population's spiritual life.[73] Since regular attendance at Mass and the reception of communion was not common at this time, it is possible that the populace was not too inconvenienced by the disruption of the liturgical calendar in some regions due to censures, interdicts, and excommunication.[74] The purchasing of papal briefs to attend Mass during times of censure or interdict, however, indicates that, for some individuals, regular attendance at religious services and the reception of the Sacraments were important.[75] The suspension of services, then, had some impact on the people, and the reaction of some royal officials suggests that the lack of religious services upset both the crown and the people.

At least three instances of *cesación a divinis* (1519, 1533, and 1556) occurred during Charles V's reign. In both 1533 and 1556, the *cesación a divinis* was a response to force, for the clergy would not accept violations of their property without a struggle. In 1533, the crown moderated its position slightly to reach a final agreement through consensus. Coercion, therefore, played a role in the political process, but the ministers' ambivalence and the clergy's resistance suggest that the state's monopoly of force did not alone guarantee fiscal support.

---

[73] See Maureen Flynn, *Sacred Charity: Confraternities and Social Welfare in Spain, 1400–1700* (Ithaca: Cornell University Press, 1989), pp. 64–69.
[74] Personal conversation with Henry Kamen in Madrid (May 1994).
[75] B.N. Ms. 9175 ff. 159v–160.

CHAPTER FOUR

NEGOTIATIONS FOR THE SUBSIDY, 1533–1534

After the serious difficulties in the summer of 1533, there was undoubtedly much hope that the Assembly of the Clergy meeting in Alcalá de
Henares would quickly reach an amenable agreement with the king
for the payment of a subsidy. Instead, the meeting became the longest
Assembly of Charles's reign, lasting from October 10, 1533, until March
18, 1534. The duration of this Assembly allows us to better understand
political practice and see how crown and clergy reached consensus in
sixteenth-century Castile. The present chapter examines the differences
between the crown and the Assembly, the means of applying pressure
within the context of these negotiations, the role of consultations as
both a stratagem and hindrance to successful negotiations, and finally
the rifts within the ecclesiastical estate.

Pending Negotiations

On September 15, 1533, Alonso de Fonseca, the archbishop of Toledo,
informed the king that his chapter had convened the Assembly of the
Clergy and expected some representatives to arrive in Alcalá by September 20. The chapter advised him, however, that some chapters refused
to send representatives, claiming that the sequestration of ecclesiastical
rents prevented them from leaving their churches or that Assemblies
customarily met at court, so they should meet there, not in Alcalá. The
absence of representatives from an unspecified number of chapters
worried both the archbishop and chapter of Toledo. Consequently, in
his letter to Charles, the archbishop hinted that the Assembly should
probably meet at court, since the archbishop's ill health and age would
prevent him from taking a firm hand in the negotiations and potentially
cause delays.[1]

Even more problematic for the pending negotiations was the sequestration. Some chapters had not sent representatives because of it,

---

[1] AGS, E leg. 27, f. 225.

others had ordered their representatives not to discuss anything until it ended, and still others had ordered their representatives to return to their churches if it was not lifted. Consequently, on September 28, the archbishop of Toledo advised the king to lift the sequestration immediately. In addition to placating the clergy, the archbishop believed, lifting the sequestration was strategically wise. That way, he said, force would still be an option if negotiations bogged down later. He also asked the king for clear instructions on what would serve him in the negotiations. Otherwise, the archbishop explained, the need for regular consultations between royal ministers in Alcalá and the king in Aragon would prolong the negotiations. Finally, the archbishop again asked for license to leave Alcalá on account of his health, adding that from his bed he would be able to do little in the negotiations and did not want his ill health to prevent their quick and successful conclusion.[2]

Absent chapters, lifting the sequestration, clear instructions, and the archbishop's health were not the only potential sticking points in the negotiations. In separate reports at the end of September, Cardinal Tavera, archbishop of Santiago and president of the royal council, and Juan de Enciso, a treasury official, outlined several more. First, the representatives proposed serving the king voluntarily with a free gift and not being obliged to pay anything on account of the bull of the *medios frutos*. Second, they wanted a guarantee from the king not to ask for a subsidy without a good cause and papal permission. Yet, Enciso reported, some representatives disagreed over the usefulness of such a guarantee. Third, they wanted the king to procure a papal brief to include all exempt clergy who had contributed in the last subsidy. They opposed the papal brief that exempted benefices worth less than 12 ducados, explaining that it would be time consuming and costly, if not impossible, to investigate the values of these benefices to determine which were truly exempt. For these reasons, the representatives recommended including all exempted clergy in the present contribution. Tavera noted that, given the large number of poorer benefices, especially in Galicia and northern Castile, the crown would either have to include them or else provide discounts, as it had in the past. Fourth, most representatives opposed reapportioning the subsidy to relieve the

---

[2] AGS, E. leg. 27, f. 228; PR leg. 20, f. 36. On October 1, Charles approved moving the Assembly to Madrid where the climate might be better for the archbishop, but his response apparently arrived too late to make a difference. See AGS, E leg. 26, f. 243.

churches of Santiago and Mondoñedo and the military orders, and they recommended that the king relieve those churches individually after the general apportionment of the subsidy. Fifth, the pope had told the Assembly's agents in Rome that this subsidy should not exceed the last subsidy, and thus Tavera recommended that Charles accept the same size subsidy as he had in 1530. Finally, the representatives wanted a longer period of payments than the king desired.[3]

On October 4, Charles outlined his basic position for the negotiations in three lengthy letters to the cardinal president, the archbishop of Toledo, and the bishop of Zamora. First, he believed that keeping the sequestration in place would force the clergy to reach a quick conclusion, but, in light of his ministers' advice, he agreed to lift it. Now, he told them, he expected the Assembly to serve him so that force would be unnecessary. Second, Charles did not want the Assembly to discuss the exemption of benefices worth less than 12 ducados, the reduction of those worth less than 24 ducados to a *decima*, or the exemption of other clergy. Third, he stated that more revenue could have been generated in the last contribution if it had been based on *frutas* and not reduced to a subsidy. Consequently, he wanted a better agreement so that he would receive more money than in the last subsidy. Fourth, he wanted the terms of payment to be just, but not overly long. Finally, he wanted a reapportionment to relieve the churches of Santiago and Mondoñedo, plus any other clergy or hospitals that were aggrieved in the last subsidy.[4] A week later, Charles told his ministers not to consent to the clergy's request to grant the contribution by their own volition, because it would weaken papal authority and be harmful to future negotiations. He also did not want the representatives to discuss the guarantee of ecclesiastical liberty.[5]

Going into the negotiations, many representatives held starkly different positions from the king, and Charles only made one concession—lifting the sequestration—that his ministers recommended. This did not bode well for a quick conclusion. Another problem was that the king's point man for the negotiations, the archbishop of Toledo, was severely ill and would die before the negotiations finished. Except for one letter to the king, complaining about his health at the start of the negotiations,

---

[3] AGS, E leg. 27, f. 330; PR leg. 20, f. 36.
[4] AGS, E leg. 26, ff. 237–239, 241, and 264–267.
[5] Ibid., f. 244.

it is unclear from the documents what affect his illness had on them.[6] It does not seem farfetched to assume, however, that Alonso de Fonseca's illness may have further complicated the affair. By early fall, both sides must have realized that any hopes for a speedy resolution were misplaced.

First Round of Negotiations, October–December 1533

The Assembly finally convened on October 10, 1533. Representatives from 21 chapters attended the opening session, and more arrived in the following weeks. That afternoon, Francisco de Mendoza, the bishop of Zamora and Comisario General de la Cruzada, informed the Assembly that he had ordered the lifting of the sequestration. With this action, negotiations could move forward. First, however, the Assembly had to deal with seating conflicts between Seville and Santiago and between Oviedo and Palencia; these squabbles threatened ecclesiastical unity. The case between Seville and Santiago was easily resolved, possibly because Santiago's representatives were not in attendance. After stating their claim to the seat after Toledo, Seville's representatives agreed to abide by a decision of the Assembly of 1530, requiring the two chapters to ask the pope to resolve their dispute over precedence in seating. Until then, neither Seville's nor Santiago's representatives would sit at Toledo's right hand. Rather, they were consigned to unassigned seats without prejudice to either's claim.[7]

The case between Oviedo and Palencia was more complicated and time consuming.[8] On October 22, fearing that this dispute between two minor chapters was distracting the Assembly, the other representatives asked for a judge to examine the case and for those chapters' representatives to sit next to the secretaries until the judge reached a verdict.[9] This decision only made matters worse, because Oviedo's representatives threatened to withdraw from the Assembly on October 24 and not to be bound by its decisions if they did not sit next to Burgos. Oviedo's representatives then left the room to wait for a response. The Assembly took the threat seriously, realizing that its ability to negotiate would be

---

[6] See AGS, E leg. 27, f. 231.
[7] ACS, Sec. VII, lib. 85, "Congregación del clero…1533," October 10, 1533.
[8] Ibid., October 10, 11, and 15, 1533.
[9] Ibid., October 22, 1533.

compromised if chapters were not bound by its decisions. The rest of the representatives then swore an oath not to make separate agreements with the crown for the payment of the subsidy and affirmed that the will of the majority bound all.[10]

The next day the Assembly told Oviedo's representatives that they had no special right or privilege to sit next to Burgos and that there was no precedent for returning powers (that is, Oviedo could not withdraw from the Assembly after formally entering it).[11] It also repeated that, for the time being, the representatives from Palencia and Oviedo would sit next to the secretaries without prejudice to their claims.[12] Two more weeks passed before both chapters' representatives agreed to the compromise.[13] Conflicts over precedence exposed the Assembly's fragility, and its need to placate even minor chapters suggests that internal rifts could seriously undermine its ability to function. The fact that the same problems arose in each Assembly and simmered for years suggests that the Assembly was incapable of resolving certain structural problems that likely led to more internal and personal conflicts.[14]

Seating, however, was not the only problem that threatened ecclesiastical unity. Some chapters did not send representatives and others refused to enter the Assembly. Santiago's representatives, for example, had arrived in Alcalá by late October, but their chapter prohibited them from entering the Assembly unless it promised to reapportion the subsidy. The representatives explained to the Assembly that past apportionments of the subsidy by the Assembly were more burdensome for Santiago than paying the present *medios frutos* in full would be.[15] Other chapters made the same claim later in the negotiations. Given that the Assembly wanted Santiago's representatives to enter and strengthen its negotiating position, one can understand Santiago's effort to pressure the Assembly to execute a clause in the agreement of 1530 to reassess Santiago and Mondoñedo's share of the subsidy or make some other concessions. Other chapters apparently planned to negotiate their own agreements with the crown as well. Such actions could also threaten the Assembly's position in its negotiations, because the crown often saw

---

[10] Ibid., October 24, 1533.
[11] Ibid., October 25, 1533.
[12] Ibid., October 27, 1533.
[13] Ibid., November 11 and 13, 1533.
[14] For more on this point, see Benjamín González Alonso, *Sobre el estado y la administración de la Corona de Castilla en el antiguo regimen* (Madrid: Siglo XXI, 1981), p. 49.
[15] ACS, Sec. VII, lib. 85, "Congregación del clero…1533," October 27 and 29, 1533.

separate accords with individual chapters as a way to entice others to make an agreement.[16]

Internal problems over precedence and attendance did not completely prevent the Assembly from addressing its main business. On October 11, the Assembly reviewed papal briefs from the summer and heard a report from a representative, who had been in Rome, on the pope and the College of Cardinals' disposition regarding these negotiations.[17] On October 12, the Assembly formed a committee to prepare general and particular grievances, and it notified the bishop of Zamora that it was waiting to hear from him.[18] The bishop sent Juan de Enciso to address the Assembly on October 13. Enciso reminded the Assembly that the king had responded to the clergy's supplications by lifting the sequestration and that he did not wish to use force to collect the *medios frutos*. Consequently, Enciso said, the king hoped that, recognizing the great debt he had incurred fighting the Turks, the Assembly would act accordingly. Instead, the Assembly called attention to the Castilian church's financial needs and grievances.[19]

The representatives also asked to see the bishop of Zamora's instructions. The bishop responded that his only order was to wait for the Assembly to propose a sum. Shortly thereafter, the Assembly sent deputies to inform the archbishop of Toledo and the bishop of Zamora that the representatives were not authorized to propose a sum; rather, they expected the king to propose a sum, and they would respond after consulting with their chapters. The archbishop advised the deputies that the Assembly should state the amount first to facilitate the negotiations. The deputies then returned to the Assembly to confer with the rest of the representatives, and the ministers immediately informed the king of these developments.[20]

The initial offer was crucial to move the negotiations forward, and each side hinted at why the sum should be high or low. Yet, neither side wanted to be the first to state a sum. Since the clergy had walked out

---

[16] AGS, E leg. 26, f. 293. Other rulers pursued a similar course of action in their negotiations with corporate bodies. See Matthew Vester, "Fiscal commissions, consensus and informal representation: taxation in the Savoyard domains, 1559–1580," *Parliaments, Estates and Representation* 20 (2000), p. 68.

[17] The minutes, however, do not record the representative's report. ACS, Sec. VII, lib. 85, "Congregación del clero...1533," October 11, 1533.

[18] Ibid., October 12, 1533.

[19] Ibid., October 13, 1533; AGS, E leg. 27, f. 231.

[20] Ibid.

in 1530 over what they considered too high a request, the king may have wanted to let them set the baseline for the present negotiations. The clergy, in turn, may have worried about an initial offer that would insult the king.

Nevertheless, the Assembly discussed offering between 200,000 and 250,000 florins, but held off on making that offer.[21] Instead, on October 15, the Assembly told the bishop of Zamora that it expected the crown to make certain concessions before it proposed a sum. First, it wanted the king to renew earlier decrees in which he and the Catholic Kings guaranteed ecclesiastical liberty and that a subsidy agreement would not turn the clergy into *pecheros* (taxpayers). It also asked that the Cortes and the pope confirm these decrees. Undoubtedly, the Assembly expected that the latter confirmations would make it more difficult for the crown to violate the guarantee in the future. Second, the Assembly asked for the agreements to include all exempt clergy who had contributed in the past subsidy. Third, it expected the crown to remedy both general and particular grievances.[22] By setting conditions for a subsidy, the Assembly was trying to establish the principal of redress of grievances before supply.

Royal officials were upset with the Assembly's demands. Cardinal Tavera recommended a harsh response.[23] The king also was not pleased, telling the bishop of Zamora that the Assembly was not to discuss these issues further. Finally, after a week, the bishop of Zamora and the king both rebuked the Assembly for being unreasonable and excessive in its demands and ordered it only to discuss the size of the subsidy. The bishop was especially appalled that after the king had lifted the sequestration, the representatives still made such audacious requests. He reminded them that the papal bull required the clergy to pay the *medios frutos* and that the concession was for the defense of Christendom. Therefore, he urged the representatives to make an offer: the king would then be more inclined to make them *merced* (royal favor in return for a service) and have no reason to use force. Finally, he reminded the representatives that the chapters had earlier promised to serve the king unconditionally.[24]

---

[21] ACS, Sec. VII, lib. 85, "Congregación del clero…1533," October 14, 1533.

[22] Ibid., October 15, 1533.

[23] AGS, E leg. 27, f. 127.

[24] ACS, Sec. VII, lib. 85, "Congregación del clero…1533," October 22 and 23, 1533; AGS E leg. 26, ff. 289–292, and E leg. 27, ff. 334–335.

On October 24, the Assembly wrote to the king, acknowledging his clemency and the considerable costs he had incurred defending Christendom, and stressed its willingness to offer a subsidy. The representatives, however, insisted that it was not excessive for them to ask for a decree that guaranteed ecclesiastical liberty. They pointed out that they were simply seeking confirmation of what he and his predecessors had previously conceded to the ecclesiastical estate. They also emphasized that including exempt clergy in the subsidy was necessary to prevent unrest and inconveniences in the collection. They even told the king that his failure to grant the guarantee and the inclusion would hamper negotiations. That evening at eight o'clock, the representatives repeated to the prelates that without a positive response to these two demands, they could consent to nothing. Realizing that the guarantee and inclusion were now the main obstacles in the negotiations, the representatives wrote to their chapters seeking advice on how to proceed if their demands were not met; they proposed dissolving the Assembly.[25]

After only two weeks, the negotiations had reached an impasse. The representatives would not agree to a subsidy without a guarantee of ecclesiastical liberty and the inclusion of those exempted in the bull of the *medios frutos*. For his part, the king was determined that the Assembly would no longer discuss those demands. The challenge for the royal ministers was to break this impasse without compromising royal authority by making the king appear to buckle under ecclesiastical pressure. Cardinal Tavera felt that the easiest way to reach a compromise without loss of face was for the king to permit the Assembly itself to procure the inclusion of the exempt clergy from the pope, and for the king to convey to the pope that the Assembly's request was not against his will. This option was preferable, Tavera argued, because the Assembly would not be pressuring Charles to do anything; rather, the king was simply showing the clergy his goodwill. Tavera was also certain that the pope would grant the Assembly's request. In that case, he added, the Assembly would have to address the inequitable apportionment of the subsidy to redress the unconscionable situation whereby poor clergy, hospitals, and monasteries paid more than their share and were thus burdened with what rightfully should fall on rich benefices.[26] Tavera's

---

[25] ACS, Sec. VII, lib. 85, "Congregación del clero...1533," October 24, 1533; AGS, E leg. 27, ff. 180 and 331.
[26] AGS, E leg. 27, f. 168.

advice was sound, but he must have realized that demanding a reapportionment would likely create a new impasse and possibly prevent a timely conclusion to the negotiations.

Charles recognized the impasse as well and wrote to Tavera for advice on November 5, yet he was not ready to concede to the Assembly's demands.[27] In instructions sent to the bishop of Zamora that same day, Charles said that, to avoid further delays, he would accept the same amount as the last subsidy, but he did not want the Assembly to discuss the guarantee and inclusion any more. To solicit the inclusion of the exempt clergy, he felt, would dishonor him and only lead to more delays. The pope was busy preparing to meet the king of France and Charles's allies in the College of Cardinals were absent from the city, and those individuals exempted in the original bull would try to avoid payment. He then reminded the bishop that the unequal apportionment of the last subsidy had resulted in a loss of money for the crown. It was therefore necessary to reapportion the subsidy to relieve the aggrieved churches, most notably Santiago and Mondoñedo. Finally, Charles must have learned that the representatives planned to leave, because he authorized the bishop to detain them if they tried and to execute the bull of the *medios frutos* if they left before reaching an agreement for a subsidy.[28] He also sent the Assembly a strongly worded response to its letter of October 24.[29] Except for accepting the same size subsidy as in the last agreement, the king had given little ground.

The representatives read Charles's letter during their afternoon session on November 12. Charles ordered them to desist from making unreasonable demands, adding that obedience to papal orders was the principal way to protect ecclesiastical liberty, and since the pope had ordered the payment for a just cause and he had shown such clemency to them, they should reciprocate in the subsidy. Otherwise, he warned them, the negotiations might reach the point where force

---

[27] AGS, E leg. 26, f. 295.

[28] Ibid., f. 293. Interestingly, after the clergy in the kingdom of Aragon had reached an agreement for the payment of the *medios frutos* in January 1533, Charles permitted them to petition the pope to include in the subsidy benefices worth less than 12 ducados and told his ambassador to support their petition. So the policy suggested by Tavera to break the impasse was not abhorrent to the king. Rather, the situation in Rome had changed, as Charles indicated to the bishop of Zamora, and those changes affected the negotiations in Castile. The negotiations for subsidies then always had an international dimension. For Charles's decision regarding the clergy in Aragon, see AGS, PR leg. 19, f. 34.

[29] AGS, E leg. 26, f. 294.

was necessary to fulfill the pope's order. Charles stressed, however, that using force would displease him. To reach a just accord, he authorized the archbishop of Toledo and the bishop of Zamora to negotiate with the Assembly on his behalf. After reading the king's letter, the bishop of Zamora forbade the representatives to discuss further the inclusion and the guarantee of ecclesiastical liberty. The bishop underlined the king's desire to avoid a forcible collection, blaming the clergy's earlier shameful actions for the sequestration of ecclesiastical rents from June to October. He also reminded the representatives that more than 15 months had passed since the arrival of the bull of the *medios frutos* and the delays in payment had substantially increased the king's interest charges. Nevertheless, he said, the king had shown great patience with the ecclesiastical estate and promised to address their grievances, so the representatives should declare an amount without delay. The representatives immediately told the bishop that their demands were for the good of the entire ecclesiastical estate and had been requested and granted before. The bishop then ordered them to desist and to declare a sum to avoid further delays and costs for the king and the churches.[30]

The king's letter and the exchange with the bishop caused a stir within the Assembly. The next day it again acclaimed that a majority vote bound all the chapters and made vague insinuations about unidentified representatives.[31] Even though the chapters overwhelmingly approved of the Assembly's efforts to obtain a guarantee of ecclesiastical liberty and the inclusion of exempted clergy in any subsidy, differences of opinion within the Assembly required it to give some ground to maintain unity.[32]

On November 14, the Assembly offered 400,000 florins payable over four years at 100,000 florins a year and implored the king not to seek another subsidy during the four-year payment period. The majority also swore an oath not to increase the offer without the express consent

---

[30] ACS, Sec. VII, lib. 85, "Congregación del clero...1533," November 12, 1533; AGS E leg. 26, f. 294 and E leg. 27, f. 337.

[31] ACS, Sec. VII, lib. 85, "Congregación del clero...1533," November 13, 1533. The insinuation may have referred to some representatives breaking their oath of secrecy. An undated and unsigned letter to Cardinal Tavera from either December 1533 or January 1534 indicates that at least one representative informed royal officials of the Assembly's proceedings and even suggested potential courses of action for the crown to take in the negotiations. See AGS, E leg. 27, f. 163.

[32] ACS, Sec. VII, lib. 85, "Congregación del clero...1533," November 8, 10, 11–12, 1533.

of their chapters. Notwithstanding the king's order, the representatives again asked for a guarantee of ecclesiastical liberty and the inclusion of the exempt clergy in the contribution. They stressed that the king and his predecessors had freely conceded guarantees in the past. They also repeated that it would be difficult to verify the values of the benefices worth less than 12 ducados and that their exemption would lead to lawsuits and confusion in the collection. Thus, according to the representatives, it would be simplest to include everyone in the contribution. If the king refused their offer, the representatives asked for permission to return to their churches, saying that they were not authorized to offer more than 400,000 florins, and they could not even offer that amount without the inclusion of the exempt clergy. They humbly begged the king to accept their offer.[33] This offer indicates a significant shift within the Assembly. It was much higher than what the representatives had previously discussed (200,000–250,000 florins), and although they repeated their conditions, they no longer expected redress before supply.

The bishop of Zamora and the archbishop of Toledo were pleased with the offer. That evening, the bishop wrote Cardinal Tavera that 400,000 florins was a significant first offer and demonstrated the Assembly's willingness to serve. He also recommended complying with the Assembly's demands for a guarantee and inclusion. He realized that it was the king's prerogative to grant a decree guaranteeing ecclesiastical liberty, but strongly advised doing so because the guarantee was extremely important to the clergy, and the representatives had inferred from the king's letters in the summer that he would issue it. In regard to inclusion, the prelates in Alcalá recommended it. The bishop explained that the exemption of people who had paid in the past would cause problems, because everyone would claim to be exempt, with some saying their benefices were worth less than 12 ducados even if they were worth 100, and each chapter consequently would need a chancery to deal with the appeals and lawsuits. He also thought that the pope would be amenable to the request, since it would preserve peace within the church.[34]

Tavera was pleased that the Assembly had finally made an offer but added that it should offer at least the same amount as the last subsidy.

---

[33] Ibid., November 14, 1533, AGS E leg. 27, f. 337.
[34] AGS, E leg. 27, f. 122.

He repeated that the best way to proceed would be to let the Assembly petition the pope for the inclusion, but since the king opposed this, the bishop was not to broach the subject. Tavera also recommended shortening the terms of payment: four years was too long because of accruing interest. Finally, he stated that the Assembly had to remedy the unjust apportionment of the subsidy so that the king would not have to provide further discounts and lose money.[35] The negotiations had turned a corner, but Tavera's response indicates that they still had a long way to go. More importantly, the king remained the major obstacle on at least one point, inclusion. While the rest of the royal ministers supported Tavera's compromise, Charles's recalcitrance on the matter likely complicated and prolonged the negotiations.

By December 4, nineteen days had passed since the Assembly sent its offer to the king. The delays infuriated the representatives, who complained to the archbishop of Toledo and the bishop of Zamora, as well as the archbishop of Toledo, who blamed the Assembly.[36] That day, he wrote his chapter that he had met several times with deputies from the Assembly only to discuss issues other than the subsidy. The prelate added that the lack of moderation in the Assembly's demands made it impossible for him and the bishop to respond positively and this only led to more discontent among the representatives. As a result, he informed his chapter that he was ready to dismiss the Assembly.[37] Undoubtedly, Fonseca hoped his missive would prompt his chapter to intervene with the Assembly.

Tavera, on the other hand, blamed the bishop of Zamora for the delays. Tavera informed the king that he had seen the bishop's instructions, and these instructions ought to have made further consultations unnecessary. Still, the bishop continued to seek clarification on many points, and Tavera predicted that consultations would continue until the parties reached an agreement because the bishop feared some representatives would cause a commotion. Consequently, he reported, the bishop continued to write to him even though he was absent and unable to take an effective hand in the negotiations.[38] Tavera was undoubtedly correct that the bishop of Zamora's hesitancy prolonged

---

[35] Ibid., f. 348.
[36] ACS, Sec. VII, lib. 85, "Congregación del clero...1533," December 4, 1533.
[37] AHN, Clero, leg. 7216, n°2, Cardinal of Toledo to chapter of Toledo, December 4, 1533.
[38] AGS, E leg. 29, f. 200.

the negotiations and in the process possibly created new problems. Yet, Mendoza's worries were justifiable given the *cesación a divinis* only six months earlier. Moreover, given the clergy's refusal to offer what the king wanted, the consultations allowed him to stall for time and try to find a compromise. Knowing that the crown needed a timely conclusion to secure further loans, the Assembly may have delayed making its offer to pressure the crown to concede to its demands before supply. Thus, perpetuating delays could be a useful stratagem for both sides. Yet, if this was a conscious strategy, it was also a risky one that led to recriminations and additional costs that neither side could afford.

The negotiations languished until the king's letter arrived on December 12. Charles apologized for the inevitable costs that the Assembly had incurred while waiting for his response to its offer of 400,000 florins, but he had been occupied with the Cortes in the Crown of Aragon and other important matters. He told the representatives that he wanted to conclude the negotiations without further concessions from the pope, and he felt that the exemption for poor benefices would not impede an agreement. He recognized that some confusion remained over whether the exemption for benefices worth less than 12 ducados applied only to individuals with a single benefice or to all benefices worth less than 12 ducados, including those held by large institutions or individuals with multiple benefices. He believed that the pope only wanted to help the poor with this exemption and promised to write the pontiff for clarification. Interestingly, Charles said nothing specific about the size of the offer, but the Assembly understood his silence on that matter. In a short written response, the representatives stated that offering more would go against their chapters' orders.[39]

That afternoon, the Assembly discussed its next step. Possibly fearing that the negotiation had reached a critical point and realizing that some members were leaking information, the representatives swore an oath not to reveal their deliberation to the royal ministers. They then prepared a lengthy response for the prelates. Oviedo's representatives also raised the issue of the apportionment and presented a *requirimiento* (a formal demand that could be the basis of a legal action) that called for the reapportionment of the subsidy based on the *verdadero valor* of each diocese's rents. Otherwise, given the poverty of the diocese,

---

[39] ACS, Sec. VII, lib. 85, "Congregación del clero…1533," December 12, 1533; AGS, E leg. 26, ff. 214–216 and leg. 27, f. 164.

Oviedo's representatives said, their chapter would rather pay the *medios frutos* than the subsidy. The Assembly tabled the issue, but this requirement indicates that the failure to apportion the subsidy fairly so that all churches benefited from the reduction of the *medios frutos* to a fixed amount threatened ecclesiastical unity.[40]

On December 13, the Assembly presented its response to the prelates, repeating its readiness to serve the king with a subsidy of 400,000 florins and under terms similar to 1530 without further consultations and delays that, it added, greatly increased the costs for the churches. Further, they stated plainly that the long delay had allowed them to consult their chapters, which prohibited them from increasing the offer because dearth had so diminished ecclesiastical rents that the present offer actually exceeded the past subsidy. The Assembly also claimed that the poor clergy with benefices worth less than 12 ducados were not aggrieved in the local apportionments, and to go forward without their inclusion in the subsidy would lead to costly and inconvenient lawsuits and investigations. The representatives added that people with even less wealth contribute to the *servicios* of the Cortes. Finally, they asserted, the king would be better served by a subsidy than by executing the bull forcibly, which would only create unrest and not generate any more revenue. The representatives apologized for their boldness, but they wished to conclude the negotiations; the king's response to their offer, they believed, was too vague and would only created further delays. They repeated their desire to serve the king and reach an agreement so that they could return to their churches, and the prelates agreed to respond to them as quickly as possible.[41] In the meantime, the Assembly made preparations to leave Alcalá.[42]

Charles was less vague about his wishes in a letter to the bishop of Zamora on December 7. He authorized the bishop to allow the Assembly to ask the pope to include the exempt clergy in the subsidy, and he enclosed a letter to that effect for his ambassador in Rome. If the Assembly did appeal to the pope, Charles told the bishop, he expected the representatives to offer 50,000 to 100,000 florins more than the last subsidy. He also stated that an appeal to the pope should not lead to further delays in reaching an agreement or in the actual payment of

---

[40] ACS, Sec. VII, lib. 85, "Congregación del clero... 1533," December 12, 1533.
[41] Ibid., December 13, 1533; AGS E leg. 27, ff. 164–166.
[42] ACS, Sec. VII, lib. 85, "Congregación del clero... 1533," December 13 and 16, 1533.

the subsidy. All the delays to date, Charles stressed, had forced him to incur high interest charges. He would therefore not accept a period of payments of more than two years. He also wanted the bishop to convey to the Assembly that, after an agreement was reached, he would address the guarantee of ecclesiastical liberty and respond to the Assembly's grievances. Charles, however, would make no further concessions, and he would not accept less than 471,000 florins, noting that the *medios frutos* of just those included in the papal bull would be twice as much. He also insisted on a just apportionment to avoid discounts for the aggrieved. Finally, he instructed the bishop to ask the representatives to wait until he arrived and to order them not to leave without royal license. However, if the Assembly sent deputies with full powers to meet him, Charles would allow the rest of the representatives to recess for Christmas. If they should leave under any other circumstance, he ordered the bishop to collect the *medios frutos* forcibly.[43] His instructions to the bishop indicate that significant differences persisted between the king and the Assembly, but it did give the prelates some leeway in their negotiations with the Assembly.

On December 16, the archbishop of Toledo and the bishop of Zamora proposed to the Assembly that if it offered more than 400,000 florins, the king would permit it to ask the pope to include the exempt clergy and would inform the pope that he approved of its request.[44] The Assembly did not bite, telling the prelates the next day that the present poverty of the church made it impossible to offer more. It beseeched the king to accept its offer so that the representatives could return to their churches to serve God and pray for the king.[45]

The prelates may have been taken aback by the Assembly's refusal. Two days later, the bishop of Zamora and the archbishop of Toledo told the Assembly that they too desired to conclude the negotiations, but given the great costs that the king had incurred personally leading an expedition against the Turks, it was reasonable for him to expect a larger subsidy than before. Even if the subsidy was double the last contribution, they opined, it would still be significantly less than the *medios frutos* the pope had conceded. Yet, they emphasized, the king was

---

[43] AGS, E leg. 26, ff. 204–210 and 245–249.

[44] ACS, Sec. VII, lib. 85, "Congregación del clero…1533," December 16, 1533; AGS, E leg. 27, f. 166.

[45] ACS, Sec. VII, lib. 85, "Congregación del clero…1533," December 17, 1533; AGS E leg. 27, f. 166.

willing to accept the same amount as the last subsidy. Moreover, if the clergy agreed to the previous sum, they repeated, the king would allow the Assembly itself to ask the pope for the inclusion. The Assembly immediately shot back that its offer of 400,000 florins was made in consideration of the king's needs, not the clergy's ability to pay, and the chapters had only agreed to what they considered an excessive amount on the condition that it not be increased.[46]

On December 21, after stating once more the great costs that the king had incurred defending Christendom, the prelates bluntly told the representatives that they could not accept their offer and that they could not dismiss the Assembly without first consulting the king. In the meantime, knowing the king's goodwill toward the church, they had asked Tavera to urge the king to accept the Assembly's offer. The representatives were perturbed, saying that further consultations would only cause additional delays and expenses for the churches.[47] Still, on December 22, the representatives agreed to wait for the royal license and decided not to meet until there was a new development.[48]

Between October and December, the negotiations for the subsidy hit several impasses. Both sides had to give some ground, but neither side was willing to concede completely. The Assembly probably gave the most ground, offering a sum before the king agreed to its conditions. Yet, its offer was significantly short of what the king expected. The concession that the king made regarding the inclusion was either too late or not acceptable to the Assembly. Besides the regular challenges of finding a compromise, delays were a problem. Yet, the delays may well have played into each side's hands. That is, the situation in late December likely would have been the same in November had the king's reply arrived sooner. Yet, the delays helped to prevent the clergy from walking out without an agreement and avoided the problems of a forcible collection. In late December, with negotiations stalled, the need to write to the king for license allowed the prelates to keep the clergy in place longer and left the door open to a peaceful resolution of the negotiations when the king arrived.

---

[46] ACS, Sec. VII, lib. 85, "Congregación del clero…1533," December 19, 1533; AGS, E leg. 27, f. 166.
[47] ACS, Sec. VII, lib. 85, "Congregación del clero…1533," December 21, 1533; AGS, E leg. 27, f. 166.
[48] ACS, Sec. VII, lib. 85, "Congregación del clero…1533," December 22, 1533.

Interlude

Between late December and the king's arrival in Alcalá on February 1, 1534, the Assembly waited for the king's response, threatened to leave, and addressed other matters. It was a tense and frustrating month for all involved in the negotiations. Probably the most inexplicable event occurred at the end of December. The Assembly met on December 29 to discuss several unspecified issues. Since many representatives were absent, including those from Toledo, it adjourned until the next day, and the doorman was ordered to summon the absent representatives for the next morning. When the representatives arrived the next day, they found themselves locked out of their meeting room in the archbishop's palace. They asked the doorman to unlock the door, only to learn that a representative from Toledo had taken the key away from him. Apparently expecting someone else to open the door for them, the representatives waited for a while before going to the church of Santa Justi. Instead of addressing the business from the previous day, the representatives voted to hold future meetings in Santa Justi, appointed a new doorman, and had two sets of keys made for the new meeting place. A few representatives, however, were only willing to meet in Santa Justi until they learned if the archbishop approved the change. So the Assembly consulted him, and he responded that it was up to the representatives to determine their meeting place. Whether or not to summon Toledo's representatives was more contentious. Many representatives were furious with their behavior and wanted them disciplined. In the end, they sent a summons to Toledo's representatives, who did not enter the Assembly until January 10 and only took their seats on January 13 after apologizing. The minutes do not state why Toledo's representatives took the key to begin with, except for a vague reference to a decision taken by the Assembly before Christmas.[49] The minutes also do not mention who presided over the Assembly in Toledo's absence; it is likely that, since Toledo's representatives were summoned back, no effort was made to elect a new president. Still, this odd episode highlights the tensions between representatives within the Assembly.

The representatives also complained to the bishop of Zamora about the delays in the king's reply, only to be told to be patient and wait, as

---

[49] Ibid., December 29, 30, and 31, 1534, and January 10 and 13, 1534.

the king would reply as soon as possible.[50] Finally, on January 9, they angrily told the bishop that they had waited 18 days for a response and this was unacceptable. Had they realized that there would be such a long delay, they said, they would have gone to Monzón rather than wait in Alcalá for the king's response. The representatives then accused the bishop of purposefully delaying the negotiations and claimed that such tactics were intolerable, because the churches could not offer more. They gave him four days to obtain the king's reply. Otherwise, the representatives would give what was offered under the conditions stipulated and leave.[51]

The prospect that the Assembly would dissolve shortly apparently prompted Mondoñedo's representative to present a *requirimiento* to reapportion the subsidy on the national level. He reminded the Assembly that in 1530 both Mondoñedo and Santiago were promised relief in the apportionment but received none. He then stated that the present *medios frutos* would not overly burden Mondoñedo. However, to preserve ecclesiastical liberty, he felt that the chapters needed to maintain solidarity in these negotiations and not reach separate agreements with the crown. To keep that unity, he intimated, a new apportionment was necessary so that Mondoñedo would not be more burdened by paying a subsidy than by paying the *medios frutos*. If the subsidy was not reapportioned, the representative threatened, his chapter would neither agree to it nor pay it. The Assembly again tabled the issue.[52]

Nevertheless, later that day, the representatives from Burgos, León, and Orense presented their own *requirimiento* to the Assembly. Since their dioceses had been aggrieved in the last reapportionment in 1523, they recommended using the *verdaderos valores* of all the rents in the kingdom's archdioceses and dioceses to reapportion the subsidy so that the apportionment would not cheat or aggrieve anyone. The representatives from Oviedo, Palencia, Astorga, Calahorra, and Mondoñedo joined their *requirimiento*. Representatives from Salamanca, Segovia, Plasencia, and Cádiz then contradicted the two *requirimientos* and any further proposals to change the apportionment. The rest of the representatives joined them, except for Coria's, who abstained.[53]

---

[50] Ibid., January 2 and 8, 1534.
[51] Ibid., January 9, 1534.
[52] Ibid., January 12, 1534.
[53] Ibid., January 12, 1534.

The majority opposed reapportioning the subsidy, but these *requiri-mientos* indicated that a minority felt strongly about the issue. Their petitions underscore why Santiago had prohibited its representatives from joining the Assembly and highlight the tension between chapters over the apportionment. Even though the overall burden was not oner-ous, individual dioceses clearly felt so burdened by the apportionment that leaving the Assembly and creating disunion seemed for some the only way to obtain fiscal relief. Here we see clearly the divergence between the universal interest of the clergy to maintain ecclesiastical liberty and the interests of individual dioceses to alleviate their burden in the apportionment. Local interests could threaten the unity that was necessary to maintain ecclesiastical liberty and, consequently, the Assembly's ability to speak effectively for the church on ecclesiastical contributions.

Around January 12, Charles wrote to the Assembly, expressing his astonishment that men of such prudence would propose to dissolve the Assembly without license, especially after he had shown such goodwill in the negotiations. He ordered the representatives not to leave Alcalá. He would be there soon, and he hoped that they could then conclude the negotiations. If they disobeyed him, Charles threatened to deprive the representatives of their rents and to declare them foreigners.[54] At the same time, he sent the bishop of Zamora a decree to detain them if necessary. In the meantime, he advised the bishop to refrain from discussing the relief of Santiago and Mondoñedo, fearing that the Assembly would use the reapportionment as pretext to make further demands.[55] The king clearly wanted to avoid contentious issues; he probably did not realize the serious problems within the Assembly itself over this issue. Charles informed Tavera that he approved of sending another prelate to speak with the Assembly, but opposed asking the representatives to write their chapters for authorization to grant 471,000 florins. Doing so, he felt, would only lead to further delays, since the authorizations would not come before he arrived in Alcalá.[56] By mid-January, Charles recognized the precarious situation that the negotiations had reached. Yet, he also hoped that his presence and the arrival of another ecclesiastical official might help to break the impasse.

---

[54] AGS, E leg. 26, ff. 300–301.
[55] Ibid., ff. 299–300.
[56] Ibid., f. 297.

In the meantime, the bishop of Zamora and the representatives continued to discuss the offer.[57] Finally, on January 17, the prelates informed the representatives that the king should be in Alcalá within a week and asked them to wait for his arrival. The representatives complained that further delays hurt the churches, but since the wait was so short, and possibly in consideration of Charles's threats, they agreed to wait for him.[58] The king himself wrote the bishop on January 21 from Calatayud that he had been informed of the Assembly's willingness to wait and that he anticipated arriving within eight days.[59]

Prior to Charles's arrival in Alcalá, García de Padilla, the commander mayor of Calatrava, informed the king that after speaking with several members of the Assembly, he thought that the prospects of an agreement were good, but not certain, given the diverse opinions within the Assembly.[60] The challenge for the royal negotiators was to propose terms that could pass muster with the majority of the representatives. Negotiations for the subsidy, therefore, were not simply between the crown and the Assembly. Differences of opinion within the Assembly could potentially derail the negotiations. Royal officials entered the second round of negotiations with some hope of winding them up, but also a sense of the difficulties still ahead.

Second Round of Negotiations, February–March 1534

On February 1, the representatives met the king as he entered the city, and the next day they discussed the subsidy with him.[61] At the meeting, the Assembly acknowledged the king's just need in his war against the Turks. However, it told him that it had convened not only to provide him with aid but also to preserve the privileges and liberty of the church. The representatives humbly asked the king to accept their offer so that they could return to their churches and pray for him. They also complained that the delays in the negotiations due to consultations between the king and his ministers had harmed the church by increasing the Assembly's cost. Charles retorted that he had received

---

[57] ACS, Sec. VII, lib. 85, "Congregación del clero…1533," January 16, 1534.
[58] Ibid., January 17, 1534.
[59] AGS, E leg. 29, f. 17.
[60] Ibid., f. 168.
[61] ACS, Sec. VII, lib. 85, "Congregación del clero…1533," January 29 and February 1, 1534.

the graver harms from the delays by incurring unnecessary interest charges on loans and lost opportunities because their aid had not arrived. Nonetheless, Charles wanted to reach an agreement with the Assembly. He then dismissed the representatives, telling them he wanted their answer the next day.[62]

Shortly thereafter, Francisco de Mendoza, Juan de Vozmediano, and Juan de Enciso entered the Assembly. They presented a letter from the king outlining his expectations. Charles wrote that he would accept 471,000 florins in two years. He agreed to inform the pope that he approved of the Assembly's request for the inclusion of the exempt clergy in the current subsidy. If the pope did not agree to this, the king would ask him to clarify whether the exemption for benefices worth less than 12 ducados applied only to an individual with a single benefice or to all holders of such benefices (individuals or institutions) regardless of other income. The Assembly replied that its original offer was not made lightly and that it had offered that high amount originally to avoid delays. The representatives did, however, make one concession, offering to pay 150,000 florins in each of the first two years and 50,000 florins in each of the next two years instead of 100,000 florins per year. The Assembly also emphasized that all its requests, including a guarantee of ecclesiastical liberty, had been requested and conceded in the past.[63] Both sides had given some ground.

Nevertheless, the king was not pleased with the Assembly's response. On February 3, he ordered the Assembly to vote yes or no on a subsidy of 471,000 florins in the presence of the bishop of Zamora and García de Padilla, the commander mayor of Calatrava. A short time later, the bishop and Padilla entered the Assembly, saying they had come to discuss the king's will. Pedro de la Peña, a representative of Toledo and president of the Assembly, countered that to vote in their presence would go against ecclesiastical liberty and the custom of the Assembly. On behalf of the Assembly, he asked them to leave. Padilla rejoined that kings customarily entered the chapters during the election of bishops and other crucial votes, implying that the situations were analogous. He warned the representatives not to cross the king and asked them to reach an agreement to avoid the inconvenience and harm that would result from a forcible collection. Before leaving the room, the ministers

---

[62] Ibid., February 2 and 3, 1534.
[63] Ibid., February 2 and 3, 1534.

stressed that the king expected a resolution to the negotiations that day and threatened to punish the representatives.[64]

After discussing the size of their offer, the representatives informed the royal ministers that, despite their desire to serve the king, they were not authorized to offer more than 400,000 florins, so they asked for time to consult with the chapters. The royal ministers curtly repeated that the king wanted the negotiations concluded that day, and they would wait for a response in the vestibule of the church until night. They also ordered the Assembly not to discuss any other issue. The representatives soon sent deputies to ask the ministers to confirm the guarantee of ecclesiastical liberty and the inclusion of exempt clergy in the contribution. The bishop reminded the deputies that the king had already agreed to address the guarantee, so they should not discuss it. In regard to the inclusion, the bishop replied that the military orders of Santiago and San Juan were to be exempt. After the deputies protested that those orders had contributed in the past, the bishop agreed to consult with his colleagues. He later told the deputies that the king only wanted those who had contributed in 1530 included in the present subsidy, and that the military orders of Santiago and San Juan were not to be included. The bishop and commander mayor added that the Assembly should be content with the king's generosity and not demand more. The representatives then asked for a lunch break, but the ministers replied that they could not leave until they had accepted the king's terms.[65]

The Assembly voted to offer the king 471,000 florins as long as the military orders of Santiago and San Juan were included in the subsidy. Otherwise, they would only offer 440,000 florins. They also requested that the king reimburse them for their costs, and they promised to pay as much as possible in the first years. The royal officials were not pleased. They were especially appalled that the Assembly should ask for reimbursement of costs, saying that the king, not they, should be asking for costs and damages. At that point, they demanded that the representatives publicly vote yes or no on the subsidy or face the loss of their property and naturalization. Pedro de la Peña asked to see the king's order for the representatives to vote publicly or be punished. He then gave an impromptu speech on the need to vote one's conscience,

---

[64] Ibid., February 3, 1534; AGS E leg. 12, ff. 169–170.
[65] ACS, Sec. VII, lib. 85, "Congregación del clero … 1533," February 3, 1534; AGS E leg. 12, ff. 169–170.

saying he would still vote his conscience even if threatened with losing his head. He implored the ministers to leave so that the Assembly could freely discuss serving the king. Diego López de Ayala then added that the Assembly could not vote in the presence of non-members and the representatives had sworn an oath to keep its proceedings secret. Padilla angrily replied that the king had absolved them of their oath, because with the king there could not be oaths or secrets. His reproach did not intimidate the Assembly; the rest of the representatives affirmed the remarks of Toledo's representatives. García de Padilla then began to make a statement, but before he could finish the first sentence, the representatives shouted him down, saying that the Castilian clergy had served the king more loyally than any other with their money, persons, and prayers, and they rebuked Padilla for using harsh words with them. Padilla then asked the representatives to confirm in an affidavit their contradictory response to the king's orders; if they agreed to do so, he and the bishop would not execute the punishments that the representatives had brought upon themselves. Padilla and the bishop began to leave, while the representatives swore that they had not contradicted the king's order and asked to place their case before the king. After discussing the ministers' harsh words, the representatives decided to ask the ministers, who were still in the vestibule, if the king had any other message for them. If not, they requested permission to leave, since it was six o'clock and they had not eaten anything all day. The ministers replied that they had nothing further to say and that the representatives could do as they pleased, so they left for dinner.[66] The crown's effort to force the clergy's hand failed, so it broke off official negotiations, but it did not forsake discussions completely.

On February 4, Alonso Manrique de Lara, the cardinal archbishop of Seville, met with the Assembly. He recommended that the Assembly agree to pay 471,000 florins, because failing to reach an agreement with the king would be more harmful to the ecclesiastical estate than paying an additional 30,000 florins. Pedro de la Peña thanked the cardinal archbishop for coming and promised him that the Assembly would consider his remarks. After much deliberation, the majority of the representatives voted to grant the king 471,000 florins in accordance with the agreement of 1530 as long as the exempt clergy were included. They also inserted clauses for payment over four years with most of

---

[66] ACS, Sec. VII, lib. 85, "Congregación del clero…1533," February 3, 1534.

the money paid in the first two years, for the costs of the chapters (presumably for the Assembly and the collection) to be deducted from the subsidy, and for the king to address their grievances. The secretaries invited the cardinal archbishop of Seville and the bishop of Zamora to hear their response. The cardinal said that he would come shortly, but the bishop of Zamora decline the invitation, saying that the king had ordered him not to negotiate with the Assembly. Moreover, he claimed, coming without Padilla would be discourteous. His reference to Padilla seemed to leave some wiggle room, so the secretaries went to speak with Padilla. Their conversation quickly turned to the previous day's harsh words, and Padilla sent the secretaries away, saying that he had orders not to meet with the Assembly.[67]

Later that day, the cardinal archbishop entered the Assembly. The bishop of Zamora and Padilla, however, came as far as the vestibule. Even though they could no longer negotiate with the Assembly, therefore, they still participated indirectly. This type of participation indicates that the crown desired to reach an accord and avoid a forcible collection. The Assembly informed the cardinal archbishop that it was willing to serve the king with 471,000 florins over four years and stated its terms. The cardinal was pleased with the offer but unable to comment on the terms, so he briefly left to discuss matters with the ministers. He later informed the representatives that the king would not accept payment over more than two years.[68] As an intermediator between the crown and the Assembly, the cardinal archbishop of Seville successfully put the negotiations back on track, just as the archbishop of Toledo had done in 1530. He informed the king that the representatives were willing to offer 471,000 florins, and the terms of payment, he thought, could also be reached without incident.[69] The cardinal may have been somewhat optimistic, but the chances of reaching an agreement were certainly better on the fourth than the previous day.

On February 5, the same day that the archbishop of Toledo died, Charles told the cardinal of Seville that he was willing to accept the Assembly's offer, but he expected it in the same period of payments as the last subsidy or preferably even shorter. He also told the cardinal that he wanted no more delays, not even a day or two. The cardinal

---

[67] Ibid., February 4, 1534.
[68] Ibid., February 4, 1534.
[69] AGS, E leg. 29, f. 206.

archbishop of Seville, the bishop of Zamora, and the commander mayor of Calatrava discussed the king's letter and how best to proceed with the Assembly, especially regarding the terms of payment.[70]

On February 6, the cardinal archbishop of Seville informed the Assembly's deputies that the king had accepted its offer, but with payment in three years, not four. The king also promised to address all their grievances shortly. A deputy asked about deducting costs from the subsidy, and the cardinal archbishop replied that the king's letter did not mention it. The deputies were troubled by this and asked to confer with the Assembly. The representatives apparently decided to drop the issue of the deduction. After consulting with their colleagues, the deputies only told the cardinal that the representatives did not have authorization to agree to a three-year payment plan, and they asked if the treasury officials, Juan de Vozmediano and Juan de Enciso, could meet with the Assembly to discuss the period of payments. The cardinal conferred with the bishop and commander and agreed that the two could meet with the Assembly. The treasury officials spent the rest of the day hashing out a payment plan with the Assembly. They finally reached a tentative agreement for the payment of 471,000 florins in four years: 200,000 florins in 1534; 200,000 florins in 1535; 51,000 florins in 1536; and 20,000 florins in 1537.[71]

That evening at midnight, Mendoza and Padilla wrote to the king to summarize the day's events. The bishop and commander optimistically thought that if Charles approved this payment plan, they could reach a conclusion the next day. They stressed to the king that the payment plan was similar to one the treasury officials had recommended to him earlier. They emphasized that 20,000 florins in the fourth year was a small amount, and it was more important for the royal service to bring the negotiations to a conclusion than to haggle over 20,000 florins to be paid in the fourth year. They sent the letter posthaste, hoping the king could respond the next day.[72]

On February 7, the Assembly's secretaries prepared letters for the pope and the cardinals. The minutes unfortunately do not state the content of the letters. Possibly, they were preparing their request for the inclusion. Later, the Assembly asked the cardinal that its offer be

---

[70] AGS E leg. 12, f. 177 and leg. 29, ff. 17 and 201.
[71] ACS, Sec. VII, lib. 85, "Congregación del clero...1533," February 6, 1534; AGS, E leg. 29, f. 201.
[72] AGS, E leg. 29, f. 201. For a similar note to the cardinal, see AGS, E. leg. 29, f. 205.

contingent upon a guarantee and a response to its grievances from the king. The Assembly thus made another effort to obtain redress of grievances before supply. The cardinal archbishop replied that he was doing all he could for them, and he warned the representatives that the negotiations would go badly if they tried to force conditions on the king. After hearing the cardinal's response, the representatives decided that they should reach an agreement first. Deputies worked with the ministers until three in the morning on the agreement.[73]

On February 8, royal officials and the deputies spent the entire morning clarifying details in the agreement. Around noon, the deputies returned with certain changes, including a clause for the Assembly to obtain from the pope the reduction of the bull of *medios frutos* to a subsidy. The Assembly protested to royal officials that the king, not the clergy, traditionally asked the pope for the reduction. Later, after the cardinal archbishop again pressed the issue, the representatives voted unanimously not to ask the pope themselves for the reduction of the bull.[74]

The next morning, at nine o'clock, Francisco de Mendoza, García de Padilla, Juan de Vozmediano, and Juan de Enciso entered the Assembly. They told the Assembly that the king would accept its offer of 471,000 florins and its terms, but he wanted the representatives to declare their willingness to pledge him the money. After much discussion, the representatives decided to transfer the Assembly to within two leagues of Toledo to make the pledge in person. That same day, Santiago's representatives finally entered the Assembly, stating that the king had asked them to sign the agreement and that they were willing to do so provided the Assembly reapportion the subsidy so that no one would be burdened by it. Mondoñedo's representative immediately voiced his approval of the request but the Assembly left the issue for later. With that, the representatives prepared to leave Alcalá, ordering the secretaries to transport all the documents and other papers related to the Assembly and paying the doorman, the chaplain, and the acolyte. The representatives then adjourned the Assembly.[75] That evening, the bishop of Zamora wrote to the king, saying that since no more could be done in Alcalá, the ministers would leave as soon as possible.[76]

---

[73] ACS, Sec. VII, lib. 85, "Congregación del clero...1533," February 7, 1534.
[74] Ibid., February 8, 1534.
[75] Ibid., February 9, 1534.
[76] AGS E leg. 29, f. 202.

The representatives reconvened on Saturday, February 14, in the church of Saint Mary in the village of Illescas, two leagues from Toledo. After Mass, the representatives wrote to the king, the cardinals of Seville and Santiago, the commander mayor of Calatrava, and the chapter of Toledo. In their letter to the king, the representatives repeated their offer of 471,000 florins and its terms of payments, but they also requested that the king address certain loose ends, such as the papal reduction of the bull to a subsidy, to conclude the negotiations. They asked the king to reply promptly, because they had spent nearly five month away from their churches at great expense. They also reiterated that the delay was not their fault and that they wanted to serve the king as they had in the past.[77]

The king's response arrived on February 18. He asked the Assembly to send deputies to conclude the negotiations. Similar letters arrived from the cardinals of Seville and Santiago. The Assembly appointed six deputies to go to Toledo, but it only authorized them to listen to the king, not to sign an agreement.[78]

On February 24, the Assembly heard back from its deputies. They had met with the royal ministers but were unable to obtain an audience with the king, who apparently was waiting for a resolution to the negotiations. Cardinal Tavera, however, promised to do whatever was necessary so that the king would obtain the reduction of the bull, but he also stated that the inequitable apportionment was unconscionable and that, in light of the agreement of 1530, the Assembly needed to reapportion the subsidy. The Assembly responded that it was satisfied with the cardinal's remarks concerning the reduction. Nevertheless, the representatives opposed reapportioning the subsidy to relieve Santiago and Mondoñedo because they were not authorized to charge the apportionment and a reapportionment would require more time, creating further costs for the churches and delaying the first payment to the king. Therefore, the Assembly asked the king to approve the current apportionment for the time being.[79]

On February 28, the Assembly received several royal provisions from its deputies as well as notice that the entire Assembly was to come to Toledo. The provisions were: first, the subsidy would be apportioned

[77] Ibid., f. 209.
[78] ACS, Sec. VII, lib. 85, "Congregación del clero...1533," February 14 and 18, 1534; AGS E leg. 26, f. 303.
[79] ACS, Sec. VII, lib. 85, "Congregación del clero...1533," February 24, 1534.

based on the rents for 1533; second, the king would obtain a papal
brief that reduced the *medios frutos* to a subsidy and pay to distribute
the brief; third, the subsidy needed to be reapportioned to relieve the
churches of Santiago and Mondoñedo and other burdened clergy; and
fourth, commissioners would judge appeals within dioceses over the
local apportionment, and if they determined that a person or institution
was aggrieved, then the chapter and the steward of the *mesa capitular*
would be obliged to pay the difference. The Assembly discussed these
provisions and sent letters to both its deputies and to Tavera, saying
that there was not time to change the apportionment, that the provisions were new and would require consultations with the chapters, and
that the representatives wished to return to their churches after many
months' absence and great expenses.[80]

Despite the request to come to Toledo, the Assembly did nothing
until March 3. On that day, its deputies returned from Toledo with
letters exhorting the Assembly to Toledo to conclude the negotiations.
Only then did a majority of the representatives vote to transfer the
Assembly to Toledo and to reconvene in the cathedral on Saturday,
March 7.[81] This may have been strategic foot dragging, but the minutes
do not explain the delay.

When the Assembly met in Toledo on March 7, the representatives
voted on the four provisions. They quickly voted against 1533 as a
base year for apportioning the subsidy and instead asked that each
year's payments be apportioned on that year's rents. They also wanted
a guarantee that the king would pay for the distribution costs of the
papal brief. The most contentious debates involved the third and fourth
provisions. Many representatives claimed not to have authorization to
discuss the apportionment, and Seville proposed that Santiago and
Mondoñedo be apportioned as in the past and then ask the king for
relief. Others, such as Burgos, said that any adjustment needed to
address all the aggrieved dioceses and not just two. The representative
of Oviedo, in turn, stated that since both Santiago and Mondoñedo
had accepted the conversion of the *medios frutos* to a subsidy, they were
bound by the apportionment, and any reapportionment of the subsidy
had to include all the dioceses. If Santiago and Mondoñedo's shares
were reduced without a general reapportionment, he declared that his

[80] Ibid., February 28, 1534.
[81] Ibid., March 3, 1534.

church, which was more aggrieved than both of those, would not be obliged to pay anything. Others concurred, but the majority opposed the third provision and advised the aggrieved churches to use the best remedies available to them to solve their problems. On the fourth provision, the representatives of Toledo voted to recommend removing the obligation for the stewards to pay the difference. The chantre of Seville agreed, but wanted to make sure that the chapters would still make the local apportionment and name the judges. Others voted against it outright as an innovation. The consensus, however, was to seek the removal of the obligation for the steward and to maintain the chapters' right to appoint the judges. Four representatives then brought the replies to the royal ministers.[82]

On Monday, Tavera and the other ministers presented the Assembly's deputies with a written response regarding the four provisions. Regarding provision one, the ministers rejected the Assembly's proposal, saying it went against the tenor of the one-year bull. Regarding provision two, they said that the king would issue a decree for the payment of the distribution costs. Regarding provision three, the ministers were displeased with the Assembly's response, noting that the king had made *merced* to the Assembly and expected it to provide relief to Santiago and Mondoñedo in the apportionment. They urged the Assembly to find an easy way to reapportion the subsidy. Finally, regarding provision four, they agreed to remove the obligation on the steward, but said that the bishop of Zamora as Comisario General de la Cruzada would name the judges. The representatives discussed the ministers' response and agreed to the revised second through fourth provisions, but not to the first. They were concerned that a single base year would lead to lawsuits or other inconveniences in the collection. The Assembly then reported back to the ministers, who were not pleased with the response.[83]

Over the next few days, the ministers and Assembly ironed out some of their differences, and on March 13, the deputies returned with an agreement for the Assembly to sign.[84] The terms of the agreement indicate that both sides made some concessions. First, the representatives granted the king a subsidy of 471,000 florins (each florin equaled 265 maravedís) to be apportioned and collected in accordance with

---

[82] Ibid., March 7, 1534.
[83] Ibid., March 9, 1534.
[84] Ibid., March 12, 1534.

the past agreement. The subsidy would be collected on all pensions and benefices, exempt and non-exempt, except for those of the orders of Santiago and San Juan. Second, the money would be apportioned based on the rents of 1533, and the payments would be made over four years under the following terms: 200,000 florins in 1534 (100,000 on June 15 and another 100,000 on November 30); 200,000 florins in 1535 (100,000 on June 15 and another 100,000 on November 30); 51,000 florins in 1536 (25,500 on June 15 and 25,500 on November 30); and 20,000 florins in 1537 (June 15). The king was not obliged to grant discounts for any amount that went uncollected under these terms. Third, the cathedral chapters would apportion and collect the subsidy at their own expense, except for the costs incurred collecting cardinals' pensions and vacant sees, which would be deducted from the subsidy. Fourth, lawsuits and appeals arising from the local apportionment were to go before the local commissioners in the dioceses, and until a verdict was reached, the chapters would continue to collect the subsidy on the disputed revenue. Fifth, any monies that had been forcibly collected by the crown and still not returned would be applied to the first payment in June. Sixth, for the agreement to be valid, the pope need to confirm it and to grant a brief reducing the *medios frutos* to a subsidy and another brief including in the subsidy those benefices exempted in the original concession of 1532, except for the military orders of Santiago and San Juan. The briefs were to be delivered to the chapter of Toledo within 70 days. Otherwise, the period of payment for the portion of the subsidy assessed to benefices not included in the original bull would be extended until the brief arrived. The document was then signed.[85]

The next day, the representatives apportioned the subsidy among the churches without any changes to the apportionment. Only the representative of Orense protested, arguing that his diocese was aggrieved due to an accounting error and that his church could not afford to pay any more than what it had been apportioned in 1495. The Assembly denied his request, saying that it made the apportionment according to the agreement of 1530 because the amount was the same, and that that apportionment had been based on the *verdadero de valor* of 1523.

---

[85] Ibid., March 13, 1534; AGS, CC leg. 1, "treslado de la asiento que se tomo por p^te de su mag^t con el estado eclesiastico de la corona de Castilla sobre la paga de los dichos medios frutos por el qual se obligaron de pagar cccclxxi V florins."

The Assembly added that if Orense felt aggrieved, it could ask for justice.[86]

The Assembly then apportioned the common costs, which amounted to 1,250 florins, among the chapters. There was some disagreement about the amount and how it was apportioned. For example, the representative of Astroga argued that the amount exceeded the costs of the Assembly and voted against paying it. The majority of the representatives, however, agreed to the amount and its apportionment. The Assembly then sent deputies to the cardinal of Seville to inquire about the guarantee and a response to their grievances.[87]

On Tuesday, March 17, the representatives went to see the king, saying that since they had concluded the negotiations and were only waiting for the dispatch of his decrees and response to their grievances, they would kiss his hands and go.[88] On March 18, Toledo's representatives claimed that an accounting error in the apportionment had aggrieved their church, and they recommended that four or five other chapters work to determine the values of all ecclesiastical rents to relieve all clergy burdened in the subsidy. This may have been a last minute ploy to reapportion the subsidy as the ministers requested. In the end, all the other representatives voted against it and the Assembly dissolved.

The next day, March 19, the king informed the chapter of Toledo that he would seek papal briefs to reduce the *medios frutos* to a subsidy and to include all those who paid in 1530 in the subsidy. Charles also issued a royal decree that confirmed his and the Catholic Kings' earlier guarantees of ecclesiastical liberty.[89] This guarantee was clearly valued by the clergy, as they felt such decrees to convert a *décima* to a subsidy of 100,000 florins helped their negotiating position. That is why the chapters pushed so hard to obtain a guarantee in both 1530 and 1533, and their insistence almost derailed negotiations in both years. Even Granada, which doubted its value at the beginning of the negotiations in fall 1533, still spent 102 maravedís to obtain a transcription of the guarantee the following spring.[90] Yet by the end of the decade, the renewal of the decree was no longer part of the Assembly's negotiating strategy.

---

[86] ACS, Sec. VII, lib. 85, "Congregación del clero…1533," March 14, 1534.
[87] Ibid., March 16, 1534.
[88] Ibid., March 17, 1534.
[89] Ibid., March 19, 1534.
[90] ACG, leg. 458, pieza 7.

Conclusion

These negotiations indicate that the clergy and the crown did not always see eye to eye and that their differences could lead to serious conflicts. Even though the size of the subsidy was the same in 1530 and in 1533, it would be wrong to look at the results and conclude that the negotiations were all just pro forma. It is true that the terms rarely changed and that the clergy did gradually offer more money over time. The five months from October 1533 to March 1534, however, indicate that just to maintain the status quo involved real, hardnosed negotiations and both sides were forced to make concessions. For example, the clergy had to drop their demand for a redress of grievances before supply and the crown had to grant the guarantee and allow the Assembly to seek the inclusion of exempt clergy. For an agreement to be reached, both sides had to compromise. Neither side could really claim complete victory.

Yet, historians influenced by state-building theory and concepts of absolutism often try to find a victor in such negotiations for financial subsidies. They argue that the crown's success extracting a larger contribution or obtaining better terms from a corporate body shows the growing power of the state and central authority. On the other hand, if the corporate body limited the size of the contribution or obtained better terms for its payment, scholars claim that the monarch was not strong enough to impose his will and thus was forced to rule through autonomous, intermediate bodies. These concepts, however, often obscure the compromises at the center of political practice and the political realities of sixteenth-century Castile. They also create assumptions that kings and representative institutions were adversaries and reduce negotiations to a zero-sum game between the crown and parliamentary bodies. Instead, we should view these negotiations as a partnership between political elites, marked often by conflict as well as collaboration. Only that way can we start to unravel the elite interactions that are central to understanding how the political kingdom acted and how the elites sustained their privileges through negotiations.[91]

---

[91] J.B. Owens, *"By My Absolute Royal Authority": Justice and the Castilian Commonwealth at the Beginning of the First Global Age* (Rochester, NY: University of Rochester Press, 2005), pp. 237–238.

CHAPTER FIVE

VERIFICATION AND REDISTRIBUTION
OF THE SUBSIDY, 1540–1542

Since the economic vitality of the dioceses changed over time, the Assembly made periodic adjustments in the apportionment of the subsidy, though the frequency of reassessments cannot accurately be gauged.[1] Tarsício de Azcona notes, for example, that in 1523 the Assembly adjusted the payments to the *verdadero de los beneficios* (the true values of the benefices); this was the first allusion to what much later would be known as the *veros valores*, or "true values," of the ecclesiastical rents. In 1532, in an attempt to alleviate the financial burdens of Santiago and Mondoñedo, the Comisario General de la Cruzada unsuccessfully asked the chapters of Toledo and Seville to provide him with the values of the Castilian dioceses' ecclesiastical rents. In 1541, the Castilian clergy reached an agreement for the verification of the values and a more equitable apportionment of the subsidy. Nevertheless, the Assembly of 1546 again addressed the issue and prepared new instructions for verification. Later, in 1555, the chapters strongly opposed the Comisario General's attempt to carry out a new verification. The Assembly of 1566 finally made a new assessment that lasted for fifty years. Yet, by the 1590s, the Comisario General once again called for a new assessment, and the chapters again resisted, complaining about the time, costs, and difficulties of verifying the *veros valores*. The next reassessment did not occur until 1616, when the Assembly again verified the values to reapportion the subsidy and decided to let it stand for another fifty years. The Assemblies of both 1566 and 1616

---

[1] Juan Carretero Zamora refers to similar adjustments of the *servicio* among the cities during Charles V's reign. See "Los servicios de las Cortes de Castilla en el reinado de Carlos I (1519–1554): Volumen, Evolución, Distribución" in *Las Cortes de Castilla y León. 1188–1988* (Valladolid, 1990) and "Fiscalidad y presion fiscal en La Mancha durante el reinado de Carlos I (1519–1554): El servicio ordinario y extraordinario," *Cuadernos de Estudios Manchegos* 21 (1991), pp. 29–90. Richard Bonney notes a general resistance to tax assessments throughout Europe and an unwillingness of states to investigate. See "Revenues," in *Economic Systems and State Finance*, ed. Richard Bonney (Oxford: Clarendon Press, 1995), p. 434.

used the verification procedures of 1541.[2] The process of making these adjustments was often marked by contention and suspicion. In 1540, for instance, to correct the inequities in the subsidy apportionment, which would allow for a speedier collection and prevent excessive discounts, the crown wanted the *veros valores* of church rents verified. The chapters, on the other hand, were wary of the crown's interest in verification, fearing that royal involvement would undermine their position vis-à-vis the crown. Moreover, many chapters were reluctant to use complicated and time-consuming procedures to verify the rents of each diocese.

This chapter examines the issues and conflicts surrounding the verification of the *veros valores* and the redistribution of the church subsidy in Castile between 1540 and 1542. It begins with a review of the agreement of 1540 on verifying the *veros valores* and the reasons for its failure. It then focuses on the subsequent Castilian Assembly of the Clergy of 1541 and details the torturous negotiations on the proper procedures of verification and a more equitable apportioning of the subsidy. These contentious negotiations over verification procedures reveal significant divisions within the Assembly and illuminate the complex interactions and power relations between church and state in a critical area of royal finance.

The Agreement of 1540

Although the war with France had ended in 1539, conflict still raged in the Mediterranean against the Ottoman Turks and their piratical allies in Algiers. Charles V also had to depart Spain in late 1539 to quell a tax revolt in Ghent. The crown's financial needs, therefore, persisted throughout and after 1539. Charles left twelve-year old Prince Philip as regent, but Cardinal Juan Tavera, archbishop of Toledo, exercised real power in Charles's absence as lieutenant general of the kingdom. In 1539, Pope Paul III (1534–1549) conceded a new ecclesiastical con-

---

[2] See Tarsício de Azcona, "Reforma del episcopado y del clero de España en tiempo de los Reyes Catolicos y de Carlos V (1475–1558)" in *La Iglesia en la España de los siglos XV y XVI* vol. III/part 1 of *Historia de la Iglesia en España*, ed. Ricardo García Villoslado (Madrid: Biblioteca de Autores Cristianos, 1980), p. 202; ACT, Documentos Secretaria Cabildo, Caja 1, July 6, 1532 and February 2, 1556; BN, Ms. 10435, ff. 12v–13v; Ángel Iturrioz Magaña, *Estudio del subsidio y excusado (1561–1808): Contribuciones económicas de la Diócesis de Calahorra y La Calzada a la Real Hacienda* (Logroño: Instituto de estudios riojanos, 1987), pp. 61–63.

tribution, *dos quartas*, to aid in the war against the Turks. In October 1539, Cardinal García de Loaysa, the Comisario General de la Cruzada and archbishop of Seville, notified the Castilian chapters of the conces-sion.[3] The chapters apparently protested the concession, and the crown responded by embargoing the rents in each diocese. If the crown wanted to pressure the clergy to negotiate, its coercive measure succeeded. In January 1540, the chapters convened an Assembly in Madrid to negoti-ate the payment of a subsidy and to work out its apportionment. About half the chapters actually sent representatives.[4]

Many of the chapters expected Charles to lift the embargo after the Assembly had convened, as he had done in 1533, and thus had instructed their representatives not to discuss a subsidy agreement until the embargo was lifted. Charles, however, refused to lift the embargo until after he reached an agreement with the Assembly. Since both sides refused to budge, Loaysa feared that the representatives might leave without accomplishing anything. Fortunately for him, the representa-tives' resolve broke down after fifty days, and they began to negotiate the size of the subsidy. The negotiations, however, did not go smoothly and were not confined to the corridors of power. The representatives soon began to court public opinion, going door to door in Madrid to make their case for a small subsidy. The crown responded by sending a circular letter throughout the kingdom to justify why the clergy should pay a subsidy.[5]

---

[3] AGS, CJH leg. 13, f. 163. The church was to provide the crown with a quarter of its rents in both 1539 and 1540. Assemblies of the Clergy met in Navarre, Granada, the Canaries, and the Crown of Aragon.

[4] AGS, CC leg. 2, "...de la yglia de avila...q le cupo a pagar de susidio en los anos de dxl xli xlii." The churches present were: Toledo (it also represented Badajoz), Santiago, Salamanca, Osma, Sigüenza, Coria, Cuenca, Zamora, Ciudad Rodrigo, Plasencia, Cartagena, Palencia, Ávila, and Orense. The churches that negotiated sepa-rate agreements were Seville, Córdoba, Jaén, León, Oviedo, Astorga, Lugo, Cádiz, and the military orders of Calatrava and Alcántara. The Assembly negotiated an agreement for Toledo, Burgos, Santiago, Palencia, Zamora, Salamanca, Cuenca, Sigüenza, Osma, Calahorra, Cartagena, Plasencia, Badajoz, Ciudad Rodrigo, Orense, Tuy, Mondoñedo, Segovia, Ávila, and the abbeys of Agreda and Alfaro. The Assembly also argued that Astorga should be included in its division. Although many chapters were not represented at the Assembly, this did not mean that they were unrepresented at court. Representa-tives of Seville, for example, were at the court and interacted with the Assembly. Since the chapter of Seville reached a separate agreement, its representative never formally presented powers to the Assembly. See ACS, Sec. I, lib. 17, ff. 4, 18v, 25rv.

[5] Kristen Kuebler, "Cardinal García de Loaisa y Mendoza: Servant of Church and Emperor," (Ph.D. diss., Oxford University, 1997), pp. 163–165; ACS, Sec. I, lib. 11, f. 18v.

Finally, in place of the *dos quartas*, the representatives offered what was from the crown's perspective a minuscule amount. The royal ministers nonetheless decided to accept 500,000 ducados from all the Spanish kingdoms instead of the *dos quartas*. In April, the Assembly committed Castile to pay 418,000 ducados, even though the embargo had not been lifted. From that amount, the Assembly distributed 286,000 ducados among 20 dioceses and the abbeys of Agreda and Alfaro. The other chapters and military orders had made separate agreements with the crown to pay the remaining 132,000 ducados. The kingdoms of Aragon, Navarre, Granada, and the Canaries were responsible for the remaining 82,000 ducados. Even though the Castilian Assembly had offered its largest subsidy to date, the king rejected the offer, writing from Flanders that he would accept nothing less than 600,000 ducados from all the Spanish kingdoms, and he expected Castile to carry 540,000 ducados. The representatives were outraged and returned to their chapters in June, telling the king that he would have to take the *quarta* by force because they would not give it freely.

The Comisario General then sent orders to royal officials in all the cities authorizing them to collect the *quarta*. If the local chapter accepted the *quarta* within nine days of receiving notification of the Comisario General's orders, the chapter would make the local apportionment and collection as normal. The chapters apparently responded by saying public prayers to St. Thomas, the lawyer of the Church. Moreover, none of their tenants cooperated with the royal officials. The sequestration consequently was a failure. In September, the king finally agreed to a subsidy of 500,000 ducados from all the Spanish kingdoms.[6]

In addition to hammering out the apportionment of the subsidy in April 1540, the Assembly also outlined the procedures for verifying each diocese's *veros valores*. Although its decision concerning the apportionment of the subsidy only applied to those chapters represented at the Assembly, the Assembly's resolution that the *veros valores* be verified involved all chapters and their dioceses. The Assembly consequently decided to use the procedures set down at the previous Assembly that

---

[6] See B.N. ms. 9936, ff. 63v–66v; AGS, E leg. 48, f. 214, E leg. 49, ff. 93, 292, E leg. 50, ff. 85, 194, 260; and AGS, CC leg. 2, "...de la yglia de avila...q le cupo a pagar de susidio en los anos de dxl xli xlii." Modesto Ulloa has incorrectly suggested that the Assembly only offered 286,000 ducados in 1540. In fact, it offered 418,000 ducados but only apportioned 286,000 ducados. See Modesto Ulloa, *La hacienda real de Castilla en el reinado de Felipe II*. 3rd ed. rev. (Madrid: Fundación Universitaria Española Seminario "Cisneros," 1986), p. 600.

representatives of all the chapters had attended. Before proceeding with the actual verification, however, the chapters at the Assembly wanted a papal brief to grant their elected deputies, either canons or other clergy, the necessary jurisdiction, including the invocation of secular authority, to carry out the verification.[7] The Assembly charged the chapters of León, Ávila, and Palencia with acquiring the papal brief. Once the brief arrived, the values of all churches, monasteries, pious places, and mendicant and military orders would be verified for a five-year period from 1535 to 1539. To ensure a true and honest verification, deputies from one diocese were to verify the values of another. Toledo, for example, was supposed to verify the values of Santiago, Mondoñedo, and Lugo, while Burgos would verify Toledo's values. All the chapters were supposed to elect their deputies and send them to the designated diocese by May 1, 1541.[8] The Assembly thus allowed for a year's time between the agreement of April 1540 and the actual verification. Although some chapters resisted the agreement, the representatives thought that a year was probably sufficient to acquire the papal brief and possibly convince the unwilling chapters. The verification was to be completed by the end of February 1542. Should the chapters fail to comply with the settlement, the agreement authorized the Comisario General to proceed against the reluctant chapters and force them to carry out the verification.[9] With the *veros valores* in hand, the chapters would convene an Assembly and reapportion the subsidy. For the verification to guarantee an equitable reapportionment of the subsidy, all the chapters had to participate.

---

[7] Some ecclesiastical rents were in the possession of laymen or lay within seigniorial jurisdiction. Since the canons could not proceed against either laymen or within seigniorial jurisdiction, they sought the aid of the royal administration to carry out verification when confronted by recalcitrant laymen or lords.

[8] AGS, CC leg. 2, "...de la yglia de avila...q le cupo a pagar de susidio en los anos de dxl xli xlii." Seville verified Burgos; Ávila verified Seville and Cádiz; Jaén verified Ávila; Segovia verified Jaén; Cartagena verified Segovia; Osma verified Cartagena; Badajoz verified Osma; Astorga verified Badajoz; Orense verified Astorga; Tuy verified Ciudad Rodrigo; Zamora verified Tuy and Orense; Oviedo verified Zamora; Ciudad Rodrigo verified Oviedo; Plasencia with Ávila was to verify Seville and Cádiz; Córdoba verified Plasencia; Palencia verified Córdoba; Cuenca verified Palencia; Calahorra y La Calzada verified Cuenca; Salamanca verified Calahorra y La Calzada; León verified Salamanca; Sigüenza verified León; Santiago verified Sigüenza; Mondoñedo and Lugo verified the abbeys of Agreda and Alfaro (if they did not want to do so, they would verify Calahorra y La Calzada); Cádiz verified Coria.

[9] Ibid. The agreement, however, did not list the authority granted to the Comisario General.

A Failed Start

The first obstacle to verifying the *veros valores* was obtaining the papal brief. In February 1541, the crown expressed concern to the Marquis of Aguilar, the royal ambassador in Rome, about the pope's failure to issue the requested brief. The crown realized that further delays in issuing the brief only prolonged the inequitable apportionment of the subsidy and exacerbated the financial burden of the clergy at all levels.[10] For example, in March, a local sacristan complained to the chapter of Toledo that the current apportionment of the subsidy in the diocese was detrimental to him.[11] Since the individual chapter was responsible for the apportionment on the local level, he evidently hoped that the canons of Toledo would lighten his burden.[12] At the Assembly of 1541, the representative of Santiago suggested another reason why the crown supported the verification process: the crown had continually lost revenue by providing discounts to burdened churches. If the Castilian and the local apportionments were just and equitable, there would be less reason for the churches to ask for discounts. The crown, then, would receive the entire contribution.[13]

Complaints and discontent notwithstanding, in May 1541, without the requisite papal brief, many chapters had not named their deputies to investigate the *veros valores* as the Assembly had agreed. García de Loaysa consequently wrote a letter to all the chapters on May 26, ordering them to begin the verification. In his letter, Loaysa repeated the terms of the agreement of 1540. In order to remove the cause of complaints and ensure that future apportionments of the subsidy be just and equitable, the verification was to be completed by the end of

---

[10] AGS, E leg. 55, ff. 74–75. February 1 and 21, 1541.

[11] ACT, AC lib. 6, f. 212v.

[12] Although such complaints were recurrent, they might have played a more decisive role in 1541 than previously. Already upset with the burdensome national apportionment, many chapters probably became even more dissatisfied with it when they received complaints from the diocesan clergy about the local apportionment. For some chapters, then, this may have been an added incentive to complete the verification promptly and incorporate some of the changes into the current subsidy. Even though our present concern is the verification of the *veros valores*, we must remember that the negotiations for the *veros valores* were taking place within the context of the local apportionment and collection of the subsidy granted in 1540.

[13] ACS, Sec. VII, lib. 86 "Congregación de las Santas Iglesias 1541," Session 31. A copy of these minutes is also deposited in the Archivo Catedralicio de Toledo, see ACT, OF lib. 1344.

February 1542. He informed the chapters that the king wanted the verification carried out, and warned them that if they did not comply with his order, he would enforce the verification in accordance with the agreement and with a special papal commission. The chapters were to send notarized replies to his assistant, Juan Suárez de Carvajal, the bishop of Lugo, in Madrid within nine days of receiving Loaysa's letter. In its reply on June 21, the chapter of Sigüenza asked the Comisario General to wait for the papal brief to arrive, arguing that without this brief, it lacked the necessary authority to verify the values and the investigation would not be thorough. The canons promised Loaysa that they would promptly complete the verification as soon as the brief arrived.[14] Apparently many other chapters responded similarly, because the situation remained the same in early July. The chapters' insistence on waiting for the brief was not simply a delaying tactic; they evidently did not have the legal jurisdiction to carry out interdiocesan verification. Furthermore, they clearly felt that the agreement's provision to send deputies to another diocese by May 1 was negated until the papal brief arrived. Loaysa's attempt to threaten the canons into action consequently failed. Even if the papal brief had arrived on time, however, it is not certain that the verification would have taken place. The lack of consensus among the chapters regarding the agreement of 1540 was a further stumbling block.

Although the chapters clearly rejected his authority to force them to carry out the verification, Loaysa sent them another order on July 8, urging the chapters to name their deputies and send them to the designated dioceses. After reiterating his threat to execute the verification if they did not abide by his order, he reproached the recalcitrant chapters. Loaysa warned that each additional day waiting for the papal brief caused the clergy further harm from the inequitable apportionment. Unless the verification began immediately, they would not be able to remedy the current situation for any of the injured parties. He ordered the chapters to name their deputies within three days of receiving his letter. Within another three days, the deputies were to leave their own dioceses to begin the investigation in the assigned dioceses. They were to verify the values of all episcopal, capitular (i.e., pertaining to the chapter), and monastic rents, as well as the rents of the military and mendicant orders, particular clergy, and ecclesiastical rents in the

---

[14] AGS, CJH leg. 14, f. 147.

possession of lay people. To facilitate the initiation of the investigations, the Comisario General was prepared to delegate the power the pope granted him to the people the chapters designated to carry out the verification. He apparently thought that the authority he delegated would suffice for the clergy to execute a thorough investigation. For noncompliance with his order, Loaysa threatened excommunication.[15] There is no known documentation listing the special powers the pope granted to Loaysa. Salamanca's suspicion, discussed below, might well have been justified.

Loaysa's letter of July elicited a variety of responses from the chapters of Castile, ranging from compliance, to requests for clarification, to outright resistance. The wide array of responses indicates that the chapters were far from united on the appropriate method to verify the *veros valores* and, perhaps, whether they should even do it. A few examples illustrate the range of responses.

The chapter of Badajoz quickly complied with Loaysa's order. The canons received instructions on July 26 to verify the *veros valores* of the diocese of Osma and appointed three people to carry out the verification on July 29. To avoid Loaysa's censures, the chapter paid the expenses of the deputies associated with the verification at Osma. The chapters of Calahorra and Santo Domingo de La Calzada administered the diocese of Calahorra-La Calzada. The chapter of La Calzada immediately sent a canon to Cuenca. Calahorra evidently did not name a deputy as promptly, because the canon wrote to the chapter of La Calzada on August 12 from Madrid that he was still waiting for the canon from Calahorra. Meanwhile, the chapter of Cartagena elected Dr. Pedro de Medina, its treasurer, and the licenciado Francisco de Horozco to verify the values in Segovia. Both men, however, tried to avoid service. Medina said that he was preoccupied, as an inquisitor, with an important case, and he insisted that he was not healthy enough to make the trip to Segovia. Horozco, for his part, claimed that he was ill. Despite their protests, the chapter worried that other canons might contrive similar excuses and so sent them to Segovia.[16] Loaysa's threat evidently motivated some chapters, including those of Badajoz, La Calzada, and Cartagena, to act. The threat, however, was not strong enough to mobilize all the chapters.

---

[15] AGS, CJH leg. 7, f. 69.
[16] Ibid., ff. 70bis, 75, 78, 81, 86.

The chapter of Cuenca claimed that it had only a few canons and most were too old to make an arduous journey. So, in their reply to Loaysa, the canons of Cuenca reiterated their desire to wait for the papal brief, believing it would allow for an easier method than the one the Comisario General currently imposed on them.[17] Other chapters might have found themselves in a similar situation, as even healthy canons hesitated to accept a mission that demanded a long period of time away from home.

Loaysa's letter left the chapter of Salamanca with many questions. First, the letter arrived without the papal commission addressed to Loaysa or a publicly transcribed copy of it. The chapter was uncertain if the cardinal really had the power to delegate authority. To carry out the verification without impediments, the deputies would need a copy of the papal commission addressed to Loaysa. Second, the letter did not indicate who would pay the deputies' salaries and expenses. Would the money come from Salamanca, the chapter of Calahorra (whose rents Salamanca was to verify), or the Assembly of the Clergy? Third, many laymen held ecclesiastic rents in Calahorra. Since the chapter did not have jurisdiction over laymen, it asked the cardinal to send a bailiff with a staff of justice to administer against the laymen. If Loaysa addressed these concerns, the chapter would readily comply with his orders.[18]

Like their colleagues in Salamanca, the canons of Palencia noted the absence of a copy of Loaysa's papal commission. Moreover, the chapter reminded Loaysa that it had sent agents to Rome to obtain the brief, and while there had been problems earlier, their agents had reported on June 15 that the papal brief was forthcoming, and that it would be sent to Castile shortly. The chapter insisted on waiting for the brief. Moreover, something as important as the verification, it explained, required people with experience and authority; three days were insufficient for selecting suitable deputies. Likewise, the time allowed for traveling to distant dioceses was too short. Córdoba was 100 leagues, or approximately 560 kilometers, from Palencia, and the deputies needed time to plan their trip and make arrangements to be absent for several months. The chapter also fretted that those unaccustomed to summer travel might become sick and even die on their journey. Finally, the

---

[17] Ibid., f. 71.
[18] Ibid., f. 74. Zamora had similar concerns, see ibid., f. 76.

chapter stressed to Loaysa that it was not obstructing the verification
process out of self-interest, for it was severely burdened by the current
apportionment.[19]

The chapter of Seville, on the other hand, challenged the cardinal's
order to send representatives to Burgos and questioned his authority
to carry out the investigation himself if the canons did not comply.
The canons' principal point was that since they had neither sent representatives to the Assembly of 1540 nor affirmed the agreement, they
should not be obliged to do what Loaysa ordered. Furthermore, they
contended that the current verification process was impossible, or at
least difficult, to complete in such a short time. Moreover, the procedure
was inconvenient and expensive, and the results would be questionable.
The chapter of Seville indicated, however, that it would comply if there
was a more convenient method for verifying the values.[20]

The chapter of Toledo recognized the various problems with
verification as early as July 4. In response to Loaysa's letter of July
8, it immediately prepared an appeal and wrote a letter to the other
chapters. Two days later, the chapter nominated two canons to meet
with Cardinals Loaysa and Tavera to devise new ways of verifying
the *veros valores*.[21] Many chapters still had not even received Loaysa's
letter or responded to it. The chapter of Toledo probably realized,
however, that notwithstanding Loaysa's threats, the method from 1540
was unworkable. Unlike negotiations with the crown for the payment
of the subsidy, which individual chapters could do separately as had
happened in the 1540 agreement, the verification of the *veros valores*
required all of them to participate, because verification would provide
an equitable apportionment among all the dioceses. If a few dioceses
refused to participate, as was the case in July, the verification would
be impossible. Loaysa himself probably realized that his threats were
not moving enough chapters to act. Moreover, his experience execut-

---

[19] Ibid., f. 89.

[20] Ibid., f. 70. August 1, 1541. Although his failure with the other chapters is partially
understandable, Loaysa's utter failure to convince his own chapter needs explanation.
As mentioned in chapter 1, prior to the Council of Trent, the chapters were exempt
from their bishops' jurisdiction and almost constituted a parallel power in the dioceses.
The canons were also appointed by the popes, kings, and bishops. Thus, the canons
as a whole could not be considered clients of any one particular person. See Lucía
Carpintero Aguado, "La congregación del clero de Castilla en el siglo XVII" (Ph.D.
diss., Universidad Autónoma de Madrid, 1993), p. 16; AGS, E leg. 49, f. 135.

[21] ACT, AC lib. 6, ff. 218, 222v, and 223v–224. July 4, 14, and 16, 1541.

ing the *quarta* the previous July might have made him reluctant to use coercion a second time, especially when, in addition to public prayers to St. Thomas (the lawyer of the Church), the chapters might also initiate lawsuits against the crown. By mid-August, the Comisario General and the chapters had agreed to a new Assembly in September 1541 to revise the procedures for verifying the *veros valores* set down by the agreement of 1540.

The Assembly of 1541

The Assembly convened on September 11, 1541, in Madrid, and this time all the chapters of Castile attended. The Assembly's goal was to reach an acceptable agreement among the chapters on the proper procedures of verification in order to apportion the subsidy equitably. Many chapters worried, however, that a majority in the Assembly might force them to implement an unacceptable agreement. The chapter of Santiago, for example, said that if its representatives did not consent to an agreement that the majority reached, the chapter was not obliged to honor it. For any agreement to be binding, therefore, all the chapters had to accept and agree to it. The Assembly went to work immediately to correct inequities between the dioceses. Its first suggestion called for the solvent dioceses to take upon themselves the amount necessary to relieve the burdened dioceses. To determine if a diocese was burdened, the Assembly consulted past apportionments of the subsidy and other ecclesiastical contributions. Discussions then began on how to relieve the burdened dioceses.[22]

At the same time, the Assembly informed Cardinal Loaysa of its efforts to address the issue of the *veros valores*. Loaysa responded on September 15, saying that he was grieved that the chapters were divided on the issue and exhorting the representatives to place the common good ahead of their own dioceses and chapters' particular interests.[23]

---

[22] ACS, Sec. VII lib. 87, "Congregación…1541," Sessions 1–4 and 7.

[23] Amidst the preparations for a new Assembly in August, Francisco de los Cobos notified Juan Vázquez de Molina that Loaysa had fallen ill. He suggested that the office of Comisario General de la Cruzada be transferred to the bishop of Lugo, who already had experience in these negotiations and would be better able to carry out the work (see AGS, E leg. 51, f. 79, August 24, 1541). Whether Loaysa's sickness adversely affected the negotiations in the fall is unknown. It may explain, however, why he did not travel from Fuensalida to Madrid for the Assembly. His absence meant longer

He suspended the order that he had earlier sent to all the chapters and allowed the Assembly to come up with a better method of investigation. Loaysa warned the representatives, however, that should they fail to do so, he would have to enforce the verification even at the cost of infringing on the chapters' authority and causing further conflict. Loaysa prayed that the Assembly could bridge the difference between the chapters and agree on a suitable method of verification.[24]

On September 17, Juan de Vozmediano, auditor and royal secretary, notified the representatives that the king granted the Assembly authority to redress the injustices of the present apportionment of the subsidy and set down the proper procedures for investigating the *veros valores*. Each church or monastery on the diocesan level should pay only what it could justly afford, and all the chapters had to accept the framework for verifying the *veros valores*. This was the Assembly's mandate, and the crown wanted the issue resolved by the end of September.[25] Both Loaysa and the king supported the Assembly, but they also put pressure on it to act. The king gave the representatives only until the end of September to reach an agreement, and Loaysa made clear that without a resolution, he would grudgingly carry out the verification himself.

After making little headway, the Assembly decided to appoint a committee to hammer out a viable method of verification.[26] On October 10, Pedro Suárez de Guzmán, canon of Toledo and a committee member, presented the Assembly with three options. First, the chapters could verify the values in accordance with the 1540 agreement. Second, each chapter could verify the values within its own diocese. Third, six deputies of the Assembly could traverse the kingdom and appoint clergy in each diocese to carry out the verification. The Assembly immediately discarded the third option as impractical. It then voted on the remaining two choices. Seventeen chapters voted to adopt self-verification, and ten voted to retain the method from 1540.[27] Self-verification would reduce

---

delays in his responses to developments. He also appeared less active in the negotiations as the fall progressed.

[24] ACS, Sec. VII lib. 87, "Congregación...1541," Session 6.

[25] Ibid., Session 6.

[26] Ibid., Sessions 12 and 13.

[27] Ibid., Session 16. The following voted to change the verification method: Toledo, Córdoba, Seville, Zamora, Osma, Segovia, Ciudad Rodrigo, Lugo, Palencia, Sigüenza, Salamanca, Cuenca, Cartagena, Ávila, Coria, Badajoz, and Jaén. In their votes for changing the verification method, Córdoba and Seville spoke against the agreement of 1540 because they had not agreed to it originally. Burgos, León, Santiago, Oviedo,

costs and the inconvenience of sending deputies to a distant diocese for several months, but it could not guarantee accountability.

The next day, the representatives decided to inform the Comisario General of their vote. After a lengthy discussion, they agreed to send four deputies—two in favor of and two against changing the procedure of verification. The deputies were to relay to Loaysa the outcome of the vote and tell him why they favored one position or the other. If he agreed to the new method, the deputies were to ask him to allow a reasonable amount of time for it to be enacted. Since keeping an Assembly in session during the verification would be expensive, they would ask Loaysa for permission to adjourn. When the *veros valores* were verified, the Assembly would reconvene and use the new values to adjust the apportionment of the subsidy among the dioceses.[28]

The representatives in favor of letting each diocese verify its own values found indirect support from Cardinal Tavera. On October 13, the Assembly learned of Tavera's response to the latest vote.[29] The cardinal thought that the best option was to reapportion the subsidy without verifying the *veros valores*; he asserted that verification in accordance with the agreement of 1540 was detrimental to the Spanish ecclesiastical estate. He maintained that royal ignorance of the *veros valores* actually favored the church in its negotiation with the crown. Public verification of ecclesiastical rents could undermine the church's position, presumably because royal knowledge of the *veros valores* would allow the crown to further pressure the ecclesiastical estate during negotiations for the subsidy. Moreover, some prelates did not consent to the method of 1540 and had warned that neither they nor their dioceses would contribute to the costs of the verification. If the bishops refused to let their books be examined, it would probably be impossible to verify the diocesan rents accurately. Furthermore, some bishops indicated that the chapters would have to pay the entire cost of the verification themselves from their own treasuries; many chapters probably thought twice about taking on excessive costs. Tavera argued against any investigation of the *veros*

Plasencia, Mondoñedo, Astorga, Tuy, Orense, and Calahorra y La Calzada voted to retain the method agreed to in 1540.

[28] ACS, Sec. VII, lib. 87, "Congregación...1541," Sessions 17 and 18. There apparently were some changes between the tenth and eleventh. The bishoprics of Tuy and Orense now supported change, while Lugo was now in favor of the method agreed to in 1540.

[29] With the Comisario General and the bishop of Lugo, Tavera represented the crown in the negotiations with the Assembly.

valores as a means of rectifying the injustices of the subsidy apportionment. However, should some form of verification be insisted upon, he
conceded that it would be a lesser evil for the dioceses to verify their
own values.[30] As a royal official, Tavera was probably compelled to
push the Assembly toward a timely conclusion. By arguing persuasively
against the method of 1540, he probably hoped to eliminate one point
of contention. As a prelate, he obviously wanted to avoid any procedures
that could seriously compromise ecclesiastical liberties in the future, as
he undoubtedly thought the method of 1540 would do.

Loaysa also came down in support of self-verification. He was apparently not overly concerned with the procedure's lack of accountability
but was more concerned about staving off disgruntled clergy's complaints to the crown. In a long letter to the Assembly on October 14,
he urged the representatives to overlook minor injustices and handle
the local subsidy apportionment with care. Loaysa gave the representatives twelve days to iron out their differences. Should it fail to break the
impasse, the Assembly would have to impose self-verification and devise
a suitable method for each chapter to investigate its own diocese's *veros
valores*. Only then would Loaysa grant the representatives permission
to return to their churches.[31] Even though the Assembly had aimed
to reach a unanimous decision on the verification procedures, Loaysa
flatly told them to follow the majority decision if a unanimous decision
proved impossible.

In compliance with Loaysa's order, the representatives formed a new
committee on October 17 to hammer out a solution. On October 20,
the committee presented two options. The first option was, again, self-
verification; as the majority of the Assembly had agreed, each diocese

---

[30] ACS, Sec. VII, lib. 87, "Congregación…1541," Session 19. Some representatives, however, might not have been convinced by Tavera's argument. In its reply to
the Comisario General on August 1, for example, the chapter of Seville suggested that
the method of 1540 might not be so exact as to undermine the Assembly's negotiating
position vis-à-vis the crown in the way Tavera suggested.

[31] Ibid., Session 22. On October 19, unaware of the recent developments in Madrid,
the chapter of Seville wrote its representatives not to leave the court for Burgos or any
other place, except to consult with Loaysa, the archbishop of Seville. Its representatives
were ordered to pursue an agreement that would not harm the chapter's conscience
or treasury. At the same time, the chapter of Seville agreed to send a representative to
another diocese, if it would not cost too much to do so. First, however, the chapter had
to be contacted. Successful implementation of the method of 1540 would require the
participation of all the chapters, and Seville clearly was not a proponent of the method
of 1540. Consequently, even if the method of 1540 had won wide support within the
Assembly, it might still have been difficult to execute. ACS, Sec. I, lib. 17, f. 103.

would verify its own *veros valores*. The second option called for the creation of a new commission with fair representation from the burdened and the solvent chapters. The commission would hear declarations of diocesan values from each chapter and adjust the subsidy apportionment accordingly. Once the commission's decision was finalized, all the chapters would have twenty days to respond.[32]

The Assembly voted for self-verification and prepared a fourteen-point instruction list for the dioceses to investigate their own *veros valores*.[33] The representatives of Santiago, however, immediately opposed the plan; they argued that the instructions were an innovation and that, until the king approved them, there was no guarantee that the dioceses would complete the investigation. Astorga, Mondoñedo, and Calahorra y La Calzada concurred with Santiago.[34] In essence, royal approval implied that the king or Comisario General, or both, would delegate to the chapters authority in certain spheres outside of their normal jurisdiction (point 14). Investigating the military orders' rents (point 10), for

---

[32] ACS, Sec. VII, lib. 87 "Congregación... 1541," Session 23 and 24.

[33] Ibid., Session 25. The following fourteen-point instructions were drafted. 1) Each chapter would name canons of good standing to verify all the ecclesiastical rents in the diocese, except for the royal *tercias*, which would be valued separately. 2) Each chapter would swear an oath to elect officials to carry out the verification according to the instructions. 3) For the investigation of the tithes, the investigators would assess the monetary value of the rent conforming to the common estimation of its cash value. In those dioceses where some of the tithe was leased, the investigators would use the diocese's method for determining the value of the leased rent for verification purposes. 4) For the rents outside of the tithes, they would follow the same procedures used with the tithes. 5) For farms and other landed property of monasteries and ecclesiastical houses, the investigators would estimate the property value as if the property was leased. 6) The investigation would be limited to three years between 1535 and 1537. 7) The ecclesiastical rents, except for those used to pay diocesan priests, would meet all the costs incurred. 8) The chapters had until the end of April 1542 to carry out verification. Representatives were then to meet in Toledo to make an equitable apportionment of the subsidy. 9) The rents of the hospitals were to be verified according to the instructions. The chapters, however, were to keep the hospitals' rents separate from the other diocesan rents. 10) The chapters were to verify the rents, presumably tithes, of the military orders of Calatrava and Alcántara in their diocese. The military orders were to verify other rents and report them to the Comisario General. 11) All the chapters must use the method outlined above, otherwise the values would not be admitted at the pending meeting in Toledo. 12) Within a month of the arrival of their representatives, the chapters were to send the Comisario General their approval of the instructions. If they did not comply, the Comisario General would make the investigation at the cost of the chapter and diocese in the period indicated by the Assembly. 13) The investigators must swear to abide by the points given above. 14) The Assembly would ask the Comisario General and the crown to grant the investigators the necessary power to carry out the verification effectively.

[34] Ibid.

example, was probably outside the chapters' reach. As head of the military orders, however, the king could possibly authorize the chapters to investigate the military orders' rents without jurisdictional conflicts. Since there was no reference to obtaining a papal brief, self-verification apparently did not cross any ecclesiastical jurisdictions that necessitated papal authorization. Representatives from Tuy and Orense also challenged the instructions, arguing that the three-year time period from 1535 to 1537 would be prejudicial to their dioceses.[35] These protests temporarily blocked the self-verification option.

The debate on the proper procedure continued. The Assembly elected a committee of 12 deputies, composed of an equal number of representatives from the burdened and solvent dioceses, to devise a just and reasonable procedure for verifying the *veros valores.*[36]

Despite the committee's efforts, a resolution continued to elude the Assembly. The twelve deputies reported to the Assembly on October 24 that they could not reach an agreement. Consequently, the committee suggested proceeding with verification, presumably self-verification, as Loaysa had ordered ten days earlier. At that point, several chapters protested and called for interdiocesan verification, as the agreement of 1540 stipulated. The representative from Segovia also demanded that any decision on verification be unanimous. The differences between the majority and the minority over self-verification versus interdiocesan verification finally led the Assembly to consult with the archbishop of Toledo and the royal ministers, as well as with the Comisario General.[37]

The thorny issue of verification seemed to defy any clear and timely solution. Unable to break the impasse, the Assembly turned to adjusting the subsidy apportionment on the general level without first verifying the local rents. On October 27, the representatives discussed a proposal to use arbitration. The suggestion was simple: the Assembly would divide the dioceses into two groups, and each group of fourteen dioceses would name three or four arbiters to rectify the current apportionment. The arbiters would then impose their decisions on all the dioceses. The proposal for arbitration, however, did not go unchallenged, and other

---

[35] Ibid., Session 26. Tuy and Orense possibly opposed the three-year time period because 1535 to 1537 were actually prosperous years for their dioceses. If so, they would not receive sizable discounts using these years for verification purposes.

[36] Ibid. The twelve churches selected were: Toledo, Seville, Zamora, Salamanca, Jaén, Cartagena, Santiago, León, Oviedo, Burgos, Orense, Palencia.

[37] Ibid., Session 27 and Session 28.

representatives proposed alternative forms of arbitration. Before the Assembly could reach a decision, however, the royal auditor Juan de Vozmediano arrived with an ultimatum from the archbishop of Toledo and the Comisario General.[38]

The archbishop of Toledo and the Comisario General ordered the Assembly to produce a plan to relieve the burdened churches the next day, October 28. Should the representatives fail to agree on a feasible arrangement, they were to share the options they had discussed with the bishop of Lugo, who would determine the 'most appropriate' solution. Should the representatives refuse to comply with the ultimatum, they would be dismissed. The Comisario General, then, would enforce the verification in accordance with the agreement of 1540 and his special papal commission. In light of this grim and forbidding prospect, the representatives agreed that each chapter should simply declare the values of its own diocese before a committee of the Assembly. Based on the declared values, the Assembly would reapportion the subsidy accordingly. Claiming that they did not know the values of their respective dioceses, the representatives of Córdoba, Salamanca, Cartagena, Plasencia, and Jaén did not accept this method, but the majority agreed that the Assembly should present it to the bishop of Lugo as the only viable option. Debate raged over the arbitration committee's composition until the representatives finally agreed to a 12-member committee.[39]

On November 2, the committee made a new apportionment of the subsidy.[40] Unfortunately, in the face of opposition, the new apportionment failed to win the Assembly's approval. Some opposition came from unexpected corners. Even though 1,535,297 maravedís had been deducted from their original share in 1540, the representatives from Calahorra y La Calzada opposed the arbitration of November 2. Orense also received a substantial deduction, but its representatives still

---

[38] Ibid., Session 29. The first group comprised Toledo, Seville, Cuenca, Córdoba, Cartagena, Plasencia, Jaén, Santiago, Burgos, León, Mondoñedo, Palencia, Calahorra, and Segovia. The second group consisted of Zamora, Salamanca, Sigüenza, Badajoz, Ciudad Rodrigo, Coria, Cádiz, Oviedo, Astorga, Ávila, Lugo, Osma, Orense, and Tuy.

[39] Ibid., Session 29–30. For a complete copy of the ultimatum, see AGS, CC leg. 2, "memorial que se leyo a la congregación a 27 de octobre de 1541 anos."

[40] Ibid., Session 33. The arbitration committee had to reckon with the full subsidy of 418,000 ducados, which converted to 156,750,000 maravedís (1 ducado = 375 maravedís). See Table VI.

opposed the committee's decision. Some chapters' representatives split their votes. Even though it had to pay over a million maravedís more, one of Plasencia's representatives voted yes while the other voted no. These few examples reveal that a large subtraction did not guarantee the apportionment immediate acceptance and that a large addition did not ensure immediate opposition.

Other issues certainly played a role in the representatives' decisions. The representative of Santiago, for example, complained that the arbiters had calculated the *voto de Santiago*, which should have been excluded from the subsidy, into Santiago's rent for the apportionment.[41] He consequently refused to submit to the committee's decision. Although he opposed the apportionment, García Manrique de Lara, president of the Assembly and canon of Toledo, did not vote against it because the other representative from Toledo, Pedro Suárez de Guzmán, was a member of the arbitration committee and would be able to explain to their chapter why it received a 12 percent increase over the original apportionment. Manrique's position suggests that returning to one's chapter with either a heavy increase or too small a decrease could create problems for a representative. Since their diocese received a minuscule reduction of 803 maravedís, Osma's representative may have voted against the reapportionment for the reason suggested by Manrique. On the other hand, Ávila, Badajoz, and Córdoba voted against the committee's decision over a procedural question; they wanted to verify the *veros valores* before reapportioning the subsidy.[42] There is therefore no easy way to determine why a particular representative would support or oppose the decision made by arbitration.

On November 3, the Assembly informed Tavera of these discouraging developments. Frustrated, the representatives pleaded with Tavera for permission to return to their churches and implored him to sanction self-verification. On November 4, Tavera's response arrived. The archbishop was vexed by the Assembly's ineptitude and continued discord. He considered the Assembly's failure to reach an agreement a disservice to the crown and granted the representatives leave to go home, but prohibited them from further negotiations or actions on the *veros valores*. The crown had given up on the Assembly. It threatened

---

[41] The *voto de Santiago* was an ecclesiastical tax that the Castilian and Galician farmers paid to the archbishopric of Santiago and its benefices. For more details, see Manuel Teruel Gregorio de Tejada, *Vocabulario básico de la historia de la Iglesia* (Barcelona: Crítica, 1993), pp. 456–458.

[42] ACS, Sec. VII, lib. 87 "Congregación...1541," Session 33.

to pursue the matter unilaterally and intimated that laymen might be deployed to verify the *veros valores*. In desperation, the representatives implored Archbishop Tavera and the bishop of Lugo for permission to backtrack and proceed with verification in accordance with the agreement of 1540. Their entreaty was summarily dismissed.[43]

Rebuffed but undeterred, the Assembly decided to remain in session, convinced of the gravity of the situation.[44] It ignored the crown's order to desist from further action on the *veros valores* and recommissioned the board of arbitration to work out an equitable apportionment of the subsidy. On November 5, the board announced a new apportionment that would be valid for the next six years.[45]

The second arbitration brought about an acceptable reapportionment of the 418,000 ducados. Representatives of Mondoñedo, Calahorra y La Calzada, and Jaén, for example, supported the board's decision for the well-being of the ecclesiastical estate, but the representatives of Salamanca would not consent to the new apportionment without first consulting their chapter. The lack of complete consensus notwithstanding, the Assembly adopted the committee's decision and conveyed the new developments to the archbishop of Toledo, the bishop of Lugo, and other royal ministers.[46] After two months of negotiations, the Assembly had succeeded in transferring 8,212,553 maravedís from burdened to solvent dioceses. Overall, the percentage change was minor, at 5 percent. On the local level, however, some significant changes took place. Of the richer dioceses, Toledo's share increased by approximately 12 percent, while Burgos's share fell by approximately 16 percent. Of the poorer dioceses, Cádiz's share rose by approximately 12 percent, while Mondoñedo's share decreased by approximately 29 percent (see Table VI). More importantly, the arbitration continued the slow redistribution of the subsidy burden from north to south. With the exception of Zamora and Salamanca, all the dioceses for which there is data in Galicia and Old Castile experienced decreases, while those in New Castile and Andalusia experienced increases (see Map 3).

---

[43] Ibid., Sessions 36 and 37. Under current circumstances, Tavera's earlier advocacy of self-verification if no agreement was possible had apparently faded. See pp. 153–154 above.

[44] It may have been around this time that propaganda sheets mysteriously appeared on church doors in Madrid, portraying Loaysa as a traitor to the ecclesiastical estate. See Kuebler, "Cardinal García de Loaisa," pp. 167–168.

[45] ACS, Sec. VII, lib. 87 "Congregación…1541," Session 38. See Table VI.

[46] Ibid.

Table VI. The Redistribution of 418,000 ducados
(= 156,750,000 maravedís) in 1541.

Diocese	April 1540	November 2, 1541	November 5, 1541†	Change‡
Toledo	19,468,871□	21,801,340	21,801,340	+2,332,469 (12%)
Seville		15,299,824	15,299,924	
Burgos	13,921,021	11,677,756	11,727,756	−2,193,265 (15.7%)
Palencia	10,283,812	8,933,120	8,974,293	−1,309,519 (12.7%)
Cuenca	5,174,813	6,279,030	6,279,530	+1,104,717 (21.3%)
Calahorra	7,592,426	6,057,129	6,037,129	−1,555,297 (20.5%)
León	6,187,000	5,842,413	5,852,412	−334,588 (5.4%)
Ávila	6,024,339	5,712,500	5,663,077	−361,262 (5.99%)
Córdoba	5,250,000	5,408,487	5,408,487	+158,487 (3.0%)
Segovia	5,399,297	5,150,000	5,150,000	−249,297 (4.6%)
Salamanca	4,688,132	4,907,500	4,907,500	+219,368 (4.7%)
Osma	4,813,303	4,812,500	4,812,500	−803 (0.02%)
Sigüenza	4,386,868	4,687,500	4,687,500	+300,632 (6.8%)
Santiago	4,939,943	4,250,087	4,216,087	−723,856 (14.6%)
Zamora	3,684,637	3,863,680	3,863,680	+179,043 (4.9%)
Plasencia	2,465,634	3,525,000	3,450,000	+984,366 (39.9%)
Jaén		3,037,500	3,013,500	
Badajoz	2,651,763	2,812,500	2,812,500	+160,737 (6.1%)
Oviedo		2,774,990	2,774,990	
Cartagena	1,987,147	2,667,983	2,667,983	+680,836 (34.3%)
Coria	2,069,056	2,662,500	2,662,500	+593,444 (28.7%)
Astorga		2,592,938	2,592,938	
Orense	3,417,633	2,522,687	2,503,937	−913,696 (26.7)
Ciudad Rodrigo	1,247,122	1,237,500	1,237,500	−9,622 (0.77%)
Lugo	1,125,000	1,070,437	1,070,437	−54,563 (4.8%)
Cádiz	937,500	1,000,000	1,050,000	+112,500 (12.0%)
Mondoñedo	1,445,837	1,050,000	1,030,000	−415,837 (28.8%)
Tuy	1,081,946	1,000,000	1,000,000	−81,946 (7.6%)
Abbey of Agreda	356,383	375,000	375,000	+18,617 (5.2%)
Abbey of Alfaro	159,002	150,000	150,000	−9,002 (5.7%)
Order of Calatrava		7,312,500	7,312,500	
Order of Alcántara		6,375,000	6,375,000	
Total°	120,749,485	156,847,401	156,760,000	+6,845,216 and −8,212,553

Sources: AGS, CC leg 2; ACS, Sec. VII, lib.87 "Congregación de las Santas Iglesias, 1541," Sessions 33 and 38.

† Figures given in both Roman numerals and text. There are two discrepancies. In both cases, the text was used in the table. The Roman numerals were: Astorga 2,092,938 and the Order of Calatrava 7,213,500.

‡ The amount of change is determined by subtracting the April 1540 column from the November 5, 1541 column. The percentage of change is calculated by dividing the increase or decrease by the original sum in the April 1540 column.

□ All figures are in maravedís (1 ducado = 375 maravedís).

° In 1540, the unlisted four dioceses and the military orders carried approximately 36,000,000 mrs. In the November 5, 1541 division, these dioceses and orders paid 1,368,337 more than in the 1540 division. This amount exceeds by a 1,000 the amount necessary to close the gap between increases and decreases. The total amount adjusted through arbitration was 8,212,553.

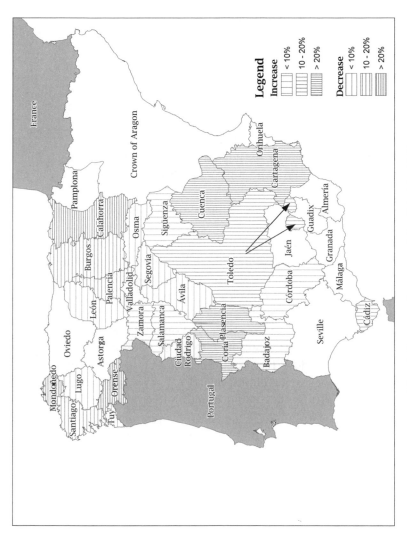

Map 3. Reapportionment of the Subsidy, 1541.

Because it relied simply on the representatives declaring the approximate value of their diocesan rents, arbitration did not guarantee the level of accountability assured by interdiocesan verifications or even self-verification prior to reapportioning the subsidy. Self-interest probably dictated that representatives declared the lowest amount possible for their diocese. The Assembly's only safeguard against flagrant dissimulation was the records from prior apportionments. At the same time, however, many chapters had a longstanding desire to rectify the inequitable apportionment.[47] In 1530, for example, the agreement between the crown and Assembly assured the relief of burdened dioceses.[48] In 1533, several chapters vigorously called for the subsidy's reapportionment. Quibbling over the method should not be seen as hostility to the concept of verification and an equitable apportionment, but rather as opposition to having either an unpalatable method forced upon them or a method that would expose the church's true wealth to an avaricious king.

With the subsidy successfully reapportioned through arbitration, the representatives began to situate their concern in a larger context. They were concerned not only about the inequitable apportionment of the contribution in Castile, but among the other Spanish kingdoms as well. In 1540, the ecclesiastical estates of the Spanish kingdoms together had to contribute 500,000 ducados to the crown. Of that, Castile was responsible for 418,000 ducados, while the crowns of Aragon, Navarre, Granada, and the Canaries together paid only 82,000 ducados. In the previous contribution of 1536, the Crown of Aragon alone had paid almost 80,000 ducados. The Castilian representatives agreed that if Aragon had previously paid 80,000 ducados, Aragon, Navarre, Granada, and the Canaries together could certainly carry more than 82,000 ducados now. On November 9, the Assembly petitioned the archbishop of Toledo to redress the unfair apportionment of the 500,000 ducados; in addition to verifying the values within the kingdom of Castile, the inequitable apportionment among the Spanish kingdoms had to be rectified as well. The undue burden thrust upon Castile aggravated the already inequitable apportionment among the dioceses.[49]

---

[47] Ibid., Session 33.

[48] ACS, Sec. II, lib. 1157 (77), Session, April 8, 1530.

[49] ACS, Sec. VII, lib. 87 "Congregación...1541," November 9, 1541. The exact process by which the 500,000 ducados was divided between the kingdoms is unclear; either the crown imposed the unequal apportionment or the Assemblies in the other kingdoms were more successful in the negotiations than Castile.

The appeal fell on deaf ears. Tavera dismissed the petition and told the Assembly that the negotiations were already too far along to raise a new issue at this point. Besides, the representatives had enough on their hands dealing with the situation in Castile. The representatives thought otherwise. García Manrique de Lara, president of the Assembly, argued that it was not too late to address the issue and suggested that the Assembly petition Tavera again. A canon of Seville went further and wanted to bring the matter to the king's attention. He proposed that the Assembly deputize certain chapters or canons to petition the king when he returned from the campaign against Algiers. The representatives agreed and decided to petition by region; the chapters of Seville, Córdoba, Jaén, and Cádiz, for example, would join together to present the petition for Andalusia.[50] The Castilian Assembly strongly felt that the current apportionment of the ecclesiastical contribution among the kingdoms of Spain was unfair. The unequal apportionment of the subsidy, not only within Castile but also among the Spanish kingdoms, had to be addressed.

As the representatives plodded along with these negotiations, they suffered a further blow on November 11. The Assembly learned that the bishop of Lugo had just discussed with the archbishop of Toledo the possibility of using prelates and religious orders to verify the dioceses' *veros valores* together with the chapters. This was entirely unprecedented; prelates or religious orders had never before been involved in the verification process. Furthermore, since the beginning of the century, the chapters alone had been responsible for collecting and apportioning the subsidy. They probably feared that the involvement of other ecclesiastical bodies in the verification process could break their monopoly over the subsidy.[51]

Alarmed by this turn of events, the Assembly appealed to the bishop of Lugo on November 12, arguing that such measures would severely prejudice the customs and authority of the Assembly and cause great discontent among the churches. They implored the bishop not to break with time-honored tradition. He was sympathetic but still directed the representatives to consult with the archbishop of Toledo. Tavera was less receptive; he merely told the representatives that it was the king's decision to use prelates and religious orders to verify the *veros valores*.

---

[50] Ibid., November 10, 1541.
[51] Ibid., November 11, 1541.

The representatives insisted that neither the chapters nor the Assembly would sanction such expedients, which violated ecclesiastical customs.[52] Whether the crown was indeed determined to bring the prelates and other clergy into the verification process is unclear. By threatening such action, however, the crown probably wanted to pressure the Assembly to reach a decisive course of action.

To the crown's dismay, the Assembly considered the move a direct affront to its authority and assumed a feisty defensive posture. Pedro Suárez de Guzmán argued that the chapters must hold their ground. They had not convened the Assembly to devise a completely new method for verification, but only to modify the procedures within the old framework. All the representatives agreed that they had to defend their authority to verify the ecclesiastical rents and to apportion the ecclesiastical contribution. The chapters fiercely guarded their privileges and even threatened to revoke, if necessary, the new subsidy apportionment the committee of arbitration had reached on November 5.[53]

The Assembly's adamant opposition apparently forestalled the crown's latest assault. On November 18, the crown once again allowed the Assembly to carry out self-verification, but reverted to the original time frame of the agreement of 1540 and ordered the chapters to complete the verification by February 1542. At that time, the chapters had to notify the Comisario General that they had settled on a new diocesan apportionment of the subsidy that was acceptable to all the diocesan clergy. Should the chapters fail to comply, the Comisario General would commission the prior of the religious order or the bishops' vicar-general to verify the values of each diocese in conjunction with the chapters' deputies.[54]

The Assembly was dissatisfied with this change in royal policy, as it was already too late to meet the February 1542 deadline. Furthermore, as the negotiations dragged on, representatives from several chapters had already left and, in their absence, the Assembly could not respond to the royal demand. The representatives immediately conveyed these concerns to the bishop of Lugo and the archbishop of Toledo. The representatives reminded the royal ministers that the Assembly had convened for the express purpose of making the verification process

---

[52] Ibid., November 12–13, 1541.
[53] Ibid., November 16, 1541.
[54] Ibid., November 18, 1541.

more just and less onerous.[55] The Assembly would not tolerate a flagrant violation of its liberty. To resist the possible intervention of prelates in the verification process, the Assembly allocated 52,638 maravedís to help defray the costs of lawsuits in both Spain and Rome.[56]

On November 19, the representatives petitioned the bishop of Lugo to dissolve the Assembly, which they believed had met its mandate. As tensions escalated, the Assembly apparently disregarded the original insistence on unanimous decisions, overcame the endless vacillations, and accepted the majority vote for self-verification (i.e., the individual chapters investigating the *veros valores* of their own dioceses). Arbitration had temporally remedied the general apportionment for six years. Hence, for the moment, the problems of verification were settled. The representatives told the bishop that they would work to ensure that all injuries were rectified, that no one would have reason to complain, and that the chapters would notify their prelates, clergy, and others who contributed to the subsidy of the changes in the local apportionment. Furthermore, they requested that the bishop not place any obstacles in their way by changing procedures in the collection of the subsidy or by imposing unrealistic deadlines for completing the verification.[57] The representatives were unequivocal with the bishop, opposing any measures that would undermine their ability to do a good job.

On November 20, the Assembly sent a letter to all chapters. In that letter, the Assembly instructed the chapters on verifying the *veros valores* and stated explicitly that if the Comisario General or his assistants proceeded in any way contrary to customs or in prejudice to customary rights, the chapters would defend their rights through all legal channels available to them.[58] The representatives then kissed the hands of the archbishop of Toledo, lieutenant general of Spain in Charles's absence, and dissolved the Assembly.[59]

---

[55] Ibid.

[56] Ibid., November 19, 1541.

[57] Ibid.

[58] The letter to the chapters did not spell out the exact procedures, and there was no reference to them in either the minutes of the Assembly or the royal documentation that I have examined. I do not think that they refer back to the fourteen-point instruction of October 21, 1541.

[59] ACS, Sec. VII, lib. 87 "Congregación…1541," November 20, 1541. Communications between the chapter of Toledo and its representatives in the Assembly on November 27 indicate that the crown made further demands on the clergy after the Assembly had been formally dissolved. The chapter directed its representatives not to

The chapters began verification almost immediately. On December 9, the chapter of Toledo elected four canons to verify the values of the archdiocese, and on December 24 the chapter of Seville charged the *chantre* (choir master) and a canon with verifying the values of the archdiocese.[60] Although Toledo and Seville, and presumably other chapters, began to verify the values, from the crown's perspective, the verification process quickly bogged down. In July 1542, for example, the bishop of Lugo notified the chapters that *veros valores* that were acceptable to the prelates and other diocesan clergy were supposed to have been calculated by the end of February 1542. If the chapters did not calculate them within fifty days, the bishop would commission the prelates to take part in the verification process.[61] Despite the bishop's threat, delays continued to plague the verification process. The chapter of Toledo, for example, was still verifying the archdiocesan rents as late as October 20, 1542, and many other dioceses took up to four years.[62] There is no indication, however, that prelates were involved in the verification or that the bishop of Lugo ordered them to take part. Verification was a long and drawn out process. Such difficulties give ample reason to doubt that the timely arrival of the papal brief in 1541 would have had any impact on the process.

Conclusion

The differences over verification make clear that the Castilian chapters were not monolithic in outlook. While all chapters acknowledged the urgent need to adjust the subsidy apportionment in order to relieve the financially strained dioceses, they did not support verification unconditionally. Even though it was burdened, the chapter of Palencia opposed Loaysa's attempt to enforce verification in the summer of 1541. Seville, on the other hand, refused to be bound by the agreement of 1540. Such division partially prevented the original agreement from being implemented and made it more difficult for the Assembly to come to an acceptable conclusion on a new procedure. Far from being united, the chapters fought over every detail that could affect their share of

---

consent to the king's latest orders, and urged them to return home. The exact nature of the king's orders is unclear. See ACT, AC lib. 6, f. 242v.
   [60] ACT, AC lib. 6, ff. 246–247. ACS, Sec.I, lib. 17 f. 110v.
   [61] AGS, CJH leg. 15, ff. 29 and 44.
   [62] ACT, AC lib. 6, f. 300; Iturrioz Magaña, *Estudio del subsidio*, pp. 61–63.

the subsidy and wrangled bitterly over reapportionment among the dioceses. Consensus then had to be reached not only between the Assembly and the crown but also within the Assembly for the distribution of taxation.[63]

Despite their internal differences, the chapters were united in defense of ecclesiastical interests against external encroachments. All the chapters of Castile easily agreed that the apportionment of the subsidy of 500,000 ducados among the kingdoms of Spain was unjust. The Assembly of 1541 protested the disproportionate burden imposed on Castile and demanded rectification by the crown. The threat to their liberties also united the chapters against the intervention of prelates in the verification process. Loaysa had recognized that such intervention would infringe on the chapters' authority, and his statement indicates that the crown was aware of the challenge it was posing. The extent to which the king was prepared to carry out his threats is unclear, but the chapters certainly took them seriously. They loudly protested the prelates' involvement in the verification and prepared for the worse. Their protests won over some of the royal ministers and temporarily averted the involvement of prelates.

Although necessary and important, verifying the *veros valores* was a process many churches wished to avoid or limit. The negotiations between 1540 and 1542 provide insight into the workings of the Assembly of the Clergy and the dynamics of the exchange between church and state. The Assembly was clearly not an united body at all times. The crown, on the other hand, did not follow through with its threats. While the king attempted to pressure the Assembly, he had refrained from using force at every point in 1541 and 1542 and avoided any direct and blatant infringement of ecclesiastical authority.

Like the Castilian Cortes, the Castilian Assembly of the Clergy was a viable representative force. The crown could not simply impose its will on the ecclesiastical estate in fiscal matters. The Assembly fiercely defended the ecclesiastical estates' control over the verification process. At the same time, the crown and the Assembly worked together to reach an acceptable consensus. Without certain authorizations from either the king or the Comisario General or both, the verification

---

[63] For more on the idea of "vertical" and "horizontal" consensus, see Matthew Vester, "Territorial Politics and Early Modern 'Fiscal Policy': Taxation in Savoy, 1559–1580," *Viator: Medieval and Renaissance Studies* 32 (2001), p. 282.

that members of the ecclesiastical estate so direly wanted could not be carried out. Of course, the partnership was not always tranquil, as this case demonstrates. The crown continually pressured the clergy and threatened ecclesiastical liberties. On the whole, however, it was reluctant to use coercion and sought to govern through consensus. The Assembly itself doggedly defended ecclesiastical liberties and tried to limit royal demands. Negotiations ensured that both parties achieved most of their objectives on reasonable terms and with fewer altercations; the king received the money that he desperately needed, while the ecclesiastical estate retained control over their rents. A fragile and conflictive consensus underlay church-state relations over the subsidy. The crown's continued reluctance to use coercive measures suggests that the connection between fiscal centralization and the monopoly of force is not necessarily a valid explanation for the growth of state finance in the sixteenth century.[64] On the contrary, this Castilian example provides further evidence that instead of fiscal centralization, the crown relied on mutual consent and fiscal devolution to the realm to pay for its wars.[65]

---

[64] Anthony Molho, "The State and Public Finance: A Hypothesis Based on the History of Late Medieval Florence," *The Journal of Modern History* 67, suppl. (December 1995), p. S98.

[65] James D. Tracy, *Emperor Charles V, Impresario of War: Campaign Strategy, International Finance, and Domestic Politics* (Cambridge: Cambridge University Press, 2002), p. 303.

CHAPTER SIX

NEGOTIATIONS FOR THE SUBSIDY OF 1546

In 1546, at peace with both France and the Ottoman Empire, Charles V finally turned his attention to the Holy Roman Empire and the Lutherans. With his victory at Mühlberg (1547), he temporarily imposed a religious settlement on Germany. A successful military campaign depended on a sound war chest, and the church played a prominent role in filling the royal coffers. In 1546, the Castilian chapters convened another Assembly to negotiate a subsidy with the crown. Although the Assembly did not haggle over the amount as it had in 1530, it did demand redress of grievances before supply. It also prepared new instructions for verifying the *veros valores*, because the agreement of 1541 had expired. Through an examination of these negotiations, the present chapter provides further information on the royal attitude towards the Assembly and indicates the limits of royal power. It examines the stratagems the crown and the Assembly used to negotiate a subsidy and discusses the internal dynamics of the ecclesiastical estate.

The Royal Position

As early as March 1545, the crown sought another ecclesiastical contribution. Having already discussed the issue with the papal nuncio, Charles V commanded Philip, his son and regent, to draw up orders for Juan de Vega, the ambassador in Rome, to seek a papal concession for the war against the Turks, which continued in 1545, as well as for the suppression of Protestants. Philip cautioned, however, that negotiations with the pope might yield no more than empty promises. The king realized this risk, and, apparently hoping to obtain a voluntary grant from the clergy without a papal concession and without delay, he ordered Francisco de los Cobos to ascertain what financial aid the bishops would offer. Rather than asking the bishops directly, Philip and Cobos first communicated the king's order to the Council of State, the cardinal of Seville, and the president of the Royal Council. The ministers concluded that to consult the bishops alone would limit the contribution to their individual rents and that the bishops gave very little. Furthermore, the ministers anticipated that some bishops might protest such a request to Rome and that, with little influence over their chapters, most bishops would be unable to persuade them to aid the king. On the other hand, the ministers feared that to ask the entire ecclesiastical estate for a voluntary grant would precipitate problems that the king wanted to avoid.[1]

The regency government consequently did not communicate the king's order to the bishops and instead recommended that, since the current contribution expired in 1547, the king should ask the pope for another concession similar to the past *medios frutos*. The nuncio's promise to assist the crown provided a further incentive to seek a papal concession. Given the dire economic situation in Spain and the probable ecclesiastical resistance to any innovation, Philip urged Charles to obtain a bull in the customary form and to justify it with suitable reasons, such as the war against the Turks. He clearly wanted to prevent the clergy from appealing innovations or questionable justifications. Philip also advised Charles to obtain briefs for the cardinals to contribute as well.[2] These preparations indicate the importance of papal approval. The regency government's assumption that the prelates would not make a voluntary grant suggests that even though the crown nominated prelates, it could not easily manipulate them once they held office; even if the crown could control the prelates, the ministers' remarks reveal that the bishops could not control their chapters. Only a papal concession would provide the necessary authority to overcome reluctant prelates and chapters. The clergy still might find fault with the bull and try to prevent its execution, but a papal concession provided the legitimacy that the crown needed to seek a contribution.

The negotiations in Rome did not end in empty promises. By March 1546, the crown had received a new bull for the *medios frutos*, but it could not start collecting the new contribution until 1547, because the bull stipulated that the past contribution, which was still being collected, must expire first. Philip informed Charles on March 30, 1546,

---

[1] *Corpus documental de Carlos V*, ed. Manuel Fernández Álvarez (Salamanca, 1975) II, p. 361. In 1530, the crown also discussed obtaining a voluntary grant from the ecclesiastical estate, but it was dissuaded from pursuing it. In 1533, the crown turned down the clergy's offer of a voluntary grant. So clearly the royal position was not fixed and expediency often determined royal policy. See chapter 2, p. 69 and chapter 4, p. 110.

[2] Ibid. For a discussion of the cardinals' exemption from the subsidy and attempts to include them, see Lucía Carpintero Aguada, "La congregación del clero de Castilla en el siglo XVII" (Ph.D. diss., Universidad Autónoma de Madrid, 1993), pp. 133–136.

that the cardinal, the bishop of Lugo, and ministers of the Treasury thought it prudent to employ the bull as in the past. They thus advised against convening an Assembly, which continually caused problems. If the chapters offered a subsidy of 500,000 ducados in lieu of the *medios frutos*, as the Assembly did in 1543, Philip recommended accepting the amount.[3] The collection would then span three years even though the crown would collect little in the third year. After the customary discounts, Philip thought that the crown would receive a subsidy of 450,000 ducados. If the chapters failed to make an offer, he would, in accordance with the bull, collect a quarter of the ecclesiastical rents in each year.[4] Philip told his father, however, that given the current dearth, a forcible collection would be difficult and would disrupt the charitable work of the church. He also reminded Charles to obtain from Rome the briefs that required cardinals with pensions in Spain to contribute to the subsidy. Furthermore, Philip warned that if he went to Aragon to convene a Cortes, as was being discussed, his absence would hamper the negotiations for the *medios frutos*.[5]

Charles agreed with Philip's assessment and said he would accept a subsidy of 500,000 ducados in the same periods of payment as the last contribution. He also agreed that a discount of 56,600 ducados

---

[3] The 500,000 ducados was for all of Spain. The Castilian dioceses were responsible for 418,000 ducados, while the dioceses of Aragon, Granada, Navarre, and the Canaries carried 82,000 ducados.

[4] From Philip's description of a quarter in each year and from other documentation, the concession appears to have been for a *dos quartas*. Philip's letter indicates that he did not make a clear distinction between the two types of concessions.

[5] *Corpus*, II, pp. 459–460, 462. A short report lists the nine cardinals with rents in Spain in 1546. They were the cardinals of Seville, Burgos, Coria, Cuenca, Jaén, Tarragona, Mantua, and Cibo, and Cardinal Poole of England. The cardinal of Mantua had a pension of 3,000 ducados in the diocese of Badajoz, that of Cibo a pension of 6,000 ducados in the diocese of Zaragoza, and Cardinal Poole a pension of 2,000 ducados in the diocese of Granada. None of these cardinals had been exempt from paying in the last contribution. Although the number of cardinals was not great, if they did not contribute, a significant amount of revenue would be out of reach. The pensions of three cardinals came to 11,000 ducados. If the contribution was for a quarter of the rents, a quarter of 11,000 ducados would be 2,750 ducados or 1,031,250 maravedís, roughly equivalent to Mondoñedo's portion of the subsidy and slightly more or less than what several dioceses paid in 1546. If the other six cardinals had comparable pensions, a quarter of all nine pensions would be over three million maravedís. Since the aggregate of these rents was substantial, the crown's pursuit of a papal brief for the cardinals to contribute to the subsidy is understandable. See AGS, E leg. 73, f. 169.

was unavoidable.[6] The current economic hardships might explain the crown's desire to avoid negotiating with the Assembly, for the ministers probably recalled the clergy's opposition to the monetary demands placed on them in 1530, also a year of dearth. The king was also more generous with discounts. In 1530, Charles had originally offered a 4.8 percent discount, while the discount in 1544 was 11.3 percent of the total subsidy; Charles was ready to offer a similar discount in 1546.[7] Since the crown's monetary needs were as great as ever, this change suggests a minor victory for the clergy against royal fiscal demands.

The king's desire to avoid an Assembly parallels the regency governments' continual desire to avoid negotiating with the Cortes.[8] Such maneuvers on the crown's part indicate that representative bodies were vibrant institutions. Like other corporate bodies, the ecclesiastical estate could and did put pressure on the crown, and it affected the government's course of action. The regency government, for example, decided not to announce the bull of Saint Peter (i.e., sale of indulgences to finance the construction of St. Peter's Basilica in Rome) at this time, because it feared that the bull would create further difficulties with the clergy.[9] Moreover, Philip made clear that a forcible collection would be difficult; the crown had to reach some form of agreement with the clergy. The important point is not whether the agreement was between the crown and the Assembly or with individual chapters, which the royal ministers favored, but that the crown needed to reach an agreement with the ecclesiastical estate for a peaceful collection even though the crown had papal authorization to collect a portion of ecclesiastical rents.

Philip next wrote Charles concerning the ecclesiastical contribution on May 9. First, he had not announced the bull for the *medios frutos* in accordance with Charles's order to announce it along with another bull

---

[6] AGS, CC leg. 4, "Copia de capitulos de carta de su magestad a su alteza de 24 abril 1546." On February 11, 1547, Charles wrote to the Comisario General with instructions for making the discount of 20,000 ducados. See AGS, CC leg. 4, "mandamiento para que se haga descuento a las hordenes de 20,000 ducados de lo que han de pagar de susidio por quanto su mag. les haze merced de ellos."

[7] For a breakdown of the discount in 1544, see Modesto Ulloa, *La hacienda real de Castilla en el reinado de Felipe II*. 3rd. ed. rev. (Madrid: Fundación Universitaria Española Seminario "Cisneros," 1986), p. 601.

[8] For more on royal attitudes toward representative institutions, see Sean T. Perrone, "Charles V and Representative Politics," paper presented at the Annual Meeting of the Society for Spanish and Portuguese Historical Studies, New York, April 27–30, 2000.

[9] AGS, E leg. 73, f. 192.

for the vassals of the monasteries, which still had not arrived. Recognizing the delicate situation of asking for another contribution from the
clergy while they were still paying the present one, the crown believed
that the bull for the vassals might mitigate some of the uproar over
the *medios frutos* and thus wanted to announce both bulls at the same
time. Second, Philip informed Charles that Juan Suárez de Carvajal,
the bishop of Lugo, had replaced García de Loaysa, cardinal of Seville,
who had died in April, as Comisario General de la Cruzada. Although
he might not need it, Philip advised Charles to obtain a papal brief
to confirm the bishop as Comisario General. He also asked the king
to provide the bishop with a pension because he had little income.[10]
Philip's advice was prescient, for the bishop of Lugo's replacement of
the cardinal of Seville did become a point of contention later in the
negotiations as some chapters tried to use Suárez's lack of formal papal
approval to their advantage.

A week later, the regency government began to make preparations to
notify the chapters, after it decided not to wait for the other bull. The
reason for the sudden change is unclear, but it is possible that the crown
received unfavorable news from Rome about the status of the bull for
the vassals of the monasteries. In any case, the regency government
now needed to consider how to address ecclesiastical hostility to the
new concession. In a letter of May 18, Cobos assured Charles that if
the crown clearly articulated the reason for the new contribution, the
clergy would contribute.[11] Cobos thus advocated effective propaganda
to overcome clerical reluctance.

This was not the first time Charles V had to justify his actions to his
Spanish subjects. To calm irate subjects in 1535, for example, Isabel
of Portugal posted placards throughout the kingdom that justified the
king's attack on Tunis, which was more beneficial to his Italian possession, instead of Algiers, from which pirate attacks on the coasts of
Spain originated. The crown's discourses to the Cortes were also a
type of royal propaganda.[12] The king even posted broadsides in 1540
to justify to the Castilian population why the church should pay a

---

[10] Ibid., f. 119.

[11] Ibid., f. 186. On June 7, Cobos again expressed concern that the negotiations
would not be problem free. See AGS, E leg. 73, f. 168.

[12] María del Carmen Mazarío Coleto, *Isabel de Portugal: Emperatriz y Reina de España*
(Madrid: Consejo Superior de Investigaciones Científicas, 1951), p. 413; AGS, Guerra-
Antigua, leg. 8, f. 11; Manuel Fernández Álvarez, "La política exterior" in *Las Cortes
de Castilla y León en la Edad Moderna* (Valladolid, 1989), pp. 345–366.

subsidy. Clearly, then, the crown needed to make its case to the people, both those who negotiated the payments of subsidies and those who paid them. Such public relations were especially important for Charles V, because his dynastic interests often clashed with the local interests of his subjects.[13] The crown recognized the importance of persuading reluctant subjects to support its war efforts. Persuasion, of course, did not always work. The crown's efforts to persuade the clergy in the spring of 1546 are unknown, but, as we will see below, by August they had turned to threats.

Charles's letter of April 24 apparently had not arrived by May 18, because in his letter of that day, Philip reiterated that due to dearth, the crown would have to negotiate for a subsidy similar to the past *medios frutos*. Moreover, without an agreement with the clergy, he explained, no merchants—at least not the Germans—would make loans based on a potential ecclesiastical contribution. He consequently would make every effort to reach an agreement. Philip also urged Charles to provide discounts, which were even more necessary than before.[14] Even without convening an Assembly, the negotiations would not be easy because of the economic situation, and the clergy consequently would not simply renew the previous agreement. Long, drawn-out negotiations could clearly lead to financial hardship for the crown, while the clergy realized that the longer they resisted, the more the crown would be pressed to make a favorable agreement. The very use of the ecclesiastical contribution to secure and pay loans was also a sore point with both the clergy and other Spaniards. Lucía Carpintero notes, for instance, that on several occasions, the Cortes petitioned the king to use the Tres Gracias only for their expressed purpose and no other end.[15]

The chapters responded to the notification in late June and early July. Some had registered appeals, arguing that substituting the bishop of Lugo for the cardinal of Seville was invalid. Even though the royal lawyers thought it unnecessary, Philip's letter of July 3 again asked Charles, if he had not already done so, to write to his ambassador

---

[13] James D. Tracy makes the same point regarding the Low Countries, see his *Emperor Charles V, Impresario of War: Campaign Strategy, International Finance, and Domestic Politics* (Cambridge: Cambridge University Press, 2002), p. 16.

[14] AGS, E leg. 73, f. 129.

[15] Lucía Carpintero Aguado, "Iglesia y Corte Castellana en el siglo XVI," *Hispania Sacra* 41 (1989), p. 554.

in Rome for a brief that confirmed the replacement.[16] The chapters' appeals, especially those concerning the substitution, placed the crown in a difficult position. If the bishop of Lugo lacked legitimate authority, all the decrees and notifications he authorized and sent out in May might be invalid, requiring that the government begin the whole process again.[17]

Philip also informed Charles that he had signed the necessary obligations for Queen Mary, Charles V's regent in the Netherlands, guaranteeing repayment of a loan of 300,000 escudos from the *medios frutos*, the sale of monasteries, and the sale of offices of Grand Master.[18] This reference is important for two reasons: First, it indicates that loans taken in the Netherlands were charged to the ecclesiastical contribution and that the merchants or bankers needed a guarantee that revenues from the kingdom of Castile were allocated before they would make a loan to Charles. Second, it shows that the crown negotiated loans on the ecclesiastical contribution before reaching an agreement with the clergy.[19]

On July 31, Charles related his satisfaction that the chapters had been notified of the *medios frutos* and expressed his desire to renew the agreement of 1543. Since the concession was for the service of God and the holy Catholic faith, Charles presumed that the clergy would willingly and quickly reach an agreement.[20] In view of the prolonged negotiations with the Assembly on previous occasions, Charles's letter displays a certain naiveté. Although they saw victory over the Protestants as important and worthy of prayer (the chapter of Toledo, for example, organized a procession to assure the king's victory), the clergy did not necessarily feel that the king's war justified their monetary aid, especially in a time of dearth.[21] Rather, the clergy's foremost duty was to pray. Charles was clearly correct that the clergy played an important role in the defense of Christianity and the spread of Catholicism, but

---

[16] For more on the papal brief approving the substitution, see AGS, E leg. 73, f. 140.

[17] *Corpus*, II, pp. 476 and 478.

[18] Ibid. In a letter of June 19, Mary had informed Philip that no one would make the loan without his signature guaranteeing the payment from these three sources.

[19] For more information on the crown's use of the subsidy to secure loans, see Ulloa, *La hacienda*, pp. 605–606 and Ramón Carande, *Carlos V y sus banqueros* (Madrid: Sociedad de Estudios y Publicaciones, 1949), p. 476.

[20] *Corpus*, II, pp. 483–485.

[21] ACT, AC lib. 7, f. 157v.

his identification of royal interests with religious interests may have led him to misconstrue the proper relationship between the two.[22]

On September 27, Philip informed Charles that the brief ordering cardinals with pensions in Spain to contribute in the *medios frutos* had arrived. Since the ambassador did not know whom the king had named Comisario General, the brief was directed to the nuncio, authorizing him to delegate the powers to the bishop of Lugo so that he could make arrangements for the cardinals to pay.[23] Although the brief concerned the cardinals, it probably solved the problem of the Comisario General's legitimacy. Once the nuncio delegated the authority of the office to Suárez, there would be no question about his right to administer the contribution.

The Chapters' Position

By mid-June, the chapters had begun to receive notification of the *medios frutos* and started to formulate their replies.[24] A lively debate ensued in Burgos on June 18 over the proper response. In opposition to the tone of the discussion, the dean walked out of this meeting.[25] Though the minutes do not record the final decision the chapter made, the dean's action indicates that debates on ecclesiastical contributions could be contentious.

Individual chapters also consulted each other. On July 5, the chapter of Burgos received letters from the chapters of Toledo and Santo Domingo de la Calzada and also appointed a canon with salary to handle all business relating to the contribution.[26] Such exchanges generally dealt with how to appeal the bull and whether to assemble.

---

[22] John Lynch, "Philip II and the Papacy," *Transactions of the Royal Historical Society* 5th series. 2 (1961), p. 42.

[23] *Corpus*, II, p. 504. Despite the papal brief, the cardinals were reluctant to pay. A year later, on September 29, 1547, the bishop of Lugo ordered the cardinals to contribute their portion of the subsidy. In case the cardinals and their agents were unsure of the concession and their duty to pay, he inserted the papal brief including their rents in the contribution. The bishop of Lugo then exhorted them to comply with the brief and warned them that if they did not, he would forcibly collect the entire *dos quartas* from their rents. See AGS, CC leg. 4, "traslado de la carta que dio el obpo de lugo para que los cardenales paguen subsidio esta ynserto el breve que su santidad dio para ello."

[24] ACB, R lib. 48, f. 260v; ACT, AC lib. 7, f. 148.

[25] ACB, R lib. 48, f. 262.

[26] Ibid., f. 268. The minutes record the letters' receipt but not their content.

Roughly six weeks after the notification, the Castilian chapters agreed to convene an Assembly. Following the normal procedures, Toledo obtained positive responses from the other chapters before it convoked an Assembly for September 20 at the prince's court.[27] The documents provide no indication that the chapters consulted the prince prior to their decision, but they did subsequently petition for a royal license to meet. Since the crown wanted to avoid such a reunion, royal consent was not forthcoming. As I mentioned in chapter one, the role of royal consent was ambiguous. When there was not a strong consensus to assemble, the lack of royal consent might have persuaded individual chapters not to send representatives. When there was widespread support, the importance of royal consent diminished. In 1546, the chapters were more likely to agree to an Assembly without royal consent, because ecclesiastical contributions were the Assembly's purview. A year earlier, on the other hand, the chapter of Toledo's attempt to convene an Assembly to address the Council of Trent had failed in the face of royal opposition.

In early August, almost all the chapters—most of them persuaded by Toledo—again appealed the bull. The bishop of Lugo heard their appeals but did not yield, threatening instead to execute the bull as was his right. He also sent a decree of the prince to all the Castilian chapters as well as to those in the Crown of Aragon, ordering them to accept the king's offer by the end of August and thus avoid a forcible collection. It also stated that the Comisario General would make sure that the poor monasteries and impoverished clergy were not injured. Cobos, on the other hand, believed that an agreement was possible and advised against a rigid stance, because the Comisario General could not execute the bull until after the current contribution ended in May 1547. Cobos urged the king to obtain papal briefs to reduce the concession to a subsidy.[28] The chapters were in a favorable position to appeal a bull, which could not be executed until May 1547, while the crown's ability to pressure the ecclesiastical estate by threatening a forcible execution was greatly weakened. If the clergy continued to resist payment in May 1547, on the other hand, the royal ministers

---

[27] ACT, AC lib. 7, f. 153.

[28] AGS, E leg. 73, f. 200. From Cobos's perspective, the papal briefs clearly were essential for reaching an agreement. John A.F. Thomson's suggestion that such briefs were simply a formality cannot be sustained in light of the Castilian example. For more on the Roman angle to these negotiations, see chapter 8.

would have a legitimate reason to seize the portion of their revenues that the pope had conceded. The crown needed a quick agreement, however, to secure loans.

On August 11, the Alcalde Mayor of Toledo presented the chapter with the royal decree, mentioned above, ordering it to pay the *medios frutos* without convening an Assembly, to avoid excessive costs. In exchange for their cooperation, the crown would allow the chapters to provide a subsidy similar to that of 1543. In its response, on August 12, Toledo complained that the decree's August deadline made it difficult for the chapters to serve the king willingly, because they had no time to consult each other. Furthermore, the chapter had already called an Assembly for September 20. According to Toledo, the chapters needed to assemble to resolve the many problems the contribution created, from its apportionment to its collection. In contrast to the crown's notion that the Assembly was troublesome, the chapter posited that Assemblies not only offered the crown what they could but also provided for an orderly and peaceful payment process. A forcible collection, according to the chapter, would only create vexations and challenges for the crown. The chapter acknowledged that an Assembly was expensive, but added that it was more cost effective than not having one, because without an Assembly lawsuits and other difficulties would plague the collection. It urged the king to reconsider, reminding him that a forcible collection would entail many problems, such as arresting clergy, forcibly taking their account books, announcing embargoes to tenants, and not being able to collect a tenth of what the clergy peacefully collected in a short time.[29] Moreover, according to the chapter, experience had shown that the harsh treatment of the clergy in previous executions had scandalized the people and God. On August 13, the chapter had two representatives deliver the letter to the prince and sent copies to all the chapters.[30]

---

[29] Philip Hoffman and Kathryn Norberg have argued that "[i]n the end, representative institutions, not absolute monarchy, proved superior in revenue extraction. Where representative bodies held the ultimate authority, as in the Netherlands or eighteenth-century England, they facilitated taxing....Where forceful representative institutions were absent, though, fiscal paralysis was almost inevitably the result." See *Fiscal Crises, Liberty, and Representative Government, 1450–1789* (Stanford: Stanford University Press, 1994), p. 306. The chapter's remarks corroborate this conclusion, but the chapter may have exaggerated when it stated that the crown could only collect a tenth of what the clergy could collect.

[30] B.N., ms. 1293 ff. 95–2° to 96v; ACT, AC lib. 7, f. 154rv; and ACS, Sec. VII, lib. 86, Session 1.

By informing the other chapters of its action, Toledo cemented opposition to the crown. Its letter also may have given pause to many royal officials, who still remembered the serious problems with forceful executions in both 1533 and 1540. Although the chapter did not mention suspending Holy Offices, it does not seem farfetched to assume that that possibility was in the back of many officials' minds. Thus Toledo made a convincing case that an Assembly was required to maintain the internal order of the kingdom.

Whether in response to the original letter of convocation or Toledo's letter of August 13, the chapter of Burgos sent a canon to the court on August 21. Together with representatives from Toledo and other chapters, that canon was empowered to petition Philip to authorize an Assembly of the Clergy.[31] The chapters then orchestrated a general campaign and their efforts paid off: the prince finally granted the chapters license to assemble. In a letter of September 27, Philip briefed Charles on his meeting with the representatives from Toledo. In their petition to assemble, he noted, the representatives expressed their desire to serve the king; he added that representatives from other chapters were arriving as well with similar petitions. After consultations, Philip wrote, he granted license for the chapters to assemble, provided that each would send no more than one representative to keep down costs, that the representatives would accept the king's offer to provide a subsidy similar to the past *medios frutos*, and that the Assembly would take place in October. Philip explained to his father that since the bull could not be executed until May 1547, the Assembly, far from being an inconvenience, would actually be beneficial to the royal service.[32]

By mid-September, preparations were under way for the Assembly.[33] The powers granted to the different representatives varied; some had complete powers while others did not. Although this often caused delays in the negotiations, the lack of full powers meant that the crown could not pressure the representatives into making an unacceptable agreement, because the chapters still had to sanction the agreements.

---

[31] ACB, R lib. 48, f. 283v.

[32] *Corpus*, II, p. 504. Philip's rationale for consenting to the Assembly is understandable, but the crown wanted to limit the number of representatives and have them come with complete powers. The crown, however, was unable to dictate terms to the chapters. Toledo, for example, sent two representatives, while other representatives continually had to consult their chapters.

[33] See ACB, R lib. 48, ff. 294 and 296v; ACT, AC lib. 7, ff. 162, and 163; AGS, CC leg. 4, "Obispado de Calahorra/susidio/anos de dxlvii dxlviii dxlix."

The Assembly

The Assembly convened its first session on October 8 in the church of San Martín. Representatives from seventeen chapters and the abbey of Agreda were present; representatives from the other chapters, except for Astorga and Cartagena, arrived in the following days and weeks. In his opening speech, the dean of Toledo reprimanded the representatives for their past divisiveness. As long as they placed the particular interests of their chapters above the universal interests of the ecclesiastical estate, he stated, the Assembly would be unable to remedy the harms inflicted on the church, and he urged them to work together to reach an agreement.[34] The dean's remarks demonstrate that the divisions between the chapters over verification, discussed in chapter five, were not the only issues that could divide them. Despite similar backgrounds as clerics and cathedral canons, the representatives did not constitute a unified 'power elite.' They often disagreed because of regional differences or other interests, which weakened their ability to negotiate with the crown and reach a satisfactory resolution among themselves. With a few exceptions, however, the dean's exhortation for unity was effective in 1546.

On October 11, the Assembly opened debate. The first matter of discussion was whether the representatives should accept the crown's offer to collect the subsidy according to the agreement of 1543 or try to negotiate better conditions. Second, if the concession was reduced to 500,000 ducados for all of Spain, the representatives wanted a more equitable division between the kingdoms, with Aragon, Valencia, Catalonia, Navarre, Granada, the Indies, and the Order of Santiago contributing their proper share. Third, the Assembly debated whether the representatives should discuss—as past Assemblies had suggested—a remedy to the crown's continual demand for tribute from the church, especially since the Council of Trent was in session.[35] Fourth, since the apportionment of 1541 had lapsed, the representatives needed to make arrangements to verify the values and equitably redistribute the subsidy.

---

[34] ACS, Sec. VII, lib. 86, Session 1.
[35] Possibly the chapters hoped that the Council would issue a decree limiting ecclesiastical contributions, similar to the Council of Constance, which established that "universal tenths were to be levied only for great and arduous causes which concerned the utility of the entire church." See Philip H. Stump, "The reform of Papal taxation at the Council of Constance (1414–1418)," *Speculum* 64 (1989), p. 77.

Fifth, they needed to make arrangements to pay the outstanding debts owed to Toledo for the common costs of past Assemblies. Sixth, all the representatives would report their dioceses' grievances, which the Assembly would then use to petition the crown for relief. Seventh, the representatives wanted either to proceed with a pending lawsuit against the commanders for tithing from areas outside their own districts or for the ministers to correct the violation. The Assembly immediately addressed questions of past debts and made a motion that representatives with outstanding debts should contact their chapters without delay and pay Toledo before the Assembly dissolved.[36] The Assembly's agenda makes clear its desire to remedy certain wrongs against the church as well as to put its own house in order.

Before they began to discuss the contribution, the representatives wanted to examine the original bull, evidently hoping to find inconsistencies between the bull and the notification they had received. Any contradictions would justify appealing the bull and delaying the negotiations. The dean of Toledo reported, however, that the bishop of Lugo had said that he could not transfer the original bull to the Assembly without the prince's express permission, but he would permit members of the Assembly to read or copy it. Nevertheless, the Assembly dispatched further emissaries to ask the bishop to transfer the bull. The bishop repeated that he would not transfer the original bull to the Assembly, but would permit representatives to read it at his residence. This time the Assembly accepted the invitation and sent deputies to examine the original bull. They reported that the bull conformed to the copy in the notification, so the whole Assembly did not need to see it.[37]

With the validity of the bull recognized, the Assembly turned to the contribution. On October 14, the dean of Toledo prudently advised that, given the king's great need and the defense of Christendom, the Assembly should not resist and had little choice but to reach an agreement. After a lengthy but unrecorded debate, the Assembly agreed to provide a subsidy. It then discussed fifteen grievances, such as the inequitable division of the subsidy between the kingdoms, the suspension of payments, and the inclusion of hospitals in the apportionment of the

---

[36] ACS, Sec. VII, lib. 86, Session 3. The failure of the chapters to pay the cost of the Assembly promptly was a recurrent problem. See chapter 1, p. 46.

[37] Ibid., Sessions 4–6. In view of the Assembly's demand to examine the original bull, the bishop requested to see their powers. The bishop, however, appears not to have succeeded.

subsidy. The Assembly appointed a committee to draw up a shorter list of grievances, and it agreed to demand redress before supply.[38]

The committee presented a list of six grievances the next day, and the Assembly sent them to the bishop of Lugo. The first complaint was that only the kingdom of Castile had seen its share of the subsidy increased in 1540, while the other Spanish kingdoms continued to pay 82,000 ducados. The Assembly wanted to rectify this situation so that each kingdom paid its fair share. Second, the Assembly wanted the crown to lift all suspensions of payments and to allow lawsuits pertaining to them to proceed. It also asked that those individuals who contributed in the past do so in the present collection. If someone was over-assessed, the chapters would return the excess amount, and the crown did not need to intervene or suspend payments. Third, it wanted rents from *tercias* that had been sold or given to private individuals to be included in the subsidy, arguing that these were tithes like any other. Fourth, the Assembly wanted the bishop to order confraternities that claimed exemption to contribute their share. It made the same request of hospitals. Fifth, the Assembly wanted assurance that the chapters would name those responsible for the collection. Sixth, if the bishop of Lugo conveyed these grievances to Cobos, the Comendador Mayor of León, the Assembly wanted him to relate its complaint against the commanders for tithing outside their districts. It also wanted license for the pending lawsuit against the commanders to proceed.[39]

The bishop, however, would not address the Assembly's complaints until it agreed to pay the king a subsidy of 500,000 ducados. By placing its grievances first, he explained, the Assembly had started where the negotiations were supposed to end. Since they did not obtain redress from the bishop, the representatives decided to consult the nuncio, the president of the Council, and other ministers. At that very moment, a servant of the bishop of Lugo arrived, summoning deputies to meet with him regarding their grievances.[40]

In the end, the Assembly only sent deputies to meet with the bishop of Lugo and the nuncio on that day. These deputies reported back to the Assembly on October 19. The interview with the bishop was counterproductive. He was aghast that the Assembly presented such

---

[38] Ibid., Session 6.
[39] Ibid., Session 7.
[40] Ibid., Session 8.

grievances and declared that what they said about the apportionment among the kingdoms was untrue. The representative of Seville retorted that the 500,000 ducados were neither justly nor proportionately divided among the kingdoms. Although he did not know all the details, the representative knew that the dioceses in the kingdom of Granada only paid 8,000 ducados, and this was unfair to those in Castile. The bishop disputed the point, whereupon the representative calmly told him that the Assembly would not speak with him any more but would rather go directly to the king.[41]

The bishop later sent a report to the Assembly outlining how the past two subsidies had been divided among the kingdoms. According to the bishop's report, the contribution of the other kingdoms and the military order of Santiago had increased from 35,000 ducados to 82,000 ducados, while that of Castile rose from 333,000 ducados to 418,000 ducados.[42] The bishop's report clearly stated that the other kingdoms had a greater proportional increase than Castile. The Assembly of 1541 had argued, however, that the kingdom of Aragon alone provided 80,000 ducados in 1536, while Aragon, Navarre, Granada, and the Canaries combined only paid 82,000 ducados in 1540. The current Assembly stuck by these numbers, as both sides juggled figures to make their cases.

The interview with the nuncio, on the other hand, was more productive. The deputies presented him with a copy of their grievances and asked him to convey them to Cobos. The nuncio offered to do whatever he could to bring the negotiations to a successful conclusion and arranged for the deputies to meet with himself and Cobos at the monastery of San Jerónimo; after that meeting, Cobos promised to discuss the Assembly's grievances with the bishop. After hearing these reports, the Assembly decided not to send copies of its grievances to the other ministers until the bishop responded.[43] It probably considered Cobos's intervention with the bishop on its behalf sufficient, but the Assembly was still prepared to appeal to other ministers if the bishop's response was unsatisfactory. The Assembly clearly looked to different ministers for support and probably hoped to manipulate the differences among them to its advantage.

---

[41] Ibid., Session 9.
[42] Ibid.
[43] Ibid.

Despite the representative of Seville's declaration that the Assembly would not speak with the bishop of Lugo, the dean of Toledo visited the bishop on the nineteenth. He told the bishop that the Assembly would immediately prepare an agreement once it received his response to its grievances. The dean stated that the representatives did not want to prolong the negotiations; they suffered from bad lodgings and, with winter approaching, wanted to return home. The bishop, however, did not take the bait, telling the dean that the representatives should not delay further, because he did not intend to respond to their grievances until they agreed to pay a subsidy under the same terms as in 1543.[44] The bishop clearly was not going to budge.

The bishop sent an official response on October 20. He wrote that the Assembly only sought redress to delay the negotiations and that he would not respond to its grievances. Moreover, he declared that representatives of Aragon and Catalonia also asked to be relieved in the past apportionment but that he had not lightened their burden.[45] The bishop's response did not satisfy the Assembly, and it clearly found his effort to demonstrate his even-handed treatment of the clergy in both kingdoms unconvincing. On October 21, the Assembly sent deputies to consult Cobos and the nuncio on the matter. It instructed those deputies to assure the nuncio of the Assembly's willingness to serve the king, but also to stress its desire to find a remedy to its grievances.[46]

A representative from Seville reported on October 22 that the nuncio had met with the royal ministers concerning the grievances, but the ministers would not respond to them until the Assembly agreed to pay 500,000 ducados. Given the crown's reluctance to redress their grievances, the representatives decided to discuss reducing the size of the subsidy and lengthening the period of payments. They also discussed verification of the *veros valores* and decided that self-verification was the best method.[47] The Assembly then appointed a committee of eight to draw up an instruction similar to that of 1541 for self-verification.

---

[44] Ibid., Session 11. The representatives may also have wanted to reach an agreement because the costs of living in Madrid were much greater than normal. Due to this, the chapter of Seville augmented the salaries of its representatives. See ACS, Sec. I, lib. 20, ff. 10–11.

[45] Ibid., Session 10. The dean of Toledo proposed a method of verification at the session, but the Assembly thought that it was better for everyone to reflect on the issue before making a decision.

[46] Ibid., Session 11.

[47] Ibid., Session 12.

The committee was to consult the minutes from previous Assemblies as well as the current minutes to calculate the most convenient method to verify the values in each diocese without harming the clergy.[48] Despite the problems with self-verification debated in 1541, the representatives in 1546 considered no other options. Although they began to make preparations for reaching an agreement and apportioning the subsidy, they did not give up hope of obtaining redress of grievances before supply.

Philip's arrival in Madrid on October 22 allowed the Assembly to make its case directly to the prince. At an audience with Philip on October 24, the dean of Toledo declared the church's willingness to serve the crown, but he also told Philip that, in a time of scarcity, a subsidy similar to the preceding one was excessive and the periods of payment were too short. Consequently, in light of dearth and the fatigue of the poor clergy, he asked for a reduction in the amount and an extension of the payment period. He reminded Philip that the foundation of good government began with the protection of the church; the Catholic Kings, he noted, made donations and gifts to the church, which brought them victories and created the powerful kingdoms that the king now ruled. The prince was happy to hear of their willingness to serve, but said that the bishop of Lugo and Cobos were handling the negotiations.[49] Philip was not going to intervene directly and consequently did not break the impasse with the bishop of Lugo, as the Assembly had hoped.

From the nuncio, however, the Assembly learned of the bishop and Cobos's reaction on reviewing its grievances. Concerning the inequitable apportionment of the subsidy between the kingdoms, the ministers would make no changes because the clergy of Aragon and Catalonia had complained that they were burdened from contributing to both the *servicio* of the Cortes and the subsidy. The ministers, however, would try to alleviate the Castilian dioceses' burden through the third payment. Concerning the suspension of payments of those who claimed to be over-assessed, the bishop replied that he would still suspend 12,000 maravedís. Concerning the *tercias*, the ministers said that people who possessed *tercias* and customarily paid would still pay, while those with

---

[48] Ibid., Session 13. The representatives of Segovia and Seville each made suggestions for the instruction at later sessions. See Sessions 16 and 19.

[49] Ibid., Session 14.

tercias that the king sold or gave away freely would not be included. Concerning the confraternities and hospitals, the ministers replied that the hospitals would either pay or not in accordance with the bull. The appointment of collectors, the bishop said, was his prerogative, even though the collectors would always be appointed with the chapters' approval. Concerning the tithes of the commanders, the ministers said they would simply do what they could.[50]

The ministers' deliberations did not please the Assembly. Even worse was their failure to give an official response to the Assembly's grievances after privately discussing them. This so offended the Assembly that it felt the failure constituted a new grievance, and it once more sent a deputy to ask the bishop for a response.[51]

With no solution in sight, the representatives discussed offering 500,000 ducados, as the bishop had asked, but resolved to do so only after procuring a reduction and better periods of payment, with an equal amount being paid each year and after the rents were collected. The representative of Ávila stressed that his chapter would only agree to a subsidy under those terms. He also urged the Assembly to procure an order similar to that of 1544 that authorized the corregidores and other justices to collect the subsidy from recalcitrant contributories for the present collection.[52]

On October 26, the Assembly presented Cobos with its terms. It stressed to him that dearth made it extremely difficult to reduce the papal concession to a subsidy of 500,000 ducados for all of Spain, and the Assembly could only offer such a sum with difficulty. It implored Cobos for the crown to redress its grievances, to accept what the dioceses could pay, to distribute the payments over four years as in 1534, and to make the payments equal for each year and made after the rents were collected.[53] Although it still sought changes to the most recent agreement and wanted its grievances redressed, the Assembly had dropped its demand for redress of grievances before supply. Yet the crown had only won a slight victory over the Assembly, which still demanded that its other conditions be met before payment.

---

[50] Ibid., Session 15. Cobos's position here is not exactly clear, given his earlier support to hear and consider the grievances. Nevertheless, the Assembly still saw Cobos as a potential advocate for its position, as we will see below.
[51] Ibid.
[52] Ibid., Session 15.
[53] Ibid., Session 16.

The Assembly's offer was a major turning point. Cobos agreed to discuss it with the president of the Council and the bishop of Lugo, and to do what was feasible. The nuncio also agreed that the terms were good.[54] They apparently satisfied the bishop of Lugo, as well; on October 29 the ministers finally responded to the grievances and terms for the subsidy. To the Assembly's displeasure, however, they made no major concessions, saying reducing the size of the subsidy and the issue of the tithes of the commanders were up to the king. The ministers only made a few minor concessions, such as agreeing to have the Comisario General name canons and *racioneros* of the chapters to carry out the collection, while delaying the first date of payment from April to June 15. Given its good will and the justifications it presented, the Assembly was upset with the crown for failing to meet all its demands. Some representatives even advocated dissolving the Assembly rather than face further affronts, while others suggested that since the king's great need meant that they could not challenge the sum, the Assembly should not concede a subsidy until the current one lapsed in 1547 and unless it received a guarantee of equal payments after the rents were collected. Those representatives who lacked full power to make an agreement wrote to their chapters for advice. Meanwhile, all representatives agreed to reflect on the most suitable way to expedite the negotiations.[55] Although they finally breached the impasse with the bishop, the results were undoubtedly a letdown for the representatives.

Negotiations came to a standstill at the beginning of November because Philip left Madrid for a few days and Cobos was ill. Philip's absence was especially detrimental because, on November 3, the Assembly decided to petition him to meet its latest demands. Deputies, who finally met with the prince on November 6, beseeched him to accept the payment over four years, after the rents were collected, and requested that everyone who had customarily paid contribute and that the collectors be members of the chapters. The prince received the petition and expressed gratitude for the Assembly's desire to serve the king, but declared he could only provide concessions that conformed to the king's will.[56]

---

[54] Ibid., Session 17.
[55] Ibid., Session 18.
[56] Ibid., Sessions 20–21, 24.

The committee of eight meanwhile presented a 26 point instruction for verification, and on November 3, the Assembly voted on each of its points. The point to include oblations, stole fees, and offerings brought to the altar provoked a lengthy discussion. The representative of Coria wanted these fees included because they constituted most of the rents in his diocese, while the representative of Palencia deferred to the papal bull, saying that if these fees were included in the bull he would vote yes, and if not he would vote no. The representative of Segovia, who also served on the committee, strongly opposed the provision to include these fees in the verification of the values. They had not been included in previous subsidies and, according to him, were not proper rents, but fees for the administration of the church and the Sacraments. Despite his plea, the representatives voted 19 to 6 to include these fees in the verification.[57]

A formal vote on the entire 26 point instruction for verification took place on November 6.[58] The representatives of Toledo, Zamora, Sala-

---

[57] Ibid., Session 21. In Germany, Wolfgang Perke has found that oblations and stole fees, "along with offerings brought to the altar, made up a significant portion of clerical income (up to 75 percent!)." See Peter A. Dykema, review of *Kirche und Gesellschaft im Heiligen Römischen Reich des 15. und 16. Jahrhunderts*, ed. Hartmut Boockmann, in *Sixteenth Century Journal* 27 n. 4 (1996), p. 1227. Since the Castilian situation was possibly similar, the Assembly's desire to verify these fees is understandable. Coria's support for verifying these fees might seem counterproductive; if the overall wealth of the diocese increased, the diocese would probably be assigned a larger portion of the subsidy. On the other hand, an accurate assessment of diocesan rents would allow the chapter to make a more equitable division on the local level.

[58] Ibid., Session 24. The following 26 point instruction was discussed: 1) Within two months of receiving the instruction, each chapter was to elect one or two people to carry out the investigation and calculate the value of all types of ecclesiastical rents, as the instruction ordered. 2) They were to swear not to announce or tell any person the amount of the values except when necessary. The oath was to be made at the beginning of the investigation and later with the notification. 3) The investigation would be limited to the three years between 1535 and 1537. 4) The investigation would calculate the amount of each specific tithe, such as bread, wine, olive oil, and so forth. If the tithe could not be liquidated, the price of the lease would be used. 5) The investigation would calculate all monetary rents derived from property, inheritances of property, foundations, donatives, and property held in patronage. 6) All revenue—belonging to friars and nuns or of other clergy, and even belonging to the Orders of Calatrava and Alcántara—that was derived from farms in the diocese would be valued by the lease. 7) The Orders of Calatrava and Alcántara would calculate their values according to the instruction and bring them to the Assembly. 8) All the *tercias* belonging to the King or those sold or given to others would be calculated. The investigator would specify the source of the *tercias*. 9) The first fruits would be valued even though they included bonuses and oblations, stole fees, and offerings brought to altar for the administration of the Sacraments. 10) The true value of chaplaincies, elected and not, and those endowed with anniversaries would be valued without counting the salary of chaplains

manca, Cádiz, Coria, Tuy, Orense, and the abbey of Agreda voted in favor. Those from Osma, Lugo, Ciudad Rodrigo, and Sigüenza had investigated the values according to the procedures of 1541 and would make the necessary changes to correspond with the present procedures. The representatives from Ávila and Calahorra generally agreed with the instruction but thought that the years used (1535–1537) were too distant. León and Santiago wanted the years to correspond with what their churches had already done even though they did not know the exact dates. Cuenca's representative thought that the instruction was acceptable except for the stole fees. The representative of La Calzada questioned the verification of the stole fees and oblations and also thought that the years were too distant for verification. The representative

---

as well as the rents of the sacristies. 11) All monasteries with no exception for any Order would have their rents valued, including bonuses, all farms (even those where the monks worked the land themselves), and other types of rents, as well as the value of chaplaincies located in the monasteries and the reason for each chaplaincy. 12) All the rents pertaining to hospitals and confraternities would be investigated. Those rents used for hospitality would be calculated separately. 13) All rents and *votos*, like those of Santiago and of any other monastery, hospital, church, chapel, or pious place, were to be valued. Santiago was to report all its *votos* and how much corresponded to each diocese. 14) All annual rents that the prelates or others received from notaries or attorneys, stamps, cases, requests to court, bulls rewarding benefices, etc. would be valued. 15) The investigators were to take great care to report each type of tithe in remote places. If the tithes were *tercias* of other persons or benefices of hospitals, the amount was to be calculated separately. 16) Since a rule or report could not be given for all the various types of tithes, the Assembly left it up to those who were verifying to make sure all the values were included. 17) In many areas, *tazmias* (measurement of grain or a benefice) could not be determined for the three years, either because it was not the custom to value them or when done no reliable witness existed. Consequently, the figures from eyewitnesses and other sources did not tally up correctly. (Apparently, the *tazmias* would not be valued, but the instruction is not clear). 18) They would determine the common price of the bundles of grains and other products during the three years in which they were gathered and price recorded. 19) Each chapter would notify Toledo when it had finished the investigation, and they agreed to meet in Toledo on March 1, 1548, with the values. 20) If a chapter did not carry out the investigation, the closest chapter would investigate, with the negligent chapter paying the costs, and if the chapter did not finish within the time limit, the Assembly could apportion it a reasonable amount. 21) The cost of the investigation would be placed in the division of the subsidy, and the chapters should try to make the salaries moderate. 22) The investigators would not discount the amount of money taken from the ecclesiastical rents to pay for the collection. 23) The apportionment of the present subsidy would correspond to the past one, and after the verification the Assembly would redistribute the subsidy and relieve those burdened by it. 24) Chapters that made the verification conforming to the instruction of 1540–1541 were to make changes so that it conformed to the present instruction. 25) The chapter of Toledo was to notify the absent chapters about the instructions. 26) The instruction also applied to the abbeys of Agreda and Alfaro.

of Oviedo would agree only if the verifications were limited to rents included in the bull. The representatives of Seville, Segovia, Jaén, Córdoba, Mondoñedo, Sigüenza, and Palencia all had to consult their chapters before committing to the instruction.

On November 8, the Assembly continued to discuss the verification, voting on whether to investigate the values by a papal brief or a commission from the Comisario General. Representatives from 12 chapters voted for the brief, while those from 9 voted for the commission. Córdoba's representatives split, with one voting for the brief and the other voting for the commission. The Assembly then sent some deputies to consult with the bishop on the possibility of obtaining a brief. Though delays in obtaining the papal brief in 1541 had hindered the verification in that year, the debate shows that most representatives preferred a papal brief authorizing verification to an order from the Comisario General. Since many of the representatives had to consult their chapters, the Assembly decided to leave the final vote for a later session.[59]

Nevertheless, on November 10, the Assembly again debated the years 1535–1537 selected in the instruction for the verification. A representative of Toledo supported using these years because they had been selected in 1541 and some dioceses had already made the verification using them. On the other hand, the representatives of Santiago, Calahorra y La Calzada, Ávila, and Agreda felt that the years were too distant, and that dioceses should use more recent account books. Many representatives, however, wanted to wait until they heard from their chapters. The representative of León, for example, declared that he had only written his chapter two days ago and could not expect a response so quickly. He wondered why the Assembly did not wait several days, as it had agreed to earlier. Despite these differences, a majority of the representatives voted to use these years.[60]

Since the crown had made no major concessions to the Assembly, the dean of Toledo proposed a vote on November 13 on whether to pay a subsidy of 418,000 ducados or face a forcible collection. Twenty-three representatives voted to provide the subsidy, but several of those votes came with qualifications. In accepting the subsidy, for example, the representatives of Lugo, Mondoñedo, Oviedo, and Orense stipulated

---

[59] Ibid., Session 25.
[60] Ibid., Session 27.

that the sum allocated to their dioceses be based on the *veros valores* of 1541. Five representatives left the decision up to the majority, while one abstained until he heard from his chapter. No representative voted against the offer of 418,000 ducados.[61] The Assembly's already weak resolve to resist clearly had dissipated. The representatives probably realized that, except for the few concessions already made, the negotiations had reached a standstill. Most probably preferred to offer a subsidy rather than endure a forcible collection. An execution was a nuisance not only for the crown but also for the ecclesiastical estate, which would suffer various harms, from loss of revenue to prison terms.

The bishop of Lugo accepted the Assembly's offer to provide the king with 418,000 ducados and promised to do all within his power to bring the negotiations to a favorable end. In view of his response, the Assembly on November 15 again sought redress for its grievances from the bishop in hopes of facilitating the collection. It also formed a committee to apportion among the dioceses the subsidy (conforming to the apportionment of 1541), the 4,000 florins earmarked for the representatives to Rome, and the common costs of the Assembly. Most of the session, however, dealt with the instruction for verification, for which a majority voted in favor with minor alterations. The years 1535–1537 would be used for most calculations, but new farms, new endowments, and improvements which increased the value of villages and estates would be calculated using 1546. To redistribute the subsidy, the Assembly would reconvene in Madrid, if the court was not present; otherwise it would meet in Guadalajara.[62]

The next day, the Assembly read the apportionment of the subsidy, and several representatives protested. The representative of Ávila, for example, complained that his diocese was unjustly assigned 36,000 maravedís more than in the past apportionment.[63] On November 17, several representatives from chapters in Galicia and elsewhere protested the apportionment, saying that it assessed them more than they could pay.[64] The representatives of Lugo, Mondoñedo, Orense, Oviedo, and the Abbey of Agreda even appealed the apportionment to the bishop

---

[61] Ibid., Session 29.
[62] Ibid., Session 30. The Assembly's decision on the location for the next meeting suggests two possibilities: it was either trying to avoid the high costs of court and Toledo or either the prospect of the crown or the chapter of Toledo putting pressure on it.
[63] Ibid., Session 31.
[64] Ibid., Session 32.

of Lugo. On November 18, an official of the Council of the Cruzada informed the Assembly that the bishop planned to hear the appeal but that he had not yet had time to examine the agreement because he was busy with other issues. The Assembly, in turn, dismissed these representatives and discussed their appeal. It later informed the bishop that these representatives had little reason to complain, because the Assembly had decided to verify the values of all the dioceses to alleviate the current inequities.[65]

Before he dismissed the appeal, the bishop asked on November 19 to examine the apportionment of 1541 and asked what the current Assembly had done to relieve the burdened dioceses. The Assembly complied with his request and in turn asked him to return the draft agreement so that they could reach a conclusion, but the bishop would not do so. To avoid another impasse, the Assembly sent the dean of Toledo to speak with the bishop. The dean persuaded the bishop to dismiss the appeal and to return the draft agreement. To the Assembly's surprise, the returned agreement did not conform to what the Assembly had sent the bishop, so it sent four representatives to meet with him to iron out the differences.[66]

Finally, on November 20, the differences were corrected and the Assembly and the crown reached an agreement. A total of 418,000 ducados was to be collected from the rents of 1547 and 1548. All the dioceses of Castile, as well as the military orders of Calatrava, Alcántara, and the Dominicans of the province of Castile, would participate in the payments. As in the past subsidy, the Dominicans would be separated from the others and carry out their own collection and payment. Second, the contribution would be made in five payments over three years. The first payment of 50,630,250 maravedís would be made by June 15, 1547; the second payment of 50,630,250 maravedís by the end of November 1547; the third payment of 22,258,500 maravedís by June 15, 1548; the fourth payment of 22,258,500 maravedís by the end of November 1548; and the fifth payment of 10,972,500 maravedís by June 15, 1549. The appropriation of the subsidy among the dioceses conformed to the past division. After the verification of the *veros valores* was completed, each diocese would pay the new amount assigned to it. Third, each chapter was to grant an obligation conforming to the past

[65] Ibid., Session 33.
[66] Ibid., Session 34.

subsidy. Fourth, the cardinals were to contribute to the subsidy. Fifth, the Comisario General would receive the entire subsidy that fell to vacant sees during the five payments. Sixth, he would name as judges prebends of the cathedrals. Seventh, he would order the local chapter to investigate all complaints in the local division; without consulting the chapters he would not suspend the payment of any individual unless the payment lay expressly outside the bull. Eighth, the prince would provide orders for the secular justices to proceed against those who refused to pay. Ninth, the Comisario General would make the necessary arrangements to determine the values of the kingdom of Granada within fifteen months. All representatives then accepted the agreement, which included many of the Assembly's demands.[67]

Although the focus here has been on negotiations in the Assembly, negotiations also took place between the Assembly and the chapters.[68] In one series of correspondence starting on October 20, the Assembly urged the chapter of Toledo, as head of the Castilian church, to send a representative to Rome. Past Assemblies, it noted, had discussed the issue and recommended that all the chapters send representatives to Rome. Consequently, in 1546, only a few chapters still had not sent representatives, and Toledo was one. The chapter's absence was detrimental to ecclesiastical interests, the Assembly stated, because only Toledo could galvanize the representatives in Rome and speak with authority.[69] The chapter of Toledo thought otherwise. On October 24, it responded that sending representatives to Rome was the Assembly's duty, not the chapter's duty. Moreover, the chapter thought there was no remedy in Rome at this time and that the Assembly would accomplish more in Spain through its goodwill in the negotiations.[70]

Toledo's response did not deter the Assembly. On October 27, the representatives decided to give Toledo a year to send a delegate to Rome, and they wrote the chapter again three days later, asking it to send a representative to join those from the other chapters to protest the excessive tributes placed on the Castilian church and to petition the

---

[67] ACS, Sec. VII, lib. 86, Session 34 and AGS, CC leg. 4, "Concordia que se tomo con los procuradores de las iglesias de la corona de castilla e leon sobre la paga del subsidio de las dos quartas que se concediaron a su magestad el ano de XLVI por la qual se obligaron de pagar CCCCXVIII V ducados en los anos de DLVII DLVIII DLIX."

[68] ACT, AC lib. 7, ff. 172rv; ACB, R lib. 48, f. 310v.

[69] ACS, Sec. VII, lib. 86, Session 10, see also Session 9.

[70] Ibid., Session 16.

pope and the College of Cardinals for redress. The Assembly insisted that Toledo comply and stated that it would not dissolve until Toledo did.[71]

The Assembly won over the chapter of Toledo, which on November 8 agreed to send a representative to Rome.[72] Whereas the chapters usually pressured the Assembly, in this case, the Assembly as an institution put pressure on one of its major component parts. In particular cases, therefore, the power dynamics between the Assembly and the chapters favored the Assembly. Assemblies were undoubtedly convened for just such a reason. Without an Assembly, for example, it would have been impossible to hammer out instructions for verification; the Assembly was probably able to persuade reluctant chapters more successfully than individual chapters.

The Confirmation of the Agreement

With the agreement in hand, the representatives returned to their chapters to report the outcome. On November 30, Burgos's representative reported to his chapter and presented a letter from the Assembly. That chapter met on December 1 to discuss whether it should accept the apportionment of the subsidy and the obligation to pay for the entire bishopric. Since their representative had already signed the agreement, the Archdeacon of Lara declared that the chapter had no choice but to accept it. After some debate, the canons ratified the agreement because all the other chapters had already done so. At the same time, the chapter tried to remedy certain grievances through further negotiations with the crown, preparing a letter for the bishop of Lugo and another minister concerning the injuries that the diocese had received and its conditions for accepting the agreement.[73]

On December 3, the chapter of Burgos sent a canon to Madrid to petition the bishop of Lugo and other ministers not to suspend a particular individual's payment of the subsidy, and to ask them to allow lawsuits begun by the chapter to proceed without impediment in exchange for Burgos's acceptance of the subsidy.[74] Even after the crown

---

[71] Ibid., Sessions 17 and 19.
[72] ACT, AC lib. 7 f. 175v.
[73] ACB, R lib. 48, ff. 318rv.
[74] Ibid., f. 319v.

and the Assembly reached an agreement, then, negotiations still took place between the crown and the individual chapters. The chapter of Burgos's discussion indicates that the chapters might even reject the Assembly's agreement. The implications of rejecting the agreement are not clear. Presumably, the crown would have had a tax farmer collect the entire *medios frutos* in accordance with the papal bull. Still, given the crown's desire for local institutions to carry out the collection, it seems likely that the chapters were able to make some minor changes to the agreement in their letters of obligation in light of local needs.

The letters of obligation were a type of mini-agreement between individual chapters and the crown, and they resembled the agreement made between the Assembly and the crown. In a sense, they ratified what a chapters' representative(s) had agreed to in the Assembly. The fact that several months passed before some chapters issued their letters of obligation—Córdoba, for example, issued its on March 31, 1547—suggests that there may have been several exchanges with officials at court before all the details were settled.

Most letters of obligation followed a general form. Córdoba's letter, for instance, listed all the canons, *racioneros, medio racioneros*, and other officials who were present for the obligation. It further stated that the chapter spoke for all clergy, plus secular people, who were obligated to contribute to the subsidy in the diocese. In addition, it briefly rehashed the events from the notification of Pope Paul III's bull to the Assembly's agreement to pay a subsidy of 418,000 ducados. It then listed the amount Córdoba had to pay (5,408,487 maravedís) and the amount due in each of the five payments. The obligation certified that the collection would follow the conditions the agreement had set out.[75]

In its obligation, Granada listed the periods of payment and stated that the payment would go to either the crown or whomever the bishop of Lugo appointed to receive it; that anyone with an ecclesiastical rent, including cardinals, had to pay this subsidy; and that exemptions would only go to the military orders, functioning hospitals, and poor nuns. To prevent the subsidy from becoming a burden, the obligation stated, the apportionment in the diocese was to be equitable. Finally, the obligation asked that the judges of the bishop of Lugo proceed with rigor against those individuals who refused to pay their portions

---

[75] AGS, CC leg. 4, "Obispado de Cordoba/subsidio/anos de dxlvii dxlviii dxlix/obligation otorgo el cabildo de cordoba sobre la paga del dicho subsidio."

of the subsidy to the collectors the chapter named. The obligation also requested royal assistance to collect the subsidy from seigniorial areas.[76] Resistance to payment then did not end with the agreement. Both the local clergy and laymen with ecclesiastical rents still sometimes refused to pay their portion. Royal officials often assisted the chapters in the collection. The agreement between the crown and the Assembly only ended one round of negotiations; a second round of negotiations for the subsidy then began on the local level.

Conclusion

The negotiations for the subsidy provide many insights into the nature of government, finance, church-state relations, and the internal dynamics of the church. From the evidence, we can make several general observations about early modern Castile's political culture. First, the regency government's ambivalence toward the Assembly of the Clergy reveals the limits of monarchical power—representative institutions did constrain the crown. The crown also needed to win public opinion. It could not simply demand a contribution without justification. These clearly were not the actions of an absolutist monarch. This evidence suggests a need to rethink concepts of absolutism and the nature of governance in sixteenth-century Castile.

Second, the subsidy was an important source of royal revenue. Even before an agreement was reached, the crown used the subsidy to guarantee loans. Some bankers, however, were reluctant to make a loan without an agreement between the Assembly and the crown. This reluctance pressured the crown to reach an agreement and indicates that a papal bull was not guarantee enough for financiers that an ecclesiastical contribution was forthcoming. Negotiations for the subsidy, then, had an impact on royal finances throughout Europe.

Third, the negotiations suggest greater parity between the church and the state than scholars typically assume. Despite gaining the right to appoint prelates and control the church in Granada and America, the crown's influence over the Castilian church was still limited. The crown may not have redressed all of the Assembly's grievances, but it did make concessions. Moreover, the chapters convoked an Assembly

---

[76] AGS, CC leg. 4, "obligation de Granada...subsidio...1547–1549."

despite royal opposition. The chapters maintained their autonomy and in the process served as a counterweight to increasing royal control over the church.

Fourth, the negotiations reveal many divisions within the ecclesiastical estate. Philip's letter of March 1545 indicated that the bishops had little control over their chapters. In turn, the chapters' influence within the dioceses was limited—else why call on the secular arm to help collect the subsidy? The debates both within the Assembly and the chapters demonstrate clear differences of opinion among the canons themselves, though Burgos's vote to accept the obligation also shows a tendency towards conformity.

CHAPTER SEVEN

THE FAILED NEGOTIATIONS FOR THE SUBSIDY OF 1555

In the spring of 1556, on learning of the forcible collection of ecclesiastical rents by Spanish officials, Pope Paul IV (1555–1559) exclaimed: "They are heretics there that they have treated the clergy so badly!"[1] The pope's declaration referred not only to secular officials, but also to the Comisario General de la Cruzada, Bishop Juan Suárez de Carvajal. This chapter examines the events that led to the pope's exclamation. It starts with the failed negotiations between the crown and the Castilian Assembly of the Clergy for an ecclesiastical contribution in 1555. This failure led Suárez to seize ecclesiastical rents by force, incurring the wrath of Paul IV. This case study further demonstrates the importance of consensus between the crown and the Assembly and indicates that a clear demarcation between church and state is not always possible when prelates were at the center of royal policies towards the church.[2]

In the spring and fall of 1554, both Prince Philip and Princess Juana[3] advised the king to order his ambassador in Rome to obtain the bull for the subsidy for the next triennium (1555, 1556, and 1557) quickly, because they had already drawn on most of the anticipated revenue.[4] The fact that the crown had secured loans on the subsidy long before the pope conceded it indicates that, by the 1550s, the crown saw the subsidy as a regular source of revenue.[5] These loans also indicate that financiers were less wary of making loans without a signed agreement between the Assembly and the crown than previously. Still, royal officials realized that too great a delay in obtaining a papal concession and reaching an agreement with the Assembly for the payment of the subsidy could lead to serious financial problems. Delays were not the only

---

[1] AGS, E leg. 883, f. 18.
[2] For a discussion of these events within the wider context of governmental policy in the 1550s, see M.J. Rodríguez-Salgado, *The Changing Face of Empire: Charles V, Philip II, and Habsburg Authority, 1551–1559* (Cambridge: Cambridge University Press, 1988), pp. 226–231.
[3] Charles V's daughter, Juana of Portugal, was the regent at this time.
[4] AGS, E leg. 103, ff. 144, 238, and 340.
[5] Ibid., ff. 52–56 and 396.

potential obstacle: Princess Juana also expressed concern in December 1554 that Charles had used the pending subsidy and *cruzada* to secure loans for expenses other than Mediterranean defenses.[6] In the end, the main obstacles in the negotiations of 1555 were not delays and misappropriation of funds, but rather the validity of the papal concession. Nevertheless, the correspondence from 1554 reveals that even before the negotiations with the Assembly began, royal officials felt intense pressure to obtain a papal concession and to reach an agreement with the clergy for its payment.

In October 1554, Pope Julius III (1550–1555) finally conceded a *dos quartas* to the king. In January 1555, the bull arrived in Spain, and in February, the Comisario General sent notification of the new concession to the chapters.[7] Toledo received its notification on February 18, 1555. It immediately prepared an appeal, and the canons swore an oath to keep secret all the chapter's discussions relating to the negotiations for the *dos quartas*. The chapter also ordered the canons to attend all meetings that addressed the present subsidy and ways to prevent future subsidies; those who did not attend would face a fine. Clearly, after nearly forty years, the crown's unending demand for subsidies and its treating them as ordinary revenue had become intolerable for the chapter of Toledo. On February 25, Toledo wrote the other chapters for their input on how to proceed, and three days later, it sent two canons to court to present its appeal to the bishop of Lugo.[8] By March, the chapters were discussing the new concession and the appropriate response. Finally, on May 2, the chapter of Toledo sent letters to all the chapters convening the Assembly for June 20 in Valladolid. After receiving the letters of convocation, the chapters elected representatives, assigned them salaries, prepared their instructions, and granted them powers.[9]

In the meantime, Bishop Juan Suárez de Carvajal began to execute another bull, which arrived with the new concession for him to verify the values of ecclesiastical rents and to reapportion the subsidy. He ordered royal officials throughout Castile to seize account books and arrest clergy who impeded their actions. It is not clear when these seizures and arrests began or where they took place, but they became

---

[6] Ibid., f. 381; E leg. 109, f. 145.
[7] AGS, E leg. 109, f. 46 and PR leg. 20, f. 34 (I).
[8] ACT, AC, lib. 9, f. 239v, 240rv, and 242rv.
[9] ACB, R lib. 49, ff. 747, 753–756; ACS, Sec. I, lib. 23, ff. 43, 45, 46v; ACT, AC lib. 9, ff. 254v and 259–262v.

a point of contention between the Assembly and the crown after the Assembly convened.[10]

In late June, the representatives began to arrive in Valladolid. According to Toledo's representatives, Suárez tried to divide them before the Assembly got under way. First, he appealed to self interest, offering representatives from individual dioceses better agreements for their churches than what they traditionally obtained through the Assembly and promising to reapportion up to 30,000 ducados from the burdened to the unburdened dioceses. Second, he warned them that they did not have royal license to meet. He failed, however, to divide the representatives, and the Assembly held its first session on June 25, 1555.[11] Until this time, the death of Julius III on March 23 did not impede the negotiations or create a unique situation. Everything was routine, from the clergy's initial appeals, to the crown employing some force against them, to the meeting of the Assembly.

Yet the Assembly of 1555 would be anything but normal.[12] After the opening formalities, Rodrigo Zapata, a representative of Toledo and president of the Assembly, urged the other representatives to find a way to prevent the ecclesiastical estate from being burdened by future subsidies. Two days later, on June 27, he proposed that the session of July 3 be devoted exclusively to discussing a remedy to the continual subsidies.[13] Zapata's speech clearly set the tone for the Assembly and reveals the clergy's frustration over the regularity of papal concessions and the crown's treating them as taxpayers.

The Assembly next notified royal officials that it was in session. The initial responses of the three officials who would conduct the negotiations on behalf of the crown are worth noting. Bishop Antonio Fonseca, the president of the council, expressed surprise, saying that until the deputies informed him, he had known nothing about the Assembly convening, but promised to do all in his power for the ecclesiastical estate. Secretary

---

[10] ACS, Sec. VII, lib. 85, "Congregación del clero...1555," Sessions 9 and 12, July 6 and July 10, 1555. In 1562, the Comisario General again tried to seize the account books from the chapters and again faced opposition from the chapters. See ACS, Sec. IX, leg. 111, n.1, f. 247.

[11] ACT, Documentos Secretarias Cabildo, caja 1, "Al dean y cabildo de Toledo de capellan mayor de Toledo y Francisco de Silva. Valladolid 30 de junio de 1555."

[12] In addition to the subsidy, the Assembly also discussed how best to respond to the Tridentine decrees and to seek royal permission to lease the ecclesiastical rents.

[13] ACS, Sec. VII, lib. 85, "Congregación del clero...1555," Sessions 1 and 3, June 25 and 27, 1555.

Juan Vázquez de Molina likewise offered to assist the Assembly in the negotiations. Suárez was also open to negotiations, but chided the chapters for assembling too late and without the permission of the princess. Nonetheless, he stated, he would accept the same amount as in the last subsidy. The deputies countered that if they simply planned to grant the same amount as before, the chapters could have done so without the costs of assembling. The bishop did not respond, and he went on to ask for the accounts of past subsidies so that he could carry out the verification and reapportionment of the subsidy for the benefit of the ecclesiastical estate. The deputies replied that the Assembly did not convene for him to reapportion the subsidy and asked for his permission to do it themselves.[14] These responses highlight the tensions between Suárez and the Assembly, but also indicate that Fonseca and Vázquez were more amiable to the body. This dynamic would eventually allow the Assembly to play the ministers off one another.

On June 27, the Assembly went to kiss Princess Juana's hand. Zapata addressed the princess on the Assembly's behalf, and noted that the clergy had willingly served the king in the past, but that dearth and the intolerable burden of past subsidies prevented them from paying more at the moment. He thus asked the princess to delay payment until 1556. Otherwise, he emphasized, the present subsidy would be unbearable for everyone, not just the poor clergy. He also complained that royal officials were seizing the chapters' account books and arresting the clergy. Princess Juana responded that the king also had great needs, as they well knew. With that, the audience was over.[15]

During the next two weeks, the Assembly appointed committees to determine if on the death of Julius III the concession lapsed and to find a remedy to prevent future subsidies. It repeatedly appealed to the bishop of Lugo to suspend his provision for the seizure of account books and to release those clerics who had been arrested. It also inquired of Vázquez whether the princess had appointed ministers to negotiate with it.[16]

On Monday, July 1, the committee looking into the concession's validity reported that it was still valid despite Julius III's death. Since six lawyers disagreed, however, the committee recommended that all the

---

[14] Ibid., Sessions 2 and 3, June 26 and 27, 1555.
[15] Ibid., Session 3, June 27, 1555.
[16] Ibid., Sessions 4 , 6, 7, and 9, June 28 and July 3, 4, and 6, 1555.

lawyers in attendance study the documents. The Assembly concurred and asked for a further report from all the lawyers.[17] The Assembly also successfully persuaded the bishop of Lugo to post the original papal concession in his apartments for the representatives to consult and to send an authentic transcription to the Assembly.[18] It was less successful in its efforts to persuade the bishop to stop seizing account books and imprisoning clergy.[19] The bishop insisted that he could not order the release of incarcerated clergy on hearsay alone; he needed authentic testimony.[20] The Assembly finally received a notarized testament from an incarcerated canon in Astroga. On being presented with the document, the bishop of Lugo agreed to examine the case. On July 11, he informed the Assembly that orders had been issued for the release of clerics, but he would not countermand his earlier provision without first obtaining unspecified guarantees from the Assembly and consulting with his lawyers.[21] This did not satisfy the Assembly, which continued to barrage him with requests to suspend his order and even informed Fonseca and Vázquez of Suárez's unsatisfactory response. The bishop, however, stood firm: he would issue a provision for the release of prisoners in all the dioceses, but would not nullify his orders for the seizure of books and arrest of clergymen. He also pressed the Assembly to discuss the verification of the accounts. Eventually, the Assembly brought him the account books for the general apportionment of the last subsidy, but not the more extensive documentation that he requested.[22]

Finally, on July 6, the Assembly learned that the princess had appointed the president of the council, the bishop of Lugo, and Juan Vázquez to negotiate with it. The representatives then sent deputies to meet with the ministers and to set a date to begin negotiations.[23] Yet the ministers were unprepared to start negotiations. In fact, the president still had not received orders from the princess to take a hand in the negotiations, but told the deputies that he would be willing to do

---

[17] Ibid., Session 5, July 1, 1555. ACT, Documentos Secretarias Cabildo, caja 1, "Al dean y cabildo de Toledo de los senores Francisco de Silva y Capellan Mayor de Toledo. Valladolid 16 de julio de 1555."

[18] ACS, Sec. VII, lib. 85, "Congregación del clero...1555," Session 7, July 4, 1555.

[19] Ibid., Session 8, July 5, 1555.

[20] Ibid., Session 10, July 8, 1555.

[21] Ibid., Sessions 12 and 13, July 10 and 11, 1555.

[22] Ibid., Sessions 13, 14, 15, and 16, July 11, 12, 13, and 15, 1555.

[23] Ibid., Session 9, July 6, 1555.

so even though he had little experience with these negotiations. The
representatives then decided to prepare their grievances, especially
over the account books, for the ministers to address before offering a
subsidy.[24]

Just when it appeared that the negotiations might begin in earnest,
the Assembly received news from Rome via the chapter of Palencia
on July 15 that, with Paul IV's election on May 24, a rule of the papal
chancery had invalidated all ecclesiastical contributions granted by previous popes, including Julius's concession of the *dos quartas*. This letter
confirmed conclusions presented to the Assembly the very same day
from its lawyers as well as lawyers in Salamanca. The revocation of a
bull after negotiations had begun was an unprecedented development.
The Assembly ordered all the representatives to send a copy of the letter to their chapters, asking them to study it and advise the Assembly
on how to proceed in the negotiations, especially if the royal ministers
denied that the bull had been revoked.[25]

On July 16, Toledo's representatives duly wrote their chapter. They
communicated that the bull had been revoked and therefore that the
bishop of Lugo had no authority to proceed against the chapters. Consequently, Rodrigo Zapata and Francisco de Silva wrote, the Assembly
could not negotiate a subsidy payment in good conscience for fear
of incurring ecclesiastical censure and because no representative had
authority to negotiate a subsidy payment without a valid bull. Even
though they respected the legal knowledge of their colleagues in the
Assembly, Zapata and Silva still asked their chapter to consult its lawyers
discreetly on the legal issues, especially the royal ministers' claim that a
general revocation did not apply to bulls with lead seals or to concessions made to the emperor. The representatives noted, however, that
the ministers showed them nothing to support their claim.[26] In light of
the revocation, Zapata and Silva wrote, the Assembly needed to decide
if it should dissolve. In that case, they noted, some muttered that the
crown would then forcibly collect the money, and every diocese would
have to endure two years of deprivation. Zapata and Silva believed
that a long sequestration might be too much for many, but that they

---

[24] Ibid., Session 11, July 9, 1555.
[25] Ibid., Session 16, July 15, 1555. The various rules of chancery were entered into
the minutes on August 26. See Ibid., Session 42, August 26, 1555.
[26] This exchange with the ministers apparently took place outside of the Assembly,
because the minutes of July 15 and July 16 do not refer to such a discussion.

had no other choice, given the regularity of the subsidies. They still did not know the Assembly's views on the matter, however, and were consequently reluctant to insist on dissolving the Assembly. They were especially concerned that if papal confirmation of the bull arrived, the representatives would be forced to return shortly after dissolving, and they reminded their chapter that the back-to-back Assemblies in 1540 and 1541 had been very expensive for the churches. Zapata and Silva also worried that the churches would fare worse from a forcible collection than the crown would, even though it would collect little. They concluded their letter by asking their chapter to respond quickly with advice.[27] Toledo's representatives clearly realized that this was a crucial moment for the ecclesiastical estate. The clergy needed to stand firm against an invalid bull, but not all chapters had the means to do so. If the confirmation arrived, they would have incurred the king's wrath and additional costs for nothing.

Prior to hearing from his chapter, Zapata asked the representatives whether, in view of the revocation, they should discuss the size of the subsidy and its period of payments.[28] He felt that under the circumstances, the Assembly could not negotiate a subsidy payment in good conscience. After discussing the issue, the representatives resolved to inform the ministers of the revocation before doing anything else. They then charged Zapata and the lawyers with preparing a petition for the ministers.[29]

On July 23, the representatives reviewed the petition for the ministers. The petition denounced the concession, stating that the dates of

---

[27] ACT, Documentos Secretarias Cabildo, caja 1, "Al dean y cabildo de Toledo de los senores Francisco de Silva y Capellan Mayor de Toledo. Valladolid 16 de julio de 1555."

[28] On July 22, the chapter of Toledo charged two canons with preparing a response, but the minutes do not record it. ACT, AC lib. 9, f. 270v.

[29] ACS, Sec. VII, lib. 85, "Congregación del clero...1555," Session 20, July 19, 1555. In addition to preparing the petition, the representatives attended to several other issues during the rest of July and early August. They wrote several letters to the pope regarding the jurisdiction of the chapters, future subsidies, and the Council of Trent. They asked royal officials to address a controversy over ecclesiastical leases, and they asked the president and Vázquez to intervene with the bishop to prohibit him from forcing the chapters to bring their account books to court. The representatives also worked on a more equitable apportionment of the common costs. They also lodged a protest with the nuncio and prepared a letter to the pope about the arrest of clergy by the bishop of Lugo. Finally, they waited for any news from Rome that would be advantageous to the ecclesiastical estate. See Ibid., Sessions 18, 19, 20, 22, 29, and 31, July 17, 18, 19, and 23, and August 3 and 8, 1555.

payment (June 24 and November 30) were impossible to meet and that
the crown was unrealistic to expect the clergy to pay money before they
had collected their rents. The petition also criticized Suárez's conduct,
especially his refusal to send the original bull to the Assembly, show it
to its deputies, or make a transcription of it for the Assembly. In the
petition, the representatives stated that without seeing the original papal
bull that named Suárez Comisario General in the *dos quartas*, they could
not presume that he held the office. So they asked the other ministers
to order Suárez to show them his documents regarding the concession,
because they understood that a rule of the papal chancery rescinded
all ecclesiastical contributions granted by previous popes. Unless the
king had a confirmation of the *dos quartas* from Paul IV, they stressed,
the Assembly could not continue to negotiate for the subsidy without
incurring ecclesiastical censure. They asked the ministers to respond
positively to their requests and underlined their desire to serve the
king. After the petition was read to the Assembly, the representatives
unanimously approved it and recommended that a copy be sent to
each minister. They put off sending it, however, until the president of
the council returned from a short trip.[30]

By August 7, Bishop Fonseca still had not returned to Valladolid, so
the Assembly sent the petition to Suárez and Vázquez.[31] On August 9,
the bishop of Lugo rejected their petition and upbraided the representatives for asking to see his papal documents. The Assembly consequently
decided to focus its efforts on Fonseca, who was expected to return
shortly, and Vázquez.[32]

The president met with the representatives immediately upon returning to Valladolid on August 12. He was good-natured, agreeing that
many lawyers thought that the concession had been revoked but also
noting that many others disagreed. Regardless of the bull's status, the
president advised the representatives to demonstrate their willingness
to serve the king by offering a subsidy. Juan Vázquez concurred, saying

---

[30] Ibid., Session 22, July 23, 1555. It is worth noting that the minutes of July 3
indicate that the bishop of Lugo had made the original bull available to them and
sent a transcription to the Assembly. Whether there is an error in the minutes or the
representatives were referring to another document in this petition is unclear. Perhaps,
though, they intended to impute the Comisario General's character.
[31] Ibid., Session 30, August 7, 1555.
[32] Ibid., Session 32, August 9, 1555.

that the king's needs were so great that the clergy should still serve him with a subsidy even if the concession were revoked.[33]

On August 15, Suárez briefed the king on the negotiations. To break the impasse with the clergy, he wrote, he had asked the regent to write the royal ambassador in Rome to obtain a brief verifying the concession. He recommended this plan as the best way to bring the negotiations to a successful conclusion. Given the poor agricultural conditions, he also advised the king to make the habitual discounts to the clergy. By order of the regent, Suárez had consulted with Fonseca and Vázquez, and they all agreed that Charles should seek a smaller sum than usual. They also advised against a forcible collection, which would be toilsome and costly to the crown and upsetting to the people and the clergy. Besides, the crown would not obtain much more than the usual sum through a sequestration. All the ministers recommended a quick conclusion so that the clergy could depart. Given the representatives' current stance, Suárez stressed, an agreement was impossible without confirmation from Rome.[34]

Nevertheless, after meeting with their lawyers, Suárez and the other ministers concluded that the bull was valid and ordered the Assembly to work on an agreement for its payment. Otherwise, Suárez had bluntly told the representatives, they could go home. If the ministers were trying to pressure the Assembly, knowing that documents from Rome might take months to arrive, they failed. The Assembly responded by having its lawyers draft a brief for the ministers, outlining why the bull was revoked. In the cover letter accompanying that brief, the Assembly reiterated that the bull was revoked by a rule of chancery and that without papal confirmation, the representatives would incur censure if they negotiated a subsidy. Consequently, they would return to their churches, because there was nothing further to do.[35]

On August 18, Toledo's representatives informed their chapter that the negotiations had come to a standstill. The royal ministers simply ignored the Assembly's argument that the concession was revoked, they explained, but failed to substantiate why they thought it was valid. Even if it was revoked, the ministers had still advised the Assembly to grant the king a subsidy. The Assembly, however, was reluctant to grant a

---

[33] Ibid., Session 33, August 12, 1555.
[34] AGS, E leg. 109, f. 286.
[35] ACS, Sec. VII, lib. 85, "Congregación del clero... 1555", Session 36, August 17, 1555.

subsidy in the absence of a valid bull and to set a wrong precedent by doing so. Toledo's representatives also reported that the ministers had written the royal ambassador in Rome, probably for confirmation of the concession. Zapata and Silva asked their chapter for further advice, but in the meantime they promised to vote with the majority as the chapter had previously ordered them.[36] This letter indicates significant monitoring of royal actions, but also a fair amount of politicking within the Assembly itself. How else would Toledo, which voted first, know the sense of the majority?

Princess Juana also wrote both King Charles and Prince Philip on August 18. She recapitulated the events to date and described how they had reached an impasse over the bull's validity. She stressed the need to obtain a brief to confirm the concession, explaining that the Assembly would not negotiate a subsidy payment without it. She advised against a forcible collection, as dearth would make it difficult to collect more than previously and a forcible collection would be impossible without much toil, cost, and delays. Moreover, she warned, coercion would create unrest and discontent among the clergy, which would be counterproductive. She asked for a quick response, because the representatives were at court at their own expense and wanted to return to their churches.[37] Juana clearly wanted the king or prince to intervene with the ambassador before the regency government found itself pushed too far into a corner—if the bull was delayed too long, the clergy would have to go home because the costs of the Assembly would be too great and the fiscal needs of the crown would make a forcible collection inevitable.

The papal nuncio also joined the discussion over the status of the concession. On August 20, the nuncio told the Assembly that he was certain that Paul IV would confirm Julius's concession. Therefore, he advised the Assembly to begin negotiations for a subsidy. He believed that such negotiations were in the best interests of the ecclesiastical estate, and he knew that some representatives agreed. The representatives responded that they were not authorized to reach a subsidy agreement with the king without a papal concession; to do otherwise would be prejudicial to the ecclesiastical estate. After hearing this response,

---

[36] ACT, Documentos Secretarias Cabildo, caja 1, "Al dean y cabildo de Toledo de Rodrigo Zapata y Francisco de Silva. Valladolid 18 de agosto de 1555."

[37] AGS, E leg. 109, ff. 67, 291, 306.

the nuncio tactfully reversed himself, saying that it was best to comply first with God and then one's prince. He then pledged his good will to the Assembly.[38] Undoubtedly, the Assembly had hoped for more support from the nuncio, but the exchange indicates how uncertain things were. The nuncio thought that the bull would be renewed, and his remarks make clear that some unnamed representatives had spoken to him and expressed their desire to serve the king.[39] Clearly, then, a small number of representatives favored reaching an agreement, regardless of the bull's status. They either hoped to avoid the additional costs of assembling at a later date or felt that their loyalty to the king obliged them to serve.

Although the ministers told the Assembly on August 17 that the bull was valid, they still had not responded formally to the Assembly's petition of August 7. The Assembly therefore inquired of the bishop of Lugo on August 30 why it still had not received a response and requested permission to leave. The bishop brushed the question aside, expressing his doubt that the bull had been revoked and telling the Assembly to ask the princess directly for license to leave. After hearing this, the Assembly discussed once again how best to proceed in this unprecedented situation. It decided to send further inquiries to the chapters and to wait for the ministers' response before doing anything. The representatives also sent more deputies to speak with Vázquez and Suárez to insist that the ministers respond to their petition.[40] The delays infuriated the representatives, who sent further messengers on September 9 to tell the ministers that making the Assembly wait so long was unconscionable, because it cost the churches 500,000 maravedís every 10 days. The Assembly's mounting costs concerned the crown, which feared that the poor clergy would bear the brunt of these expenses, and thus the representatives' remark may have gotten its attention.[41]

Finally, on September 11, the president of the council summoned the Assembly's deputies to the Prado monastery to receive the ministers' reply to its petition. The meeting was not positive. After apologizing for

---

[38] ACS, Sec. VII, lib. 85, "Congregación del clero…1555," Sessions 38 and 40, August 20 and 22, 1555.

[39] Relations of these negotiations for the *dos quartas* in royal archives indicate that representatives from several chapters, including Burgos and Calahorra, wished to provide a subsidy. See AGS, PR leg. 20, f. 34 (I and II).

[40] ACS, Sec. VII, lib. 85, "Congregación del clero…1555," Session 44, August 30, 1555.

[41] Ibid., Session 51, September 9, 1555; AGS, PR leg. 20, f. 34 (I).

the delays caused by his illness, the president told the deputies that he had examined the petition and consulted many learned lawyers, including a former auditor at the Roman Rota. These lawyers disagreed with the Assembly on the bull's status and said that a bull with a lead seal could only be revoked by another bull with a lead seal. A simple rule of chancery, therefore, could not revoke Julius III's concession. Consequently, the president asked the Assembly to negotiate the payment of a subsidy, given the king's great needs. The deputies then asked the president to allow his lawyers and those of the Assembly to confer on the legal issues. The ministers approved, but urged the Assembly in the meantime to work on an agreement to avoid a forcible collection.[42]

The representatives, however, decided to take no action for the moment and to wait to see if the bull was executed. This irritated the bishop of Lugo, who drew up orders for the execution of the *dos quartas*. These orders clearly stated the following: first, that the bull was not revoked because it came with a lead seal; second, that the revocation was general and did not include the prince; and third, that Julius and Charles had a contract in the concession stipulating that it could not be revoked by his successor. For this last reason, the king had already spent the money and the crown would collect it.[43]

On September 20, despite his earlier advice against sequestering ecclesiastical rents, Suárez wrote to the king that the royal ministers had decided to proceed with a forcible collection. He acknowledged that this action would hurt the churches and that there would be complaints, but he believed that it was necessary to compel the clergy to reach an agreement. The sequestration, however, would be limited at first to the rents of the bishops, chapters, and secular clergy. The officials would also sequester the rents of rich orders of friars who could afford to pay. If the clergy came around, as he expected they would, Suárez wanted to reach a quick agreement to avoid their spending more money at court or delaying payment through further negotiations. He thus urged the king to inform him of his terms for an agreement right away.[44] At this point, then, Suárez clearly saw force as just one tactic

---

[42] ACS, Sec. VII, lib. 85, "Congregación del clero...1555," Sessions 53 and 54, September 11 and 12, 1555.

[43] Ibid., Sessions 55 and 61, September 13 and 20, 1555.

[44] AGS, E leg. 109, f. 285. The sequestration would not touch at this point the rents pertaining to the Dominicans and Augustinians, and it would also not touch the rents of the military orders.

in the negotiating process, but he also recognized that without clear instructions from the king, any advantage gained through force could easily be lost by delays.

The representatives themselves were also beginning to take stock of their options in the event of a forcible collection. The nuncio's secretary informed the Assembly that the royal officials planned to execute the *dos quarta* with only the bull of Julius III, claiming that the rules of chancery had no authority unless they came with a lead seal. He advised the Assembly to write to Rome right away to obtain a properly sealed document, and the Assembly immediately formed a committee to write the letter. The representatives must have been buoyed by the recent news that agents of ten chapters had met with the pope for more than one hour. They informed the pope of the abuses that the chapters had suffered from the prelates and royal officials, and secured his promise to address them. Although the news from Rome did not touch on the subsidy itself, it boded well for the Assembly that the pope had spent so much time with the chapters' agents. The Assembly also appointed a committee to determine how the ecclesiastical estate should respond to a forcible collection and whether it would be wise to prepare instructions for the churches.[45]

On September 30, the Assembly reviewed a letter to the chapters, which provided a brief synopsis of the events to date. It also reported that the bishop was ready to execute the bull but was refraining in the hope that a dispatch from Rome would confirm the bull's validity and that the representatives would then serve the king voluntarily. The representatives stressed to the chapters that very good lawyers had told them that the bull had been revoked and that, according to law, they could not make any agreement without papal license. If the bishop should execute the bull, the representatives stated, he would act unlawfully. The Assembly recommended using all legal responses available to the clergy and to report any violation directly to Rome. The Assembly also recommended that the clergy protest to the king any harms inflicted on them by the bishop's illegal actions, having confidence in the king's clemency and his knowledge of their past service. The representatives closed by saying that they had waited for four months for the

---

[45] ACS, Sec. VII, lib. 85, "Congregación del clero…1555," Sessions 62, 63, 64, and 66, September 23, 24, 25, and 28, 1555. The issue about the appropriate response to a forcible collection was raised again on October 8. See Session 73, October 8, 1555.

confirmation so that they could serve the king. Since no word had arrived, they would return to their chapters confident that the king would not allow them to be harassed for what they would have done freely with papal authorization.[46]

While a conflict appeared imminent to the Assembly at the end of September, Suárez still did not proceed against the clergy with force. Instead, the royal ministers continued to try to convince the representatives that the bull was valid.[47] Between October 2 and 10, deputies meet with the president of the council three times. Although the president was searching for a way to break the impasse over the status of the bull, he also chided the representatives for spending so much time and money assembled without making any preparations for payment in case the bull was valid or a confirmation arrived.[48] Clearly, each side was procrastinating, probably hoping that either the confirmation or an indisputable revocation would arrive soon. Otherwise, the clergy would have left already and the ministers would have begun the sequestration. In a sense, both sides were cornered; without news from Rome, their only options would lead to conflict, which was something both sides wanted to avoid.

On October 15, a servant of the bishop of Lugo summoned four representatives from four different chapters to appear before the princess at 9:30 to discuss the negotiations. The Assembly then appointed six deputies from the chapters of Toledo, Seville, Burgos, León, and Salamanca to meet with the princess. When the deputies arrived at the palace, the princess, who scolded them for having accomplished nothing since June, ordered the representatives to reach an agreement within three or four days and then to return to their churches. If she hoped to intimidate the Assembly's deputies into submission, she was disappointed. Rodrigo Zapata responded that the chapters had convened the Assembly in good faith, but shortly after the representatives had signaled their willingness to serve the king and to negotiate with his ministers by kissing the princess's hand in June, they had learned that the bull had been revoked. Without papal license, Zapata stressed, the clergy could not negotiate the payment of a subsidy for fear of

---

[46] Ibid., Session 67, September 30, 1555. See also B.N., Ms. 9937, ff. 161–163v and Biblioteca de San Lorenzo del Escorial, Ms. V II 4, f. 460.

[47] AGS, E leg. 109, f. 284 and E leg. 113, f. 92.

[48] ACS, Sec. VII, lib. 85, "Congregación del clero…1555," Sessions 69, 71, 72, and 76, October 3, 5, 7, and 11, 1555.

censure. The princess shot back that the bull was valid and that they had no reason to say otherwise. She implored them to serve the king with a subsidy within three to four days. Zapata unhesitatingly repeated that, according to the Assembly's lawyers, the bull had been revoked. Otherwise, he said, the representatives would have served the king with alacrity. In that case, the princess told them to return to their churches and excused the deputies. Later, at the Assembly, the representatives began to discuss their next step. If the princess's order had shaken anyone's resolve, a letter from the chapter of Salamanca approving the Assembly's actions to date in defense of ecclesiastical liberty must have given them heart.[49]

The next day, after further discussing the princess's order, the representatives reaffirmed their earlier decision not to make an offer without a new papal concession and not to do anything novel in the negotiations. Consequently, they decided to make preparations to dissolve the Assembly. The decision to dissolve, however, was not unanimous. Seville's representatives recommended consulting the chapters before leaving. The Assembly then prepared a letter for each chapter to explain why it had dissolved, and it turned to the common costs. It also charged the chapter of Toledo, in its absence, with coordinating the exchange of information regarding the *dos quartas*. The Assembly also appointed two deputies to make one final appeal to the bishop of Lugo not to execute the bull of the *dos quartas*.[50]

On October 18, the Assembly sent deputies to bid farewell to the princess and each of the royal ministers. Seville's representatives again opposed leaving without royal license and before hearing back from the chapters, fearing such actions would harm the ecclesiastical estate and create disunion. Several other representatives agreed, but the majority voted to dissolve the Assembly. Later that day, the representatives who met the bishop of Lugo reported that he was not pleased with the Assembly's response to the princess, and he castigated the representatives for spending so much money assembling and not accomplishing anything.[51] The princess was unhappy but more polite: she thanked the deputies for notifying her and said that the representatives had

---

[49] Ibid., Session 79, October 15, 1555. Similar letters of support had arrived from other chapters on the previous days, see Ibid., Sessions 77 and 78, October 12 and 14, 1555.

[50] Ibid., Session 80, October 16, 1555.

[51] Ibid., Session 82, October 18, 1555.

her permission to leave.[52] Juan Vázquez was also unhappy with the Assembly's decision.[53] The nuncio, on the other hand, promised to do all that he could for the ecclesiastical estate.[54]

The Assembly then reviewed a lengthy letter to the chapters, explaining its decision to dissolve in light of recent events.[55] It also examined more legal documents, including three legal instruments for appealing the execution if it was carried out. Unfortunately, the minutes do not transcribe these documents.[56] Finally, the Assembly sent several deputies on October 21 to present a long letter to the bishop of Lugo that detailed why the bull had been revoked and why he had no authority in the matter. The bishop was not pleased and said that he would respond later. The Assembly, however, did not wait for his response, but rather dissolved itself that afternoon.[57]

The crown did not act immediately. In early November, a debate ensued over who should carry out the sequestration. Suárez advocated using lay officials, as precedent dictated, while the president and other ministers recommended using ecclesiastical officials instead. Despite his reservations, Suárez ordered ecclesiastical officials to collect the rents. Factional politics may partially explain Suárez's action. He knew that the king regarded the president highly, and Suárez did not dare to break with him and be accused of damaging the negotiations. He stated clearly to the king, however, that he was reluctant to engage ecclesiastical officials.[58]

The princess also wrote to her father on November 11 that because they could not reach an agreement with the Assembly and because of its costs, she had ordered the representatives to return to their churches and let the Comisario General carry out the execution. In order not to embitter the pope, the Comisario General would use ecclesiastical and not secular officials to collect the money. In the meantime, she said, the king should write to his ambassador in Rome to obtain either a new concession or the confirmation of the present one, and send it

---

[52] Ibid., Session 83, October 19, 1555.
[53] Ibid., Session 84, October 20, 1555.
[54] Ibid., Session 84, October 21, 1555.
[55] Ibid., Session 83, October 19, 1555.
[56] Ibid., Session 84, October 20, 1555.
[57] Ibid., Session 84, October 21, 1555.
[58] AGS, E leg. 109, f. 284 and E leg. 113, f. 92. Later, after ecclesiastical officials had already been dispatched, the president changed his mind and agreed to send laymen. AGS, E leg. 113, ff. 96–97.

immediately, because the clergy insisted that the bull had been revoked. She also noted the bishop of Lugo's opposition to sending ecclesiastics to carry out the sequestration, fearing that such an innovation would not be advantageous. The princess also expressed concern that the clergy might complain to the pope.[59] The princess's letter reveals that the crown's anticipation of papal reaction to the sequestration and potential clerical appeals to Rome influenced royal policy.

Even though ecclesiastical officials served the king in a wide range of capacities, Suárez had a hard time finding anyone who was willing to sequester ecclesiastical rents. In his memoir, Diego de Simancas, the future Bishop of Zamora, recalled being appointed to the task in Toledo. He noted that Suárez tried to tempt him with the prospect of winning royal favors through the commission. Simancas, however, still refused because it would be against his conscience.[60] The licenciado Santillana, a justice of the *Chancillería* of Valladolid, finally accepted the commission.[61] In the end, Suárez employed both ecclesiastical and lay officials to carry out the sequestration. Even though he found the quality of the officials wanting, Suárez had to pay them higher salaries than normal. These problems notwithstanding, he still hoped that the sequestration would bring the clergy back to the negotiating table. To that end, Suárez emphasized the importance of obtaining unequivocal verification from Rome. He recognized the risk of a papal revocation, in which case the crown would have to concede. He was certain, however, that Paul IV would reprimand the clergy, allowing the king to reach an agreement with them, especially considering that many clergy were ready to negotiate.[62]

As Comisario General, Suárez had to balance many contending interests. To discourage further resistance, he advocated swift punishment of anyone who disobeyed. An unequivocal use of force would erase any perception of royal weakness or any suggestion that the bull had been rescinded. His letter to the king on November 10 illustrates that, for Suárez, the purpose of using force was not to encourage excessive royal demands, but to steer the clergy to the negotiating table. His

---

[59] AGS, E leg. 109, ff. 218–221.

[60] Manuel Serrano y Sanz, ed., *Augobiografías y memorias* (Madrid: Editorial Bailly-Bailer, 1905), p. 153. I am grateful to J.B. Owens for directing me to this work.

[61] Sebastian de Horozco, *Relaciones históricas toledanas*, intro. y trans. de Jack Weiner (Toledo: Instituto Provincial de Investigaciones y Estudios Toledanos, 1981), p. 143. I am grateful to Laura Canabal Rodríguez for directing me to this work.

[62] AGS, E leg. 109, f. 284, E leg. 113, f. 92, and PR leg. 20, f. 34 (I and II).

strategy also represented an attempt to reassert the authority of his own ministry. Over the years, the office of Comisario General had lost to the treasury sole control over the disbursement of the ecclesiastical contribution. The treasury often used the contributions to pay the king's debts in northern Europe, and such misappropriation of the funds earmarked for war in the Mediterranean was a constant sore point with the clergy. Suárez used the clergy's resistance in 1555 as an opportunity to justify to the king why his ministry should have full authority over the collection and use of this money. If the king restored his jurisdiction, Suárez implied, he might entice the clergy to comply. In the process of restoring his own authority, this reform might also in the long run protect the ecclesiastical contributions from the royal treasury.[63]

The situation improved momentarily for the crown in late December when a papal brief arrived confirming the concession. Suárez was furious, however, that the ambassador in Rome had waited until November to send the brief issued on July 31. If the brief had arrived while the Assembly was still in session, he stated, the crown and the representatives would have reached an agreement in days. Nevertheless, the brief offered the crown a new opportunity to negotiate a settlement with the clergy. Suárez immediately sent copies to all the dioceses and began to negotiate with individual chapters for a contribution. In the meantime, royal officials suspended the sequestration. During Christmastide, however, another letter arrived from the ambassador in Rome, reporting that the brief of confirmation was revoked.[64] The news of the revocation terminated the negotiations with many chapters. Still, Suárez did manage to reach separate agreements with Cartegena and Calahorra for payment of the subsidy as in the past. Since he had not seen a copy of the revocation, however, he was determined to proceed with the execution, believing that the clergy had tricked the pope into granting it.[65]

On January 9, the chapter of Toledo received the brief and immediately sent notarized copies to the other chapters. To prevent the sequestration from continuing, the chapters then informed the Comisario

---

[63] AGS, E leg. 109, f. 284 and E leg. 113, f. 92.

[64] By revoking the brief confirming the concession, Pope Paul IV did not clarify whether the bull was valid or not. The situation in Castile returned to what it had been since July: the clergy held the bull to have been revoked, and the Crown held it to be valid.

[65] AGS, E leg. 113, ff. 96–97, PR leg. 20, f. 34 (I and II).

General's officials on the local level that the brief had been revoked.[66] Then, in mid-January, representatives from Toledo brought the original brief to court. Notwithstanding his earlier pledge to abide by a revocation, Suárez stood firm on the need to collect the contribution and advocated a propaganda campaign in Rome to counter the clergy's lies and let the pope know what really was happening in Spain.[67]

Despite the brief of revocation, therefore, royal officials continued to sequester ecclesiastical rents. In protest, the clergy began to suspend services in Salamanca and Zamora in early February.[68] The new crisis further highlighted the conflicts between Suárez and other royal ministers. Suárez ordered the clergy to lift the suspension (arguing that the clergy had no legal cause to suspend services) and demanded that the participants report to court to be punished. He even wanted to send bailiffs to arrest those causing the problems, but once again, Suárez complained, the other ministers impeded him in his designs. The Royal Council also ordered the clergy to lift the suspension but would not issue a further decree to order the recalcitrant clergy to court. The crown's mixed messages, Suárez argued, strengthened the ecclesiastical estates' resolve: the chapters of Salamanca and Zamora, for example, would not lift the suspension. While they awaited word from the king, Suárez suggested to the regent that, to break the impasse between the ministers, she convene lawyers to determine whether the crown's cause was just or not.[69]

Four days later, on February 15, Suárez offered proof that Salamanca and Zamora's actions had stiffened resistance in other dioceses that previously had not protested. Using some old bulls, for instance, Toledo named a *juez conservador* (a judge who defended the Church against violations of its rights) to proceed against royal officials who sequestered ecclesiastical rents in the archdiocese. On the same day, the *juez conservador* imposed a *cesación a divinis* in the archdiocese of Toledo. The judge apparently had a sense for the dramatic, because he began

---

[66] ACT, AC lib. 10, f. 9rv; ACS, Sec. I, lib. 23, f. 161; AGS, E 113, f. 99. Toledo's minutes say that the brief revoked Julius III's concession, not the brief of confirmation as the letter from the ambassador implies. This might explain some of the continued confusion over the status of the original bull during the spring of 1556.

[67] ACT, AC lib. 10, ff. 9v–10; AGS, E leg. 113, ff. 96–97.

[68] BN, Ms. 9937, f. 164; A minority of canons in Salamanca opposed the *cesación a divinis*, see AGS, PR leg. 20, f. 34 (II). For a more detailed examination of a suspension of Holy Offices, see chapter 3.

[69] AGS, E leg. 113, f. 94.

the *cesación a divinis* by tolling the bells of the cathedral and all the other churches in the city nine times. Although the clergy still baptized children and provided last rites for the sick, the people of Toledo were inconsolable over the action, especially as it came during Lent.[70] Suárez was furious and sent orders to arrest the judge. Yet shortly thereafter, León and Cuenca also suspended Holy Offices. As news spread, more and more dioceses participated in the *cesación a divinis*, and royal officials blamed Toledo for instigating the other chapters.[71] This situation greatly worried the princess, who asked the prelates to intervene with their chapters to prevent further disorder.[72]

At this point, Suárez realized that his own actions were under scrutiny, and he assured Philip that reports of excesses in the sequestration were untrue—there were neither significant arrests nor extortion. He added that Salamanca and Zamora complained because some ministers pampered them; the policies of these officials only created obstacles to a suitable resolution of the negotiations. By mid-February, however, Suárez was slowly becoming isolated in his advocacy of force. The president, for example, had called for suspending the sequestration and any other action that the royal officials took against the clergy. Suárez, on the other hand, strongly opposed such a measure, because it would be equivalent to confessing that the bull had been revoked. He thought that this would be an inappropriate sign of weakness and harm the crown's position in the future. He would do nothing of the sort until he heard from the king or the regent.[73]

Suárez did not have to wait long. On February 27, Princess Juana ordered him to suspend the sequestration. He complied, but noted to Philip that the clergy were not content even with this and, seeing the crown's weakness, had not lifted the suspension.[74] The *cesación a divinis*, however, did not last much longer, for Salamanca finally lifted it on

---

[70] ACT, AC, lib. 10, f. 15; Horozco, *Relaciones*, pp. 143–144.

[71] BN, Ms. 9937, f. 164; AGS, PR leg. 30 f. 34 (III). Suspensions also took place in Segovia, Seville, Badajoz, Córdoba, Plasencia, Coria, Cartagena, and Ávila, see Rodríguez-Salgado, *Changing Face*, p. 229.

[72] AGS, E leg. 109, f. 86 and E lib. 73, February 22, 1556.

[73] AGS, E leg. 113, f. 98. On the same day, Bishop Antonio de Fonseca wrote to Philip that the sequestration was excessive and many clergy had been arrested; some churches responded with a *cesación a divinis*. After the arrival of the recent brief of revocation, he added, the Council thought it was necessary to temper the fury with which Suárez wanted to proceed. See AGS, E leg. 113, f. 233.

[74] AGS, E leg. 113, f. 98.

March 2 and Toledo and Zamora on March 11.[75] The princess's relief was clear in her response to Fr. Domingo de Soto's news that Toledo had lifted the *cesación a divinis*.[76] In the end, open resistance by many chapters had been sufficient to curtail the crown's offensive against the clergy and to rattle royal nerves.

It was not enough, however, to check royal efforts to collect the subsidy. Princess Juana still sought to collect the money. She wrote to her father on March 3 that she had ordered the ministers to seek agreements with individual chapters to pay the *quarta* or a portion of it. By lifting the sequestration, she explained, the crown might induce some chapters to come back to the negotiating table. Juana was not overly optimistic, however, and she pinned much hope on positive news from Rome that never arrived.[77] By the end of April, the princess complained that the chapters had hindered the collection process by casting doubt on the bull's validity. Such a hold-up jeopardized the entire subsidy of 500,000 ducados, she said, and would cost the crown greatly in interest charges. Moreover, she stated, it also endangered the crown's ability to collect a subsidy in 1558 and 1559; much of that money was already consigned and accumulating interest charges.[78] The dire financial situation might explain why royal officials declared on June 13 that Julius III's concession had not been revoked and proceeded to implement the collection. They sent orders to the chapters asking them to pay the subsidy as they had in the past or else to send representatives to court to negotiate its payment. If the chapters did not comply, the Comisario General would carry out the execution.[79]

The news from Rome, however tardy, was not positive. Despite Suárez's assertions that the clergy were treated moderately, the pope did not see it that way. The clergy clearly influenced him with stories of atrocities and the extortion of a million ducados from the church. The crown's attempt at damage control did not arrive soon enough for the pope to retract his declaration that "they are heretics." In fact, on April 22, the pope demanded that Suárez personally present himself

---

[75] AGS, PR leg. 20, f. 34 (III); Horozco, *Relaciones*, p. 144. Yet, at least one chapter, Osma, suspended Holy Offices later in March. So the situation remained somewhat unpredictable for the near future. See AGS, E leg. 114, f. 103.

[76] AGS, E leg. 114, f. 93.

[77] AGS, E leg. 112, f. 65.

[78] AGS, CJH leg. 29, f. 120.

[79] José Goñi Gaztambide, *Historia de la Bula de la Cruzada en España* (Vitoria: Editorial del Seminario, 1958), p. 532; ACT, AC lib. 10, f. 32v; ACG, leg. 11, pieza 11.

in Rome to defend his actions.[80] That injunction was no more effective than Suárez's earlier demands that the rebellious clergy appear in court. Nevertheless, the deterioration of the royal cause in Rome did not bode well for the crown. In May 1556, Paul IV revoked the concession outright. Even though the crown doubted that Paul IV had the authority to revoke Julius III's concession, it gave up its effort to obtain a subsidy. Instead, it instructed the archbishop of Toledo to negotiate with the prelates and chapters for the payment of a loan.

On July 3, royal officials stopped executing the *dos quartas*, and the crown returned the money it had already collected. The chapter of Córdoba, for example, had 644,045 maravedís returned to it.[81] The papal revocation of the subsidy and clergy's failure to provide a voluntary grant in lieu of the subsidy undermined the entire fiscal system of the monarchy and helps to explain the royal bankruptcy of 1557.[82]

The clergy's momentary success against royal claims may have influenced royal negotiations with other corporate bodies. In July, Suárez advocated some demonstration of royal authority so that other kingdoms would know that the king could enforce his will in a justifiable case, and so that the common people in Castile would not oppose the king without just cause.[83] For Suárez, then, the crown's response to clerical resistance not only affected church-state relations but also had an impact on governance in general. We must weigh his advocacy of a firm policy, however, against the potential calamities to the realm caused by a long-term suspension of Holy Offices and clerical hostility. Philip II clearly recognized the dangers and was adamant in December 1556 that there was to be no Assembly to discuss a loan from the clergy for a campaign against Algiers and Bugia while he was out of the country, because he wanted no further trouble with the chapters.[84]

The failed negotiations in 1555 confirm the independence and autonomy of the Assembly in the face of royal pressure, as I discussed

---

[80] AGS, E leg. 113, f. 130.

[81] See Goñi, *Historia de la Bula*, pp. 532–540; Juan Gómez Bravo, *Catalogo de los obispos de Córdoba, y breve noticia historica de su Iglesia Catedral, y obispado* (Córdoba: Juan Rodriguez, 1778), II, p. 453.

[82] David Alonso García, "Poder y Finanzas en Castilla en el tránsito a la modernidad (Un apunte historiográfico)," *Hispania* 66 (2006), p. 176.

[83] AGS, E leg. 113, f. 126. Although Suárez advocated force, he clearly was not a supporter of absolutism. His remarks suggest that on certain occasions subjects did have the right to resist their monarch.

[84] AGS, E leg. 512, ff. 149–150.

in previous chapters. I would therefore like to conclude this chapter with a few observations about the Comisario General and his office, as well as the role of the papacy in the negotiations between the Assembly and the crown. First, the Comisario General did not operate independently of the other ministers. Suárez constantly consulted them on policy initiatives and on several occasions accepted policies that he thought were counter-productive. The constant involvement of other royal ministers in these negotiations suggests some encroachment on the Comisario General's prerogatives. Disagreements over policy might also indicate that factional politics were seeping into the negotiations for the subsidy.

Second, the turbulent negotiations in 1555 gave Suárez the opportunity to reassert his prerogatives. He beseeched the king to order that all subsidies pass through his coffers and be used for the defense of Spain. If, as some scholars suggest, the councils became the true guarantors of societal liberties in Castile by protecting their own judicial rights and prerogatives, then Suárez's efforts to reassert the rights of his office and council in the collection process would have prevented the misappropriation of ecclesiastical rents.[85] To this extent, the Comisario General would impede the royal treasury from centralizing and disposing of all rents, despite restrictions on their use. Such a situation would not only favor his council but presumably the entire ecclesiastical estate.

Third, as a servant of both church and state, Suárez's action in these negotiations often blurred the lines between the two. Early on, he advised against a forcible collection and suggested accepting a smaller amount than normal to reach an agreement. Yet, when the die was cast, he had no qualms about using force against the clergy, especially when the failure to do so made the clergy more rebellious. He did, however, limit the scope of the sequestration so that the poor clergy would not be harmed. The Comisario General's position, of course, varied with each incumbent. An earlier Comisario General, for example, showed great reluctance to use force against the clergy in 1533 for fear of a suspension of Holy Offices. Other ecclesiastical officials also had qualms about sequestering ecclesiastical rents. Clearly, at times, some ecclesiastical officials in the royal service could not execute the crown's

---

[85] See I.A.A. Thompson, "Castile: Absolutism, Constitutionalism, and Liberty" in *Fiscal Crises, Liberty, and Representative Government, 1450–1789*. ed. Philip T. Hoffman and Kathryn Norberg (Stanford: Stanford University Press, 1994), p. 217.

will against the church with a clear conscience. Others, however, could act against the church on the crown's behalf without scruple. This situation raises several questions: How are we to assess church-state conflicts when clergy were the principle agents on both sides? Should we see these conflicts as royal encroachment on ecclesiastical power, as conflicting views among the clergy on the church's place in society, or as one ecclesiastical faction using the crown to displace another? I have not tried to answer these questions here, but only present them as something to ponder for future discussion on prelates in politics and the nature of regalism in the Spanish monarchy.

Finally, we cannot overlook the role of the pope and papal authorization of ecclesiastical contributions. The negotiations came to a standstill in 1555 because Rome gave no clear indication on the validity of Julius III's concession. With the brief of confirmation, several chapters immediately began to negotiate agreements for payment of the contribution. Two made agreements before the brief that revoked the brief of confirmation arrived, which once more placed the bull's validity in question. It should be noted that once a brief revoking the original concession arrived, the crown ceased to pursue the subsidy and even returned money collected during the sequestration. The behavior of both the crown and the clergy clearly indicates the continual importance of papal authorization of ecclesiastical contributions in Castile, as we will see in greater detail in the next chapter.

CHAPTER EIGHT

SPANISH DIPLOMACY AND THE CHURCH SUBSIDY

In 1563, Cardinal Borromeo wrote from Rome to the nuncio in Spain that "agents of the Spanish clergy shout to the sky of the harms done to them by the exaction of the subsidy, complaining that it would be not only difficult but impossible for them to pay the sum...the pope cannot avoid hearing them because they are on every corner shouting; wherever the pope goes he encounters them."[1] Even though Borromeo may have exaggerated in his letter, he underscored how insistent the clergy were in their appeals to Rome. This did not bode well for Spanish ambassadors, who already had to contend with frequent papal hostility toward making a concession; for example, after the Turks were expelled from Malta in 1565, Cardinal Pacheco on his own initiative asked Pope Pius IV (1559–1565) to grant the king a subsidy. The pope responded: "Send him the *quinquenio*? He will be lucky if he gets it when he asks me for it."[2] Negotiations for subsidies, then, were never limited to Spain. A recurrent duty of the Spanish ambassadors in Rome was to negotiate for ecclesiastical concessions and a recurrent duty of the ecclesiastical agents was to oppose the concessions. The popes retained considerable control over royal access to ecclesiastical taxation, and papal concessions gave the popes leverage on the Spanish kings. To understand fully the negotiations between the crown and the Assembly, we must consider the papal dimension.[3]

This chapter addresses three aspects of the negotiations in Rome for papal concessions between 1529 and 1556. First, it examines the obstacles, ranging from reluctant popes to French objections, that the ambassadors had to overcome to obtain these concessions. These

---

[1] Ignasi Fernández Terricabras, *Felipe II y el clero secular: La aplicación del concilio de Trento* (Madrid: Sociedad Estatal para la Conmemoración de los Centenarios de Felipe II y Carlos V, 2000), p. 355.

[2] Cardinal Pacheco to Philip II, September 23, 1565, *CODOIN* vol. CI, pp. 106–107, quoted in Fernand Braudel, *The Mediterranean and the Mediterranean World in the Age of Philip II*. vol. II, trans. Siân Reynolds (New York: Harper and Row, 1973), p. 1020.

[3] For a broader view of Spanish diplomatic activities in sixteenth-century Rome, see Michael J. Levin, *Agents of Empire: Spanish Ambassadors in Sixteenth-Century Italy* (Ithaca: Cornell University Press, 2005), especially chapters 2–5.

obstacles illustrate the often hostile diplomatic climate in Rome and Spanish attempts to maneuver within it. Second, the terms and conditions for each concession were central to these negotiations, because they could determine the size of the concessions, how the concessions were used, and the ease with which the monies were transferred to royal coffers. Consequently, both sides tried to obtain through the negotiations what they considered the most suitable and advantageous terms. Third, the chapter examines the Assembly's efforts to appeal to and to influence the pope. Royal ambassadors, in turn, monitored the Assembly's agents in Rome, countering their assertions of royal excesses or abuses. The papacy then acted as arbiter between the crown and the clergy.[4]

The Obstacles

The Spanish crown could not obtain ecclesiastical contributions without the requisite papal bull.[5] Such contributions provided the crown with 3,666,000 ducados between 1519 and 1555, but in each case the crown had to negotiate with the papacy. Maintaining amicable relations with the popes, then, was essential to securing the desired concessions. The Italian wars of the League of Cognac (1526–1529) between Pope Clement VII (1523–1534) and Charles V created a six year hiatus between concessions, while the hostility and subsequent war between Pope Paul IV (1555–1559) and Philip II created nearly four years of uncertainty concerning the validity of the previous concession and the possibility of future ones.[6] In normal circumstances during Charles V's reign, however, the popes conceded either an ecclesiastical contribution or a *cruzada* approximately every three years. These grants were nominally for the war against Islam. Although the impetus for a new concession could come from either the crown or the papacy, the correspondence

---

[4] For a discussion of similar negotiations for the cruzada during Charles V's reign, see José Goñi Gaztambide, *Historia de la Bula de la Cruzada en España* (Vitoria: Editorial del Seminario, 1958), pp. 476–501.

[5] An ecclesiastical contribution, or subsidy, is not the same thing as an ecclesiastical loan to the crown. A papal bull was not needed to negotiate a loan with the ecclesiastical estate. In 1556, when Paul IV revoked Julius III's bull for a *dos quartas*, the crown sought an ecclesiastical loan. For the 1556 loan, see Goñi, *Historia de la bula*, p. 541.

[6] On August 4, 1559, Paul IV finally agreed to concede a *cruzada*. He died, however, before the bull was issued. Ibid., pp. 544–545.

of Spanish cardinals and ambassadors suggests that Spanish officials generally initiated the discussion.[7]

The popes did not always make concessions enthusiastically, and at times they used the negotiations to extract concessions from the crown. In March 1529, Francisco de Quiñones, the Cardinal of St. Croce,[8] informed Charles that the bull for the *cruzada* was ready, but it contained a clause prohibiting its use until imperial forces surrendered certain papal fortresses.[9] By connecting his demand for the return of papal possessions occupied by Imperial forces with Charles's need for money, Clement VII effectively used the concession of the *cruzada* as a bargaining chip.[10] Papal concessions provided a ready source of revenue for the crown, but such concessions also provided the popes with leverage against secular rulers. Naturally, at a time when many rulers had broken openly with Rome, such leverage had to be used adroitly.

Simple bureaucratic problems also delayed the issuing of bulls. In the spring of 1529, papal officials claimed to no longer have a copy of the bull for the *quarta* Hadrian VI (1522–1523) granted in 1523 and refused to prepare a new bull without seeing it first. This did not bode well for the timely conclusion of the negotiations, because, according to the cardinal of St. Croce, papal officials had little desire to do anything

---

[7] The Spanish crown was not alone in seeking ecclesiastical contributions from the popes. Whenever the Turks prepared a naval expedition, the Venetian ambassador asked the pope to grant the Republic two tithes of the present year's ecclesiastical rents to help maintain the Venetian fleet that protected Venice and Christendom. See Kenneth M. Setton, *The Papacy and the Levant (1204–1571)* (Philadelphia: American Philosophical Society, 1984) vol. IV, p. 606.

[8] The Cardinal Protector of Spain in 1529 was Pompeo Colonna. None of his letters appear in the Spanish correspondence from Rome concerning the ecclesiastical contribution. Those cardinals involved in the negotiations in Rome on behalf of Spain were generally Spanish cardinals, but none appears to have been the Cardinal Protector.

[9] AGS, E leg. 848, f. 114. Presumably the pope referred to the occupation of Ostia and Civita Vecchia by Imperial forces, which had been a sore point since January. The troops, however, refused to leave until they were paid. So they too used the occupation as a bargaining chip in their negotiations for wages. Around Easter, the fortresses were finally returned, and Clement VII wrote a letter to Charles on May 7, 1529, thanking him for surrendering the fortresses. See Ludwig Pastor, *The History of the Popes: from the close of the middle ages*, ed. by Ralph Francis Kerr (London: Kegan Paul, Trench, Trubner, & Co., 1938) vol. X, pp. 38–39, 43, 48, 55.

[10] Other popes also used the concession of the *cruzada* to put pressure on the king. For example, Philip II eventually sent Bartolomé de Carranza to Rome for trial because the pope was reluctant to grant a *cruzada* until it was done. See John Lynch, "Philip II and the Papacy," *Transactions of the Royal Historical Society*, 5th series, 2 (1961), p. 31.

unless they were forced to.[11] Consequently, Micer Mai, the royal ambassador, tried to find a copy of Hadrian VI's concession himself in the records of the lawyers, representatives, and solicitors of the king. He even asked Secretary Pérez in Naples to look for a copy in his records. Although he failed to find a copy of the actual bull, Mai did locate a brief from 1523 that outlined the substance of the concession. Using this brief, he prepared a draft for a new *quarta*. The pope rejected the proposed concession, claiming that it would exceed 500,000 ducados and harm the clergy. He also noted that Hadrian VI's bull did not amount to more than 100,000 or 150,000 ducados.[12] Furthermore, the inclusion of an unspecified clause in Mai's draft outraged papal officials. To defuse the situation, the ambassador withdrew the clause and promised that the crown would accept what the pope offered. Papal officials did not respond to his overture, and Mai complained bitterly to the king that Clement VII's behavior was unfriendly and inimical to a timely conclusion of the negotiations. He also insinuated that the pending papal voyage to Spain to negotiate the peace treaty appeared to be a hoax.[13] Despite his difficulties with the pope and many papal officials, Mai was still hopeful because Lorenzo Pucci, the cardinal of St. Quattro Coronati, who drew up the bulls and briefs for papal concessions, had offered to secure a copy of Hadrian VI's bull for him. With a copy of the bull in hand, Mai thought that he could bring the negotiations to a close.[14]

The absence of the previous bull was a real obstacle, because Clement wished to grant a *quarta* under the same conditions as Hadrian VI

---

[11] AGS, E leg. 848, f. 36.

[12] In 1523, the Castilian Assembly of the Clergy and the crown agreed to a subsidy of 250,000 florins, roughly equivalent to 177,000 ducados. Mai's draft then proposed a contribution much larger than the final agreement between the Assembly and the crown. See Tarsício de Azcona, "Estado e Iglesia en España a la luz de las asambleas del clero en el siglo XVI," *Actas del congreso internacional Teresiano* (1983), pp. 305, 314–315.

[13] In May 1529, Clement sent a nuncio to Barcelona to negotiate the treaty. The nuncio then ironed out the final details for the papal concession and other terms of the treaty. Mai, then, was regulated to a secondary position for the final phase of the subsidy negotiations between the papacy and the crown that year. It is important to remember that these negotiations could take place in both the papal and the royal courts, and undoubtedly the reports back from the papal nuncio influenced the popes' positions in these negotiations just as much as the reports back from the royal ambassadors in Rome influenced the kings' positions. For more on the Treaty of Barcelona, see Thomas James Dandelet, *Spanish Rome, 1500–1700* (New Haven: Yale University Press, 2001), p. 41; Levin, *Agents of Empire*, pp. 48, 50.

[14] AGS, E leg. 848 ff. 8, 25, and 26.

had in 1523. The papal officials' reluctance to work with the ambassador or look for a copy of the previous bull also created unnecessary delays. Bureaucratic inertia did not make the negotiations easier, but might have been a useful 'tool' for either the pope or a faction within the curia to prevent a timely conclusion to the negotiations. Prolonging the negotiations might have been a papal strategy to gain more leverage with the crown. Mai, for example, was ready to accept whatever was offered in late March 1529 to avoid further delays. On the other hand, the Roman curia was full of factions and parties that supported various kings, princes, or familial groupings with their own interests in preventing or delaying the issuance of the requisite bull.

The French, for example, obstructed both Spanish attempts to gain a concession and to include certain clauses in the bull. On April 3, 1529, for example, Mai identified the French as one barrier to the concession of the *quarta*. Since financial constraints partially explained the end of hostilities between France and Spain in 1529, he related, the French ambassador had warned the Pope that a concession to Charles V would allow him to continue the war with France.[15] Moreover, if the French did not completely oppose a concession, they might oppose certain clauses. When the Spanish ambassador informally asked that cardinals contribute to the subsidy in 1535, the pope replied that the king of France opposed the participation of any French cardinal, and the ambassador consequently decided not to solicit the inclusion of any cardinals.[16]

The Spanish ambassadors, of course, also prevented the French kings from receiving papal concessions. Micer Mai, for example, managed to nullify a papal concession of a *décima* to France in 1532.[17] Rome was a diplomatic hub where ambassadors from all countries curried favor with the pope, who tried to balance their wishes and thus keep Roman

---

[15] Ibid., f. 34. In 1523, Martín Salinas, Archduke Ferdinand's ambassador to the imperial court, reported that the king had sufficient money to finance his military campaigns against France, because the clergy had just offered a subsidy of 210,000 florins in place of the *quarta*. See *El Emperador Carlos V y su corte según las cartas de Don Martín de Salinas: embajador del Infante Don Fernando (1522–1539) con introducción, notas é indices*, ed. Antonio Rodríguez Villa (Madrid: Establecimiento Tipográfico de Fortanet, 1903–1905), p. 147. Salinas reported a smaller subsidy than Azcona found for 1523, see note 12 above. Later, in 1535, the French argument that Charles would use the Spanish armada against Marseilles and not against Barbarrosa may partially explain why Paul III delayed granting a concession. See AGS, E leg. 864, f. 91.

[16] AGS, E leg. 864, f. 93.

[17] AGS, E leg. 857, f. 11.

Catholic unity intact. As Paolo Prodi explains, the hostilities between Charles V and Francis I left the pope with no choice except to take a neutral position; only where the larger interests of the church and faith were concerned would the pope depart from this rule.[18] Thus, the Spanish ambassadors had to contend not only with the popes' political maneuvers, but also with the political schemes of Charles's adversaries.

There was also the question of timing. All concessions were ostensibly for the war against Islam, and in July 1532, Mai wanted to conclude the negotiations for a new concession quickly, fearing that either a royal victory or a truce with the Turks would create a further impediment.[19] The bull finally conceded in 1532 was specifically for defense against the Turkish advance, but by the time it arrived in Spain the immediate threat had diminished.[20] This situation partially explains the Castilian chapters' resistance to the concession in 1532 and 1533. The tides of war, then, could affect papal readiness to grant a concession, and the Castilian church's willingness to pay.

In his attempt to extract a concession from the crown in July 1554, Pope Julius III (1550–1555) also skillfully used delaying tactics. He argued that since the past subsidy was still current, he could not grant a new one. Fernando Montesa, secretary to the ambassador, corrected him, pointing out that the previous subsidy was for 1552 and 1553 and no longer current, but to no avail. He later learned that the problem was not the past subsidy but Julius's desire to deduct the repayment of his loan of 200,000 ducados from a new ecclesiastical contribution.[21] The secretary did not want to link the concession of the subsidy directly to the repayment of the loan, possibly fearing a dangerous precedent for future negotiations. He therefore complained to Cardinal Montepulciano that the pope's position was inappropriate for negotiating with a king who never took anything from the ecclesiastical estate without

---

[18] Paolo Prodi, *The Papal Prince: One body and two souls: the papal monarchy in early modern Europe*, trans. by Susan Haskins (Cambridge: Cambridge University Press, 1987), p. 178.

[19] AGS, E leg. 857, f. 120.

[20] María del Carmen Mazarío Coleto, *Isabel de Portugal: Emperatriz y Reina de España* (Madrid: Consejo Superior de Investigaciones Científicas, 1951), p. 356.

[21] In 1551, Charles V had provided Julius III with a loan of 200,000 ducados, plus soldiers and other supplies for the pope's military campaign against Ottavio Farnese, the duke of Parma. For more on the War of Parma and Charles's larger diplomatic and strategic goals in supporting the pope, see Levin, *Agents of Empire*, pp. 60–63.

papal authorization. In contrast, he said, the king of France habitually took ecclesiastical wealth without papal authorization, and the king of France would never have made a loan to the pope.[22] Nonetheless, to show Spain's goodwill, Montesa recommended to Montepulciano that after an ecclesiastical contribution was freely conceded, the pope could then begin discussions through either himself or the nuncio on a suitable way to repay the loan. Although Montepulciano approved of the proposal, it apparently had no legs.[23]

On August 23, 1554, the secretary reported that the pope now refused to make a concession because he feared it would further enrage the chapters already outraged by the Council of Trent's decree that granted bishops visitation rights in the cathedrals.[24] Montesa insisted that only a few chapters were upset, and if the papal concession and the Tridentine decree arrived separately, the clergy would not create a tumult. Furthermore, he stressed that the pope had to consider the crown's dire financial need, but Julius was determined not grant a new ecclesiastical contribution until the chapters were calm. According to Montesa, the pope's apprehension over the chapters' discontent was only a pretext; his real concern was still the repayment of the loan. Realizing that he was making no headway with the pope, the secretary advised Charles V that either he or Antoine Perrenot, the bishop of Arras, should forcefully communicate the king's position to the nuncio.[25] Julius shrewdly used the potential unrest in Castile caused by the Tridentine decrees to postpone making a concession. Even when they did not specifically refer to ecclesiastical contributions, the chapters' complaints provided the popes with legitimate reasons for withholding a concession. Of course, in 1554, Julius III did not necessarily act out of consideration

---

[22] The secretary's comparison of Charles V's actions to support the papacy and France's failure to do so was regularly made by Spanish officials who were angry at the pope's unequal treatment of the two monarchs. Between the sixteenth and eighteenth century, the Spanish felt that the Holy See treated them unjustly despite their gallant efforts to spread and to defend the faith. See Ismael Sánchez Bella, "Iglesia y estado español en la edad moderna (siglos XVI y XVII)," in *El estado español en su dimensión histórica*, ed. Manuel J Peláez et al. (Barcelona: Promociones y Publicaciones Universitarias, 1984), pp. 155–159.

[23] AGS, E leg. 881, f. 46.

[24] The decree challenged the chapters' autonomy, and they successfully appealed it in Rome. See Feliciano Cereceda, S.J., "El 'litigio de los cabildos' y su repercusión en las relaciones con Roma (1551–1556)," *Razón y Fe* 130 (septiembre-octubre 1944), pp. 215–220.

[25] AGS, E leg. 881, f. 48.

for the plight of the Spanish clergy; the pope withheld the concession primarily to obtain the crown's forgiveness of his loan.

Even though royal officials demanded that the papal concession be made freely without strings attached, in time, they finally accepted Julius III's terms—200,000 ducados would be deducted from the concession to repay the loan.[26] Yet, had the king not reached an agreement with the pontiff, he would have been unable to raise any money at all from the clergy to finance the campaign against Bugia in North Africa, except in the form of a loan. The stalling tactics of a pro-Imperial pope, who just a few years earlier had written a warm letter of thanks to Charles V for his assistance in the War of Parma, indicates that all popes used the negotiations for concessions to achieve their own political objectives.[27]

The examples discussed above—papal reluctance, bureaucratic delays, French opposition, and timing—clearly suggest that princes did not simply demand and obtain a papal concession as a matter of course. Negotiations were often protracted and obstacle-laden. Some attempts might even have ended in failure, which may explain Francis I's demand for a double tithe in 1532 under threat of apostasy.[28] Obtaining a papal bull was not just a routine formality for princes in the early sixteenth century. Nor would it be for the rest of the Habsburg period. Alexander VII (1655–1667), for instance, did not renew the *cruzada* on one occasion and only renewed the subsidy and *excusado* with much resistance, because the crown was misappropriating the funds.[29]

---

[26] Ibid., f. 57. This concession became the bone of contention between the papacy, the crown, and the chapters in 1555 and 1556, which is discussed in chapter 7 and the final section of the present chapter.

[27] Dandelet, *Spanish Rome*, p. 51.

[28] Pastor, *The History*, vol. X, p. 198. Although Secretary Montesa's remarks from 1554 support the claim of Martin Wolfe that "the pope's right to consent to such levies [in France], even formally, vanished," the evidence from 1532 indicates that Francis I still sought a papal concession, and papal approval was evidently deemed important: why else threaten apostasy? Moreover, at the "contract" of Poissy (1561), the clergy demanded formal papal consent to the contract and later in 1579 they again brought up the issue of papal consent to a new subsidy. This evidence suggests that royal control in France over the tenths probably was not as complete as historians have thought in the sixteenth century. See Martin Wolfe, *The Fiscal System of Renaissance France* (New Haven: Yale University Press, 1972), pp. 100 and 124; Matthew Vester, "The Bresse Clergy Assembly and Tithe Grants, 1560–80," *Sixteenth Century Journal* 35 (2004), p. 779 n. 21.

[29] BN VE 186–7, f. 12.

The Terms

The ambassadors had to persuade the popes not only to grant a concession, but also to include the terms most favorable to the crown in the
requisite papal bull. The crown often provided its ambassadors with
detailed instructions on the terms it wanted. In 1535, for example, the
crown ordered its ambassador to seek a bull for the prelates (including
cardinals), all the clergy, and any other people who possessed ecclesiastical rents or pensions to finance 15 galleys at approximately 6,000
ducados per galley, for a total contribution of 90,000 ducados. To
prevent the clergy from convening an Assembly, the king asked Paul III
(1534–1549) to authorize the cardinals of Toledo, Seville, Burgos, and
Sigüenza, along with the nuncio and bishop of Palencia to apportion
the 90,000 ducados among the dioceses.[30] In order to apportion the
money effectively and justly, the king wanted a clause that required the
diocesan clergy to present their rent books for the past three years or
make verbal declarations of their rents before designated officials. The
king also asked the pope to include a clause that prohibited the clergy
from appealing the bull or offering another sum, as well as another
that allowed secular authorities to help carry out the collection. Finally,
the crown sought a separate brief that would be sent secretly, allowing the designated officials to reach an agreement, if necessary, with
the Spanish ecclesiastical estate for a sum different than what the bull
specified. Apparently, the crown worried that the clergy would be more
reluctant to pay the stated sum if they knew that the crown might
accept a smaller amount.[31]

These proposed clauses served several purposes. First, including the
cardinals increased the number of contributories, allowing the amount
to be more equitably distributed upon a larger economic base, and
would possibly lessen protests by the clergy.[32] Second, naming prelates
to apportion the subsidy would allow the king to bypass the Assembly

---

[30] Francisco Mendoza, formerly Bishop of Zamora, was Bishop of Palencia in 1535.
He was also the Comisario General de la Cruzada.

[31] AGS, E leg. 863, f. 25.

[32] To placate the clergy, García de Loaysa, for example, desired the arrival of a bull
obligating the cardinals to contribute in 1543. Later, in 1563, Philip II ordered his
ambassador to seek the inclusion of the cardinals for the well-being of the ecclesiastical
estate even though they were exempt in the original bull. See Kristen Kuebler, "Cardinal
García de Loaisa y Mendoza: Servant of Church and Emperor," (Ph.D. diss., Oxford
University, 1997), p. 168; ACS, Sec. IX, leg. 111, n. 1, f. 289.

of the Clergy. Third, the clauses would prevent excessive appeals that would hinder the collection. Fourth, the clauses would prevent delays in the collection by allowing royal officials to intervene when and where necessary. Although the documents do not refer to the negotiations of 1533–1534, the events in those years likely influenced this set of proposals.

Royal attempts to dictate the terms of a bull, however, often failed and, at times, created further problems. On July 3, 1539, the king instructed his ambassador, the Marquis of Aguilar, to solicit without delay a bull for a new concession from the king's Spanish and Italian possessions. The king ordered the ambassador to press for the inclusion of all the necessary clauses, especially a provision for cardinals to contribute, and to ensure that the bull be sent out as soon as possible.[33] By August 1539, the papacy had prepared a draft of a bull, but it fell short of royal specifications. Paul III had reserved for himself the *décimas* of Italy and offered the king only Spain's.[34] The ambassador contended that since the king had spent large sums of money on the defense of Christendom, he should be entitled to the *décimas* from his Italian kingdoms and subjects as well. The pope replied that he did not want to set a precedent for other princes in the future to demand similar concessions of Italian rents for themselves. The ambassador found the pope's response persuasive in light of the Holy League. Nonetheless, he wanted to hear from the king before dropping the royal demand to include the Italian *décimas* in the concession.[35]

The pope, however, did not want to wait, and he assured the ambassador that if the king opposed the terms of the bull, he would amend it later. Realizing that the pope would not budge on the *décima*, the Marquis of Aguilar turned to Charles V's request to insert a clause to carry out the *veros valores* in the bull. Here again, he was thwarted. Using Clement VII's bull of 1532 as a template, Paul III ordered that the calculation for the amount be based on the common estimate of the ecclesiastical rents' value in 1539. The ambassador protested, saying that Clement VII had amended the bull of 1532 so that the exaction would

---

[33] AGS, E leg. 868, f. 124.

[34] This action strengthens Prodi's suggestion that while the popes delegated or were delegating certain ecclesiastical powers to princes, the papacy tried to increase its control over the Italian church, even outside the Papal States. See *Papal Prince*, p. 173.

[35] AGS, E leg. 868, f. 6. For more on the Holy League of 1538, see Dandelet, *Spanish Rome*, p. 48 and Levin, *Agents of Empire*, pp. 19–23 and 159–160.

be based on the *veros valores*, as in the concession of 1529. Moreover, he stressed, the king did not want to use this clause to extract more money from the clergy but to better apportion the subsidy. If the pope did not want to place the clause openly in the bull, the ambassador stated, the king would accept a secret brief for an assessment based on the *veros valores*.[36] The pope was resolved, however, neither to add this clause nor grant a secret brief.

The ambassador also failed to persuade the pope to include other terms favorable to the crown. So, in the final draft of the bull, the cardinals and the Order of San Juan were still exempt from paying and the amount of money that the king would collect was smaller than expected; the pope estimated 470,000 florins. If the exaction was calculated on the basis of the *veros valores*, the ambassador told Charles, the amount would be 600,000 florins. This calculation seems to belie his earlier remark to the pope that the king did not seek the *veros valores* to extract more money from the clergy. He informed Charles on August 20, however, that the pope was determined to finalize the draft without further changes.[37] Although the crown obtained a concession in 1539, the Marquis of Aguilar's letter reveals the crown's utter failure to procure all the terms it desired. Setting the terms, the popes pursued their own political objectives both within and outside of Rome. The exemption of the cardinals, for instance, probably assured the pope support within the College of Cardinals and among those cardinals who held Spanish pensions. Moreover, the exemption may have touched on the

---

[36] A division and collection based on the common estimation would not entail the detailed and complex methods of verification discussed in chapters 5 and 6. Negotiating over the method or the base year to assess the values of ecclesiastical rents to determine the size of the contribution was typical of these negotiations. These were not mundane issues, and all parties took them seriously. In the late 1560s, for instance, an important point in the negotiations between the papal nuncio and Venetians for an ecclesiastical contribution was whether an assessment from 1536 or 1538 would be used to calculate the size of the contribution. At this time, the papal nuncio to Venice was concerned that the Spanish and Venetians may have conferred on their respective negotiations with the papacy for contributions. Possibly, he feared that their sharing strategy or information on the year of assessment might weaken the papal negotiating position. It is important to remember, then, that the Spanish ambassadors were not the only ones seeking papal concessions, and the popes were often involved in similar negotiations with other princes simultaneously. This undoubtedly led to ambassadors sharing strategies and information, and possibly using the grants to other princes as precedent for their own negotiations. See Vester, "The Bresse Clergy," pp. 777–778.

[37] AGS, E leg. 868, f. 6. As seen in chapter 5, the crown negotiated a subsidy of 500,000 ducados, well above both the pope's and ambassador's estimates for the subsidy.

longstanding conflict between popes and kings over the presentation rights of church pensions.[38]

If the ambassador failed to obtain acceptable terms in the original concession, the crown would try either to renegotiate the bull or, more likely, to amend it through papal briefs. At present, there are no known examples in which the Spanish crown returned a bull because of unfavorable papal conditions or where the crown seized ecclesiastical income on its own authority. The French, however, might have done so in 1535.[39] The possible French action gives credence to Thomson's assessment that the lack of a papal grant would not hinder a prince from seizing church income. The Spanish case, however, suggests that the prince would try to work with the papacy to obtain a bull with the most favorable conditions.

Although he had little luck dictating the terms of the bull in 1539, the Marquis of Aguilar had slightly more success amending it. On October 21, he related that Paul III had issued a brief for the Comisario General de la Cruzada to estimate the *medios frutos* in order to avoid inconveniences, doubts, and differences within the ecclesiastical estate itself. Unfortunately, since the brief had to correspond to the bull, Cardinal Jeronimo Ghinucci was unable to remove the stipulation 'following common estimation.' Nonetheless, this gave the crown a little more control over the apportionment, and a papal official told the ambassador that the royal ministers should be content with it. Another brief was also prepared for the cardinals, informing them that if necessary, they would be required to contribute. The ambassador did not have complete success, however. The pope wanted both his nuncio and the cardinal of Seville to administer the concession, and a brief allowing the crown and the clergy to reduce the *medios frutos* to a subsidy was still not forthcoming.[40] Yet, the pope made one major concession. He

---

[38] Dandelet, *Spanish Rome*, pp. 50, 91, and 97.

[39] AGS, E leg. 864, f. 4. On February 15, 1535, Paul III conceded two-tenths of the ecclesiastical rents to Francis I on the condition that the king would aid the pontiff with either money or ships. See Pastor, *The History*, vol. XI, p. 223.

[40] During the reign of Charles V, with the exception of 1536, the papal concessions consisted of a proportion of ecclesiastical rents, ranging from a tenth to half. The crown and Assembly of the Clergy, however, normally agreed to the payment of a subsidy worth less than the original papal concession. Since papal approval was necessary to reduce the concession into a subsidy, the crown always sought a brief to that end. It normally kept the brief secret, presumably in order to negotiate the highest subsidy possible with the Assembly. In 1530, the crown was concerned that the chapters might not make the first payment of the subsidy if the papal brief did not arrive on time (See

allowed Charles to collect a *décima* from the clergy of Naples.[41] The briefs, then, made up for many deficiencies in the original bull. Unfortunately, the briefs could only correct problems to a certain degree. The original clause in the bull concerning estimation, for example, limited the authority that a brief could concede to the Comisario General.

The process of amending a bull might also open the door to further obstacles. On October 31, 1532, Mai reported that the recently granted bull of the *medios frutos* was more typical of Italy than Spain.[42] While he acknowledged that it might create problems in Spain, he advised the empress to accept the bull without changes. Otherwise, he worried that in retaliation for Mai persuading the pope to rescind a bull conceding *décimas* to the king of France, the French ambassador would hamper his effort to revise the bull of the *medios frutos*. Mai also advised the empress that the pope might be unwilling to amend the bull. Finally, he feared that if the crown did not accept the present bull immediately, the Turks might withdraw before it could be amended. For these reason, Mai accepted the bull and recommended that regency government do the same.[43] From the ambassador's perspective, he had obtained the best bull possible under the circumstances.

Nevertheless, the regency government in Spain still wanted changes, because it feared that the current bull would create more delays in negotiating with the Assembly of the Clergy than the time necessary

---

chapter 2, p. 82.) John A.F. Thomson misinterprets the Portuguese request for a similar brief in 1517. He found it surprising that "the pope was brought in at all, because the practical compromise between the king and clergy had been reached without him. Nevertheless, it was clearly felt desirable that Roman approval should be obtained, a sign that however much papal claims were flouted in practice, some form of lip-service was still paid to them." The Spanish situation makes clear that within the context of the negotiations between the crown and the Assembly, papal approval to reduce the concession into a subsidy was not just desirable but essential. See Thomson, *Popes and Princes, 1417–1517: Politics and Polity in the Late Medieval Church* (London: George Allen & Unwin, 1980), p. 178.

[41] AGS, E leg. 868, f. 17. Later, in the 1560s, Pius V revoked the Catholic King's right to a *décima* from clergy in his Italian possession. There was no guarantee then that popes would renew concession in perpetuity. See María Antonietta Visceglia, "Convergencias y conflictos. La monarquía católica y la santa sede (siglos XV–XVIII)," *Studia Historica. Historia Moderna* 26 (2004), p. 173.

[42] The Spanish churches normally provided a *quarta* of one year's rents to the crown and not the *medios frutos* (or half) of one year's rents. Moreover, Italian churches apparently sold ecclesiastical properties to pay the concession. Some cardinals were opposed to extending the sale of ecclesiastical properties to Spain. See AGS, E leg. 858, ff. 120 and 123, and leg. 859, f. 35.

[43] AGS, E leg. 857, f. 11.

to amend it in Rome. First, the ambassador was instructed to remove the exempt status of the four mendicant orders from the bull. In turn, the crown promised the pope that it would provide discounts to burdened monasteries. Second, the ambassador was to amend the bull of *medios frutos* for one year into a *quarta* for two years, or *dos quartas*, which would be more suitable for the royal service.[44] If it would take too much time to amend the bull, the ambassador was to procure a papal brief to convert the *medios frutos* into a concession of *dos quartas*. Third, Mai was to make sure that only the bishop of Zamora was named administrator of the concession in the revised bull. He was not to be co-administrator with Giovanni Poggio, the apostolic collector and nuncio, because such a scenario would set a bad precedent for the future.[45] The regency government believed that Poggio's involvement would give the papacy the opportunity to be more intrusive in the local negotiations and collection in Castile.

On November 29, Mai informed the king that he had received instructions from Spain to amend the bull of the *medios frutos*. Before proceeding with the regency government's order, however, he wanted to know if the king also wanted him to solicit a new bull. Mai thought that the briefs he had already sent from Rome, such as one for the Comisario General to reach an agreement with the ecclesiastical estate for the payment of a subsidy instead of the *medios frutos*, sufficed to make the necessary corrections.[46] The ambassadors then had to contend not only with the diplomatic situation in Rome but also with potential conflicts of interest between Charles V and the regency government in Spain. In this particular case, it seems that Charles decided not to seek further changes to the bull.

Even though the popes heeded their nuncios' advice to make concessions to the princes, they never offered unconditional access to ecclesiastical rents, seeking to restrain royal demands and maintain papal authority.[47] Consequently, the terms the popes laid down were often

---

[44] The amount would be the same as the *medios frutos*, but spreading it over the rents of two years would make the contribution less of a burden for the clergy. The latter consequently would not protest as loudly.

[45] AGS, P.R. leg. 20, f. 69. This document is undated. From the context, however, it appears to be from 1532.

[46] AGS, E leg. 857, ff. 182 and 191–192.

[47] Paolo Prodi found that, confronting the schism with England in 1534, Girolamo Aleandro, a papal diplomat, advised the pope to make any concessions necessary so that the princes would not break with Rome. To cement its alliances, which "was the

at odds with royal objectives, and the Spanish crown regularly tried to amend them or persuade the popes to provide the most favorable terms to begin with. Other princes, however, might have threatened to defy papal authority or even break with Rome. The popes then had to deftly navigate these treacherous negotiations. For the most part, in regard to Spain, the popes continued to dictate the terms of the papal concessions and retained the upper hand in matters relating to ecclesiastical contributions.

The Chapters' Appeals

The Castilian chapters also appealed the bulls to the Holy See, protesting the undue burden the concession itself or specific clauses placed on them. The chapters appealed every concession, sending either representatives to Rome or instructions for their permanent agents already in the eternal city. Given the tense situation in Castile between the crown and the chapters, the crown found such action disconcerting and ordered its ambassadors to keep an eye on the clergy's activities. It even went so far as to ask the popes to order all Spanish clergy to leave Rome during the negotiations for papal concessions.[48] Clearly, then, the clerical presence was an important factor that could impinge on royal diplomacy in Rome.

Consequently, the Assembly of the Clergy often debated the best way to maintain its presence in Rome. Most often it simply sent agents to Rome to address specific issues of general concern to the ecclesiastical estate. For example, in 1555, the Assembly sent agents to Rome for one year.[49] Yet, from time to time, the Assembly discussed establishing a more permanent institutional presence in Rome. In 1533, the Assembly discussed three options: establishing its own permanent procurator general in Rome, hiring a solicitor, or employing a cardinal protector.[50]

---

surest way to defend power against religious and political rebellion," the papacy had to make concessions. See his *The Papal Prince*, pp. 162–163 and 168–169.

[48] ACS, Sec. VII, lib. 85, "Congregación del clero…1533," November 25, 1533 and February 5, 1534; ACT, AC lib. 5, ff. 110v and 111v; AGS, E leg. 27, ff. 29 and 184 and E leg. 60, f. 177; Fernández Terricabras, *Felipe II*, p. 355; Dandelet, *Spanish Rome*, pp. 69, 149.

[49] ACS, Sec. VII, lib. 85, "Congregación del clero…1555," Session 25, July 29, 1555.

[50] ACS, Sec. VII, lib. 85, "Congregación del clero…1533," October 20 and 21, 1533, and January 15, 1534.

Apparently, these options were considered too expensive or redundant, because the Assembly continued to send ad hoc agents and to employ agents of individual chapters already in Rome until 1592. In that year, the Assembly finally decided to establish permanent procurators general at both the papal and royal courts. Procurators general continued to represent the Assembly of the Clergy into the eighteenth century.[51] Through its appeals and agents, the Assembly tried to limit the number and size of the concessions and to prevent the crown from infringing on the rights and privileges of the chapters as well as the rest of the ecclesiastical estate.

In the 1550s, the chapters' and Assembly's representatives in Rome became more effective, especially in regard to nullifying the Council of Trent's decrees that gave the bishops greater authority over their chapters. With respect to the Council's decrees, the popes and cardinals became convinced that the Spanish bishops were a threat to papal authority and that the chapters were the defenders of the pope. Consequently, they wanted to limit the enforcement of the Tridentine decrees that increased episcopal authority. In time, the conflict between the chapters and bishops over Tridentine reforms became intertwined with conflicts between the popes and king. The popes began to see the chapters as the only counterweight to ever-increasing royal control over the Spanish church. As we have already seen, Julius III used the chapters' outrage as an excuse to delay conceding a contribution to the crown in 1554.[52]

In 1555 and 1556, the focus of the rest of this section, the chapters were well positioned to lodge their complaints in Rome, especially with the new anti-Spanish pope, Paul IV (1555–1559), who used their complaints to bolster his anti-Spanish policies.[53] Paul IV, who was hostile to Spanish control over Naples, formed an alliance with Henry II of France to expel Spain from Italy. It seems that the political alignment had shifted sufficiently in 1555 and 1556 to give the chapters'

---

[51] Very little is known about the procurator general at the papal court. For more on the establishment of both positions, see Sean T. Perrone, "The Procurator General of the Castilian Assembly of the Clergy, 1592–1741," *Catholic Historical Review* 91 (January 2005), pp. 32–34.

[52] Cereceda, "El 'litigio,'" p. 228; Fernández Terricabras, *Felipe II*, p. 305.

[53] Two agents of the Spanish chapters were particularly well placed at this time: Agustín Castrillo, a canon from Burgos, had free access to the papal lodgings; and Burgos's lawyer in Rome, Juan Bautista Osio, was an intimate of cardinal Serracino, the pope's nephew. Fernández Terricabras, *Felipe II*, p. 307.

representatives the upper hand in Rome, because if he responded positively to their appeals, Paul IV would achieve one of his foreign policy objectives—to weaken Spain. In October 1556, for example, the Spanish ambassador noted that by revoking the concession, the pope had hoped to weaken Spanish defenses and create dissent among the king's subjects.[54] The clergy's complaints, then, provided Paul IV with a justification to carry out his foreign policy objective.

With the death of Marcellus II (April 30, 1555), after only a month in office, and the election of Paul IV in May 1555, the ongoing negotiations in Castile for the payment of a subsidy ground to a halt. The Assembly held that, through a rule of the papal chancery, the election of a new pope annulled Julius III's concession. The crown disagreed. In time, both sides appealed to Rome. By November 1555, the situation concerning the validity of Julius III's concession to the crown hung in the balance. On November 20, Don Fernando Ruiz de Castro, the Marquis of Sarría and ambassador, elatedly wrote to Princess Juana of Portugal, the regent of Spain, that the pope had issued a brief confirming the concession. The representatives of the clergy, however, made significant headway in Rome in the next few days; on November 28, the ambassador informed her that the pope had revoked the brief and that the status of the original concession was unclear. The ambassador advised the princess that if she intended to proceed with collecting the subsidy, she would need to reach a favorable agreement with the clergy, even if such an agreement meant accepting a subsidy no larger than the last one. Otherwise, he feared, the clergy would complain to the pope, and the crown would lose the entire subsidy, because Paul IV, who had always favored the ecclesiastical estate and was averse to the concession in the first place, might revoke the concession outright. As we will see, the ambassador gave prescient advice. The pope's support for the ecclesiastical estate might not have been based solely on lofty ideals; rumor had it that the clergy had offered the pontiff 20,000 ducados to revoke the concession.[55]

---

[54] AGS, E leg. 883, ff. 46–48.

[55] AGS, E leg. 882, ff. 77–78. From the brief "Ad Romani Pontificis" located in the Cathedral Library of Pamplona, Jose Goñi Gaztambide dates Paul IV's revocation of the brief of revalidation to November 17, 1555. The ambassador's November letters, then, provide a clear sequence of events but not precise dates. See Goñi, *Historia de la Bula*, p. 529.

The chapters and other Spanish clergy succeeded in gaining the pope's ear, as Pedro Pacheco, the cardinal of Sigüenza, confirmed in a letter to the princess on November 28. Paul IV told him that he had information from the chapters and others in high positions that attested to the mistreatment of the clergy. Among other things, royal officials had sequestered account books and arrested clergy. The pope found such abuse intolerable and suggested that he might order the royal ministers to Rome. The cardinal replied that the pope was misinformed and implored him to disbelieve the falsities uttered by the Spanish clergy. In response, Paul IV offered to show the letters to the cardinal after excising the signatures. The cardinal also reported to the princess that the concession did not appear to be revoked by the rules of the chancery.[56] Even in Rome, therefore, some lawyers believed that Julius's concession was still valid. The regency government in Spain certainly welcomed this news.

On December 3, the Marquis of Sarría confirmed that many in Rome believed that the concession had not been revoked by a rule of chancery and that a brief of confirmation was not necessary. He therefore advised the princess not to use the brief of confirmation dated July 30, because the clergy would then use the brief *Ad Romani Pontificis*, which revoked the confirmation. Such actions would only create further confusion about the status of the concession.[57] Although the crown still felt that it had a strong case for collecting the ecclesiastical contribution, the papal response did not provide the crown with the reassurance necessary to forestall clerical resistance to the collection. John A.F. Thomson, then, is correct about the princes' use of papal authorization to pressure the clergy to pay. These events also suggest, however, that if the Spanish clergy questioned a bull's validity at all, they would not simply acquiesce to royal demands.[58] In fact, through their diplomatic efforts in Rome, the chapters were able to pressure the crown and influence the negotiations.

Although the crown continued to collect the *quarta*, it recognized the questionable legality and morality of its action. In fact, Juana of Portugal consulted several theologians regarding the execution of Julius III's bull. The general consensus was to obey the recent papal order

---

[56] AGS, E leg. 882, f. 180.
[57] Ibid., ff. 82–83.
[58] Thomson, *Popes and Princes*, p. 180.

and cease implementation of Julius's concession. Friar Melchor Cano, however, argued that the crown could proceed with the execution. Disregarding the caution of other theologians, the bishop of Lugo, Comisario General de la Cruzada, followed Cano's advice and continued with the collection.[59]

The bishop of Lugo's action, however, did not bode well for the crown. Already, in April 1556, the cardinal of Sigüenza urged the princess to reach an agreement with the clergy, assuring her that any order or intervention from the pope would be a setback. When a scathing letter from the chapter of Toledo arrived in mid-April, the situation deteriorated even more. The chapter complained to the pope about mistreatment by the royal ministers, especially the bishop of Lugo.[60] It claimed, for instance, that the crown had rejected its offer to pay the subsidy, as it had in the past, and that the ministers had forcibly taken the account books to investigate the *veros valores* and arrested many canons. Not content with the customary 500,000 ducados, the chapter stated, the crown had exacted more than a million ducados from the clergy. Toledo's letter so provoked Paul IV that he decided to revoke the concession made by Julius III and suspend the *cruzada*. The pope also ordered the bishop of Lugo and Friar Melchor Cano, who said that Paul IV could not revoke the concession made by Julius III, to appear personally in Rome. Since the cardinal of Toledo was probably unaware of what his own chapter had written to the pope, the cardinal of Sigüenza urged Juana to have the cardinal himself write to the pope about what had really transpired in Spain.[61]

On May 6, the cardinal of Sigüenza again proposed that Juana and the cardinal of Toledo write to the pope, telling him the truth to counteract the many falsities the clergy had related.[62] The crown then made an effort to gain the pope's ear. First, the ambassador and the cardinal of Sigüenza presented the crown's case directly to the pope. Second, the crown tried to influence the cardinals so that they might indirectly convey the royal message to the pope: Juana, for instance, wrote to Giambattista Cicala, the cardinal of St. Clemente. Third, the princess

---

[59] Goñi, *Historia de la Bula*, pp. 529–530.

[60] In addition to writing the pope, the chapters had also suspended Holy Offices during Lent to protest the forceful and unlawful collection. See chapter 7, pp. 218–219 and B.N., Ms. 1293, ff. 96v–100; Ms. 9175, ff. 159v–160.

[61] AGS, E leg. 883, ff. 17, 18, and 21; Fernández Terricabras, *Felipe II*, p. 308.

[62] AGS, E leg. 883, ff. 19 and 20.

wrote directly to the pope, asking him to confirm Julius III's concession and stressing that the problems that had occurred in the bishop
of Lugo's execution of the bull were due to the clergy's resistance and
disrespect. She then asked the pope to discipline the recalcitrant clergy
who had laid false charges against their king.[63] The crown's attempts
to dissuade the pope, however, were unsuccessful.

On May 8, the ambassador reported that Paul IV still had not
revoked the bull. He did not think, however, that there was any question
about the pope's position. Within the limited time that remained, he
recommended that the princess reach an agreement with the clergy.[64]
Unknown to the ambassador, the pope had that very day issued briefs
revoking the *quarta* and suspending the *cruzada*; he only learned of this
on May 21.[65] According to Francisco Robuster, the royal solicitor in the
Rota, one brief suspended the *quarta* and even ordered the restitution
of all or some of the money already taken, while the other suspended
the *cruzada*. The cardinal of Toledo was entrusted to execute both
briefs.[66]

Upon learning of the revocation, the Marquis of Sarría immediately tried to block the arrival of the briefs in Spain. He advised the
Marquis of Tarifa to direct all mail from Rome to the court. The measure, however, did not succeed; the briefs or copies of them arrived in
Salamanca and then were sent to Toledo. Despite the revocation, the
crown still wrote to the chapters asking them to concede a subsidy, as
they had in the past.[67] The ambassador's attempt to circumvent the
briefs' arrival suggests that the briefs were not hollow documents. Even
though the crown still tried to reach an agreement with the chapters
for the payment of a subsidy, the revocation of the concession clearly
had an adverse impact on the negotiating process and affected domestic
policy in Castile.

Although the regency government was certain that Paul IV could not
revoke the concession, it officially stopped executing the *quarta* on July

---

[63] AGS, E leg. 866, ff. 134, 136, and 137. For a short minute on what the letter to
the pope should contain, see E leg. 866, f. 133.
[64] AGS, E leg. 883, f. 21.
[65] Goñi, *Historia de la Bula*, p. 531.
[66] AGS, E leg. 883, f. 22.
[67] AGS, E leg. 866, f. 135. Blocking the mail from Rome apparently was common.
Cereceda cites a similar occurrence in 1555 (Cereceda, "El 'litigio,'" p. 221).

3 and began to return the money it had already collected.[68] Nevertheless, the crown made further entreaties in Rome for papal confirmation of Julius III's original bull or another suitable concession. On August 11, Juana instructed the cardinal of Sigüenza to seek confirmation of Julius's concession even though Paul had recently revoked it, because some chapters were ready to make an agreement with the crown. The ambassador was given similar instructions.[69] On August 28, the cardinal of Sigüenza replied that there was no reason to speak further with the pope on the matter—the clergy had convinced him.[70]

The complete diplomatic triumph of the clergy in 1555–1556 was a first. Prior to Paul IV, the clergy's complaints to the popes had little impact on the overall course of the financial concessions.[71] This victory clearly encouraged the clergy to continue sending complaints of fiscal oppression to Rome. In 1559, for example, Paul IV denied a new *cruzada* in part because of these letters.[72] The presence of representatives of the Assembly in Rome was the norm until at least the mid-eighteenth century. Even though these representatives generally failed to obtain a complete revocation of an ecclesiastical contribution, they complicated the ambassadors' job and perhaps even convinced the popes to be less generous to the crown. Since the clergy continually appealed every new concession in Rome, they must have felt that their agents had achieved enough success to make this endeavor worthwhile. Given Philip II's frequent requests that Spanish clergy leave the city during negotiations for papal concessions, it is clear that the crown agreed.[73]

Conclusion

The negotiations in Rome were complicated. Far from a forgone conclusion, they were essential to obtaining an ecclesiastical concession. The negotiations between the Spanish monarch and the popes between 1529 and 1556 indicate that the princes had not superseded the popes

---

[68] See Goñi, *Historia de la Bula*, pp. 532–540; Juan Gómez Bravo, *Catalogo de los obispos de Córdoba, y breve noticia historica de su Iglesia Catedral, y obispado* (Córdoba: Juan Rodríguez, 1778), II, p. 453.

[69] AGS, E leg. 883, f. 34; for draft of this letter see E leg. 866, f. 131. For the letter and draft to the ambassador, see E leg. 883, f. 33 and leg. 866, f. 139.

[70] AGS, E leg. 883, f. 35.

[71] Goñi, *Historia de la Bula*, p. 527.

[72] Fernández Terricabras, *Felipe II*, p. 309.

[73] Dandelet, *Spanish Rome*, p. 149.

in controlling church finances. The papacy had lost significant power during the fifteenth century, but through deft negotiations, the papacy could still extract various concessions from princes. By supporting the chapters, the popes could hinder royal attempts to exact concessions without papal sanctions. Moreover, by periodically naming the nuncio to administer the subsidy together with the Comisario General de la Cruzada, the popes were able to keep a hand in the negotiations in Spain. Papal authority was not just limited to making the concession; the popes also had a direct role in Spanish internal policy. This position allowed the papacy to retain some extraterritorial jurisdiction. The negotiations in Rome thus not only expose the limitations on Spanish power and influence in the eternal city, but they might also provide another vantage point to examine the limitations of royal power within Spain itself.[74]

Any discussion of the subsidy and the Assembly of the Clergy must consider the Roman dimension, because the pontiffs played a central role in the concession of the grants and the terms under which they were made. The evidence from 1529–1556 indicates that royal control over ecclesiastical rents at the end of the Renaissance was not as secure as Thomson suggests. At the same time, it is worth remembering that the papacy received financial and other benefits from Spain in exchange for papal concessions. For example, 65 percent of all funding for building St. Peter's between 1529 and 1620 came from Spanish imperial lands. The crown could prevent those monies from flowing to Rome just as easily as the pope could prevent the ecclesiastical rents from flowing to royal coffers. In a sense, there was a certain amount of mutual financial dependency between the Spanish monarchy and the papacy.[75]

---

[74] Levin, *Agents of Empire*, pp. 200–208.

[75] Thomas James Dandelet, "Paying for the New St. Peter's: Contributions to the Construction of the New Basilica from Spanish Lands, 1506–1620," in *Spain in Italy: Politics, Society, and Religion, 1500–1700*, edited by Thomas James Dandelet and John A. Marino (Leiden: Brill, 2007), p. 194; See also A.D. Wright, *Catholicism and Spanish Society under the Reign of Philip II, 1555–1598, and Philip III, 1598–1621* (Lewiston, NY: E. Mellen Press, 1991) pp. 26–28, 32, 55–56, 144. More detailed studies are needed to understand the mechanism for the transfer of funds between Spain and Rome, the actual volume of papal rents in Spain, and the struggles between the crown and papacy to control these rents. Juan M. Carretero Zamora has begun to fill this gap, see Carretero, "La colectoría de España en época de Carlos V: Cuentas del nuncio y colector general Giovanni Poggio (1529–1546)," *Cuadernos de Historia de España* 78 (2003–2004), pp. 103–135.

Although Spain has been the focus of this chapter, other ambassadors engaged in similar negotiations. The Venetians, for instance, had to present their great needs to the pontiff to justify requests for ecclesiastical contributions. The French also received grants from the pope, at least until 1535, and they too saw concessions either revoked or filled with unacceptable conditions. The basic points addressed here concerning obstacles, terms, and appeals were probably familiar to other princes negotiating for papal concessions. The Spanish example provides a point of reference for understanding negotiations that all or most Catholic powers engaged in in Rome. Moreover, the Spanish example presents solid evidence that papal bulls and briefs were central to negotiations with the Castilian Assembly of the Clergy for ecclesiastical contributions. If the negotiations between other ecclesiastical Assemblies and monarchs were similar to those in Castile, the fiscal relations between popes and princes needs to be reevaluated.

CHAPTER NINE

CONCLUSION

During Charles's reign, the Castilian church convened thirteen Assemblies of the Clergy, but, despite its frequent meetings, the Castilian Assembly of the Clergy has remained a relatively unknown institution in Spanish and European history. Through the preceding case studies, this book has examined the structure and function of the Castilian Assembly of the Clergy in order to provide a better understanding of finance, governance, political practice, and church-state relations in sixteenth-century Castile.

To expand their financial base, the 'new monarchies' often turned to the church. Some negotiated for the contributions with the pope or the clergy or both, while others broke with Rome and placed themselves at the head of the church. John Lynch asserts that by the second half of the sixteenth century:

> [Philip's] methods were probably more effective than those of Protestant rulers who confiscated church property. The English crown sold monastic land for ready cash and failed to derive a long-term revenue from it. Philip II, on the other hand, by maintaining and extending church property and then taxing a prosperous institution ensured that the Spanish state possessed yet another source of revenue...[1]

Despite the twists and turns of negotiations with the Assembly and papacy, the Spanish crown benefited from its financial relations with the church. By the mid-sixteenth century, the *cruzada* and subsidy together provided more money than the *servicio* of the Cortes. By the early seventeenth century, the Tres Gracias still provided the crown with 13.3 percent of royal revenue, more money than the *servicio* of the Cortes (3.7 percent) but less than the *millones* tax (18.6 percent). The Assembly itself negotiated the payments of just over 6 percent of royal

---

[1] John Lynch, *Spain Under the Habsburgs* (New York: New York University Press, 1981) vol. I, p. 138.

income (670,000 *ducados* out of a total annual income of 10,750,000 *ducados* in 1621).[2]

The growth of the size of the subsidy payments corresponds roughly to the growth of the *servicio* payments during Charles V's reign. Between 1519 and 1556, the church transferred roughly 1,187,250,000 maravedís in subsidies to the crown. Between 1519 and 1537, 437,250,000 maravedís was collected (37 percent of the total) and between 1538 and 1556, 750,000,000 maravedís (63 percent). If Julius III's concession had not been revoked in 1555, the breakdown would have been slightly different: 437,250,000 maravedís (31.8 percent) for 1519–1537 and 937,500,000 maravedís (68.2 percent) for 1538–1556.[3] These hypothetical proportions during the first and second period would have corresponded almost exactly to the percentages of the *servicio* the Cortes paid in the same periods, which was less than one-third for 1519–1537 and over two-thirds for 1538–1556.[4] The financial burden on the Spanish kingdoms, then, increased dramatically after 1538, and both secular and ecclesiastical assemblies paid more in the second period than in the first, indicating that both experienced a similar proportional increase in taxation. The Assembly of the Clergy, therefore, did not necessarily fare any worse than the Cortes in its negotiations with the crown. At the same time, increasing fiscal demands made both representative institutions more important partners in government, especially as guarantors of royal credit.[5]

Nevertheless, judging by monetary figures alone, the Assembly's record for limiting the fiscal demands of the monarchy appears mixed. Between 1519 and 1555, the subsidy increased seven-fold, from

---

[2] These calculations are adapted from Helen Rawlings, *Church, religion and society in early modern Spain* (London: Palgrave, 2002), pp. 135–137.

[3] Tarsício de Azcona's figures were used to calculate the total contribution made during Charles V's reign. These totals include both the crowns of Castile and Aragon, and Azcona includes 500,000 ducados for 1555 even though the crown returned the money to the Castilian dioceses in 1556. For a point of comparison, I have both included and excluded that amount in the calculations above. See "Estado e Iglesia en España a la luz de las asambleas del clero en el siglo XVI," *Actas del congreso internacional Teresiano* (1983), pp. 314–315.

[4] Constance Jones Mathers, "Relations between the City of Burgos and the Crown, 1506–1556" (Ph.D. diss., Columbia University, 1973), p. 304.

[5] For a similar development with the French Assembly of the Clergy, see Jotham Parsons, "Assemblies of the French Clergy from Philip the Fair to Louis XIII," *Parliaments, Estates and Representation* 23 (2003), p. 9.

26,500,000 maravedís to 187,500,000 maravedís for all of Spain. The largest setback came in 1530, when the subsidy doubled. On the other hand, the crown often demanded contributions far larger than those actually received. In 1530, for example, it sought 700,000 florins from the Assembly but settled for 471,000 florins, while in 1540 it requested 600,000 ducados but agreed to 500,000 ducados (418,000 from Castile and 82,000 from the other kingdoms). In negotiations for the *quarta*, *dos quartas*, and *medios frutos*, the Assembly successfully offered amounts less than what the crown desired, even though it failed to make the crown honor royal decrees limiting the subsidy to 100,000 florins. Furthermore, even as the crown's monetary needs increased, the Assembly maintained the subsidy at 500,000 ducados for all of Spain from 1540 until 1562, successfully curtailing royal fiscal demands for over 20 years. Throughout the early modern period, the fiscal demands of the monarchy always fell disproportionately on the kingdom of Castile; this was true for the ecclesiastical contribution as well. Its complaints to the contrary notwithstanding, the Castilian Assembly nevertheless managed to limit the growth of royal exactions after 1530 proportionally more than did the Assemblies in the other Spanish kingdoms. Between 1530 and 1540, the subsidy for all of Spain increased from 132,500,000 to 187,500,000 maravedís. Although Castile carried roughly 58 percent of this increase, or 31,935,000 maravedís, the other kingdoms saw their share of the subsidy quadruple from 7,685,000 to 30,750,000 maravedís.

The effectiveness of the Assembly and the chapters in restraining the fiscal demands of the crown cannot be measured in maravedís alone. The Assembly was an independent institution, and the crown could not prevent it from convening. Consequently, with every contribution, the crown had to deal with the clergy's complaints. Moreover, the Assembly retained control over the apportionment of the subsidy and the verification of the ecclesiastical rents. Whenever the crown tried to abrogate these rights, the Assembly put up stiff resistance and usually prevailed, at least with respect to the structuring of the financial demand. Thus, even though the size of the subsidy increased, the Assembly continued to control the collection of taxes. The crown failed to gain complete control over ecclesiastical finances because it was constantly dealing with a viable political body that could restrain royal action. At the same time, a symbiotic relationship existed between the crown and the Assembly; that is, without those royal fiscal demands, there would have been no rationale for the Assembly. The Assembly was the administrative

instrument that made possible these wealth transfers and therefore kept
the cathedral chapters at the center of political and fiscal life in Castile
for centuries after the Council of Trent.

The crown used coercion and the threat of it to pressure the clergy to
act, but the outcome of negotiations was not determined by a powerful
state exerting its will over a defenseless church. The clergy could and
did resist the crown, using the suspension of Holy Offices, public prayers
to St. Thomas, sermons against the crown, appeals to Rome, and even
placards against royal officials. Consequently, the use of coercion by the
crown had mixed results. In 1533, the crown broke the clerical resolve
to suspend Holy Offices, and the clergy came to the negotiating table.
On the other hand, in the summer of 1540, the clergy's determination
to pay no more than 500,000 ducados finally forced the crown to end
its sequestration and accept the offer. Moreover, the crown's failures in
1540 may have made the royal ministers reluctant to carry out their
threats in 1541.

Furthermore, forcible collections were not necessarily as lucrative as
reaching agreements with the Assembly. The chapter of Toledo stressed
this point in August 1546, while royal ministers urged Charles to reach
an agreement with the clergy for payment rather than using force. The
corregidores also doubted that they would be able to collect much
through the sequestration of ecclesiastical rents in 1533 because the
clergy had already either hid or spent their money. Moreover, forceful
measures generally precipitated resistance by the clergy, creating the
internal disruptions that the crown wished to avoid. Coercion then
was an option in the negotiating process, but it did not guarantee a
positive outcome.

The correspondence of the regency governments of Isabel, Philip II,
and Juana with Charles V confirm that the crown sought to avoid
conflict with the clergy and did not undertake these negotiations lightly,
especially when Charles was absent from Spain. The non-confronta-
tional approach taken by the regency government of Isabel is exempli-
fied in the negotiations between the fall of 1532 and the spring of 1533;
at this point, only Tavera advocated a confrontational policy. In 1530,
the archbishop of Toledo advised against using a bull to give prelates
a greater say in the negotiations for ecclesiastic contributions because it
would only inflame the chapters. As these examples demonstrate, even
the expectation of opposition by the clergy could curtail royal policy.

Charles shared their opinion. In 1535 and 1546, he wanted to avoid
Assemblies altogether and reach settlements directly with individual

chapters. Charles was also aware of the potential pitfalls of pressing for too much at once and advised against seeking a voluntary grant beyond the subsidy in 1530. Whenever possible, the crown dealt circumspectly with the ecclesiastical estate. I.A.A. Thompson blames the 'bankruptcies' of 1557 and 1560 on "the failure of Charles V's political nerve after 1520."[6] Although Thompson is probably referring to negotiations with the Cortes after the Comunero Revolt, his statement is also valid for negotiations with the Assembly. Had Charles been more confrontational with the clergy, he might have extracted even more from the church. Confrontation with the church, however, could have been even more pernicious than with other institutions, because the church was a central pillar of society and of legitimacy for the monarchy. If the clergy preached against the monarch or suspended Holy Offices, they could severely weaken monarchial authority and possibly even stir rebellion. To maintain internal calm and avoid a situation that might undermine his authority, Charles had to cooperate with preexisting institutions. Thus, while the crown's authority was paramount, it was not absolute, and the crown continually had to work within a pluralistic institutional framework.

The negotiations for the ecclesiastical contribution also provide insights into governance under Charles V. Increased bureaucratization and professionalization neither resulted in a more effective and centralized government nor eliminated autonomous bases of power. The various ministers and councils often had different outlooks on how to proceed and vied with one another to retain and expand their jurisdiction and privileges. The archbishop of Toledo, for example, severely reprimanded a minister in 1530 for his conduct in the negotiations, while the council of Orders supported exempting the Order of Santiago in opposition to other ministers that same year. Divisions and divisiveness often prevented the consolidation of very much power in any one person's hands. The structure of government created new autonomous bases of power, often with overlapping jurisdiction, within the royal administration itself. In fact, the crown intentionally extended such a system to the colonies so that no one minister or institution

---

[6] I.A.A. Thompson, "Castile: Polity, Fiscality, and Fiscal Crisis," in *Fiscal Crises, Liberty, and Representative Government, 1450–1789*, ed. Philip T. Hoffman and Kathryn Norberg (Stanford: Stanford University Press, 1994), p. 168.

would become too strong. A pluralistic government such as this clearly contradicts the notion of a centralized state.

The composition of the government also could have an effect on negotiations with the Assembly, because the royal ministers who negotiated with the Assembly were often ecclesiastical officials. Consequently, a clear demarcation between church and state in these negotiations is not always possible. Alonso de Fonseca, archbishop of Toledo, played an important role in the negotiations with the Assembly of 1533. Yet that summer, to the frustration of the Comisario General, he did not condemn the suspension of Holy Offices. In 1541, Cardinal Tavera, while carrying out royal orders, was mindful of the church's interests, maintaining that verification of the *veros valores*, especially under the agreement of 1540, would undermine the church's position. After the crown insisted on some form of verification, he conceded to self-verification as the lesser evil. The reluctance expressed by Cardinal Loaysa, the Comisario General, to trespass on the customary prerogatives of the church in 1541 may also help explain why the crown refrained from using force against the chapters and was willing to come to the negotiating table. At the same time, Juan Suárez Carvajal, the Comisario General, had few qualms about defying papal authority and forcibly collecting ecclesiastical rents in 1556. Some prelates and ecclesiastical officials were clearly more regalist than others. This was not lost on the Assembly as it made overtures to more friendly prelates, like the Archbishop of Toledo in 1530, to help obtain a suitable agreement. The intertwining of royal and ecclesiastical roles influenced the course of the negotiations and the dynamics of church-state relations in Castile.

These negotiations also make clear that royal appointments of prelates and attempts to reform the clergy and religious orders did not translate to greater royal control over the church. Bishops continued to exercise independence, and even those bishops allied with the crown occasionally emerged as its fiercest opponents.[7] Moreover, the ecclesiastical estate had many foci of power, and the chapters were an important one. An examination of the Assembly squarely places the chapters at the center of the church-state dialogue for ecclesiastical contributions. This examination clearly illuminates the complexity of church-state

---

[7] Helen Rawlings, "Bishops of the Habit in Castile, 1621–1665: A Prosopographical Approach," *Journal of Ecclesiastical History* 56 (2005), p. 468; Sean T. Perrone, "Clerical Opposition in Habsburg Castile," *European History Quarterly* 31 (2001), pp. 331–336.

relations and provides a greater understanding of the internal divisions and lack of centralization within the church.

The negotiations, however, were never limited to Castile. Both the crown and the Assembly turned to Rome, and the popes issued bulls and briefs at the behest of both parties. The constant participation of the Assembly's agents in the negotiations in Rome, whether to obtain briefs for the inclusion of exempt clergy in 1533 or the revocation of Julius's concession in 1555, brings into question the notion that "during the early modern period, relations between pope and clergy have almost always been mediated by the sovereign."[8] This study has shown the importance of papal bulls and briefs in the negotiations between the crown and the Assembly for the ecclesiastical contribution, and the ability of the clergy to influence their drafting. Church-state relations thus cannot be confined to the internal situation in Spain but must address the international aspect of the Roman Catholic Church.

Understanding the papal position demands further investigation into the Roman dimension of these negotiations. Greater attention, for instance, must be given to the nuncio and his role. In 1545, both Charles and Philip discussed a new contribution with papal nuncios. The Spanish documentation, however, provides few details on these discussions, except that the nuncio in Spain offered to help the crown. Later, in 1555, the Assembly turned to the nuncio to support its claim that the bull was revoked. On other occasions, nuncios participated in the negotiations and co-administered the collection with the Comisario General. By studying their instructions and correspondence, the nuncios' role in the negotiations, from the granting of the papal concession to its payment, should become clearer.

Papal documentation should also provide a better understanding of the negotiations between the papacy and Spanish ambassadors. Such documents will highlight the international context within which these concessions were made, because papal decisions to grant Spain concessions had implications for the Spanish clergy, for papal relations with other princes, and for all countries at war with Spain. Subsidy negotiations, then, were automatically European in scope. Consequently, further examination of papal documents should elucidate relations between popes and other princes during the Reformation and possibly

---

[8] Hélène Millet and Peter Moraw, "Clerics in the State," in *Power Elites and State Building*, edited by Wolfgang Reinhard (Oxford: Claredon Press, 1996), p. 175.

allow us to use the Spanish case to reevaluate the papacy's continual political importance in the early modern period.

Since Assemblies of the Clergy in other Catholic countries were similar to the Castilian Assembly, more research on other Assemblies and other intermediary ecclesiastical bodies will likely show that political developments under other 'new monarchies' did not lay the foundations for the victory of regalism in Catholic Europe. In a short overview of royal attempts to survey and tax ecclesiastical property in eighteenth-century Europe, Robert Villers noted that royal policy in France took a slightly different turn on account of fierce resistance by the Assembly of the Clergy.[9] More than likely, new research will show that other ecclesiastical Assemblies also stymied royal policies. Assemblies were incorporated into the monarchical structure of government but not subsumed by the monarchy. In fact, like other corporate bodies, the princes continually had to reach compromises with Assemblies for taxes.

Despite the similarities, there were substantial differences in the composition, structure, and prerogatives of the different Assemblies of the Clergy, and thus more research is needed on the non-French Assemblies before substantial comparative studies can be written.[10] These studies are especially important, however, because Assemblies of the Clergy and cathedral chapters within the Spanish monarchy did occasionally communicate with each other and even exchange strategies.[11] The crown

---

[9] See Robert Villers, "L'imposition des biens d'église dans les grands pays catholiques au XVIII° siècle (Contribution à l'étude des relations entre l'Église chrétienne et les pouvoirs séuliers," *Études d'histoire du droit canonique, dédiées à Gabriel Le Bras, doyen honoraire de la Faculté de droit et de sciences économiques de Paris, membre de l'Institut,* (Paris, 1965) Vol. 1, pp. 743–751.

[10] For an initial effort at such a comparison, see Sean T. Perrone, "Assemblies of the Clergy in Early Modern Europe," *Parliaments, Estates and Representation* 22 (2002), pp. 45–56.

[11] In 1555, canons from Barcelona and Valencia asked the Castilian Assembly of the Clergy for information on the status of its negotiations with the crown for the *dos quartas*. See ACS, Sec. VII, lib. 85, "Congregación del clero...1555," Session 72, October 7, 1555. In 1587, the Assembly agreed to help the chapter of Evora, Portugal, to end various privileges and exemptions enjoyed by the Jesuits. See BN 3/18355, "Congregación de las yglesias metropolitanas y catedrales de los reynos de Castilla, y León, que se celebro en la villa de Madrid el ano de mil y quinientos y ochenta y seys, con ocasion del quatro quinquenio de Excusado," f. 40v. In 1648, the chapter of Tarazona sought the Assembly's help to prevent the collegiate chapter of Calatayud from being elevated to a cathedral. See BN 3/13076 "Assientos de la congregación que celebraron las santas iglesias metropolitanas, y catedrales de los reynos de la corona de Castilla y León desde 20 de julio de 1648 hasta 12 de Marzo de 1650," f. 21.

also looked at negotiations for ecclesiastical subsidies in other kingdoms for guidance. In 1535, a report to the empress noted that the French clergy paid more than the Spanish clergy, while after the debacle in 1555 and 1556, one royal ambassador offered to gather information on how the French king compelled his clergy to contribute.[12] Comparative research on Assemblies of the Clergy, then, will offer a useful means to understand church-state relations and the clergy's concerns throughout the Spanish monarchy and potentially throughout Europe.

Concepts such as state building and absolutism only obscure early modern political and social realities. By examining the negotiations for ecclesiastical contributions between the crown and the Assembly, we can clearly see the limitations of the state-building model. To note simply that the Castilian Assembly of the Clergy successfully withstood royal attempts to centralize authority and break down the preexisting corporate order and that it continued to obstruct royal attempts to control the finances of the church is only to take the first step toward a new interpretative framework. Unfortunately, much of the scholarship, including the present study, seems stuck at that first step, repeatedly knocking down the 'state-building' and 'absolutism' straw men, even though specialists have long recognized that these concepts are inadequate to describe political realities. In order to make the next step and truly develop a new, more useful interpretative framework, future studies on corporate bodies and representative institutions need to abandon the master narratives of absolutism and state-building as a starting point and instead employ a narrative that emphasizes the pluralistic nature of power—that is, the relationships between royal officials, elites, and corporate bodies.[13] We need to examine how princes tried to build consensus with corporate bodies and representative institutions and reach accords acceptable to all parties. Only then will we truly understand governance and political practice in the early modern period. By concentrating on the negotiations for the subsidy, this book sheds light on the dynamics of church-state relations and political practice in the early modern period. It adds further evidence that the 'new monarchies' ruled through consultations and consensus with autonomous corporate bodies.

---

[12] AGS E leg. 113, f. 99 and E leg. 1563, ff. 88–89.

[13] J.B. Owens, *"By My Absolute Royal Authority": Justice and the Castilian Commonwealth at the Beginning of the First Global Age* (Rochester, NY: University of Rochester Press, 2005), pp. 237–238.

BIBLIOGRAPHY

Primary Sources

Archivo Catedralicio de Burgos
  Registro, libros 37, 41, 43, 44–46, 48, 49
Archivo Catedralicio de Granada
  Actas Capitulares, libros 2, 3
  Legajos 10, 11, 22, 29, 52, 69, 458
Archivo Catedralicio de Sevilla
  Seccion I, libros 10–24
  Seccion II, libro 1157 (77)
  Seccion VII, libros 85, 86, 87
  Seccion IX, legajos 107, 111, 182, 195
Archivo Catedralicio de Toledo
  Actas Capitulares, libros 4–10
  Documentos Secretaria Cabildo, Caja 1
  Obras y Fabrica 1336, 1344, 1350
Archivo General de Simancas
  Comisario de Cruzada, legajos 1–6
  Consejos y Juntas de Hacienda, legajos 7–10, 13–18, 22, 29
  Estado, legajos 11, 12, 19–21, 24, 26, 27, 29, 45, 48–51, 55, 60, 70–73, 103, 109,
    112, 113, 114, 512, 848, 857–860, 863, 864, 866, 868, 873, 881–883, 1563
  Estado, libro 73
  Guerra-Antigua, legajo 8
  Patronato Real, legajos 19, 20
Archivo Historico Nacional
  Clero, legajo 7216
Biblioteca de San Lorenzo del Escorial
  Manuscript V II 4 f. 460
Biblioteca Nacional (Madrid)
  General Collection 3/13076, 3/14341, 3/18355
  Manuscript 1293, 1778, 2029, 9175, 9936, 9937, 10435
  V.E. 24–1, 25–83, 186–7
Memorial Library, Special Collections, University of Wisconsin-Madison
  Porter Collection of Spanish Literature, Item 736

Secondary Sources

Aldea Vaquero, Quintín. "La resistencia eclesiástica." In *La España del conde duque de Olivares*, edited by John Elliott and Angel García Sanz. Valladolid: Universidad de Valladolid, 1990.
———. "La economía de las iglesias locales en la Edad Media y Moderna." *Hispania Sacra* 26 (1973): 27–68.
Alonso García, David. "Poder y Finanzas en Castilla en el tránsito a la modernidad (Un apunte historiográfico)." *Hispania* 66 (2006): 157–197.
———. "¿Pagar o no pagar? En torno al fraude fiscal eclesiástico en el Madrid del antiguo regimen." *Cuadernos de Historia de España* 77 (2001–2002): 187–206.
Álvarez Vázquez, José Antonio. "La contribución de Subsidio y Excusado en Zamora, 1500–1800." In *Haciendas forales y hacienda real: Homenaje a D. Miguel Artola y D. Felipe*

Ruiz Martín, edited by E. Fernández de Pinedo. Bilbao: Universidad del País Vasco, 1990.

——. "El memorial del estamento eclesiástico en 1691 sobre la baja de la tasa de interes en fueros y censos." *Hispania* 38 (1978): 405–435.

Azcona, Tarsício de. "Estado e Iglesia en España a la luz de las asambleas del clero en el siglo XVI." *Actas del congreso internacional Teresiano*, coordinated by Teófanes Egido Martínez. Salamanca: Ediciones Universidad de Salamanca, 1983.

——. "Reforma del episcopado y del clero de España en tiempo de los Reyes Catolicos y de Carlos V (1475–1558)." In *La Iglesia en la España de los siglos XV y XVI* vol. III/part 1 of *Historia de la Iglesia en España*, edited Ricardo García Villoslado. Madrid: Biblioteca de Autores Cristianos, 1980.

——. "Las Asambleas del clero de Castilla en el otoño de la Edad Media." *Miscelánea José Zunzunegui (1911–1974)* I (Estudios Historicas, I) Vitoria, Editorial ESET, 1975: 203–245.

Barrio Gozalo, Maximiliano. "La iglesia peninsular de los Reyes Católicos a Carlos V (1490–1530)." In *De la union de coronas al Imperio de Carlos V*, coordinated by Ernest Belengeur Cebriá. Vol. 1. Madrid: Sociedad Estatal para la Conmemoración de los Centenarios de Felipe II y Carlos V, 2001.

——. "Perfil socio-económico de una élite de poder. VII: los obispos de Cartagena-Murcia (1556–1834)." *Anthologica Annua* 39 (1992): 103–167.

——. "Perfil socio-económico de una élite de poder, VI. Los obispos de Pamplona, 1556–1834." *Anthologica Annum* 38 (1991): 43–106.

Bernardo Ares, José Manuel de. "Parliament or City Councils: The representation of the kingdom in the Crown of Castile (1665–1700)." *Parliaments, Estates and Representation* 25 (2005): 33–54.

Bilbao, L.M. "Ensayo de reconstrucción histórica de la presión fiscal en Castilla durante el siglo XVI." In *Haciendas forales y hacienda real: Homenaje a D. Miguel Artola y D. Felipe Ruiz Martín*, edited by E. Fernández de Pinedo. Bilbao: Universidad del País Vasco, 1990.

Bizzocchi, Roberto. "Church, Religion, and State in the Early Modern Period." *The Journal of Modern History* 67, Supplement, (December 1995): S152–S165.

Bonney, Richard. "Revenues." In *Economic Systems and State Finance*, edited by Richard Bonney. Oxford: Clarendon Press, 1995.

Brandi, Karl. *The Emperor Charles V: The Growth and Destiny of a Man and of a World-Empire.* Translated by C.V. Wedgewood. London: Jonathan Cape, 1939.

Braudel, Fernand. *The Mediterranean and the Mediterranean World in the Age of Philip II*, 2 vols. Translated by Sian Reynolds. New York: Harper & Row, 1973.

Bulst, Neithard. "Rulers, Representative Institutions and their Members as Power Elites: Rivals or Partners?" In *Power Elites and State Building*, edited by Wolfgang Reinhard. Oxford: Claredon Press, 1996.

Burgos Esteban, Francisco Marcos. "El poder de la fe y la autoridad de la palabra. Iglesia y fiscalidad en la época del conde duque de Olivares." In *Iglesia y Sociedad en el Antiguo Régimen*, edited by Enrique Martínez Ruiz and Vicente Suárez Grimón. Las Palmas: Universidad de las Palmas de Gran Canaria, 1994.

Carande, Ramón. *Carlos V y sus banqueros: La Hacienda Real de Castilla.* Madrid: Sociedad de Estudios y Publicaciones, 1949.

Cárceles de Gea, Beatriz. "La contribución eclesiástica en el servicio de millones (1621–1700)." In *Iglesia y Sociedad en el Antiguo Régimen*, edited by Enrique Martínez Ruiz and Vicente Suárez Grimón. Las Palmas: Universidad de las Palmas de Gran Canaria, 1994.

Carpintero Aguado, Lucía. "La congregación del clero de Castilla: un organismo mediatizado por la fiscalidad." In *Política, religión e inquisición en la España moderna: Homenaje a Joaquín Pérez Villanueva*, coordinated by P. Fernández Albaladejo. Madrid: Ediciones de la Universidad Autónoma de Madrid, 1997.

——. "Las décimas eclesiásticas en el siglo XVII: un subsidio extraordinario." In *Monarquía, imperio y pueblos en la España moderna*, coordinated by Pablo Fernández Albaladejo. Alicante: Universidad de Alicante, 1997.

——. "La contribución del clero castellano a los servicios de millones." *Revista de Historia Moderna* 15 (1996): 271–297.

——. "La congregación del clero de Castilla en el siglo XVII." Ph.D. diss., Universidad Autónoma de Madrid, 1993.

——. "Iglesia y Corte Castellana en el siglo XVI." *Hispania Sacra* 41 (1989): 547–567.

——. "La iglesia primada y el poder politico en el siglo XVII." *Congreso de Historia de Castilla-La Mancha*. 8, no. 2. Toledo: Junta de Castilla-La Mancha, 1988.

Carretero Zamora, Juan M. "La colectoría de España en época de Carlos V: Cuentas del nuncio y colector general Giovanni Poggio (1529–1546)," *Cuadernos de Historia de España* 78 (2003–2004): 103–135.

——. "Fiscalidad y presion fiscal en La Mancha durante el reinado de Carlos I (1519–1554): El servicio ordinario y extraordinario." *Cuadernos de Estudios Manchegos* 21 (1991): 29–90.

——. "Los servicios de las Cortes de Castilla en el reinado de Carlos I (1519–1554): Volumen, Evolución, Distribución." In *Las Cortes de Castilla y León. 1188–1988*. Valladolid: Cortes de Castilla y León, 1990.

Castejon y Fonseca, Diego de. *Primacia de la Santa Iglesia de Toledo*. Toledo, 1645.

Catalán Martínez, Elena. "El fin de un privilegio: La contribución eclesiástica a la hacienda real (1519–1794)." *Studia Historica. Historia Moderna* 16 (1997): 177–200.

——. "La participación de la Iglesia en el pago de las deudas de la Corona, 1543–1746." In *Iglesia, sociedad, y estado en España, Francia e Italia (ss. XVIII al XX)*, edited by Emilio La Parra López and Jesús Pradells Nadal. Alicante: Diputación Provincial de Alicante, 1991.

Cereceda, Feliciano, S.J. "El 'litigio de los cabildos' y su repercusión en las relaciones con Roma (1551–1556)." *Razón y Fe* 130 (septiembre–octubre 1944): 215–234.

Cloulas, Ivan. "Le 'subsidio de las galeras,' contribution du clergé espagnol à la guerre navale contre les infidèles de 1563 à 1574." *Melanges de la Casa de Velazquez* 3 (1967): 289–326.

Cruz Arroyo, Dolores. "El Consejo de la Cruzada: Siglos XVI–XVII." Thesis, Universidad Autónoma de Madrid, 1988.

Dandelet, Thomas James. "Paying for the New St. Peter's: Contributions to the Construction of the New Basilica from Spanish Lands, 1506–1620." In *Spain in Italy: Politics, Society, and Religion, 1500–1700*, edited by Thomas James Dandelet and John A. Marino. Leiden: Brill, 2007.

——. *Spanish Rome, 1500–1700*. New Haven: Yale University Press, 2001.

Dios, Salustiano de. "Sobre la génesis y los caracteres del estado absolutista en Castilla." *Studia Historica* 3 (1985): 11–46.

Domínguez Ortiz, Antonio. *Las clases privilegiadas en el Antiguo Régimen*. 3rd edition. Madrid: Ediciones ISTMO, 1985.

——. "Un alegato de los párrocos de la dioceses toledana contra el desigual reparto de los diezmos." *Hispania Sacra* 33 (1981): 533–539.

Doucet, R. *Les institutions de la France au XVIe siéle*. 2 vols. Paris: Editions A. Et J. Picard, 1948.

Dykema, Peter A. Review of *Kirche und Gesellschaft im Heiligen Römischen Reich des 15. und 16. Jahrhunderts*. ed. by Hartmut Boockmann. In *Sixteenth Century Journal* 27, no. 4 (1996): 1227–1228.

Ertman, Thomas. *Birth of the Leviathan: Building States and Regimes in Medieval and Early Modern Europe*. Cambridge: Cambridge University Press, 1997.

Espinosa, Aurelio. "The Spanish Reformation: Institutional Reform, Taxation, and the Secularization of Ecclesiastical Properties under Charles V." *Sixteenth Century Journal* 37 (2006): 3–24.

Fernández Albaladejo, Pablo. *Fragmentos de Monarquía*. Madrid: Alianza Universidad, 1992.

──. "Iglesia y configuración del poder en la monarquía católica (siglos XV–XVII)." In *Etat et Eglise dans la Genese de L'Etat Moderne*. Madrid: Bibliotheque de la Casa de Velazquez, 1986.

Fernández Álvarez, Manuel. *Poder y sociedad en la España del Quinientos*. Madrid: Alianza Universidad, 1995.

──. "La Emperatriz Isabel." *Boletín de la Real Academia de la Historia* 190, no. 2 (May–August 1993): 223–233.

──. "La política exterior." In *Las Cortes de Castilla y León en la Edad Moderna*. Valladolid: Cortes de Castilla y León, 1989.

──. "Los Austrias Mayores, Monarquía Autoritaria o Absoluta?" *Studia Historica* 3, (1985): 7–10.

──. *Charles V: Elected Emperor and hereditary ruler*. trans. J.A. Lalaguna. London: Thames and Hudson Ltd., 1975.

Fernández Álvarez, Manuel ed. *Corpus Documental de Carlos V*, 5 vols. Salamanca: Ediciones Universidad de Salamanca, 1973–1981.

Fernández Collado, Ángel, *La catedral de Toledo en el siglo XVI: Vida, arte y personas*. Toledo: Diputación Provincial de Toledo, 1999.

Fernández de Madrid, Alonso. *Silva Palentina*, edited by Jesús San Martín Payo. Palencia: Ediciones de la Excma. Diputación Provincial, 1976.

Fernández Terricabras, Ignasi. *Felipe II y el clero secular: La aplicación del concilio de Trento*. Madrid: Sociedad Estatal para la Conmemoración de los Centenarios de Felipe II y Carlos V, 2000.

Flynn, Maureen. *Sacred Charity: Confraternities and Social Welfare in Spain, 1400–1700*. Ithaca: Cornell University Press, 1989.

Fortea Pérez, José Ignacio. "Las ciudades, las Cortes y el problema de la representación política en la Castilla moderna." In *Imágenes de la diversidad: el mundo urbano en la Corona de Castilla (s. XVI–XVII)*, edited by José I. Fortea Pérez. Santander: Universidad de Cantabria, 1997.

──. "The Cortes of Castile and Philip II's fiscal policy." *Parliaments, Estates and Representation* 11 (1991): 117–138.

──. *Monarquía y Cortes en la Corona de Castilla: Las ciudades ante la politica fiscal de Felipe II*. Salamanca: Cortes de Castilla y León, 1990.

García, Heliodoro. "El reformismo del 'Pastor Bonus' de Juan Maldonado." *Hispania Sacra* 35 (1983): 193–218.

Garzon Pareja, Manuel. *Diezmos y tributos del clero de Granada*. Granada: Archivo de la Real Chancilleria, 1974.

Gelabert, Juan. "The Fiscal Burden." In *Economic Systems and State Finance*, edited by Richard Bonney. Oxford: Claredon Press, 1995.

Genet, Jean-Philippe. "Introduction: Which State Rises?" *Historical Research* 65, no. 157 (June 1992): 119–133.

Gibson, William. *The Church of England, 1688–1832. Unity and Accord*. New York: Routledge, 2001.

Gil, Xavier. "Parliamentary Life in the Crown of Aragon: Cortes, Juntas de Brazos, and other Corporate Bodies." *Journal of Early Modern History* 6 (2002): 383–384.

Gilchrist, J. "Cathedral Chapter." *New Catholic Encyclopedia*. vol. 3. New York: McGraw-Hill Book Company, 1967.

Giron, Pedro. *Cronica del Emperador Carlos V*. edited by Juan Sanchez Montes. Prologue by Peter Rassow. Madrid: Consejo Superior de Investigaciones Científicas, 1964.

Gómez Álvarez, Ubaldo. *Revisión histórica de la presión fiscal castellana (siglos XVI–XVIII) Tomo I: Análisis tributario del caso de la provincia de León, sus partidos y concejos en el s. XVII*. Oviedo: Universidad de Oviedo, 1996.

Gómez Bravo, Juan. *Catalogo de los obispos de Córdoba, y breve noticia historica de su Iglesia Catedral, y obispado*. 2 vols. Córdoba: Juan Rodríguez, 1778.

Goñi Gaztambide, José. *Historia de la Bula de la Cruzada en España*. Vitoria: Editorial del Seminario, 1958.

González Alonso, Benjamín. *Sobre el estado y la administración de la Corona de Castilla en el antiguo regimen*. Madrid: Siglo XXI, 1981.

Green, Vivian Hubert Howard. *Medieval Civilization in Western Europe*. London: Camelot Press Ltd., 1971.

Griffiths, Gordon. "The State: Absolute or Limited?" In *Transition and Revolution: Problems and Issues of European Renaissance and Reformation History*, edited by Robert M. Kingdon. Minneapolis, Minn.: Burgess Publishing Co., 1974.

——. *Representative Government in Western Europe in the Sixteenth Century*. Oxford: Oxford University Press, Clarendon Press, 1968.

Gutiérrez, M. "Congregación del clero de Castilla y de León." In *Diccionario de Historia Eclesiastica de España*, edited by Q. Aldea, T. Marin Martinez, and José Vives Gatell. Suplemento I. Madrid: Consejo Superior de Investigaciones Científicas, 1987.

Haliczer, Stephen. *The Comuneros of Castile: The Forging of a Revolution 1475–1521*. Madison: University of Wisconsin Press, 1981.

Headley, John M. *The emperor and his chancellor: A study of the imperial chancellery under Gattinara*. Cambridge: Cambridge University Press, 1983.

Hendricks, Charles David. "Charles V and the Cortes of Castile. Politics in Renaissance Spain." Ph.D. diss., Cornell University, 1976.

Hernández Borreguero, José Julián. "Impuestos sobre la renta de los eclesiásticos: El subsidio y excusado (Diócesis de Sevilla, mediados del siglo XVII)." *De Computis: Revista Española de Historia de la Contabilidad* 7 (December 2007): 80–99.

Hoffman, Philip T. and Kathryn Norberg, eds. *Fiscal Crises, Liberty, and Representative Government, 1450–1789*. Stanford: Stanford University Press, 1994.

Horozco, Sebastian de. *Relaciones históricas toledanas*, Intro. and trans. by Jack Weiner. Toledo: Instituto Provincial de Investigaciones y Estudios Toledanos, 1981.

Ibañez de Ibero, Carlos. *Carlos V y su politica Mediterranea*. Madrid: Consejo Superior de Investigaciones Científicas, 1962.

Irigoyen López, Antonio. "El clero murciano frente a la presión fiscal. Un documento de 1668." *Contrastes: Revista de Historia* 11 (1998–2000): 183–208.

Iturrioz Magaña, Ángel. *Estudio del Subsidio y Excusado (1561–1808). Contribuciones económicas de la Diócesis de Calahorra y La Calzada a la Real Hacienda*. Logroño: Instituto de Estudios Riojanos, 1987.

Jago, Charles. "Philip II and the Cortes of Castile: the Case of the Cortes of 1576." *Past and Present* no. 109 (1985): 24–43.

——. "Habsburg Absolutism and the Cortes of Castile." *American Historical Review* 86 (April 1981): 307–326.

Jover, José María. *Carlos V y los Españoles*. Madrid: Ediciones Rialp, S.A., 1963.

Kagan, Richard L. *Lucrecia's Dreams: Politics and Prophecy in Sixteenth-Century Spain*. Berkeley: University of California Press, 1990.

Kamen, Henry. *Spain 1479–1714: A Society of Conflict*. London: Longman, 1983.

Kerin, C.A. "Excommunication, Canonical." *New Catholic Encyclopedia*. vol. 5. New York: McGraw-Hill Book Company, 1967.

Kirshner, Julius. "Introduction: The State is 'Back In'." *The Journal of Modern History* 67, Supplement, (December 1995): S1–S10.

Koeningsberger, H.G. *Estates and Revolutions: Essays in Early Modern European History*. Ithaca: Cornell University Press, 1971.

——. *The Habsburgs and Europe 1516–1660*. Ithaca: Cornell University Press, 1971.

Kuebler, Kristen. "Cardinal García de Loaisa y Mendoza: Servant of Church and Emperor." Ph.D. diss., Oxford University, 1997.

Ladero Quesada, Miguel Angel. *El siglo XV en Castilla: Fuentes de renta y política fiscal.* Barcelona: Editorial Ariel, 1982.

La Fuente, Vicente de. *Historica eclesiástica de España.* 5 vols. Madrid, 1874.

Lawlor, F.X. "Ecomunication." *New Catholic Encyclopedia.* vol. 5. New York: McGraw-Hill Book Company, 1967.

Levin, Michael J. *Agents of Empire: Spanish Ambassadors in Sixteenth-Century Italy.* Ithaca: Cornell University Press, 2005.

Loperraez Corvalan, Juan. *Colección diplomática citada de la descripción histórica del obispado de Osma.* 3 vols. Madrid: Imprenta Real, 1788.

Lynch, John. *Spain Under the Habsburgs.* 2 vols. New York: New York University Press, 1981.

———. "Philip II and the Papacy." *Transactions of the Royal Historical Society* 5th series. 2 (1961): 23–42.

Mann, Michael. "The Autonomous Power of the State: Its Origins, Mechanism, and Results." In *States, War and Capitalism: Studies in Political Sociology.* New York: Basil Blackwell, 1988.

Mansilla, D. "Geografía eclesiastica." *Diccionario de Historia Eclesiastica de España*, edited by Quitin Aldea Vaquero, Tomas Marin Martinez, José Vives Gatell. 4 vols. Madrid: Consejo Superior de Investigaciones Científicas, 1972.

Marín López, Rafael. *El cabildo de la catedral de Granada en el siglo XVI.* Granada: Universidad de Granada, 1998.

Martín Martín, Theodoro. "La resistencia fiscal del clero en el antiguo regimen: Análisis de un manifesto-protesta." *Hispania* 48 (1988): 1075–1084.

Martínez Caados, José. "Los Cortes de Castilla en el siglo XVI." *Revista de la Universidad de Madrid* 6 (1957): 583–605.

Martínez de Campos, Carlos. *España belica el siglo XVI.* 2 vols. Madrid: Aguilar, 1965.

Martínez Millán, J. and C.J. de Carlos Morales. "Los origenes del Consejo de Cruzada (siglo XVI)." *Hispania Sacra* 51 (1991): 901–932.

Marzahl, Peter. "Communication and Control in the Political System of Emperor Charles V. The First Regency of Empress Isabella." In *The World of Emperor Charles V*, edited by Wim Blockmans and Nicolette Mout. Amsterdam: Koninklijke Nederlandse Akademie van Wetenschappen Verhandelingen, Afd. Letterkunde, Nieuwe Reeks, deel 188, 2004.

Mathers, Constance J. "The Life of Canons in Sixteenth-Century Castile." In *Renaissance Society and Culture: Essays in Honor of Eugene F. Rice, Jr*, edited by John Monfasani and Ronald G. Musto. New York: Italica Press, 1991.

———. "Relations between the City of Burgos and the Crown, 1506–1556." Ph.D. diss., Columbia University, 1973.

Mattingly, Garrett. *Renaissance Diplomacy.* London: Jonathan Cape, 1962.

Mazarío Coleto, María del Carmen. *Isabel de Portugal: Emperatriz y Reina de España.* Madrid: Consejo Superior de Investigaciones Científicas, 1951.

Menendez Pidal, Ramón. *Idea Imperial de Carlos V.* Buenos Aires: Espasa-Calpe Argentina, S.A. 1941.

Millet, Hélène and Peter Moraw. "Clerics in the State." In *Power Elites and State Building*, edited by Wolfgang Reinhard. Oxford: Claredon Press, 1996.

Molho, Anthony. "The State and Public Finance: A Hypothesis Based on the History of Late Medieval Florence." *The Journal of Modern History* 67, suppl. (December 1995).

Muto, Giovanni. "The Spanish System: Centre and Periphery." In *Economic Systems and State Finance*, edited by Richard Bonney. Oxford: Claredon Press, 1995.

Myers, A.R. *Parliaments and Estates in Europe to 1789.* London: Thames and Hudson Lt., 1975.

Nader, Helen. *Liberty in Absolutist Spain.* Baltimore: Johns Hopkins University Press, 1990.

Navarro Miralles, Luis J. "Subsidio de galeras y excusado: una aportación al estudio de la contribución fiscal eclesiastica (1567–1796)." *Pedralbes* 1 (1981): 21–49.

Nicolas Crispin, María Isabel, Mateo Bautista Bautista, and María Teresa Gracía Gracía. *La organización del cabildo catedralicio Leones a comienzos del s. XV (1419–1426)*. León: Universidad de León, 1990.

Nieto Soria, José Manuel. "Propaganda and Legitimation in Castile: Religion and Church 1250–1500." In *Iconography, Propaganda, and Legitimation*, edited by Allan Ellenius. Oxford: Clarendon Press, 1998.

———. *Iglesia y génesis del estado moderno en Castilla (1369–1480)*. Madrid: Editorial Complutense, 1993.

Oestreich, Gerhard. *Neostoicism and the early modern state*. Edited by Brigitta Oestreich and H.G. Koenigsberger. Translated by David McLintock. Cambridge: Cambridge University Press, 1982.

O'Keefe, Cyril B. "The French Assembly of the Clergy and the Provincial Councils, 1750–1788: A Frustrated Proposal for Ecclesiastical Reform in the Ancient Regime." *Proceedings of the Annual Meeting of the Western Society for French History* 6 (1978): 144–152.

Owens, J.B. *"By My Absolute Royal Authority": Justice and the Castilian Commonwealth at the Beginning of the First Global Age*. Rochester, NY: University of Rochester Press, 2005.

Parker, David. *The Making of French Absolutism*. London: Edward Arnold, 1983.

Parres, C.L. "Censures, Ecclesiastical." *New Catholic Encyclopedia*. vol. 3. New York: McGraw-Hill Book Company, 1967.

Parsons, Jotham. "Assemblies of the French Clergy from Philip the Fair to Louis XIII." *Parliaments, Estates and Representation* 23 (2003): 1–16.

Pastor, Ludwig. *The History of the Popes: from the close of the middle ages*, edited by Ralph Francis Kerr. 40 vol. London: Kegan Paul, Trench, Trubuer, & Co., 1938.

Pérez, Joseph. "Moines frondeurs et sermons subversifs en Castille pendant le premier séjour de Charles-Quint en Espagne." *Bulletin Hispanique* 67, no. 1–2 (1965): 5–24.

Pérez de Lara, Alonso. *Compendio de las Tres Gracias de la Santa Cruzada, Subsidio y Excusado*. Madrid, 1610.

Pérez-Prendes, José. *Cortes de Castilla*. Barcelona: Editorial Ariel, 1974.

Péronnet, M. "Les assemblées du Clergé de France et la révocation des édits de religion (1560–1685)." *Bulletin de la Société de l'Histoire du Protestantisme Français* 131 (1985): 453–479

Perrone, Sean T. "The Procurator General of the Castilian Assembly of the Clergy, 1592–1741." *Catholic Historical Review* 91 (January 2005): 26–59.

———. "Assemblies of the Clergy in Early Modern Europe." *Parliaments, Estates and Representation* 22 (2002): 45–56.

———. "Clerical Opposition in Habsburg Castile." *European History Quarterly* 31 (July 2001): 323–352.

———. "The Castilian Assembly of the Clergy in the Sixteenth Century." *Parliaments, Estates and Representation* 18 (1998): 53–70.

———. "The Road to the *Veros Valores*." *Mediterranean Studies* 7 (1998): 143–165.

Phillips, Carla Rahn. "Local History and Imperial Spain." *Locus* 2 (Spring 1990): 119–129.

Pizarro Llorente, Henar. "Facciones cortesanas en el Consejo de Cruzada durante el reinado de Felipe II (1562–1585)." *Miscelánea Comillas* 56 (1998): 159–177.

Prodi, Paolo. *The Papal Prince: One body and two souls: the papal monarchy in early modern Europe*. Translated by Susan Haskins. Cambridge: Cambridge University Press, 1987.

Rady, Martyn. *The Emperor Charles V*. London: Longman, 1988.

Rasler, Karen A. and William R. Thompson. *War and State Making: The Shaping of the Global Powers*. Boston: Unwin Hyman, 1989.

Rawlings, Helen. "Bishops of the Habit in Castile, 1621–1665: A Prosopographical Approach," *Journal of Ecclesiastical History* 56 (2005): 455–472.

——. *Church, religion and society in early modern Spain*. London: Palgrave, 2002.
——. "The Secularisation of Castilian Episcopal Office Under the Habsburgs, c. 1516–1700." *Journal of Ecclesiastical History* 38 (January 1987): 53–79.
Reinhard, Wolfgang. "Introduction: Power Elites, State Servants, Ruling Classes, and the Growth of State Power." In *Power Elites and State Building*, edited by Wolfgang Reinhard. Oxford: Claredon Press, 1996.
Reyes Gómez, Fermín de los. "Los libros de nuevo rezado y la imprenta española en el siglo XVIII." *Revista General de Información y Documentación* 9 (1999): 117–158.
Ríos, Juan Miguel de los. *Historia de las Tres Gracias pontificias de Crusada, Subsidio y Excusado*. 2 vols. Madrid, 1849.
Rodríguez-Salgado, M.J. *The Changing Face of Empire: Charles V, Philip II and Habsburg Authority, 1551–1559*. Cambridge: Cambridge University Press, 1988.
Rogister, John. "Some New Directions in the Historiography of State Assemblies and Parliaments in Early Modern and Late Modern Europe." *Parliaments, Estates and Represntation* 16 (1996): 1–16.
Rubin, Miri. *Corpus Christi: The Eucharist in Late Medieval Culture*. Cambridge: Cambridge University Press, 1991.
Rumeu de Armas, Antonio. "El Cardenal Tavera, Gobernador General de España." *Boletín de la Real Academia de la Historia*. 203 (2006): 163–188.
Sánchez Bella, Ismael. "Iglesia y estado español en la edad moderna (siglos XVI y XVII)." In *El estado español en su dimensión histórica*, edited by Manuel J. Peláez et al. Barcelona: Promociones y Publicaciones Universitarias, 1984.
Sánchez Herrero, José. "Sevilla del Renacimiento." In *Historia de la Iglesia de Sevilla*, edited by Carlos Ros. Seville: Editorial Castillejo, 1992.
Sánchez Montes, Juan. *1539. Agobios carolinos y ciudades castellanas*. Granada: Universidad de Granada, 1975.
Sandoval, Prudencio de. *Historia de la vida y hechos del Emperador Carlos V*, edited Carlos Seco Serrano. Madrid: Biblioteca de Autores Españoles, 1955.
Sanjuán, J. Gil. "Lucha de los cabildos castellanos por su autonomía y libertad (1553–1555)." *Espacio, Tiempo y Forma, Serie IV, Historia Moderna* 7 (1994): 275–295.
Santa Cruz, Alonso de. *Crónica del Emperador Carlos V*. 5 vols. edited by Ricardo Beltrán y Rózpide and Antonio Blázquez y Delgado-Aguilera. prol. Francisco de Laiglesia y Auset. Madrid: Imprenta del Patronato de huérfanos de intendencia é intervención militares, 1920–1925.
Schiera, Pierangelo. "Legitimacy, Discipline, and Institutions: Three Necessary Conditions for the Birth of the Modern State." *The Journal of Modern History* 67, Supplement (December 1995): S11–S33.
Schmale, Wolfgang. "The Future of 'Absolutism' in Historiography: Recent Tendencies." *Journal of Early Modern History* 2 (1998): 192–202.
Schmitz, Timothy J. "The Spanish Hieronymites and the Reformed Texts of the Council of Trent." *Sixteenth Century Journal* 37 (2006): 375–399.
Schulze, Winfried. "The Emergence and Consolidation of the 'Tax State.' I. The Sixteenth Century." In *Economic Systems and State Finance*, edited by Richard Bonney. Oxford: Claredon Press, 1995.
Serrano y Sanz, Manuel, ed. *Augobiografias y memorias*. Madrid: Editorial Bailly-Bailer, 1905.
Setton, Kenneth M. *The Papacy and the Levant (1204–1571)*. vol. IV. Philadelphia: American Philosophical Society, 1984.
Soriano Triguero, Carmen. "Iglesia, poder y sociedad: Notas historiográficas sobre el clero española en la edad moderna." In *Poder y mentalidad en España e Iberoamérica*, coordinated by Enrique Martínez Ruiz. Madrid: Ediciones Puertollano, 2000.
Spach, Robert C. "Juan Gil and Sixteenth-Century Spanish Protestantism." *Sixteenth Century Journal* 26 (1995): 857–879.

Steiner, W.J. "Assemblies of French Clergy." *New Catholic Encyclopedia*. vol. 1. New York: McGraw-Hill Book Company, 1967.

Stump, Philip H. "The reform of Papal taxation at the Council of Constance (1414–1418)," *Speculum* 64 (1989): 77.

Teruel Gregoria de Tejada, Manuel. *Vocabulario básico de la historia de la Iglesia*. Barcelona: Crítica, 1993.

Tilly, Charles. *Coercion, Capital, and European States, AD 990–1992*. Cambridge, MA: Blackwell, 1992.

Thompson, I.A.A. "Castile: Polity, Fiscality, and Fiscal Crisis." In *Fiscal Crises, Liberty, and Representative Government, 1450–1789*, edited by Philip T. Hoffman and Kathryn Norberg. Stanford: Stanford University Press, 1994.

———. "Castile: Absolutism, Constitutionalism, and Liberty." In *Fiscal Crises, Liberty, and Representative Government, 1450–1789*, edited by Philip T. Hoffman and Kathryn Norberg. Stanford: Stanford University Press, 1994.

———. *Crown and Cortes: government, institutions, and representation in early modern Castile*. Brookfield, VT: Variorum, 1993.

Thomson, John A.F. *Popes and Princes, 1417–1517: Politics and Polity in the Late Medieval Church*. London: George Allen & Unwin, 1980.

Tracy, James D. *Emperor Charles V, Impresario of War: Campaign Strategy, International Finance, and Domestic Politics*. Cambridge: Cambridge University Press, 2002.

Ulloa, Modesto. *La hacienda real de Castilla en el reinado de Felipe II*. 3rd. ed. rev. Madrid: Fundación Universitaria Española Seminario "Cisneros," 1986.

Vester, Matthew. "The Bresse Clergy Assembly and Tithe Grants, 1560–80," *Sixteenth Century Journal* 35 (2004): 771–794.

———. "Territorial Politics and Early Modern 'Fiscal Policy': Taxation in Savoy, 1559–1580," *Viator: Medieval and Renaissance Studies* 32 (2001): 279–302.

———. "Fiscal commissions, consensus and informal representation: taxation in the Savoyard domains, 1559–1580," *Parliaments, Estates and Representation* 20 (2000): 59–74.

Villers, Robert. "L'imposition des biens d'église dans les grands pays catholiques au XVIIIᵉ siècle (Contribution à l'étude des relations entre l'Église chrétienne et les pouvoirs séuliers," *Études d'histoire du droit canonique, dédiées à Gabriel Le Bras, doyen honoraire de la Faculté de droit et de sciences économiques de Paris, membre de l'Institut*. Paris, 1965. vol. 1, pp. 743–751.

Visceglia, María Antonietta. "Convergencias y conflictos. La monarquía católica y la santa sede (siglos XV–XVIII)," *Studia Historica. Historia Moderna*, 26 (2004): 155–190.

Wolfe, Martin. *The Fiscal System of Renaissance France*. New Haven: Yale University Press, 1972.

Wright, A.D. *Catholicism and Spanish Society under the Reign of Philip II, 1555–1598, and Philip III, 1598–1621*. Lewiston, NY: E. Mellen Press, 1991.

INDEX

Studies in the History of Christian Traditions

(formerly Studies in the History of Christian Thought)

Edited by Robert J. Bast

110. Bast, R. J. (ed.). *The Reformation of Faith in the Context of Late Medieval Theology and Piety*. Essays by Berndt Hamm. 2004.
111. Heering, J. P. *Hugo Grotius as Apologist for the Christian Religion*. A Study of his Work *De Veritate Religionis Christianae* (1640). Translated by J.C. Grayson. 2004.
112. Lim, P. C.- H. *In Pursuit of Purity, Unity, and Liberty*. Richard Baxter's Puritan Ecclesiology in its Seventeenth-Century Context. 2004.
113. Connors, R. and Gow, A. C. (eds.). *Anglo-American Millennialism, from Milton to the Millerites*. 2004.
114. Zinguer, I. and Yardeni, M. (eds.). *Les Deux Réformes Chrétiennes*. Propagation et Diffusion. 2004.
115. James, F. A. III (ed.). *Peter Martyr Vermigli and the European Reformations*: Semper Reformanda. 2004.
116. Stroll, M. *Calixtus II (1119-1124)*. A Pope Born to Rule. 2004.
117. Roest, B. *Franciscan Literature of Religious Instruction before the Council of Trent*. 2004.
118. Wannenmacher, J. E. *Hermeneutik der Heilsgeschichte*. *De septem sigillis* und die sieben Siegel im Werk Joachims von Fiore. 2004.
119. Thompson, N. *Eucharistic Sacrifice and Patristic Tradition in the Theology of Martin Bucer, 1534-1546*. 2005.
120. Van der Kool, C. *As in a Mirror. John Calvin and Karl Barth on Knowing God*. A Diptych. 2005.
121. Steiger, J. A. *Medizinische Theologie*. Christus medicus und theologia medicinalis bei Martin Luther und im Luthertum der Barockzeit. 2005.
122. Giakalis, A. *Images of the Divine*. The Theology of Icons at the Seventh Ecumenical Council – Revised Edition. With a Foreword by Henry Chadwick. 2005.
123. Heffernan, T. J. and Burman, T. E. (eds.). *Scripture and Pluralism*. Reading the Bible in the Religiously Plural Worlds of the Middle Ages and Renaissance. Papers Presented at the First Annual Symposium of the Marco Institute for Medieval and Renaissance Studies at the University of Tennessee, Knoxville, February 21-22, 2002. 2005.
124. Litz, G., Munzert, H. and Liebenberg, R. (eds.). *Frömmigkeit – Theologie – Frömmigkeitstheologie – Contributions to European Church History*.
125. Ferreiro, A. *Simon Magus in Patristic, Medieval and Early Modern Traditions*. 2005.
126. Goodwin, D. L. *"Take Hold of the Robe of a Jew"*. Herbert of Bosham's Christian Hebraism. 2006.
127. Holder, R. W. *John Calvin and the Grounding of Interpretation*. Calvin's First Commentaries. 2006.
128. Reilly, D. J. *The Art of Reform in Eleventh-Century Flanders*. Gerard of Cambrai, Richard of Saint-Vanne and the Saint-Vaast Bible. 2006.
129. Frassetto, M. (ed.). *Heresy and the Persecuting Society in the Middle Ages*. Essays on the Work of R.I. Moore. 2006.
130. Walters Adams, G. *Visions in Late Medieval England*. Lay Spirituality and Sacred Glimpses of the Hidden Worlds of Faith. 2007.
131. Kirby, T. *The Zurich Connection and Tudor Political Theology*. 2007.
132. Mackay, C.S. *Narrative of the Anabaptist Madness*. The Overthrow of Münster, the Famous Metropolis of Westphalia (2 vols.). 2007.
133. Leroux, N.R. *Martin Luther as Comforter*. Writings on Death. 2007.
134. Tavuzzi, M. *Renaissance Inquisitors*. Dominican Inquisitors and Inquisitorial Districts in Northern Italy, 1474-1527. 2007.
135. Baschera, L. and C. Moser (eds.). *Girolamo Zanchi, De religione christiana fides* – Confession of Christian Religion (2 vols.). 2007.
136. Hurth, E. *Between Faith and Unbelief*. American Transcendentalists and the Challenge of Atheism. 2007.
137. Wilkinson R.J. *Orientalism, Aramaic and Kabbalah in the Catholic Reformation*. The First Printing of the Syriac New Testament. 2007.
138. Wilkinson R.J. *The Kabbalistic Scholars of the Antwerp Polyglot Bible*. 2007.
139. Boreczky E. *John Wyclif's Discourse On Dominion in Community*. 2007.
140. Dowd C. *Rome in Australia: The Papacy and Conflict in the Australian Catholic Missions, 1834-1884* (2 vols.). 2008.
141. Perrone S.T. *Charles V and the Castilian Assembly of the Clergy*. Negotiations for the Ecclesiastical Subsidy. 2008.

Prospectus available on request

BRILL — P.O.B. 9000 — 2300 PA LEIDEN — THE NETHERLANDS